D1383516

Adobe®
Photoshop® CS2

in 24 Hours

Carla Rose
Kate Binder

SAMS 800 East 96th Street, Indianapolis, Indiana, 46240 USA

Sams Teach Yourself Adobe Photoshop CS2 in 24 Hours

International Standard Book Number: 0-672-32755-4

Library of Congress Catalog Card Number: 2004097756

Printed in the United States of America

First Printing: May 2005

08   07   06   05   4   3   2   1

Trademarks

Warning and Disclaimer

Bulk Sales

Sams Publishing offers excellent discounts on this book when ordered in quantity for bulk purchases or special sales. For more information, please contact

U.S. Corporate and Government Sales
1-800-382-3419
corpsales@pearsontechgroup.com

For sales outside of the U.S., please contact

International Sales
international@pearsoned.com

Acquisitions Editor
Betsy Brown

Development Editors
Betsy Brown
Jonathan Steever

Managing Editor
Charlotte Clapp

Project Editor
Andy Beaster

Indexer
Ken Johnson

Proofreader
Paula Lowell

Technical Editors
Kate Binder
Doug Nelson

Publishing Coordinator
Vanessa Evans

Interior Designer
Gary Adair

Cover Designer
Alan Clements

Page Layout
Kelly Maish

Contents at a Glance

Table of Contents

Sams Teach Yourself Adobe Photoshop CS2 in 24 Hours

Part VII: Appendix

About the Authors

Carla Rose started her photography career at the age of 8 with a Brownie Hawkeye. A graduate of the School of the Museum of Fine Arts in Boston, she has been a TV news photographer and film editor, as well as an advertising copywriter and graphic artist, before discovering the Macintosh. She has written all or part of about thirty computer books, including *Maclopedia, Adobe InDesign for the Mac, Sams Teach Yourself Digital Photography in 14 Days, Scrapbooking with Adobe Photoshop Elements 3, The Whole Mac, Managing the Windows NT Server, PageMaker 6.5 Complete, Sams Teach Yourself Digital Photography and Adobe Photoshop Elements 3 All in One, Mac Online, The First Book of Macintosh, The First Book of PageMaker 4 for Macintosh, It's a Mad, Mad, Mad, Mad Mac, Turbocharge Your Mac,* and *Everything You Ever Wanted to Know About the Mac.* She is a contributing editor to *Photoshop User* magazine and has also written for publications ranging from the *Atlantic Fisherman* to *Adobe Magazine* to *The New Yorker.* She lives near Boston, with her husband, audio guru Jay Rose, and three large, friendly cats. She welcomes e-mail addressed to author@graphicalcat.com.

Kate Binder is a graphics expert who works from her home in New Hampshire. She has written articles on design tools and techniques, publishing workflows, and photography for magazines including *Publish, PEI,* and *Desktop Publishers Journal.* Kate is also the author of several books, including *The Complete Idiot's Guide to Mac OS X, Easy Mac OS X 10.4 Tiger,* and *Easy Adobe Photoshop Elements 3,* and she is the coauthor of several more books, including *Microsoft Office: Mac v.X Inside Out, SVG for Designers,* and *Get Creative: The Digital Photo Idea Book.* To those interested in a successful career as a designer, photographer, or computer book writer, Kate recommends acquiring several retired racing greyhounds (find out more about www.adopt-a-greyhound.org—she finds her four greyhounds extraordinarily inspirational. Kate can be reached via her website at www.prospecthillpub.com.

Dedication

This one's for the dogs—both the thousands of greyhounds who've found a loving home and the thousands who never will.

Acknowledgments

Thanks most of all to Carla Rose, who laid the strong foundation on which this book is built. I also owe a great deal to my friends at Sams, especially Laura Norman, who just keeps coming back for more.

We Want to Hear from You!

As the reader of this book, *you* are our most important critic and commentator. We value your opinion and want to know what we're doing right, what we could do better, what areas you'd like to see us publish in, and any other words of wisdom you're willing to pass our way.

You can email or write me directly to let me know what you did or didn't like about this book—as well as what we can do to make our books stronger.

Please note that I cannot help you with technical problems related to the topic of this book, and that due to the high volume of mail I receive, I might not be able to reply to every message.

When you write, please be sure to include this book's title and author as well as your name and phone or email address. I will carefully review your comments and share them with the author and editors who worked on the book.

Email: graphics@samspublishing.com

Mail: Mark Taber
           Associate Publisher
           Sams Publishing
           800 East 96th Street
           Indianapolis, IN 46240 USA

Reader Services

For more information about this book or another Sams title, visit our website at www.samspublishing.com. Type the ISBN (excluding hyphens) or the title of a book in the Search field to find the page you're looking for.

Introduction

Photoshop CS2 is the latest and greatest version of a program that has set the standard for image manipulation since 1987. The new version has lots of new features, including Smart Objects, a beefed-up File Browser that's been renamed Bridge, a new Red Eye tool, Reduce Noise and Smart Sharpen commands for cleaning up photos, and a lot of "under-the-hood" enhancements that make your work easier and quicker. If you've used an earlier version of Photoshop, you'll be amazed at how much more powerful this one is. If this is your first experience with Photoshop, you'll be blown away. It's that good! The big surprise for first-time users is that it's really not as difficult to work with as it looks. If you have used any other Adobe software, the Photoshop interface will be immediately familiar to you. If this is your first step into creating digital graphics, you'll find the going easier if you work on the hours of this book one at a time and don't skip the activities or exercises.

Also, please be aware that this book was written using beta versions of the software. As such, some of the figures might be slightly different from what you see on your screen. Nevertheless, every possible effort has been made to keep the book as accurate as possible.

 By the Way

> ### Download the Pictures!
>
> I've provided a few of the source images for the book's exercises on the Sams website dedicated to this book. To download the images, point your Web browser to www.samspublishing.com, and type the book's ISBN: 0672325926. (Note: Don't use any hyphens.)
>
> After the main book page has loaded, click the Downloads link to get to the files.
>
> Please be aware that all images are protected by copyright and cannot be used for any purpose other than to work on the exercises.

There's honestly no way to become an overnight expert, be it in Photoshop or anything else, but *Sams Teach Yourself Adobe Photoshop CS2 in 24 Hours* will get you up and running in 24 hours or less. It's divided into 24 one-hour lessons, rather than chapters. Each lesson should take you about an hour to complete. Some lessons might need more time; others, less time. Please don't try to do it all in one 24-hour day, even if you could. The best way to learn is to take an hour or two between the lesson sessions to try out what you've learned. You'll want to simply poke around, and see what's on the menus and what happens when you click here and there.

Here's one for you to start with: Open the About Photoshop window and wait for a minute. You'll see it start to scroll through the list of all the people who worked on the program. Watch carefully for the very last name on the list. It's a pleasant surprise.

Ready? Let's get to work.

Conventions Used in This Book

This book uses the following conventions:

	By the Way
	By the Way presents interesting information related to the discussion.

	Did You Know?
	Did You Know? offers advice or shows you an easier way to do something.

	Watch Out!
	Watch Out! alerts you to a possible problem, and gives you advice on how to avoid it.

PART I

Getting Started

HOUR 1

The Basics

Photoshop is *still* the ultimate graphics program, although it's far different from the first version released about 15 years ago. Even though it's mainly used for photo retouching and image manipulation, you can also use it to create original art, either from scratch or based on a photograph. You can even use it to set type and turn plain fonts into gleaming metal or three-dimensional puffy satin, or whatever you like. It's much more fun than a video game and much less difficult than you might think.

Finding Your Way Around

When you first open Photoshop, you'll see its toolbox on the left side of the screen, the Tool Options bar just under the menu headings at the top of the screen, several sets of floating palettes on the right, and a Welcome Screen in the middle with links to some introductory Help topics. (You'll also see your desktop, or whatever else is open at the time, if you use a Mac.) You won't see a work area because Photoshop, unlike many other programs, doesn't automatically open a new document for you. This actually makes sense because most of your work in Photoshop will be done on pictures that you have brought in from some other source. Maybe you'll be using digital images from your digital camera or scanner. Possibly you'll work on files you've downloaded from the Internet or on photos from a CD-ROM. In Hour 2, "Opening and Saving," you will learn all about opening these pictures. Right now, let's create a blank image document so that you can try some of Photoshop's tools.

Starting a New Image

File→New is the first item on the first Photoshop menu. When you choose it, you open the New dialog box, shown in Figure 1.1. You can enter a title for your new file at the top of the dialog box, such as New Image, or leave it untitled for now. The following sections provide a brief overview to get you started setting up a new file.

FIGURE 1.1
Use the New dialog box to create a blank document.

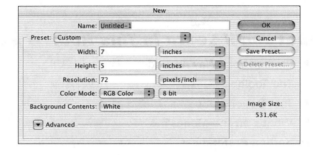

Image Size

The simple way to choose an image size is to use the Preset pop-up menu. It lists common American and European paper sizes, monitor sizes, and DVD screen sizes. Photoshop CS2 also includes a wide selection of TV and video formats, including PAL and HDTV screen sizes. Of course, you can also specify the size of your image—width and height—in pixels, inches, centimeters, points, picas, or columns across. These units are available in pop-up menus that you can access by clicking the small arrow next to the unit of measurement. See Figure 1.2.

For now, choose Default Photoshop Size. This gives you a 7×5 inch work area, a convenient size for most projects.

It's Magic!

If you have an image copied on the Clipboard, when you create a new document, the dialog box will automatically show the size of the copied image.

Resolution

Resolution refers to the number of dots-of-ink-per-inch (if you're printing) or pixels-per-inch (if you're looking at the computer screen). It's important because the resolution of the image determines the quality. Higher resolution gives you a better quality image but uses more memory. Most images that you see in print have a resolution of 150 ppi to 300 dpi (dots per inch).

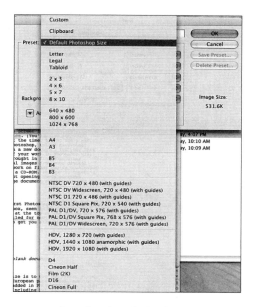

FIGURE 1.2
If the paper or screen size you need isn't listed, choose Custom and enter the dimensions.

Your computer's monitor, on the other hand, displays 72 ppi, which is substantially fewer than 300. Therefore, you always set the resolution depending on what your output will be. For now, keep the resolution at 72 ppi because we're just looking at the screen. For the same reason, set the Mode to RGB Color, as shown in Figure 1.1. RGB color is the kind of color that monitors display. (You'll learn all about color modes in Hour 5, "Color Modes and Color Models.")

Set the Background Contents to White. This gives you a white "canvas" to paint on.

Plan Ahead...

If you intend to publish your images on the Web, ignore resolution completely. Rather than thinking of an image as "so-many-inches by so-many-inches at 72 ppi," think of the image as being "this-many-pixels by this-many-pixels." Consider how much of the Web page the image will cover. If, on the other hand, you are printing to a high-quality color inkjet or laser printer, set the resolution to 200 ppi. You should use 300 ppi only if you need to create professional color prints.

Did you Know?

After you click OK in the New dialog box, you will see a new window. This is the *active window*, and the *canvas* is the large white square within it. You can have more than one window open within Photoshop at the same time, but only one can be the active window. The active window is always in the foreground. This is where you create and edit images.

Set your mouse pointer at the lower-right corner of the window, and then click and drag. The window expands, but notice that the canvas size stays the same. After you have created a new file, you can change the size of the canvas only by choosing Image→Canvas Size. This command enables you to specify a new height and width for the canvas, as shown in Figure 1.3. The Anchor section enables you to specify the base area from which the canvas expands or shrinks, by clicking any of the nine squares. (Changing the image size, obviously, changes the size of the canvas, too. The difference is that changing the canvas size gives you more room around your existing image.)

FIGURE 1.3
Click a white square in the Anchor proxy to locate the contents of your current canvas in the corresponding part of the new canvas.

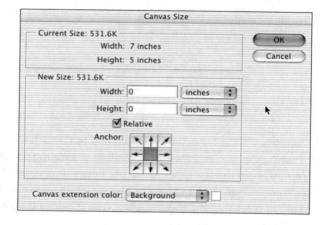

The Relative check box is a very useful tool. Checking the Relative box enlarges the canvas to create a border effect around the contents. It's useful if you have several differently sized photos and want to place them all in identical frames for a web page or printed document. Choose an appropriate size, such as 2% for a narrow frame, and enlarge all your pictures by the same percentage.

The Toolbox

The toolbox, like an artist's work table or paint box, holds all the tools you'll use to draw, paint, erase, and otherwise work on your picture. If you've used a previous edition of Photoshop, you might be in for a few surprises. Some of the tools have changed locations, and gained new capabilities, and there are some very nifty new ones. There are four categories of tools in Photoshop's toolbox:

▶ Selection tools   ▶ Path, Text, and Shape tools

▶ Painting tools   ▶ Viewing tools

Let's take a quick look at these tools. (We'll talk about them in detail later.) Figure 1.4 shows the toolbox with the tools labeled.

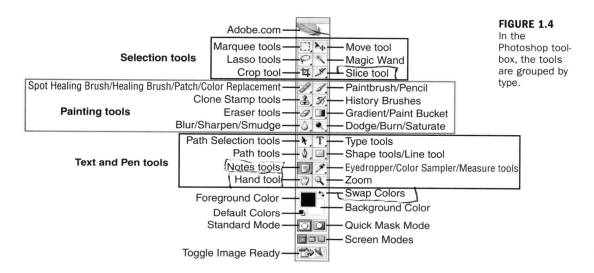

FIGURE 1.4
In the Photoshop tool-box, the tools are grouped by type.

What's That Thing?

Notice that some of the tool icons have a tiny black triangle in the lower-right corner of their icons. This means that there are more tools of the same general kind available on a pop-up menu. Point to any tool that has a triangle, click, and hold down the mouse button to see what other tools are available.

By the Way

Selection Tools

At the top of the toolbox is a group of tools called *Selection tools*. They are used to select all or part of a picture. There are three kinds: the Marquees, the Lassos, and the Magic Wand. A selected area is indicated onscreen by a blinking selection border, called a *marquee* after the movie theater marquee lights that flash on and off. Click and drag the Marquee and Lasso tools over the part of an image you want to select. Figure 1.5 shows the pop-up menus for the Marquee and Lasso Selection tools.

The Magic Wand selects by color. You can set the degree of similarity it demands, and just click to select all pixels of that color, or only the adjacent pixels that match. The final tool in this set is the Move tool. After you have made a selection, use the Move tool to move the selected area to another place in the image.

FIGURE 1.5
The Marquee
and Lasso
Selection tools.

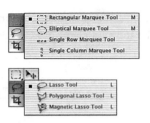

Painting Tools

Within the set of Painting tools are a Brush, Pencil, and Clone Stamp (which works like a rubber stamp). These all apply "paint" to the screen in one way or another, just like the real tools they imitate. The Pencil and Brush can change width and angle. The Pencil tool and Brush tool share a space in the toolbox. There's a button on the Tool Options bar to turn the Brush into an airbrush, and a slider to adjust the paint flow, just like in a real airbrush. The Clone Stamp tool picks up and copies a brush-shaped piece of the background and "stamps" it wherever you click. There are also various erasers that, as you might expect, take away part of the picture. You can use a Block Eraser, or erase with any of the Brush shapes. There are two special-purpose erasers: the Background and Magic Erasers. Use them to automatically erase a background or selected color.

Four special retouching tools are part of the Painting set: the Healing Brush (which looks like a Band-Aid), the Spot Healing Brush (a Band-Aid overlapping a round selection), the Patch (which looks as if it belongs on the knees of my blue jeans), and the Red Eye tool (a single-function tool introduced in Photoshop CS1).

The Spot Healing Brush and regular Healing Brush tools are better than the Clone Stamp for retouching small areas on a picture because they work only on the spot, wrinkle, or scar you want to remove without affecting the surrounding area.

The Patch covers a larger area, and its results blend evenly into the background. The Red Eye tool is essential for fixing eye color (red eye in photos of people and green eye in photos of animals).

The History Brush is a very useful tool that, combined with the History palette, gives you the capability to selectively undo and redo as many of your changes or individual brush strokes as you want. The Art History Brush imitates different painting styles.

The Gradient tool lets you create backgrounds that shade from one color to another, or even all the way through the rainbow. The Paint Bucket, which shares space with the Gradient tool, pours paint (the foreground color) into any area you select.

Finally, there are tools that move, blur, and change the intensity of the image. These are the Blur/Sharpen/Smudge tool and the Dodge/Burn/Sponge tool. The second and third options of each set are found on pop-up menus. These tools are covered in detail in Hour 7, "Paintbrushes and Art Tools," Hour 8, "Digital Painting," and Hour 9, "Moving Paint."

Path, Type, and Shape Tools

These tools aren't as easy to classify as the Painting tools or the Selection tools. They do different, useful things. The letter *T* represents the Type tool, which puts type on your picture. The Path tools, represented by a pen icon, draw paths, which are a means of drawing a line or shape. After you have drawn a line or shape, you can use the tools to select a portion of your path and reshape it. Path tools can be used as both Selection tools and as Painting tools. In Hour 13, "Paths," you learn how to work with all of the Path tools.

The Shape tools can draw both filled and unfilled shapes, including rectangles, ellipses, polygons, and custom shapes. The Line tool is also part of this set. It draws straight lines which, when you hold down the Shift key, can be constrained to 45- or 90-degree angles, just as if you had used an artist's or architect's T-square and triangle. Figure 1.6 shows the Shape tools and some of the custom shapes.

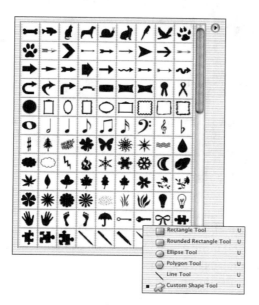

FIGURE 1.6
You can create your own custom shapes, too.

The Notes tool works like the yellow stickies it resembles. Use it to place notes on your documents while you're working on them. The note can go either on the canvas, or in the area adjacent to it. You can even use voice annotations, if your computer has a microphone plugged in. The notes are invisible when you print the image.

Viewing Tools

There are two Viewing tools: the Hand tool and the Zoom tool. The Zoom tool is shaped like an old-fashioned magnifying glass, and the Hand, not surprisingly, like a hand. The Zoom tool lets you zoom in by clicking the tool on the canvas to see a magnified view of your picture, or zoom out by pressing Option (Mac) or Alt (Windows) as you click the image. You can also click and drag the Zoom tool to enlarge a specific part of the image. When you zoom in, the picture is usually too big to see all at once. The Hand moves it within the window and is helpful after you use the Zoom tool to enlarge the picture. Use the Hand, as shown in Figure 1.7, to slide the part of the picture you want to see or work on into a convenient spot. You will also use it to slide objects or type on layers, but we'll get to that later on, in Hour 11, "Layers."

Hand Tool in Navigator window

FIGURE 1.7
The Hand moves an image within its window. You can use the Hand either on the main screen or, as seen here, in the Navigator window.

Within this category, we can also include the Eyedropper tool, the Color Sampler tool, and the Measure tool. The Eyedropper tool picks up a sample of any color on which you click, making it the active color, so you can paint with it. The Color Sampler tool places a reference point on the screen when you click, and puts all of the color information about that spot in the Info palette. You can keep information on as many as four samples at a time. The Measure tool can be used to measure dimensions and angles in the picture. Click and drag a line to measure a distance between two points, and see it displayed in the Info window. To measure an angle, first create a measured line. Then place your cursor on one of its two endpoints. Hold down the Option (Mac) or Alt (Windows) key while clicking and dragging from the endpoint of the first line in the direction of the angle.

Tool Shortcuts

Every one of these tools can be selected by clicking its icon in the toolbox, but Photoshop gives you another, even easier way to access the tools. Instead of clicking the tools you want to use, you can type a single letter shortcut to select each tool. To toggle through the available tools where there are pop-up menus, press Shift plus the shortcut letter until you reach the tool you want. Table 1.1 lists the tools with their shortcuts. Dog-ear this page so that you can refer to the table until you have memorized the shortcuts.

TABLE 1.1 Tools and Their Shortcuts

Tool	Shortcut
Marquee	M
Lasso	L
Crop	C
Healing Brush/Patch	J
Clone Stamp	S
Erasers	E
Blur/Sharpen/Smudge	R
Path/Direct Selection	A
Pen	P
Notepad	N
Hand	H
Switch Colors/Background/Foreground Colors	X
Move	V
Magic Wand	W
Slice/Slice Select	K
Brush/Pencil	B
History/Art History Brush	Y
Gradient/Paint Bucket	G
Dodge/Burn/Sponge	O
Type	T
Shape	U
Eyedropper/Measure	I
Zoom	Z
Default Colors	D

Tool Options Bar

In early versions of Photoshop, tool options were set on a palette just like Layers or History. With version 6, users learned to reach for the Tool Options bar instead. As you change tools, the bar changes according to whatever options are available for that tool. If it's been turned off, choose Options in the Window menu, or simply double-click any tool to open its Options bar.

There's an option on the bar called the Tool Preset menu. It's at the far left of the toolbar, which is shown in Figure 1.8 with the Brush Options active. You can use tool presets to save specific option sets for tools you use often.

FIGURE 1.8
Any toolbar component with an arrow has a pop-up menu.

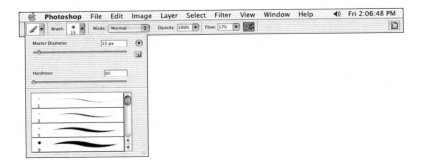

What's on the Menus?

The menus across the top of the screen contain the commands that enable you to open and manipulate files. They are accessed just as you would access any other menu, by clicking to open the menu and choosing the desired command from the list. Whenever you see an arrow or an ellipsis to the right of a menu command, it indicates that there is either a submenu, in the case of the arrow, or a dialog box, in the case of the ellipsis.

File and Edit Menus

The first two menus are File and Edit. Photoshop's File and Edit menus will be mostly familiar to anyone who has used other Macintosh or Windows programs. The File menu lets you work with files: opening, closing, saving, importing and exporting, printing, and, of course, quitting the program. There are also several time-saving automation features that you'll learn about in Hour 18, "Special Effects and Useful Tricks."

The File Browser, first introduced in Photoshop 7, has been renamed the Bridge in this version, and it's been beefed up considerably. Naturally, you can see all the data about your photo or scanned image while you preview it, and you can add your own keywords to help the Bridge locate and open your files. In addition, you can search Adobe's online stock photo collection and save groups of images that you want to open at the same time. When you open the Bridge, you can search any of your graphics folders by selecting them. After you've found the folder you want, all its pictures will appear as if they were slides on a sorting table. Figure 1.9 shows the setup. To open a picture, just double-click it. You'll also see all the information available about the picture, including its size, color mode, date and time it was shot, make and model of camera used, and a lot more than you'll ever need to know.

The Edit menu includes all the editing commands you're familiar with from other applications: Cut, Copy, Paste, Clear, and the most important one—Undo. It also contains the Transform tools, to scale, skew, distort, and rotate selections.

Mac users take note

As of Photoshop CS, the Preferences command moved to the far left Photoshop menu in Mac OS X; in Windows, it's still under the Edit menu.

By the Way

FIGURE 1.9
The Bridge lets you see thumbnails of all the images in a folder.

The menus that you might not be as familiar with (unless you've spent a lot of time working in other graphics programs) include

- ▶ Image
- ▶ Filter
- ▶ Layer
- ▶ View
- ▶ Select
- ▶ Window

The Image Menu

The Image menu, shown in Figure 1.10, has several submenus. The first of these, Mode, enables you to select a color mode in which to work. Most of the time, you will be working in RGB mode because that's what your monitor displays. Color modes are discussed in detail in Hour 5. The second submenu, Adjustments, is one you'll probably use on every photo you work on. It's the source for all kinds of color adjustments, from automatic level and color corrections to sliders that let you tweak contrast, change red roses to blue ones, and so on. You will learn how to use the tools on the Adjustments submenu in Hour 6, "Adjusting Color."

FIGURE 1.10
The
Adjustments
submenu.

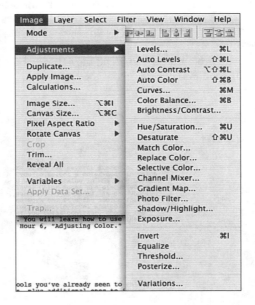

The Image menu also has the tools you've already seen to enlarge an image or the canvas it's on, plus additional ones to invert colors, posterize, and even correct color and saturation by example.

The Layer Menu

Arguably the most powerful feature of Photoshop is the capability to work on different layers. This enables you to combine images, create collages, and make corrections without fear of damaging the original picture. Think of it as working on sheets of transparent plastic. Each layer is totally separate from the others. You can paint on a layer, change its opacity, or do whatever you want with it without disturbing the background or other parts of the picture on other layers.

The Layer menu opens dialog boxes to create new layers. It also has many commands to merge and work with layers, applying layer effects, styles, and color adjustments. Figure 1.11 shows what's on the Layer menu. Hour 6 and Hour 11, "Adjusting Color" and "Layers," will teach you how to work with all kinds of layers.

FIGURE 1.11
The Layer menu.

The Select Menu

You have Selection tools, so why do you need a Select menu? The Select menu works with the tools to let you modify areas you have selected. You can grow or shrink the selected area by as many pixels as you want, or feather its edges so the selection appears to fade into a background on which you have pasted it. In Hour 3, "Making Selections," you'll learn all the tricks for selecting parts of a picture and working with them.

The Filter Menu

Filters are the tools that make Photoshop fun. The Filter menu lists more than a dozen categories of filters: Some blur or sharpen the picture, some distort it, and some turn it into imitation paintings, colored pencil drawings, or neon light sculptures. There's so much for you to do with filters that we'll spend Hours 14, "Filters that Improve Your Picture," 15, "Filters to Make Your Picture Artistic," and 16, "Filters to Distort and Other Funky Effects" applying them to your pictures.

> **Filter Fact**
>
> Photoshop filters are plug-ins, and many work with other graphics programs as well. If you install third-party filters, such as Alien Skin's Eye Candy or Andromeda filters, they'll appear at the bottom of the Filter menu.

The View Menu

Like the Zoom tool, the View menu has commands that let you zoom in on and out of the picture. As you can see in Figure 1.12, it also has the commands governing rulers, guides, and grids that enable you to measure and place objects precisely within the work area. The Show command opens a submenu that gives you access to grids, guides, notes, and slices.

FIGURE 1.12
The View menu.

You can set the rulers to measure in pixels, inches, centimeters, points, or picas, or by percentage. Choose the measurement with which you're most familiar. The setting is done in a Preferences dialog box; open the dialog box by choosing Photoshop→Preferences→Units & Rulers (for Mac OS X) or Edit→Preferences→Units & Rulers (for Windows). The unit of measure selected with the Units & Rulers preference also determines the unit of measure for the New dialog box (refer to Figure 1.1). When creating for the Web, consider setting your rulers to pixels.

Guides are lines that you place over your picture to position type or some other element that you're going to add to the picture.

Try it Yourself

Placing a Guide

To place guides, follow these steps:

1. Choose View→Rulers. This makes the rulers visible at the edges of the canvas.

2. To place a horizontal guide, put the mouse pointer on the ruler at the top of the screen and drag downward. You'll see a line scrolling down the canvas as you drag. The left ruler shows you the position of the line.

3. To place a vertical guide, put the mouse pointer on the ruler at the left of the screen and drag across. You'll see a line scrolling across the canvas as you drag. The top ruler shows you the position of the line. See Figure 1.13 for an example of a vertical guide.

4. To switch the orientation of a guide as you drag, hold down the Option (Mac) or Alt (Windows) key.

FIGURE 1.13
Guides let you place type or objects right where you want them.

After you have placed a guide, you can't move it unless you use the Move tool. (You can place a guide regardless of what tool is selected.) You can hide it by choosing View→Show→Guides to remove the check mark. To get rid of the guides, choose View→Clear Guides. To lock guides in place, press Option+Command+; (semicolon) (Mac) or Alt+Control+; (Windows).

The Show Grid command, which is also found on the View menu (View→Show→Grid), places an entire grid of guidelike lines over your image, rather like a layer of transparent graph paper. The Snap To commands make it easier to position an element, such as a block of type. In effect, they make a guide or gridline "magnetic," so that when you place the element near it, the line pulls the element right up against it.

The Window Menu

Most of Photoshop's commands can be accessed in several ways. The easiest way, generally, is to use the palettes. Photoshop's palettes give you information about your picture, and character and paragraph controls for the Type tool. The palettes contain options for many of the tools in the toolbox, a choice of brush sizes and shapes, colors, as well as access to Layers, Paths, and Channels. There are also Actions and History palettes to help you work more efficiently, and to see what you've done and step backward when necessary. The Window menu (shown in Figure 1.14) shows and hides these palettes. If there are some palettes, such as Actions, that you're not ready to use, close them to keep your screen uncluttered.

FIGURE 1.14
You can also click the tabs on the palettes to bring them forward.

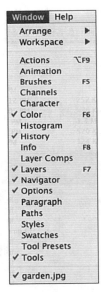

The Help Menu

The final menu is the Help menu, which gives you access to Photoshop's comprehensive help database, which is essentially the entire manual, with a good search function. I use it frequently.

Setting Preferences

As you become more familiar with Photoshop, you might want to change the ways it handles certain tasks. You might want to use the System Color Picker instead of the Photoshop version. You might decide to measure in inches for one project and centimeters for another. You might need to change the color of the guides because they're too much like the background in your photo. All these changes and many more are made in the Preferences dialog box, which is now accessible under the Photoshop menu in the current Mac OS X version (in Windows, it's still accessed via the Edit menu). The General Preferences dialog box is shown in Figure 1.15.

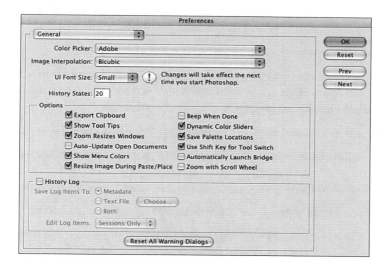

FIGURE 1.15
Set preferences here.

Use the Next button to scroll through the Preferences dialog boxes. You might encounter some preferences that you don't understand. For now, leave the default settings. As you learn more about the program, you can come back and change preferences as necessary.

Summary

You are starting to learn your way around the Photoshop screen, and you learned how to create a new image document during this hour. You looked at the toolbox and Photoshop's menus, and learned about grids and rulers. Finally, you learned about setting preferences.

Workshop

Q&A

Q *What are foreground and background colors?*

A The foreground color is the uppermost of the two colored squares in the toolbox. It's the color the brush applies. The background color is the lower square. It's the color you see when you erase "paint" from the canvas.

Q *What's the purpose of the picture at the top of the toolbar?*

A It's the Adobe Photoshop logo. If you have an Internet connection, clicking the logo will take you to Adobe's website, where you can find ideas, tips, late-breaking Photoshop news, and, of course, product info.

Q *Why are there trash cans at the bottom of the History and Layers palettes?*

A Clicking the trash on the Layers palette deletes a selected layer. Similarly, clicking the trash on the History palette deletes a selected history state. You'll learn more about this when we look at undoing in Hour 2, and layers in Hour 11.

Q *How can I draw a box around some words I've put on my picture?*

A That's one of the neat things the Shape tools can do for you. You'll learn how to use them in Hour 13. There are even pre-drawn word balloons in the Custom shapes palette.

Quiz

1. How do you zoom in for a closer look at the page?

    a. Place the Zoom tool on the part of the picture you want to see, and click.

    b. Press Option/Alt and click the Zoom tool.

    c. Press Shift and type **zoom**.

    d. Press Shift and the plus key.

2. How do you zoom out to see the whole page?

    a. Press the Shift and minus keys.

    b. Type **zoom out**.

    c. Press Option/Alt and click the Zoom tool anywhere on the picture.

Quiz Answers

1. a. Click again to magnify more.

2. c. You'll see the symbol inside the icon change to a minus.

Exercises

1. Open a new page and try some of these tools. Click the Brush and draw some squiggles and lines. Click an eraser and erase part of them. Try dragging the Smudge tool across one of the lines. Select a piece of line with one of the Selection tools and move it to another part of the page. Explore. You're not going to break anything.

2. If you have an Internet connection, click the Adobe logo at the top of the toolbar. Visit Adobe's website and see what's there.

HOUR 2

Opening and Saving

What You'll Learn in This Hour:

▶ Working with Files
▶ Saving Your Work
▶ Undoing and Redoing

Before you can do anything exciting with Photoshop CS2, you need to learn how to open and view files. Photoshop can open a wide variety of file formats, so you can work on pictures from many sources. If you have a scanner or a digital camera, you can bring in pictures that you've taken. You can also use photos from CD-ROM collections or images that you have downloaded from some online or Internet source. This hour will also cover methods of saving your work because, if you don't save, all the changes you make will be lost.

Working with Files

Photoshop can open and save images in many file formats. *Formats* are ways of saving the information in a file so it can be used by other applications, printed, or placed on a Web page for use on the Internet.

In the Windows world, file formats are defined by three-letter extensions to filenames, such as .doc for a word processing document and .bmp for a bitmapped graphic. Because you can toggle off the extension codes in Windows, you actually might not see extensions to known file types. Rest assured, they are there.

Macintosh users really only need to use file extensions if they're sharing files with someone on a PC, or are posting them on a Web page. You can toggle Append File Extension on or off in the Preferences→File Handling dialog box.

The most commonly used file format in Photoshop is its native format. The extension is `.psd` (Photoshop document). The drawback to working in "native Photoshop" (`.psd`) is that other applications might have trouble opening this format. To move files between applications, to print, or to publish on the World Wide Web, you must save your files in a compatible format.

A new file format called Large Document Format (`.psb`) was introduced in Photoshop CS. It's meant to be used for handling very large files. (You might remember the extension more easily if you think of it as Photoshop Big.) This format was developed to meet the needs of all of the multi-mega pixel digital cameras in use, and to let you work with, and save, multiple layers in a large document. Because it's new, it's not backwards compatible. Anything you save as a `.psb` file can only be opened in Photoshop CS. You can toggle the format on or off in the Preferences→File Handling dialog box. If you share files with users of older editions of Photoshop, leave it off.

The following are some common formats with brief definitions of their uses. Note that Photoshop can handle many other graphics formats as well.

- ▶ Bitmap (`.bmp`). This is a standard graphics file format for Windows.

- ▶ GIF (`.gif`). GIF stands for *Graphics Interchange Format*. It is one of the three common graphics formats you can use for Web publishing. Because it is a compressed format, it takes less time to send by modem.

- ▶ JPEG (`.jpg`). JPEG stands for *Joint Photographic Experts Group*. JPEG is another popular format for Web publishing.

- ▶ PDF (`.pdf`). Adobe Acrobat's *Portable Document Format*, a system for creating documents that can be read cross-platform.

- ▶ PNG (`.png`). Stands for *Portable Network Graphic*. It's a newer and arguably better format for Web graphics, combining GIF's good compression with the JPEG's unlimited color palette. However, older browsers don't support it. (We'll discuss these formats and their use in Web publishing in Hour 24, "Photoshop for the Web.")

- ▶ TIFF (`.tif`). TIFF stands for *Tagged Image File Format*. These files can be saved for use on either Macintosh or Windows machines. This is also often the preferred format for desktop publishing applications, such as InDesign and QuarkXPress. When you save a TIFF file, you can choose whether to include layers. If you do include layers in a TIFF file, the image might not be compatible with all desktop publishing programs.

▶ EPS (.eps). *Encapsulated PostScript* is another format often used for desktop publishing. It uses the PostScript page description language, and can be used by both Macintosh and PC.

▶ Raw (usually .raw). This format saves image information in the most flexible format for transferring files between applications, devices (such as digital cameras), and computer platforms.

These file formats, and some less common ones such as Targa and Scitex CT, are available in the Save dialog boxes—File→Save and File→Save As. Just look for the Format pop-up menu. Figure 2.1 shows the Save As dialog box with the formats available.

If you work on a Macintosh and need to share files with non-Macintosh users—or if you just like to stay on the safe side—go to the Preferences→File Handling dialog box. Click the check boxes to add an extension and to keep it in lowercase (as required by some older software).

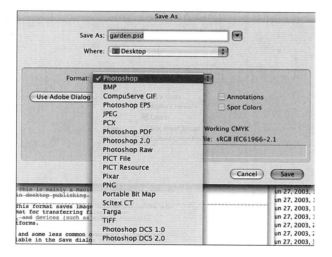

FIGURE 2.1
Photoshop CS2 can save your work in any of these formats.

Opening Files

Opening a file in Photoshop is as easy as opening it in any other application. You can open as many images as you want or as many as your computer's memory can hold. If a file is of the proper type (a file format that Photoshop recognizes), all you have to do is double-click it with your mouse to not only open it, but to launch Photoshop as well. (If Photoshop is already open, you can either double-click a file or use the File→Open command.) You can also drag and drop a compatible file onto the Photoshop CS2 icon to open the file.

Windows Users Take Note

A technical note for Windows users: Double-clicking an image file will open Photoshop only if the extension (`.bmp`, for instance) is associated with Photoshop. Sometimes, installing new applications will change the extension mapping to other programs. GIFs and JPEGs are notoriously remapped to Microsoft Internet Explorer, whereas BMP is usually grabbed by Paint. If double-clicking doesn't work for you, check your extensions.

When you open the dialog box, Photoshop displays all the files that have formats it can open. Figure 2.2 shows the Photoshop Open dialog box. As you can see, if you click Preview, Photoshop will display a thumbnail of the selected image. To create previews, go to Preferences→File Handling, and choose Always Save Image Previews.

FIGURE 2.2
Any file that's shown can be opened in Photoshop.

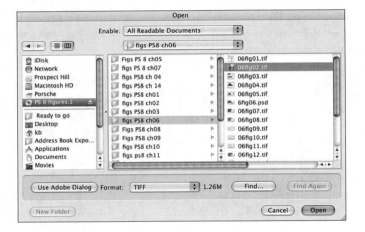

A *thumbnail* or *thumbnail sketch* is an artist's term for a small version of a picture, so called because they are often no bigger than a thumbnail.

▼   ## Try it Yourself

Open a File

As you've seen, Photoshop supports most graphics formats. You must have some graphics files somewhere on your hard drive, so let's practice finding one and opening it.

1. Choose File→Open or press Command+O (Mac) or Control+O (Windows) to display the Open dialog box.

2. Use the dialog box to locate the file on which you want to work.

▲   3. Select it and double-click, or click Open.

Using Bridge

If you have only a few graphics files, and if you're really good at keeping things organized, finding the document you're looking for isn't difficult. If, however, you're like me, your files are all over the place, and saved with the apparently random numbers the camera assigns. That's why Photoshop CS2's Bridge is one of my favorite features. To open it, use File→Browse. See Figure 2.3.

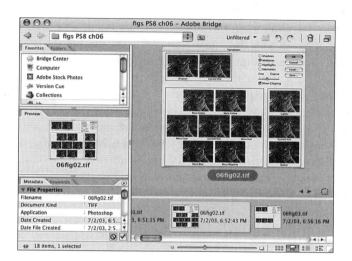

FIGURE 2.3
The three frames at the left of the window will change size if you drag the dividers.

Click a tab at the upper left (Favorites or Folders) and navigate through the folder hierarchy to locate the folder you want. As soon as one is selected, you'll see all its images displayed as if on a slide viewer. If there are folders nested inside the one you originally opened, you'll see them as folder icons. The upper-left section of the window shows the location of the file you opened. If your digital camera or scanner saves information about the selected image, you can scroll through the lower section to determine what lens and shutter settings the camera used, whether the exposure required a flash, and the precise minute and second the picture was taken—virtually everything you need to know except where it was shot. Actually, there are now some special-purpose digital cameras with GPS connections that *can* tell you where the picture was taken.

Then just scroll through the folders and the images within them until you find the one you want. Double-click the thumbnail image in the right section of the window or the preview on the left to open the original.

Importing a File

The Import command (File→Import) lets you open files that have been saved in formats that use plug-in import modules, as well as files that aren't on your hard drive. Typically, these include images created with your scanner or digital camera and special image types such as PICT resources (Macintosh only).

Importing from Digital Cameras

Most digital cameras can import pictures directly into Photoshop. The plug-in filter or photo browser comes with the camera. Drop it, if the directions say to, into the Plug-ins folder. (Remember that you must quit the application before you install plug-ins. If you install while Photoshop is running, it can't see the new plug-in until you quit and restart the program.) To import a picture, you simply plug the camera cable into the computer's USB port. Then choose File→Import and whatever camera you are importing from. Pictures in the camera are displayed, as in the Photoshop Browser, as if they were slides on a sorting table. You can view a larger image and find out more about it by selecting a picture and double-clicking or choosing Get Info. You can't click the picture and expect it to open into Photoshop, however. It will open into its own full-screen display. To work on it in Photoshop, you must open it from within Photoshop.

Mac OS X users can also open photos from iPhoto, a Mac application that doesn't require any additional software to download from all kinds of digital cameras. Figure 2.4 shows a small collection of photos imported directly from a Nikon CoolPix 5700. It's very easy to build photo libraries with this program, and you can import the pictures you have worked on in Photoshop for an easy slideshow.

Camera Raw

Camera Raw is a format that Adobe added as a plug-in in 2002, and sold separately. Because it proved to be useful and popular, it's included in Photoshop CS2. Essentially, what it does is enable direct downloads from a digital camera, without translating the file into JPEG. It takes the raw camera data, and gives you, in effect, a digital "negative." You can assign color corrections, sharpen the focus, compensate for spherical lens aberrations, and make other needed corrections picture by picture as they are copied into the computer.

Importing Files with the TWAIN Interface

The TWAIN Acquire and TWAIN Select commands found under the File→Import submenu don't actually import images. Instead, they enable you to open the appropriate scanner software to be used from within Photoshop and to use it to import the scanned images. Photoshop supports TWAIN, TWAIN32, and TWAIN_32 standards for scanning. Consult the scanner manual for more information.

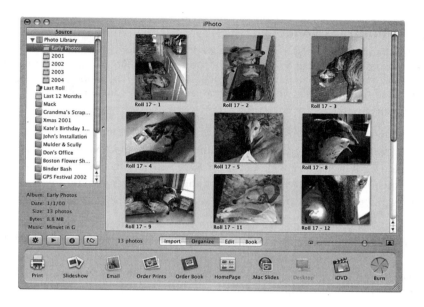

FIGURE 2.4
You won't find
this application
in Windows.

Saving Your Work

There's one very important thing to know about saving your work: Do it often! Computers are prone to unexpected shutdowns and errors. Saving takes only a couple of seconds, and it can make the difference between having to do your work all over again or just reopening it if the computer shuts down.

The first time you save a picture, you'll see the Save As dialog box, as shown in Figure 2.5. Give the file a name and select an appropriate format to save it in from the pop-up menu. After this, click Save or just press Command+S (Mac) or Control+S (Windows) to save the file.

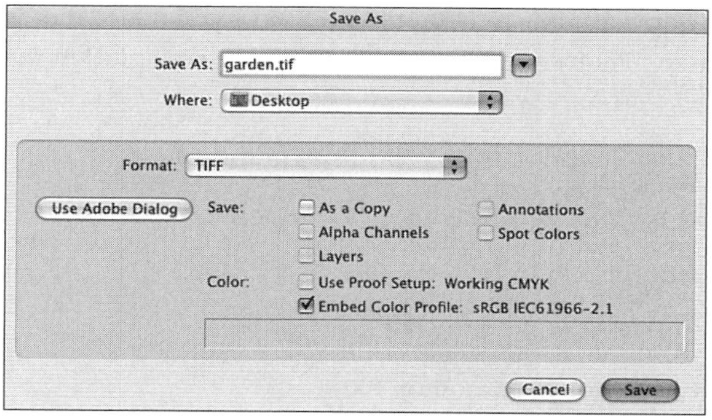

FIGURE 2.5
Saving a file in
Photoshop.

Cross-Platform Concept

For Macintosh users only: If you have to work cross-platform, that is, on both a Macintosh and PC, you should always choose to include file extensions with your files. This option is found in the Preferences dialog box. Also, always check Use Lowercase to be sure that your file is Windows and UNIX compatible.

In addition to the familiar Save and Save As commands, Photoshop has more Save commands, such as Save a Copy. This option is found in the Save As dialog box—check As a Copy to use it. Save a Copy, like Save As, lets you save the file with a new name and in a new location. The difference is that after you use Save As, you're working in the new file.

If you use Save a Copy, you save a copy of the file as it is at that moment, but you'll still be working on the original file, not the copy. Save a Copy is especially useful for making a backup copy before you try a drastic change, such as reducing color depth or increasing JPEG lossiness, or for saving the file in a different format. Suppose that you create a logo for your business and want to use it in print and on the Web. You'd save it as a TIFF or EPS file to print from, and you'd save a copy as a JPEG or PNG file for your Web page. The word copy is automatically added to the filename.

The final Save option, located in the File menu, is Save for Web. It contains the settings you need to optimize the image for Web use, including letting you see and select the amount of JPEG compression to apply, so you can get the smallest file that won't compromise the image quality too much. You can save Web images either in Photoshop or in ImageReady. It makes little difference, unless animation and other special Web effects are involved, in which case you'll probably want to use ImageReady. You'll learn about these options in detail in Hour 24.

Reducing File Size

As you start to work with different Photoshop files, you'll notice that your hard drive is starting to fill up. Photoshop files can become large very quickly. You can make your files smaller in several ways:

► Reduce the resolution or the physical size of the image

► Reduce the number of colors in the image palette

► Use a format that compresses the file

► Use a compression utility after the file is saved

► Merge layers in native Photoshop files

► Delete any alpha channels that are no longer needed

Reducing the resolution is not a good idea if you're going to print the image. If the picture is going to be viewed only on your computer screen or on the Web, reduce the resolution to 72 dpi. Be aware, though, that increasing the resolution again, if you change your mind, reduces image quality. You can change the resolution in the Image→Image size dialog box. Don't make it less than 72 dpi.

Reducing the number of colors means reducing the bit depth. This can make your colors look blotchy onscreen and in print. If you are working in grayscale (no color in the picture), reduce the bit depth to 8 bits by choosing Grayscale in the Image Mode submenu. This gives you 256 shades of gray, which is more than a printer can print.

Using a compressed format means choosing a file format, such as TIFF with LZW compression, that automatically shrinks the file down as small as possible when it saves. It does this by a means called *lossless compression*, so there's no image degradation or blotchy color. LZW compression (named for its inventors, Lempel, Ziv, and Welch) is also used by GIF and PDF formats.

There are also formats, such as JPEG, that use *lossy compression*. Lossy means, as you might guess from the name, that some of the data that makes up the image is lost in the compression process. Instead of 20 shades of blue in the sky in a TIFF file, the same image in a JPEG file might have only 5 shades of blue. And, yes, you *can* see the difference. Unfortunately, compression is necessary when you are placing images on the Web, in a multimedia presentation, or in another situation where upload time or storage space is limited. JPEG saves files in the least possible amount of disk space. One point to remember is that if you save a JPEG image a second time as a JPEG, it is compressed again and loses more information. If you work on a JPEG file a lot, you can end up with an unreadable picture. If you're going to work on a picture, save it as a Photoshop file. Don't make it a JPEG until you're done with it and ready to post it on your Web page. If you have to change the image, trash the JPEG file and go back to the Photoshop version.

When you have files you want to save for future reference, you can save them in the normal way as Photoshop documents (with a .psd filename extension) or in whatever format you prefer to work in, and then compress the files with a utility such as StuffIt or PKZip or WinZip. All these file compression utilities use lossless compression algorithms and shrink your image files by anywhere from 20% to 50%. That said, compressing JPEG or GIF files is relatively useless because they're already compressed. You won't gain more than a few percent of additional compression.

Figure 2.6 shows a typical digital photograph that I saved in a number of different file types. (The original is about 5 inches wide, and saved at 200 dpi.) Table 2.1 shows the more common file types and the sizes of the files that this picture required. The version shown is a PSD, the native Photoshop format.

TABLE 2.1   File Format/File Size Comparisons for Figure 2.6

Format	File Size
Photoshop native	1.97MB
BMP	1.97MB
EPS	2.82MB
GIF	536KB
JPEG (high quality)	272KB
JPEG (low quality)	192KB
PDF (medium quality)	188KB
PNG (interlaced)	1.3MB
TIFF (LZW compression)	1.4MB

Choosing a Format

With so many possible formats, how can you decide which one to use? It's really not so difficult. As long as you are working on an image, keep saving it as a Photoshop document (.psd). This makes sense, especially after you learn to work in layers, because Photoshop's native format can save the layers, whereas most other formats require that you merge the layers into one. After you have flattened the layers, you can't split them apart again. So, bottom line, as long as you think you'll want to go back to a picture and modify it, save a copy as a Photoshop document.

When you finish working on the picture and are ready to place it into another document for printing, save a copy as an EPS file if it's going to a PostScript-compatible printer. If you aren't sure how it will be printed, save it as a TIFF because TIFF is compatible with most printers and page-layout programs. If you're going to place your picture on a Web page, choose GIF if the picture is line art, has large areas of solid color, or uses a limited color palette. Choose JPEG or PNG if the picture is a photograph or continuous tone art (lots of colors). If you want to import the picture into some other graphics program for additional work, choose Photoshop format (PSD) if the other program supports it, and TIFF if the other program doesn't recognize Photoshop files.

Undoing and Redoing

Starting with Photoshop 5, Adobe's software engineers finally responded to user demands and introduced the History palette and History Brush tool. The History palette keeps a listing of every tool you've used and every change you've made, up to a predetermined number you can set in the History Options menu. You can also take "snapshots" of the work in progress and use these as saved stages to which you can revert. Figure 2.7 shows the History palette for a picture that's had a lot of changes made to it.

FIGURE 2.7
The History palette.

You can click any previous step to revert to it if you don't like what you've done. It's more useful in some ways than multiple undo, because the History palette lets you undo and redo selectively by choosing the step you want to revert to. More importantly, it enables you to save your work as you do it and still go back and undo. In previous editions of Photoshop, and in some other programs, after you save your work, Undo isn't available. We'll discuss the uses of the History palette and the History Brush (which lets you undo as much or as little of a change as you want) in greater detail in Hour 7, "Paintbrushes and Art Tools."

Of course, you can always use Command+Z (Mac) or Control+Z (Windows) to toggle the Undo and Redo commands in a single step. For multiple undos, use Command+Option+Z for Mac and Control+Alt+Z for Windows.

Summary

Photoshop can work with many kinds of graphics files from many sources. Those that it doesn't open directly, either by double-clicking or by using the Open dialog box, can be imported through plug-in filters. If you have a digital camera or scanner, it might have a Photoshop plug-in that enables you to open the image from within Photoshop. Check your owner's manual.

Logically enough, Photoshop can also save documents in all the formats it can open (except Raw). Different formats have different purposes and different file sizes. Some are specifically intended for Web use, others for printing. Choose a format based on the intended use of the image.

The History palette saves a step-by-step list of everything you do to your picture. You can travel backward or forward through the History list and easily undo or redo your changes, even if you have already saved the document.

Workshop

Q&A

Q *Which kinds of files compress better as GIF than as JPEG or PNG?*

A Because GIF uses a limited palette, any picture that has only a few colors will give you a smaller file as a GIF than in the other formats. Such graphics items as titles in flat colors, logos, charts and graphs, or line art will make very small GIFs. Full-color photos will not.

Q *When should I use Save a Copy?*

A Use Save a Copy when you want to make a copy of the picture you are working on and then continue to work on the original instead of the copy. Suppose that I have a picture called Roses, which I have worked on and saved. If I save a copy as Roses copy, and then keep working, I will still be working on the original Roses but will also have a copy of the picture in a closed file as it was before I did the additional work.

Q *What file formats should I use for images I'll be putting in my Web page?*

A You should try to stick with native Photoshop files when creating your images. This enables you to use all the powerful Photoshop CS2 editing features, such as layers. When you've finished your image, save it as a GIF, JPEG, or PNG for use on the Web.

Q *How does color depth affect image file size?*

A Simply put, the more colors that your image's color mode can support, the larger the file size because it takes more bits to encode more colors.

Quiz

1. BMP is

   a. A PC format that stands for bitmap

   b. A Macintosh format that stands for bump

   c. A UNIX code for better management program

2. GIFs are

   a. A format used mainly on the Web

   b. The Macintosh graphics format

   c. The little images used as icons on the desktop

3. TIFF stands for

    a. Tiled Image Format

    b. Tagged Image File Format

    c. Typical Information Font

4. To use a scanned image,

    a. Use File→Open Scanner

    b. With Photoshop open, turn on the scanner

    c. Use File→Import→TWAIN (or your scanner plug-in)

Quiz Answers

1. a. Bitmaps are a pixel-by-pixel analysis of the picture. They're not necessarily large files.

2. a. GIF stands for Graphic Image Format, and was originally developed by CompuServe so members could exchange photos with each other.

3. b. When you save a TIFF, you must choose whether to save it for Macintosh or PC.

4. c. Be sure that the scanner software is installed. Its plug-in goes in the Photoshop Plug-ins folder.

Exercises

1. Open one of your own digital photos or art files and save it in different formats. See how the format affects the file size.

2. Open a new page and try some tools, as you did after the last hour. Now, look at the History palette and see what you've done. Click on an entry and watch the image revert back to what it looked like after using that tool. Click again on the last entry to restore what you did.

Making Selections

What You'll Learn in This Hour:

- ▶ The Selection Tools
- ▶ The Selection Menu
- ▶ Selecting Large Areas
- ▶ Cutting and Copying
- ▶ Cropping

Now you're making progress. You've learned how to bring images in and out of Photoshop. The next step is learning to work with images and edit them. To do this, you have to *select* a part of the picture on which you want to work. Selections are just what they seem to be—portions of the image that you have selected.

The Selection Tools

There are several ways to select a piece of a picture. You can use any of the Selection tools: Marquee tools, Lasso tools, or the Magic Wand. You have different kinds of Selection tools because you sometimes need to make selections in a particular way, such as punching a shape out of an image or selecting all of the sky. Photoshop's Selection tools give you the power to select the whole picture or a single pixel. Just to refresh your memory, Figure 3.1 shows the Selection tools. (The pop-up menus have been shifted so that you can see what's on them.) In the lower-right corner, you can also see the Slice tool, which is used for Web animation. You'll learn all about it in Hour 24, "Photoshop for the Web."

FIGURE 3.1
The Selection tools are located at the top of the toolbox.

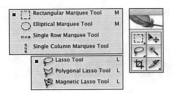

Rectangular and Elliptical Marquees

The Marquee tools, both Rectangular and Elliptical, are found in the upper-left corner of the toolbox. To select the Rectangular Marquee, just click it or press the letter *M* on your keyboard. To select the Elliptical Marquee, click and hold the Rectangular Marquee in the toolbox. When the pop-up menu appears, choose the Elliptical Marquee. Use this method to choose the Single Row or Single Column Marquee, too.

Assuming that the Rectangular Marquee is the currently selected tool, you can also press Shift+M to switch back and forth between the two. The Elliptical Marquee tool works the same way as the Rectangular Marquee tool. The icon will change accordingly on the Tool Options bar.

To experiment with its many uses, first create a new file (go back to Hour 1, "The Basics," if you can't remember how). Again, give yourself some room to work. Set the dimensions to the Photoshop default.

1. Click the Marquee tool in the toolbox.

    As you move the tool over the canvas, the cursor appears as a crosshair.

2. While the cursor is over the canvas, click and hold the mouse button, and then drag out a marquee.

    Experiment with dragging out an elliptical marquee. Try to get a sense for how marquees appear. Try dragging from different directions.

If you press and hold the Shift key *after* you've made your first selection and *before* you click again, you can make additional selections. Take care to continue holding the Shift key while making additional selections. (You'll see a plus sign beneath the crosshair.) Where the selected areas overlap, they'll merge to form one larger selected shape. Figure 3.2 shows both single marquee shapes and a combination of shapes making a selection somewhat resembling a gazebo.

To draw a perfectly square box or round circle, choose Fixed Aspect Ratio from the Style pop-up menu on the Tool Options bar and enter 1 and 1 in the width and height fields, or just press the Shift key as you drag the shape. Use Fixed Size to make multiple selections that are the same size.

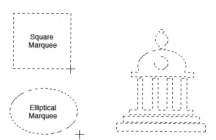

FIGURE 3.2
You can also combine square and round selections.

To deselect an area inside another area (making what graphics artists call a *knockout*), press Option (Mac) or Alt (Windows) as you drag the inner shape. (You'll see a minus sign beneath the crosshair.) For instance, if you have a circle selected and drag another smaller circle inside it while pressing Option (Mac) or Alt (Windows), the selected shape is a donut.

Pushing Your Buttons

If your memory for keyboard shortcuts is already overloaded, you'll be relieved to know you can also combine selections using the four buttons at the left end of the Tool Options bar: New Selection, Add to Selection, Subtract from Selection, and Intersect with Selection. That last one results in a selection of the common area occupied by the original selection and your new selection.

Did you Know?

The thin, horizontal (Single Row) and vertical (Single Column) marquees select a single row of pixels, either horizontally or vertically. They are often useful for cleaning up the edges of an object.

When you are dealing with selections, it is important to remember that, for good or bad, only the area within the confines of the marquee can be edited. It is the only active area of the canvas. Thus, after a selection is made, you can perform whatever action you want, but before you move on, the selection must be turned off, or *deselected*, by clicking outside the selected area with one of the Marquee tools or by pressing Command+D (Mac) or Control+D (Windows). Until you do so, you can only edit within the selection's boundaries. On the other hand, this restriction on editing can be extremely helpful if you need to draw a complex filled shape. Assemble the shape from multiple selections, as I have in Figure 3.2. Then you can pour paint into it, apply a gradient to it, or use the paintbrush with no fear of coloring outside the lines. You can even use the selection to erase a piece of the picture. If I filled the page with color or with an image and selected a shape from within it, I could easily remove the active selected piece by pressing the Backspace/Delete key.

Layer Pitfalls

If you copy or paste something onto your canvas, and then try to select a different part of the picture, you might find that the Marquee tool doesn't work. You might also get a message saying "Could not complete your request because the selected area is empty." This is Photoshop's way of reminding you that you have added another layer to your picture by pasting into it, and the part you're trying to copy isn't on that layer. Look at the Layers palette, and click the layer on which you want to work. Clicking its icon will make it the active layer. You will learn all about working with layers in Hour 11, "Layers."

Lasso

As useful as the Marquee tools and their modifier keys are, there will come times when you have to select irregular shapes. Perhaps you might need to select a single flower from a bunch or, as in Figure 3.3, remove the kitten from the table.

FIGURE 3.3
Selecting an object with the Lasso.

Lasso tool

Using the primary Lasso tool to select an object in this way requires a steady hand and good hand-eye coordination, as well as a clean mouse and mousepad or trackball. As with the Marquee tools, you can add to your lassoed selection by holding the Shift key and selecting additional parts of the object.

Slow Down, Mousie

I've found that when I am trying to make a very careful selection with the Lasso tool, and when I am using Photoshop in general, it helps to slow my mouse down. You can adjust the speed of mouse reaction time in the Mouse section of your machine's Control Panel. Start by setting the slider just a little higher than the slowest setting. Experiment to see what works best for you.

Create a Selection with the Lasso Tool

To make a selection with the Lasso tool, follow these steps:

1. Select the Lasso tool from the toolbox or press L.

2. Click and carefully drag the Lasso tool around the piece of the image you want to select. You see a solid line as you drag.

3. When you're close to completely enclosing the selection, you can release the mouse button. The two ends of the selection marquee that you have drawn around the shape automatically join together, completing the marquee. If you release the mouse button before you have traced all the way around, the ends of the lasso line will still connect, even if it means drawing a line through the center of the object. If that happens, press and hold the Shift key and use the Lasso tool again to finish drawing the shape. ▲

The Polygonal Lasso Tool

The Polygonal Lasso tool behaves in much the same way as the regular Lasso tool. The difference is, as its name implies, it makes irregular *straight-edged* selections. It's actually easier to use when you need to make detailed selections because it can be controlled more easily. Instead of simply dragging a marquee line, as you do with the regular Lasso, you click the Polygonal Lasso to place points, and Photoshop inserts a straight-line marquee between the points. You can place as many points as you need, as close together or as far apart as necessary. Figure 3.4 shows the tool in use.

FIGURE 3.4
The Polygonal Lasso tool.

▼   **Try it Yourself**

Create a Selection with the Polygonal Lasso Tool

To use the Polygonal Lasso tool, follow these steps:

1. Click the Lasso tool and hold until you see the pop-up menu.

2. Select the Polygonal Lasso tool. (You can also do this by skipping step 1 and simply pressing Shift+L until you've selected the tool.)

3. Click once in the canvas. Now move your mouse. Notice that a line follows your Polygonal Lasso wherever you move it.

4. Click again. This draws the first line and sets another point from which you can drag. Place another line and click again.

   Now with two lines set, you have an option. You can either continue to select the image, or you can double-click. This automatically finishes the selection for you.

   When the cursor nears your starting point, notice that a small circle becomes appended to the cursor. This signals that, if you click, the selection will be completed.

▲
5. Click to complete your selection.

Did you Know?

Consider All the Options
Many of Photoshop's tools, including the Selection tools, have additional options. These are found on the Tool Options bar. Whenever you select a new tool, be sure to look at its options.

The Magnetic Lasso

The Magnetic Lasso is one of my most-used tools. As you drag it around any shape with a reasonably well-defined edge, it snaps to the edge. Select it and use it just as you did the Polygonal Lasso. Because it finds edges by looking for differences in contrast, the Magnetic Lasso is most effective on irregular objects that stand out from the background. You can use the Tool Options bar to set the parameters. *Width* refers to how close to the edge you must be to have the Lasso recognize it (see Figure 3.5). *Edge contrast* determines how different the pixels must be in brightness value for the Lasso to recognize them. *Frequency* determines how often the Lasso sets its anchor points. (*Anchor points* are the points indicated by boxes on a line. Drag them to adjust the line.)

Magic Wand

The software designers at Adobe Systems must not have been able to come up with a more descriptive name for this fantastic tool, choosing instead to let it, perhaps, speak for itself—the Magic Wand. Maybe it's better that way.

FIGURE 3.5
Set the Edge Contrast value according to the amount contrast between the intended selection and what surrounds it.

The Magic Wand is a different kind of Selection tool. So far, we've looked at tools that select pixels based on their placement in the bitmap (the picture). The Magic Wand selects pixels somewhat differently; it selects them based on color values. This enables you to cut foreground objects, such as the lighthouse, out of the background. You might need to combine several selections by holding the Shift key, as done in Figure 3.6, to select the entire object.

As with the previously described tools, the Magic Wand can make and merge selections if you press the Shift key as you click the areas to select.

The Magic Wand selects adjacent pixels based on color similarities. Its tolerance can be set in the Tool Options bar. *Tolerance*, in this instance, refers to the Magic Wand's sensitivity to color differences.

The rule is easy to remember: The lower the Tolerance setting, the less tolerance the Magic Wand has for color differences. Thus, for example, if you set the Tolerance higher (it ranges from 0 to 255), it selects all variations of the color that you initially select.

Settings on the Tool Options bar allow you to select everything in the picture that matches the selected color or select only pixels that touch each other. If, for example, you have a picture with several yellow flowers and your Tolerance setting is high, you'll select as much and as many of the flowers as fits the tolerance. If you check Contiguous in the Tools Options bar, you'll select only the parts of the flower you click on that are within the tolerance *and* have pixels that touch each other. In Figure 3.7, I've set the tolerance to 32, and clicked once on each screen. The screen on the right had Contiguous selected. The one on the left did not.

FIGURE 3.6
Selections
being made with
the Magic
Wand.

FIGURE 3.7
Selecting non-
contiguous pix-
els can save
you a lot of
time.

The Magic Wand is best used for selecting objects that are primarily one color, such as the flower. It's ideal when you need to select the sky in a landscape. In a few minutes, you'll see exactly how to do this, but first, there are some other selection tricks to learn.

The Selection Menu

You might have noticed that, in addition to the Selection tools you have just learned about, there's also a Select menu, shown in Figure 3.8. Probably the most useful commands on the menu are the top four. Select All simply draws a selection marquee around the entire canvas. Deselect removes the selection marquee from the image. Reselect replaces the marquee if you have accidentally deselected something. Inverse lets you select everything but one object by selecting the object and then inverting. For instance, if I had a photo of a lemon on a plate, I could select the lemon and then choose Inverse to select the plate. Inverting is extremely useful, and you'll soon discover that it's one of your favorite commands.

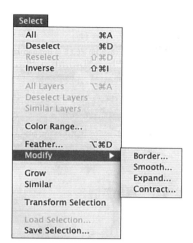

FIGURE 3.8
The Select menu and Modify sub-menu.

Feather

Feather lets you make selections with fuzzy, *feathered* edges rather than hard ones. It's very helpful when you want to select an object from one picture and paste it into another because it adds a slight blur that helps the object to blend in. You can use the Feather Selection dialog box, shown in Figure 3.9, to determine how many pixel widths of feathering to apply. Experiment with feathering selections to find out what works best.

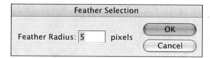

FIGURE 3.9
The Feather Selection dialog box.

Try it Yourself

Make a Feathered Selection

To make a feathered selection, follow these steps:

1. Choose an appropriate Selection tool and use it to select as precisely as possible a piece of the picture or an object within the picture.

2. Choose Select→Feather to open the dialog box.

3. Enter an amount in the window. Start with 5 and increase or decrease until the selection looks right to you.

4. Copy the selection and paste it into a new file so you can see the effect of the feathering.

Modifying Selections

The Select→Modify submenu gives you some other options for working with your selections. Border changes the selected area so that, instead of the whole object, you have selected only a border around it. You can set the width of the border in its dialog box. Smooth is helpful when you have made a lasso selection with a shaky hand. It smoothes out bumps in the Marquee line by as many pixels as you specify. Expand and Contract force, as their names suggest, your selection to grow or shrink as necessary by as many pixels as you designate in the dialog box.

Selecting Large Areas

It's often necessary to select a large part of the picture, such as the sky, so that you can darken its color or otherwise change it without changing the rest of the picture. Figure 3.10 shows a picture with a lot of sky and a very complicated object sticking up into it. There are gaps between the branches and leaves, and some of the highlights on the flowers are close to the color of the sky.

FIGURE 3.10
Selecting just the sky will be difficult.

You can download this picture from the Sams website mentioned in the Introduction. Look for crabapple.jpg. This file will open in both PC and Mac versions of Photoshop.

Try it Yourself ▼

Select a Large Area

To select the sky in this picture, follow these steps:

1. Choose the Magic Wand.

2. Set the Tolerance in the Tool Options bar to 20, as shown in Figure 3.11. This enables you to select only similar shades of blue. Be sure that Contiguous is not selected so that you can pick up the blue patches between the leaves.

FIGURE 3.11
You can set the Tolerance anywhere from 0 to 255.

3. Click the Magic Wand on a typical piece of blue (see Figure 3.12).

FIGURE 3.12
You might need to make several selections to include all of the sky.

4. Hold down the Shift key and select additional pieces of sky and cloud until you have it all.

5. Look carefully at the selected areas. Have you selected bits of blue or white that aren't part of the sky? Change the tool to the Lasso, and press Option/Alt while you draw a line around pieces of the image that you want to *deselect*. You might have to do this several times.

6. Now you can proceed to change the color of the sky, press Delete to remove it, or do whatever else you intended. Figure 3.13 shows the image with the sky completely gone. ▼

FIGURE 3.13
The entire sky is removed.

Find another picture with a lot of sky and practice this yourself. It's not difficult. Remember, if you select more sky (or whatever) than you intended, Undo will deselect the last portion selected, leaving the rest of the selection active.

Cutting and Copying

If you have used the cut or copy and paste features in any other application, you can use them in Photoshop. The commands are identical and so are the results. You'll find the Cut, Copy, and Paste commands on the Edit menu.

Cutting, copying, and pasting enable you to borrow from one picture to add to another. The example that follows takes a lonely seagull and gives him some friends. Figure 3.14 shows the seagull selected, with the feather amount set to 3 pixels to help it blend in when pasted. The picture is at a 500% enlargement. Next, you can simply use the Copy command (Edit→Copy), Command+C (Mac), or Control+C (Windows) to copy the bird to the Clipboard.

You can now paste the gull where it will fill in the empty space and improve the composition (see Figure 3.15). As long as the bird is on the Clipboard, you can place as many copies of him as you want. One seagull in Figure 3.14 is flipped horizontally to face the other way and not look quite so identical. You can also scale them to different sizes or distort them a little so they look different.

FIGURE 3.14
Before you can
copy the seag-
ull, you have to
select it.

FIGURE 3.15
The new picture,
with the added
gulls.

Cropping

Cropping is the artists' term for trimming away unwanted parts of a picture. You can
think of it as a specialized kind of selection, which is probably why the people who
created Photoshop put the Crop tool in the same toolbox section as the Selection
Marquees (see Figure 3.16). When you drag a cropping box around the part of the
image you want to keep, click Shield on the Tool Options bar to darken the rest of
the screen so that it's easier to see what's going on. Of course, you can also crop by

making a selection with the Rectangular Marquee and then using the menu command Image→Crop to trim the picture.

FIGURE 3.16
The Crop tool in use.

Try it Yourself

Crop a Picture

To crop a picture, use any image and follow these steps:

1. Select the Crop tool from the toolbox or press C on the keyboard. (It looks like two overlapped pieces of L-shaped mat board—the same tool artists use to help compose paintings.)

2. Drag it across the picture, holding the mouse button down.

3. Use the handles on the cropping box to fine-tune the selection. The area outside the box will be dimmed so that you can see what you're removing.

4. After you have the cropping box placed where you want it, double-click inside it to delete the area outside the box.

▲

You can even use Photoshop's cropping tool to correct perspective. Click the Perspective check box on the Tool Options bar. First, drag a guide from the left ruler so that you can see what's not straight that should be. (Press Command+R or Control+R to activate the rulers.) Drag the Crop tool over an image that needs perspective adjustment, like the tilting house in Figure 3.17. After you've drawn the cropping box, click to select the Perspective check box and then click one of the corners of the box and drag it until the side of the window is parallel to the side of the building. Repeat with the other side.

Click Accept to apply the changes or simply double-click inside the cropping window. Figure 3.18 shows the result. Now the building is in proper perspective, the chimney is straight, and all's right with the world.

FIGURE 3.17
Use Perspective cropping to straighten warped buildings.

Open any picture and practice cropping it. Remember, if you crop too much of the picture, you can undo. If it's too late to undo because you have already done something else, just go back to the History palette and click the step before cropping. You can also choose File→Revert to go back to the last saved version of your picture. As long as you don't close the file, you can keep cropping and using the History palette to undo as much as you want.

FIGURE 3.18
It's okay for the Tower of Pisa to lean, but not a proper Yankee house.

Summary

Some of the most powerful tools in Photoshop are the Selection tools. They enable you to edit selectively.

Try to develop a feel for when you can use selections. They can save you a great deal of time when you need to fill a space with color or an image, when you need to manipulate just a piece of an image, when you want to selectively brighten or adjust part of an image, or when you need to extract a piece of an image from a larger work.

The book refers to selections throughout the remainder of the chapters, so if you need to, dog-ear a page.

Workshop

Q&A

Q *Can I combine selections made with different Selection tools?*

A Yes. Make a selection with one of the tools, switch tools, and then press the Shift key before you add to your selection. As long as you hold down the Shift key (making a tiny plus sign visible next to the tool), you can add to your selection as many times as you want.

Q *How can I deselect part of a selection?*

A The easiest way to do this is to press Option (Mac) or Alt (Windows) key with the Selection tool active. You will see a small minus symbol next to the Selection tool. Select the part of the selection to deselect, and it is removed from the selection and added back to the picture.

Q *Can I use the marquee to draw a shape and then fill it?*

A Yes, and that's exactly how to do it. With the selection active, use the Paint Bucket to pour a color into the selected shape(s).

Quiz

1. To change from the Rectangular to the Elliptical Marquee:

    a. Go back to the toolbox and select the other one.

    b. Press Shift+M.

    c. Either a or b.

2. To select a single row or column of pixels:

    a. Hold down Control+C and the Return key, while double-clicking.

    b. Press Return as you drag the mouse.

    c. Use the Single Row or Single Column marquees.

3. How do you make the Magic Wand more precise?

    a. Insult it.

    b. Set the Tolerance to a lower number.

    c. Set the Tolerance to a higher number.

Quiz Answers

1. c. Easy, huh?

2. c. (Answer a. isn't even possible unless you have three hands.)

3. b. A lower Tolerance setting means that the Magic Wand will select only the most similar pixels.

Exercise

Most pictures can be improved by careful cropping. Try this experiment. Cut two L-shaped pieces from a sheet of paper or cardboard, as shown in Figure 3.19.

FIGURE 3.19
How to use a cropping frame.

Use these pieces as a cropping frame and look at your snapshots or at pictures in a magazine to see how different cropping affects the picture. Try finding long, narrow compositions, square ones, and rectangles.

Transformations

What You'll Learn in This Hour:

▶ Resizing
▶ Rotating
▶ Flipping
▶ Selection Transformations
▶ Warping Liquifying

It's extremely rare, if not impossible, that your pictures will always be the right size and shape for your purposes. You might need to make an object bigger or smaller as you copy it from one picture to another. You might need to straighten a tilted horizon, or even stand the Leaning Tower of Pisa upright. Perhaps you simply need to make someone face left instead of right or turn an object upside down. You can do all this and more with just a few mouse clicks or simple commands. Ready? Let's start by looking at making the whole picture bigger or smaller.

Resizing

Photoshop makes it easy to change the size of the picture or of anything in it. You have two options: resizing the image or resizing the canvas. Resizing the image makes the picture bigger or smaller. Resizing the canvas makes the picture *area* bigger, while leaving the image floating within it. You'd do this if you need more space around an object without shrinking the actual image.

Resizing an Image

To resize an image, choose Image Size from the Image menu; the dialog box is shown in Figure 4.1. You can see the pixel dimensions in pixels (logically) or percentages. You can also see the image print size (set in Output Size section of screen) in inches, centimeters, points, picas, or columns; percentages can also be found using the pop-up menus.

When you first open the Image Size dialog box, if you set the width and height pixel dimensions to Percent, you'll see the default setting of 100%. The easiest way to enlarge or reduce the image is to make sure that Constrain Proportions is checked at the bottom of the dialog box, and then simply enter new percentages in one of the fields and click OK. As if by magic, the other numbers will change to give you the correct percentage of enlargement or reduction. For now, ignore Resample Image. Leave it set to Bicubic. You'll get into what this means when you need to know it in Hour 23, "Printing and Publishing."

Scale Styles is a very helpful feature if you have applied a style such as a drop shadow or embossing to text or an object in your picture. Scale Styles makes sure that the size of the shadow, or the height of the embossing, remains proportional to the rest of the picture. Leave it checked.

FIGURE 4.1
The Image Size
dialog box.

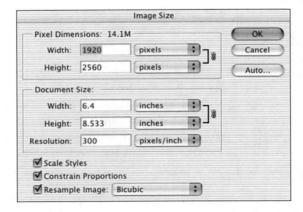

As you make changes in the Image Size dialog box, Photoshop will automatically update the file size at the top of the dialog box.

Resizing a Canvas

Resizing the canvas to a larger size gives you extra workspace around the image; it does not change the size of the image. Because resizing uses the current background color to fill in the added space, be sure that it's a color you want. I always resize with white as the background color. Resizing the canvas to a smaller size is another way of cropping the picture by decreasing the canvas area. It's not recommended because you could accidentally lose part of the picture and not be able to recover it.

To resize the canvas, choose Image→Canvas Size and specify the height and width you want the canvas to be in the dialog box (see Figure 4.2). You can specify any of the measurement systems you prefer on the pop-up menu, as you saw in the Image Size dialog box earlier. Photoshop calculates and displays the new file size as soon as you enter the numbers.

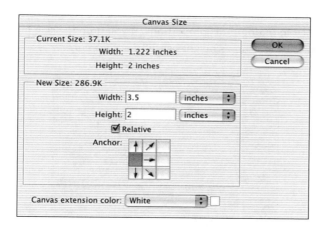

FIGURE 4.2
The Canvas Size dialog box.

Use the anchor proxy to determine where the image will be placed within the canvas. Click in the middle to center the image on the enlarged canvas, or in any of the other boxes to place it relative to the increased canvas area. Figure 4.3 shows the result of anchoring an image in the center-left of the canvas. The image size hasn't actually changed, but the canvas is bigger, making room for the type I've added. The final result is on the right.

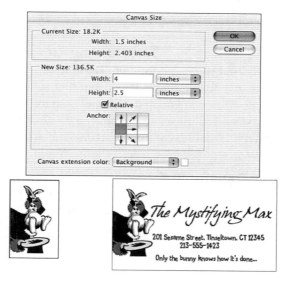

FIGURE 4.3
Before view of canvas on the left; after view on the right.

Resizing a Selection

You can also resize a selected object. To do so, first select the object or a piece of an image to be resized. Use whichever Selection tool is most convenient. With the Selection Marquee active, choose Edit→Transform→Scale. This places a box that looks like the cropping box around your selected object (see Figure 4.4). Drag any of the corner "handles" on the box to change the size of the selection while holding down the Shift key to maintain its proportions. If you drag the side handles of the box, you'll stretch the selection's height or width accordingly.

FIGURE 4.4
I drew a selection marquee around the lantern and dragged the lower-right corner to enlarge it.

Rotating

There are many reasons that you might want or need to rotate an image. If you have a scanned picture or a digital camera image that should be vertical but opens as a horizontally oriented picture, rotating it 90 degrees corrects the problem. This is a common occurrence when you use a scanner because it's usually quicker to scan with the picture horizontal, regardless of its normal orientation (see Figure 4.5).

By the Way

They Have Been Transformed

If you have used a much older edition of Photoshop, you might be accustomed to looking for the Transform commands on the Layer menu. Since Photoshop 5, they've been moved to the Edit menu.

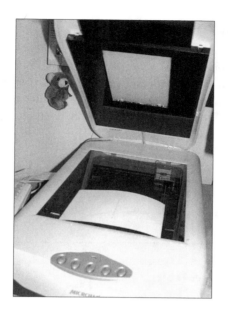

FIGURE 4.5
Placing the short side horizontally shortens the scanning time.

Rotate 180 Degrees and 90 Degrees Clockwise or Counterclockwise

To rotate the entire image, use the Image→Rotate Canvas submenu shown in Figure 4.6. Choose 90 degrees clockwise (CW) or counterclockwise (CCW) to straighten up a sideways image, or 180 degrees if you somehow brought in a picture upside down.

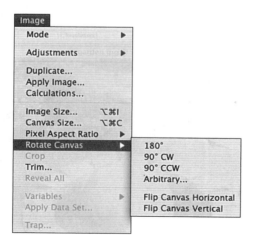

FIGURE 4.6
The Rotate Canvas submenu.

Rotate by Degrees

To rotate the canvas by something other than a right angle, choose Image→Rotate Canvas→Arbitrary to open a dialog box like the one shown in Figure 4.7. Enter the number of degrees to rotate. If you're not sure, guess. You can always undo and try again with a different number of degrees or a different direction if needed. Click the radio button to indicate the rotational direction: clockwise (CW) or counterclockwise (CCW). Then click OK to perform the rotation.

FIGURE 4.7
You can even rotate by fractions of a degree.

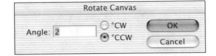

▼   **Try it Yourself**

Straightening the Horizon

Using the Arbitrary Rotation dialog box is an easy way to correct a picture that needs to be straightened. The picture in Figure 4.8 was shot just as the photographer was about to be blown off the boardwalk. Fortunately, fixing tilted horizons is an easy problem for Photoshop. Find this photo at the website and work along. It's called oldorchardbeach.jpg.

FIGURE 4.8
Oops, the horizon's not supposed to slant downhill.

You can tell just by looking at the picture that it needs to rotate counterclockwise several degrees. To straighten the horizon, follow these steps:

1. Bring a guide down from the to ruler to help you judge how crooked the image is. Click the top ruler and drag a guideline to the horizon. You can see this step in Figure 4.8. Choose Image, Rotate Canvas, Arbitrary to open the Rotate Canvas dialog box. Enter the number of degrees by which you think the horizon is "off."

2. Click the CW (clockwise) radio button to lower the right side or the CCW (counterclockwise) radio button to lower the left side of the horizon line. Figure 4.9 shows the canvas rotated by 3 degrees counterclockwise. (The setting on the tool bar is −3.) Now the horizon is level, but the edges of the picture are no longer horizontal. Cropping will square up the corners again and improve the composition at the same time.

FIGURE 4.9
You can see the background color filling in the corners of the canvas.

3. Select the Crop tool from the toolbox or press C. Drag the Crop tool across the picture to position the cropping box. Use the handles to fine-tune your cropping. Figure 4.10 shows the cropping box in position.

4. If the horizon isn't completely straight, click outside the dashed line of the cropping box. When you see a double-pointed bent arrow, you can drag the cropping box at an angle until the horizon looks right.

5. Double-click inside the cropping box when the picture looks the way you want it. Figure 4.11 shows the corrected horizon.

FIGURE 4.10
Drag the cropping box until you get rid of the listing corners of the image.

FIGURE 4.11
The horizon is level, and the composition's better, too.

Made to Measure

If you don't want to guess the proper angle for a rotation, use the Measure tool (grouped with the Eyedropper tool in the toolbox). Click at one point on the horizon (or another edge to be straightened) and drag along that soon-to-be-level line. Immediately choose Image→Rotate Canvas→Arbitrary—and the number of degrees you need to rotate is magically inserted in the dialog box by the Measure tool. Just click OK to apply the rotation. Don't worry about the measure line showing up in your image, either. As soon as you change tools, the measure line goes away.

Did you Know?

Rotate a Selection

Rotating a selection, as opposed to turning the whole canvas, is done in the same manner as resizing one. First, make the selection. Then use Edit→Transform→Rotate to place a bounding box around your selection. Drag on any of the corner handles to rotate the selection around its center point. You can see the center point as the target-shaped object in the middle of the selection in Figure 4.12. If you need to rotate the selection off-center, drag the center point to where you want it and then rotate the selection.

FIGURE 4.12
Drag any corner point to rotate the selection.

Free Transform

You can use Edit→Free Transform to make any of the changes described. Drag the handles as you press modifier keys to rotate, skew, scale, or distort as much as you want. You can also access the numeric transformations in the Tool Options bar. To distort relative to the center of the bounding box, press Alt/Option as you drag. To distort freely, press Control/Command instead. To skew, press Shift+Control (Windows) or Shift+Command (Mac). Or, if you change your mind, press Esc to cancel the transformation.

Flipping

Flipping sounds like something you'd do with a pancake, rather than a picture, but the general effect is the same. When you flip the pancake, you reverse it so the other side cooks. When you flip the image, you reverse it so you see a mirror image. You can flip horizontally or vertically. Figure 4.13 shows both.

FIGURE 4.13
The top pair of words has been flipped horizontally, whereas the bottom pair has been flipped vertically.

Flipping is different from rotating because it changes the up/down or left/right orientation of the image. Of course, sometimes you might need to do both to get the image or selected object oriented the way you want it. For comparison purposes, Figure 4.14 shows the effects of rotation. To make this composition, I typed the word *Rotate* and copied it, rotating each copy.

Watch Out!

To Flip or Not to Flip

You can flip almost any object without anyone knowing, as long as there's nothing in it that would give the viewer a clue. You can't flip a picture that has type in it, obviously. You also need to be careful about flipping pictures of people who might be wearing shirts with a pocket on one side, a wristwatch, wedding ring, single earring, or other telltale item. Also, watch out for words on signs in the background and in reflections. In many cases, it won't matter, but you might find it helpful to remove the jewelry, shirt pocket, and so on. (You'll learn how to do this in Hour 8, "Digital Painting.")

FIGURE 4.14
You can rotate an image by dragging the selection or by choosing to rotate 90 or 180 degrees from the menu, or by entering the desired rotation amount in the Tools Options bar.

Selection Transformations

Resizing and reorientation, as you've seen, can be applied either to the whole canvas or to any selected object. The transformation methods that follow can be applied only to selections, not to the whole image (unless you start by selecting the entire image).

Skewing Selections

Skew, according to my trusty *Webster's*, means "...to place at an angle." When you skew an object in Photoshop, you can do more than just slant it. You can twist, stretch, and distort it as if the object were on a sheet of rubber instead of a computer screen. The Skew command, found under Edit→Transform→Skew, enables you to twist your selection in all possible directions. Just click the handles and drag the selection. Click the toolbox to apply the setting, or double-click inside the selection, or press Enter/Return.

Skewing is related to the Perspective crop function and can be used to serve the same purpose: restoring warped perspectives. The big difference is that, because it's used on a selection instead of the whole canvas, you can straighten individual objects. Figure 4.15 shows a wedding with organ pipes about to fall on the bride's head. Because the photo was shot with a wide-angle lens, the walls and furniture appear to be slanting. In Figure 4.15, I've selected the organ cabinet with the Polygonal Lasso.

FIGURE 4.15
Selections can
be made with
any of the
Selection tools,
not just the
Rectangular
Marquee.

Now I can apply the Skew function (Edit→Transform→Skew) to the selected chest to straighten it. Figure 4.16 shows this step.

FIGURE 4.16
It usually
doesn't take
much to
straighten a tilt-
ing line.

Now, all I have to do is fill in the space where the pipes moved away from the bride, and I'm done. Because my selection is still active, I can slide it to the right a little, and move it to where it fits best. A brush full of paint fills in any remaining gaps, and the result can be seen in Figure 4.17.

Distorting Selections

All the transformation tools operate very similarly. They possess subtle differences in how they can move the selection. The Distort command (Edit→Transform→Distort) moves the selection something like the Scale command and Skew command do, but, instead of changing the size of the image, Distort crushes or stretches the image. Figure 4.18 shows one of those fashion model dolls, and the way she'd probably look if she were a real person.

FIGURE 4.17
Now the bride's not about to get clobbered.

FIGURE 4.18
Of course, you could also do the reverse, making some-body normal into a fashion model.

Select an object from one of your pictures and practice with skewing and distorting it. Remember that these commands are available to you only when the marquee is blinking, indicating that there's an active selection.

Changing the Perspective of a Selection

The Perspective command is one of the most useful functions in the Photoshop arsenal. When you want to create an image that appears to diminish in the distance, the Perspective tool can't be beat. Its movement is completely intuitive. When you drag a corner handle, the opposite corner becomes a mirror image—when you click an anchor and drag the mouse away from the selection, the mirror image moves away. When you click and drag the anchor in, it, too, follows suit.

The difference between Perspective and Distortion is that when you apply Distortion, you can do it to only one corner of the selection. Perspective automatically adjusts both corners when you drag one.

In Figure 4.19, I'm applying perspective to a shot of a gatepost. In this case, I want to make it look as though the post and the ram are about 10 feet tall instead of 5.

FIGURE 4.19
Apply the Perspective command to a selection to apply false perspective.

Warp and Liquify

Not all transformations have to be useful. The folks at Adobe have added something that's more of a wonderful toy than a tool. It's called Liquify, and it does exactly that to an image. You can swirl the image, make it bulge or shrink, and generally have fun with it. This tool is found on the Filter menu. Pick a photo, or just draw a squiggle on a blank canvas and play with it yourself. Here's my attempt (see Figure 4.20) at liquifying the fashion doll. Of course, you can also use it "seriously" to turn a frown into a smile or to widen a photo subject's squinting eyes. Use light pressure, and don't overdo it.

FIGURE 4.20
Salvador Dali
would have
loved this.

Another semi-useful but very fun feature that's new to Photoshop CS2 is Warp.
Select any portion of an image, or any layer, and choose Edit→Transform→Warp.
Then go to town! You can drag the "handles" around the warp area's edges to make
them bulge or flow, and you can drag the intersections of the interior grid to do the
same for the inner portions of the selection or layer (see Figure 4.21).

FIGURE 4.21
More methodi-
cal than Liquify,
Warp still
enables you to
push pixels
around to your
heart's content.
Here, we can
turn the level
New Orleans
skyline into a
scene from hilly
San Francisco.

Summary

Transformations are an important function in Photoshop, especially when you're combining elements from different pictures. It's often necessary to shrink or enlarge an object or the entire image. Use the Image Size and Canvas Size dialog boxes to adjust the size of the image or work area, respectively. Photoshop also lets you transform selected objects by stretching, distorting, or applying perspective to them. You can do any of these by simply applying a menu command to place a box around the object and then dragging the sides or corners of the box. Spend some time practicing the transformations. They'll be very useful later.

Workshop

Q&A

Q *When do I use Skew, versus Distort, versus Perspective? They all seem to do similar things.*

A When you know that a transformation is needed but you aren't sure what kind, use Edit→Free Transform. You can also access it by pressing Command+T (Mac) or Control+T (Windows). This command places a similar box around the object to be transformed, but it lets you rotate, distort, and drag the object in any direction, or do whatever seems necessary.

Q *I saw type that seemed to have been set standing on a mirror. The letters were reflected backward. How can I do that?*

A Set the type, make a copy of it, and flip the copy vertically. Slide the reflection into place under the original type, select it, and apply perspective until it looks right.

Q *What happens if I make a number of transformations and then change my mind about them later?*

A Using Photoshop's History palette, you can go back and undo some or all of these operations. Just go back to the state before the transformations. If you're unsure about what you're doing, it's always a good policy to work on a copy of the original picture. That way, you always have an unspoiled version if something unexpected happens.

Q *How can I tell when I've straightened the horizon enough?*

A The horizon should be level, so dragging a guide from the ruler at the top of the picture will give you something to judge it against. Remember, you can use fractions of a degree in the Rotate Canvas dialog box by typing their decimal equivalents. Half a degree is 0.5, and so on.

Quiz

1. How can you achieve the effect of a mirror appearing to the right of an object?

    a. Copy the object to be reflected, flip the copy horizontally, and move it into place. (The two images' sides should touch.) Then select the reflection and distort it, if needed for perspective.

    b. Select Edit→Mirror and then the object.

    c. You can't.

2. How can you put more white space around an object?

    a. Paint the background white.

    b. Use the Canvas Size dialog box to make the canvas bigger. (Make sure white is the background color first.)

    c. Shrink the object by selecting it and applying Edit→Transform→Scale.

3. What items should you avoid flipping?

    a. Anything containing type.

    b. Guys wearing one earring.

    c. Signs that say "This side up."

    d. Any of the above.

Quiz Answers

1. a. Edit→Mirror doesn't exist (yet).

2. b. or c. Either will work.

3. d. Don't flip anything that's obviously directional or that has clues suggesting direction, such as a watch, ring, or pocket.

Exercise

Create a new canvas. Paint a squiggle on it and select the squiggle. Practice flipping, skewing, distorting, and rotating it. Use all the tools discussed in this hour to find the ones you like best.

HOUR 5

Color Modes and Color Models

What You'll Learn in This Hour:

▶ Color Models
▶ The Modes and Models of Color
▶ Color Bit Depth and Why It Matters

Color is all around us, a blessing few of us take time to think about or recognize. It is as common as the air we breathe, but when you become aware of its presence, you become aware of the minute variations that exist in every color. Notice the shades of green on the tree outside your window. Notice how those greens differ from the green of the grass. Watch the play of light and shadow. It becomes fascinating.

In this hour, we are going to investigate the different properties of color—both in Photoshop and in life. Some of the information at the beginning might seem a little esoteric, but, in the long run, it's useful to know. After all, the more you know about color and how Photoshop addresses it, the better off you'll be. But don't worry, I'll try to keep the discussion as quick and painless as possible.

Before beginning, it must be said that the best way of learning this stuff is to have Photoshop up and running on your machine. You can glean a certain amount of information from merely reading, but the real learning won't start until you start working in Photoshop. This is for two reasons:

▶ As we all know, you remember something better when you do it yourself.

▶ Photoshop's treatment of color makes it very intuitive. Keep the Color palette open at all times (Window→Color) and keep an eye on the sliders. Notice how they change from mode to mode—the differences and similarities.

The first point to understand is that Photoshop addresses color in terms of models and modes. *Models* are methods of defining color. *Modes* are methods of working with color based on the models.

Color models describe the different ways that color can be represented on paper and on the computer screen. The color models are as follows:

► RGB (Red, Green, Blue)

► CMYK (Cyan, Magenta, Yellow, Black)

► HSB (Hue, Saturation, Brightness)

► CIE Lab

This chapter examines these models for displaying and describing color, and then turns to the Photoshop modes, which are the ways Photoshop provides for you to work with color.

Color Models

Figure 5.1 shows the Photoshop Color Picker. You can reach it by clicking either of the large blocks of color at the bottom of the toolbar. It has a graduated block of color, which you can click to select a particular shade, and text entry fields that display the numbers for any chosen color in each of the four color models. In addition, Photoshop gives you a Color palette, which is shown in Figure 5.2. Open it, if it's not already open, by choosing Window→Color. It has a strip along the bottom that covers the full color spectrum, plus black and white. Clicking anywhere on it sets the Color Picker to that range of colors.

FIGURE 5.1
The Photoshop
Color Picker.

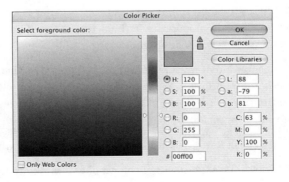

FIGURE 5.2
The Photoshop Color palette has adjustable sliders as well as a clickable strip representing the full color spectrum. Right now, it's showing pure green.

Pick a Different Picker

If your Color Picker doesn't look like this one, open Preferences to the General pane and reset the Color Picker to Photoshop.

By the Way

RGB Model

The RGB model, which computer monitors and TV screens use for display, assigns *values* on a scale of 0 to 255 for each of the three RGB primaries. As an example, pure green (as you can see in the previous figure) has red and blue values of 0, and a green value of 255. Pure white places the values of all three RGB primaries at 255. Pure black places the values of the RGB primaries at 0.

Value, in this usage, means the relative strength of the color. Because the RGB model mixes colors of light to achieve white light, the full strength is 255. When you combine all three primaries at a value of 128 (half of 255), you get medium gray.

CMYK Model

The CMYK model, used for printing, defines colors according to their percentages of cyan, magenta, yellow, and black. These are the four colors of printing inks, both in your home inkjet printer and in the fancy, high-resolution color laser printers and printing presses that service bureaus and commercial printers use. A six-color inkjet printer adds light cyan and light magenta.

Color Me Confused

A thousand years ago, when I went to grade school, every child was given a box of crayons at the start of the school year. Your grade level determined the size of the crayon box. Kindergarten and first grade students received flat boxes with eight big, thick crayons per box: the primaries, the secondaries, and brown and black. That was how we learned colors, even back then. The primaries were yellow, red,

By the Way

and blue. The secondaries were what you got when you mixed any two primaries: orange, from yellow and red; green, from yellow and blue; and purple, from red and blue. Brown was the mix of all three primaries, and black was—well, black was black.

That's how we knew them, until high school. By then, we'd outgrown crayons, of course. We filed into our physics class, and threw the previous nine years of learning out the window. The primary colors, according to the physics teacher, were red, green, and blue. And if you mixed them, you got, not brown or even the mysterious black, but—white!

Those of us still taking art classes listened to the physics lecture skeptically and went down to the art room to try mixing red, green, and blue paint. We got a sort of muddy brown, not the promised white. We asked the art teacher about this and were sent upstairs to the drama department for a demonstration. The stage lights had filters in red, green, and blue. When all the lights were on, the result was, sure enough, white light. Why? When you're dealing with light, the drama teacher explained, colors are additive. They total to white. When you're dealing with paint, you need to subtract the colors from black to get white; adding them makes that muddy brown mess. Aha! We were enlightened.

When you bought your computer system, you had to deal with this issue, whether or not you knew it at the time. Your monitor uses light to produce color. That's why it's called an RGB (Red, Green, Blue) monitor. Your printer uses ink to produce color. Not red ink, green ink, and blue ink, but a set of colors called cyan, magenta, and yellow, along with the old standby black. This color system is known by its initials, CMYK. Why K for black? For a long time, K was a mystery term, but an astute reader of an earlier version of this book explained that, "K stands for Keyline, which is a thin black line printed around colors to keep them separate." Makes sense to me....

HSB Model

When artists talk about color, they generally define it by using a set of parameters called HSB. Photoshop also includes this color model. H stands for *Hue*, which is the basic color from the color wheel; for example, red, blue, or yellow. It's expressed in degrees (0–360°), which correspond to the positions on the color wheel of the various colors. S is *Saturation*, or the strength of the color, and it's a percentage of the color minus the amount of gray in it. Pure color pigment with no gray in it is said to be 100% saturated. Neutral gray, with no color, is 0% saturated. Saturated colors are found at the edge of the color wheel, and saturation decreases as you approach the center of the wheel. If you look at the Apple Color Picker in Figure 5.3, it's a little easier to understand this. *Brightness*, the relative tone or lightness of the color, is also measured as a percentage, from 0% (black) to 100% (white). Brightness is equivalent to the value used by the RGB model.

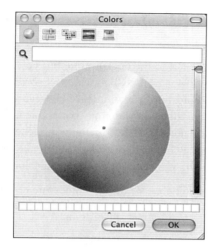

FIGURE 5.3
The Apple Color
Picker uses a
standard color
wheel.

CIE Lab Model

The most encompassing of these color models is CIE Lab. It defines a color *gamut* (a range of colors) that is broader than any of the other models. Because of its broad color gamut, Photoshop uses the CIE Lab model to convert from one color model to another. Lab color is defined as luminance, plus two components (a and b), which move, respectively, from green to red and from blue to yellow. Lab color is designed to be device-independent, meaning that the range of colors defined in this model isn't restricted to the range that can be printed or displayed on a particular device. However, this is probably not a model you will use frequently. Let's focus the attention now on the more commonly used models, and what you need to know to get up and running.

Choosing a Color Model

I suggest that you do your color work in RGB, regardless of whether your final image will be printed or viewed onscreen as, for instance, a picture on the World Wide Web. The reason for this is simple. Even if you specify CMYK as the color model, your monitor can display only as RGB. It doesn't have cyan, magenta, or yellow pixels, except as combinations of RGB light. Rather than make it perform the conversion every time you change a piece of the image, wait and convert it when you're ready to print. Actually, you needn't ever convert to CMYK for color printing, unless you're sending the image to a commercial print shop or fine arts Iris printer. Home/office inkjets are designed to work best with RGB input.

*Did you
Know?*

The Modes and Models of Color

First, forget about CIE Lab color unless you already have a background in color theory. It's there. Photoshop uses it in the background, but you needn't concern yourself with it. The other three models—HSB, RGB, and CMYK—will have much greater impact on your work in Photoshop. The difference between the modes and the models is simple. The *models* are methods of defining color. *Modes* are methods of working with color based on the models. HSB is the only model without a directly corresponding mode. CMYK and RGB have corresponding modes in Photoshop. There are also modes for black-and-white, grayscale, and limited color work.

The Photoshop modes available under Image→Mode are as follows:

- ▶ Bitmap
- ▶ Grayscale
- ▶ Duotone
- ▶ Indexed Color

- ▶ RGB Color
- ▶ CMYK Color
- ▶ Lab Color
- ▶ Multichannel

There are only four of these color modes that you'll use often: Grayscale, RGB, CMYK, and Indexed Color. Let's take a closer look at them.

Bitmap and Grayscale

Let's start with the most basic of the color modes available within Photoshop—Bitmap and Grayscale.

The Grayscale mode offers 256 shades of gray that range from white to black, whereas the Bitmap mode uses only two color values to display images—black and white (see Figures 5.4 and 5.5 for examples).

Notice the vast difference in quality. The Grayscale image has a smooth transition between values, whereas the Bitmap image does not. There are, however, a number of ways to convert to Bitmap mode, discussed later in this hour.

Whenever a picture is printed in black-and-white or grayscale—for instance, as part of a newsletter or brochure—it makes sense for you to work on it in Grayscale mode. Doing the conversion yourself, rather than sending a color photo to the printer, gives you the opportunity to make sure that the picture will print properly. You can tell by looking at it whether the darks need to be lightened or the light grays intensified to bring out more detail. You can adjust the overall level of contrast as well as work on individual trouble spots.

FIGURE 5.4
A photo rendered in the Grayscale mode.

FIGURE 5.5
The same image in the Bitmap mode.

To convert a color photo to Grayscale, simply choose Image→Mode→Grayscale. You'll be asked for permission to discard the color information. Click OK to confirm, and the picture is converted to grays. To convert the picture to Bitmap mode, as you might want to for certain effects, you must first convert to grayscale and then to bitmap.

RGB

RGB is the color mode for working on pictures that will be viewed on a computer screen. If you are preparing pictures in Photoshop that will eventually become part of a desktop presentation, a video, or a web page, stick with RGB for the best color rendition. If your work is only going on the Web, I still recommend doing the color adjustments in RGB and then converting the picture to Indexed Color if you choose to save it as a GIF in its final form. Also, if you work in Indexed Color, you can't use Photoshop's filters or layers. That's too much of a limitation!

Indexed Color

Indexed Color, when it can work for you, is a wonderful thing. Because of cross-platform compatibility issues, web designers are theoretically limited to the 216 colors shared by Macintoshes and PCs. Indexed Color is a palette or, rather, a collection of colors—256 to be exact. With this mode, you know exactly what you are getting, and if you don't like any of the palettes Photoshop supplies, you can build your own. Many web designers stick to indexed palettes to ensure consistent color. Others use any colors they want, knowing that most users don't calibrate their monitors anyway.

Indexed Color is perfect for the World Wide Web. The Indexed Color mode includes a specific Web palette. Indexed Color doesn't really limit you to 216 colors, however. Dithering takes place in Indexed Color images. From RGB mode, choose Image→Mode→Indexed Color to take a look at the Indexed Color dialog box (see Figure 5.6).

FIGURE 5.6
The Indexed Color dialog box.

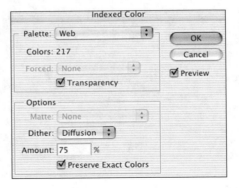

Dithering means that certain colors are combined, that is, adjacent pixels are interspersed, visually blending onscreen to create a new color although they retain their original color—or the closest index equivalent—when viewed at a large magnification.

You are given a number of palette choices when you work with Indexed Color. They are as follows:

► Exact—This option takes the colors that are in the RGB version of the image for its palette. This works only if there are fewer than 256 colors in the original image.

► System (Mac OS)—This option uses the Macintosh System palette.

► System (Windows)—This option uses the Windows System palette.

► Web—This palette uses the 216 colors discussed previously. If you are planning to publish your work on the World Wide Web, this is the "safe" palette. Otherwise, you might have problems with incompatible colors dropping out when an image is viewed with a web browser.

► Uniform—The Uniform option bases the colors in the palette on a strict sampling of colors across the color spectrum.

► Perceptual—This option creates a custom palette by giving priority to colors for which the human eye has greater sensitivity. You can use a local palette (based on the current image) or, if you switch to ImageReady, a master palette that draws colors from a group of images you plan to display on a website or CD-ROM.

► Selective—The Selective option creates a color table similar to the Perceptual color table, but favoring broad areas of color and the preservation of Web colors. Again, you can choose a local palette or a master palette.

► Adaptive—This is your best bet for most work in Indexed Color. During conversion, this option samples the most frequently used colors from the original. Adaptive usually provides you with the closest match to the original image. This option also comes in both local and master flavors.

► Custom—If none of the other options suits you, you can always build your own palette. See the Photoshop manual for instructions.

► Previous—This option simply remembers and reverts to whichever option you chose last time you converted to Indexed Color.

CMYK

As you saw earlier, CMYK mode should be used only when your image is printed commercially. By converting to CMYK before you start to print (and being aware of gamut warnings), you can make sure that your nice yellow banana or flower doesn't end up a muddy brown, or your bright blue sky doesn't print as purple.

Gamut refers to the range of colors that the combination of CMYK inks can print. Some colors are *out of gamut*, and can't be printed accurately. Very bright colors, particularly oranges and greens, are often out of gamut, and would trigger the gamut warning. The *gamut warning* shows up on the Color palette and looks like a small triangular traffic warning sign with an exclamation point in the middle.

Converting Between Modes

All you have to do to convert between modes, at least mechanically (this is not taking image degradation or changes into account), is choose Image→Mode and then choose your poison.

Although Photoshop uses the model (Lab) with the broadest gamut of color to change color modes (as if all the other modes are circles that will fit within Lab color), this is no guarantee that your colors will turn out the same in another mode as they did in the original mode.

The rule of thumb is this, and I can't stress it enough—*Do your work in RGB*, even if you are going to output your images to print. Convert a copy of your image to CMYK immediately before you send it to the commercial print shop. To see whether all your colors are within the CMYK gamut, use the menu command View→Gamut Warning. If you are going to publish your images on the Web, stick with RGB or use Indexed Color, if file size is an issue. Knowing this will save you many hours of wondering why the Web page that looks great on the office Macintosh looks funky on the Windows machine you use at home, or why the yellow in your printed piece looks brownish.

▼   **Try it Yourself**

Getting Started with Color

Just for fun, why don't we dive in with some hands-on before we go any further? Because the pictures in the book are in black-and-white, working through this exercise will give you a better idea of the concepts and ideas that we have been talking about. Let's look at a colorful image and examine how the modes affect the way the color appears.

1. First, find a colorful picture and open it. You can download the photo in Figure 5.7 from the Sams website. It's called YellowLily. To get to the website, point your Web browser to http://www.samspublishing.com/. In the Search box, type **Photoshop in 24**. Find this book in the list that appears, and click the link. On the book's main page, find and click the Related Materials link to get to the files. If your picture doesn't have the letters RGB in parentheses after the filename shown in the image window's title bar, choose Image→Mode→RGB Color. This is your starting point. If your monitor is correctly adjusted, you should see very good color.

▼

FIGURE 5.7
Yellow lily.

2. Choose Image→Mode→Grayscale. A dialog box appears, asking whether you want to discard the image's color information. Click OK. Photoshop then proceeds to examine your image and assigns all the colors to 256 shades of gray that range from white to black.

   You can monitor, using the status bar at the bottom of the picture, how the size of your file diminishes. (If you don't see the file size at the bottom of the document window, choose Show→Document Sizes from the pop-up menu.) This is because the amount of information or data in a color image is much greater than that required to display a grayscale image. In this case, the file size decreased by more than 1MB.

3. Before moving on, you need to return the image to its original RGB state. Choose File→Revert.

   This time, you're going to change the RGB image to CMYK. This process becomes enormously important if you'll be taking your images to a commercial printer. RGB can display a number of colors that CMYK, by the nature of its four inks, cannot reproduce. The inks, for instance, can only approximate neon colors.

   Before making the mode change, let's take a closer look at some of the colors in this RGB image to see whether they can be reproduced in CMYK (see Figure 5.8).

   A. Click the Eyedropper tool in the toolbox.

   B. Next, open the Color palette by choosing Window→Color.

   C. Use the Eyedropper to select (click) a color in the image. Try clicking the orange stamens in the center of the lily.

FIGURE 5.8
The triangle symbol means that the color is out of the CMYK gamut.

D. Look in the Color palette. Is there an out-of-gamut warning there? This little triangle indicates that the selected color cannot be reproduced precisely by the process colors of CMYK.

E. To get an idea how far out of gamut your colors are, choose View→Gamut Warning. This gives you an indication of the colors that will be lost or modified during the translation of RGB mode to CMYK. Figure 5.9 shows what the gamut warning looks like for this picture. Out-of-gamut areas are shown as gray patches.

FIGURE 5.9
The dark patches are out of gamut.

Hard to See the Gamut Warning?

To change the color used in the display of the Gamut Warning, open the preferences (choose Photoshop→Preferences on Mac and Edit→Preferences on Windows) and turn to the Transparency & Gamut prefs. Click the color swatch at the bottom of the dialog box and choose a color that contrasts with the colors in the picture.

By the Way

F. Click the warning triangle to select the nearest color that can be achieved with CMYK colors. You can quickly adjust a picture like this one that has many out-of-gamut colors by activating the gamut warning. You can then use the color adjustment tools you'll learn about in the next hour to bring the picture into a printable range.

4. To change the mode from RGB to CMYK, choose Image→Mode→CMYK.

5. After you've seen and perhaps printed the picture in CMYK mode, feel free to experiment with the other modes, too.

If you have a color printer, you might want to revert to RGB and print your picture and compare it to what you see onscreen. Does it look OK? If so, you're in luck. Your monitor is accurately calibrated. If not, you need to calibrate your monitor so that the images onscreen accurately display the colors as they print. Calibration is covered in a Note in Hour 23, "Printing and Publishing." If your monitor seems to need calibration, you can jump ahead to "What's Color Management" on page 441.

Color Is Critical

The human eye is extremely sensitive to even the slightest variation in color. Think for a moment about something familiar—a can of Coca-Cola. I'll bet that if you were shown two swatches of red you could, without much hesitation, select the Coke can's red and differentiate it from, say, the red used on the cover of Time magazine. If you saw cans of Coke displayed with a slightly off-color red, you'd probably think they were either outdated or perhaps counterfeit. Most people are very much aware of even slight color changes. That is why color becomes so important in product branding through advertising.

By the Way

Color Bit Depth and Why It Matters

Bit depth is a way to describe how much color information is available about each pixel in an image. It's also called color depth or pixel depth and, as with so many other things, more is better. Greater bit depth (more bits of information per pixel) means more available colors and more accurate color representation in your digital pictures. Consider this: a pixel with a bit depth of 1 has only 2 possible values, either black or white. A grayscale pixel with a bit depth of 8 has 2 to the 8th power, or 256 possible values. And a pixel with a bit depth of 24 has 2 to the 24th power, or about 16 million, possible values. Common values for bit depth range from 1 to 64 bits per pixel. You will find that your Photoshop images tend to be either 8-bit or 16-bit. More information means larger files and longer times, of course. And it also means truer color.

8-Bit Color

It's actually a little bit misleading to call 8-bit color by that name. Depending on the color mode you've chosen to work in, you have anywhere from 8 to 32 bits of information for each pixel. In RBG mode, you have 8 bits each of the red, blue, and green color channels, making 24 bits of color information. In CMYK mode, you have 8 bits each of four channels, or 32 bits in all.

16-Bit Color

In previous versions of Photoshop, not all of the tools and filters worked with 16-bit color. As of Photoshop CS2, all tools and most filters are 16-bit compatible. Does this mean you should do all your work in 16-bit color? No. Technology moves forward in uneven leaps. Even though Photoshop can work in 16-bit color, your monitor can't show you all the millions of colors your image has. And your home/office inkjet or color laser printer can't possibly reproduce them. Within a year or so, this might change as new HDTV monitors and better printing inks come on the market. Adobe has, in effect, raised the bar, and now makers of monitors and printers will have to jump that much higher. The next frontier? 32-bit color—but Photoshop's support for it at this point is still so limited that it's best to leave it alone.

Summary

Color is fun to play with, but it's also rather complicated to understand. The world in general, and Photoshop in particular, uses color models as a way of describing colors. The four color models are HSB, RGB, CMYK, and CIE Lab Color. There are also color modes, which enable you to work with color. RGB is the most useful color mode because it's the one your monitor displays. CMYK mode is used for printing, as is Grayscale.

In this hour, we discussed the color modes and the specific color models in Photoshop. We also looked at a few of the more salient issues regarding converting between modes.

In the next hour, you will delve deeper into the world of color by learning how to make tonal adjustments and general adjustments.

Workshop

Q&A

Q *What are those funny letters and numbers at the bottom of the Color Picker?*

A Those describe Web colors. The alphanumerics define the selected color in HTML.

Q *Is there ever a time when I would want to work in Lab Color?*

A Well, I've been using Photoshop since version 2, and I haven't yet found a need for Lab Color. Without knowing who you are and how you use Photoshop, I can't say you'll *never* need it, but it's unlikely.

Q *What are Web-safe colors, and why are there fewer than 256 of them?*

A Macintoshes and PCs both can use a limited palette of 256 colors. However, the two palettes aren't quite the same. Only 216 of the 256 colors are identical. These are the Web-safe colors, meaning that no matter what kind of computer you use to surf the Web, you'll see the page as its author intended.

Q *If I want to have my pictures printed on a printing press, and put them on the Web, should I be working in CMYK or RGB?*

A I'd do my work in RGB mode, and then save a copy in CMYK and check the gamut before printing it. Your video monitor can't show you true CMYK colors, no matter how many times you calibrate it. It doesn't display color that way.

Quiz

1. RGB, used by your monitor, stands for

    a. Raster (white), Gray, Black

    b. Red, Green, Blue

    c. Initials of Apple's next CEO, Roy G. Biv

2. How many colors can a Web page display precisely?

    a. Millions

    b. 256

    c. 216

3. Which color mode should you use for printed pages?

   a. CMYK

   b. HSB

   c. PANTONE

Quiz Answers

1. b.

2. c., but only because that's all Macintoshes and PCs can agree on.

3. a., if they are intended for four-color process printing. Home/office inkjet printers handle RGB conversions very well.

Exercise

Using the Photoshop Color Picker, select a nice bright red. See how it's represented in the different color models. Click at the upper-right corner of the color square. Saturation and Brightness should be 100%, regardless of which color you have selected. Red will read 0 in the Hue field. Enter **60** in the Hue field. The color square will change to yellow. Knowing that red is 0 and yellow is 60, can you predict what number pure blue will be? Look at some other colors and see how they affect the settings. Try to understand the relationship of the colors on a theoretical color wheel to the colors you see in the spectrum.

HOUR 6

Adjusting Color

What You'll Learn in This Hour:

▶ Adjusting by Eye with Variations
▶ Making Other Adjustments
▶ Adjustment Layers
▶ Understanding Channels

Are you one of those people who likes to play with the color adjustments on the television set? If you are, you're going to be absolutely astounded with Photoshop's color adjustment capabilities. If you haven't a clue as to what I mean by adjusting color, that's okay, too. By the end of this hour, you'll be able to turn red roses blue, change a sky from midday to sunset and back again, bring out the detail in shadows, and control every imaginable aspect of color manipulation.

Photoshop includes a full set of tools for making color adjustments. You can find them all on the Image→Adjustments submenu (see Figure 6.1). Some of these terms, such as Brightness/Contrast, might be familiar to you; others might not. Don't worry. You'll learn about them all in this hour.

Before you start to adjust color, you need to evaluate what kind of color you have in the picture and how you'll eventually use the image. You learned about color models and color modes last hour, so you know that RGB color is the kind that is displayed on computer screens and CMYK color is the kind that is printed. If you're going to be adjusting the color in a picture, it makes sense to adjust it according to the way it will be displayed. If your picture is going on a web page, you should work in RGB mode. If it's going to be printed on a four-color process commercial press, work in RGB to start with, but make your final adjustments (if any are needed) after you convert to CMYK mode. If you're printing on a home/office inkjet printer, stick with RGB. These printers are designed to make the conversion internally. If it's going to end up in grayscale, forget about trying to make the sky a perfect blue. Change the mode to Grayscale and make the contrast perfect instead. Just keep these few rules in mind and you won't go wrong. Table 6.1 will help you keep these options sorted out.

FIGURE 6.1
The
Adjustments
submenu gives
you all the tools
you'll need.

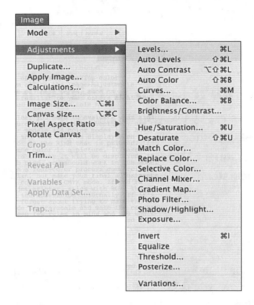

TABLE 6.1   Color Adjustment Matrix

Adjust Color In	If Output Is
RGB	Computer screen, Web, or inkjet
RGB first, and then CMYK	Process color print
Grayscale	Black-and-white print

Adjusting by Eye with Variations

The most obvious way to make a color adjustment is to compare before and after views of an image. In Photoshop, the tool for doing this is called Variations. It's the last item on the Image→Adjustments submenu. Variations combines several image adjustment tools into one easy-to-use system that shows you thumbnail images that are variations on the original image. You simply click the one that looks best to you. You can choose variations of hue and brightness and then see the result (which Photoshop calls *Current Pick*) compared to the original.

Something Missing?

If Variations doesn't appear on the Adjustments submenu, check the Image→Mode submenu to make sure you're in 8-bit color mode and that you're not using Lab or Indexed Color mode. If those settings are OK, the Variations plug-in might not have been installed. Consult the Photoshop manual for information about using plug-in modules.

Figure 6.2 shows the Variations dialog box. (See it in color in the color insert.) When you first open it, the Current Pick is the same as the original image because you haven't yet made changes. You can set the slider to the left (Fine) or right (Coarse) to determine how much effect each variation applies to the original image. Moving it one tick mark in either direction doubles or halves the previously selected amount. The finest setting makes changes that are so slight as to be almost undetectable. The coarsest setting should be used only if you're going for special effects and want to turn the entire picture to a single color. The default (middle) setting is the most practical for normal adjustments.

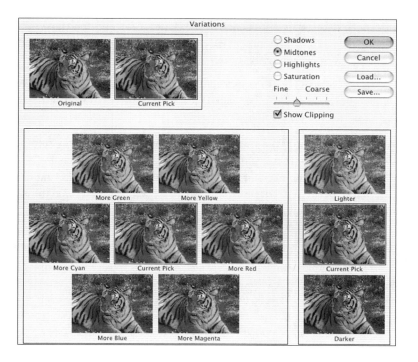

FIGURE 6.2
The seven thumbnails at lower-left adjust hue, whereas the right-side set of three adjusts brightness.

Adjusting Shadows, Midtones, Highlights, and Saturation

When you use Variations to adjust a color image, you have the option of individually adjusting shadows, midtones, highlights, or overall color saturation. *Shadows, midtones,* and *highlights* are Photoshop's terms for the darks, middle tones, and light tones, respectively, in the picture (or what would be black, gray, and white in grayscale). When you correct them with Variations, you change the color (hue) of the shadow, midtone, or highlight. Saturation affects all of them at once, increasing or decreasing the intensity of the color, although not changing it.

When you select shadows, midtones, or highlights, you adjust the hue and brightness of only that part of the picture. The advantage here is that you can adjust the midtones one way and the highlights or shadows another way, if you choose. Each setting is independent of the others, and you can, for example, set the midtones to be more blue, thus brightening the sky, yet still set the shadows to be more yellow, offsetting the blueness that they possess inherently.

Clipping is a term that describes what happens when a highlight or shadow value is adjusted so much it becomes pure white or pure black. Selecting the Show Clipping box displays a neon-colored preview of areas in the image that will be clipped by the adjustment. Clipping doesn't occur when you adjust midtones.

Remember, as you learned in Hour 5, "Color Modes and Color Models," *hue* refers to the color of an object or selection. *Brightness* is a measurement of how much white or black is added to the color.

Selecting Saturation changes the strength of the color in the image; the setting choice is simply for less or more color strength. In Figure 6.3, I'm adjusting the saturation of this photo. Remember that you can apply the same correction more than once. If, for instance, less saturation still leaves more color in the image than you want, reduce the saturation again to get even less.

▼ **Try it Yourself**

Adjust an Image Using the Variations Command

Learning to work with the Variations dialog box is an excellent way to understand how colors work.

1. Open any color image. Choose Image→Adjustments→Variations.
2. Set the radio buttons according to what you want to adjust: Shadows, Midtones, Highlights, or Saturation.
3. Use the Fine/Coarse slider to determine how much adjustment to apply.

▼

4. Watch the Original and Current Pick thumbnails as you create the desired variations by clicking the appropriate thumbnails. The following are some tips for getting the effect you want:

   ▶ To add color, click the appropriate color thumbnail.

   ▶ To reduce a color, click its opposite on the color wheel. To reduce magenta, for example, click green.

   ▶ To adjust the brightness, click the thumbnail for a lighter or darker image.

   ▶ If you're not sure exactly what you need to do, simply click the image that looks most correct to you.

   ▶ If you think you might have overdone your corrections and want to go back to the original image, press Option (Mac) or Alt (Windows) to change the Cancel button to a Reset button. Clicking the Reset button restores the settings to zero and reverts to the image saved prior to changes. (Note: This works with all adjustment dialog boxes.)

5. Click OK when you're done or click Cancel to undo all your adjustments.

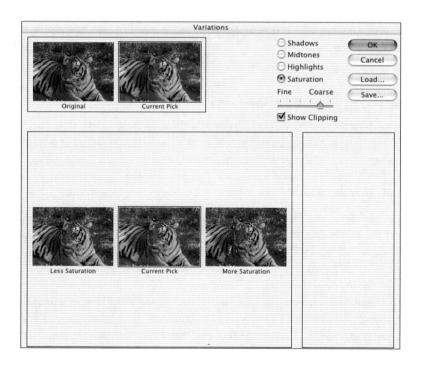

FIGURE 6.3
Less saturation gives you a duller image. More saturation gives you a more intense one. (Don't confuse saturation with brightness. Saturation changes the amount of color. Brightness adds light.)

Saving and Loading Corrections

Two other buttons appear in this dialog box, and in the other adjustment dialog boxes as well. These are the Load and Save buttons. They can save you a lot of time and effort if you have a whole series of pictures that need the same kind of corrections. Perhaps you used your digital camera to shoot several outdoor pictures with the same lousy light conditions. Maybe your scanner tends to make everything a little more yellow than you want. After you determine the settings that correct one picture perfectly, you can save those settings and then load them each time you want to apply them to another picture.

Click the Save button, and you'll see a typical dialog box that asks you to give your settings a name. You might call them foggy day fix or scanner correction. Then, when you need to apply them to another picture, use the Load button to locate and open the appropriate setting file, and your corrections will be made when you click OK in the dialog box.

Making Other Adjustments

As you've seen, Variations is the quick way to adjust color, but sometimes it doesn't give you enough control. Other times you just want to experiment. Maybe you have a picture that's mediocre, but if you play with the colors in it and beef up the contrast, you can make something out of it. These are the times when you'll want to work with individual adjustment settings.

Consulting the Histogram

Photoshop CS2's Histogram palette was once a dialog box. It doesn't actually do anything by itself, but if you learn how to use it, you can save yourself lots of time. If you ever took a course in statistics, you already know that a histogram is a kind of graph. In Photoshop, it's a graph of the image reduced to grayscale, with lines to indicate the number of pixels at each step in the grayscale from 0 to 255.

You might wonder why this is important. The main reason is that you can tell by looking at the histogram whether there's enough contrast in the image to allow you to apply corrections successfully. If you have an apparently bad photo or a bad scan, studying the histogram will tell you whether it's worth working on or whether you should throw away the image and start over. If all the lines are bunched up tight at one end of the graph, and the image isn't *supposed* to be very dark or very light, you probably can't save the picture by adjusting it. If, on the other hand, you have a reasonably well-spread-out histogram, there's a wide enough range of values to suggest that the picture can be saved. Watch out for gaps in the middle of the graph, and for ends that cut off suddenly rather than tapering down to zero. Figure 6.4 shows the histogram for a reasonably well-exposed photo.

The Histogram command has another use, which is to give you a sense of the tonal range of the image. This is sometimes referred to as the key type. An image is said to be low key, average key, or high key, depending on whether it has a preponderance of dark, middle, or light tones, respectively. A picture that is all medium gray would have only one line in its histogram, and it would fall right in the middle.

All you really need to know is that, when you look at the histogram, you should see a fairly even distribution across the graph, if the image is intended to be an average key picture. If the picture is high key, most of the lines in the histogram are concentrated on the right side with a few on the left. If it is low key, most of the values will be to the left with a few to the right.

Adjusting with the Levels Dialog Box

Adjusting levels is a method of changing the brightness of an image. As you can see in Figure 6.5, the Levels dialog box has a copy of the histogram, along with some controls that you can use to adjust the values.

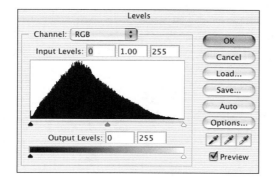

FIGURE 6.5
Be sure to check the Preview box so that you can see the effect of your changes.

Setting the *black point* (the point at the left of the histogram that represents absolutely saturated black) to match the concentration of darkest levels in the image, and setting the *white point* (at the right, indicating completely unsaturated white) to match the concentration of the lightest levels in the image, forces the rest of the levels to reassign themselves more equitably. The photo I'm using in these examples, which you can download (uncorrected) from the book's website, happens to be quite dark, but there's still ample detail. (The file is called chinadoll.jpg.)

▼   **Try it Yourself**

Adjust Brightness Using Levels

When the colors are right, but the photo seems dull or dark, adjusting the brightness helps.

1. Choose Image→Adjustments→Levels, or press Command+L (Mac) or Control+L (Windows).

2. Click the Preview box so that you can see your changes in the image window. Just for fun, you can watch the Navigator and Layers palettes change, too.

3. Create the desired level adjustments by moving the three sliders below the histogram to the left or right. The following are some tips for getting the effect you want:

   ▶ To set the black point (the darkest black) in the image, move the slider at the left side of the Input Levels histogram to the point at which the dark lines begin to cluster.

   ▶ Set the white point (the whitest tone) by moving the right Input Levels slider to the point where the light pixels begin to rise.

   ▶ Adjust the midrange by watching the picture while you move the Input Levels middle slider left or right. Figure 6.6 shows the settings for this picture.

FIGURE 6.6
Adjusting the darks helps bring out shadow detail.

4. To adjust the contrast in the image, use the sliders on the Output Levels bar. The black slider controls the dark tones; moving it toward the center lightens the image. The white slider controls the light tones; moving it toward the center darkens the image.

5. Click OK when you're done. My corrected version is included in the color plate section. It's called China Doll, Color Figure 6.6.

▲

Channeling Colors

In a color image, you can adjust the composite RGB or CMYK color image, or individual colors, by using the Channels pop-up menu. For now, stay with the composite. (You'll learn more about channels later in this hour.)

You can also use the Eyedroppers to adjust the levels. Click the white Eyedropper (on the right) and click the lightest part of your image. Then click the dark-tipped Eyedropper (on the left) to select it and click the darkest point on the image. If you're working on a grayscale image and there's an area in the image that seems to be right in the middle, click it with the midrange Eyedropper (in the middle). Avoid using the midrange Eyedropper in a color image unless it has an area that's supposed to be a neutral gray—neither reddish (warm) nor bluish (cool); if you click in an colored area, Photoshop will adjust all the image's colors so that the area you clicked in doesn't have any color.

You "Auto" Try it

If you click Auto in the Levels dialog box or choose Auto Levels from the Image→Adjustments menu, Photoshop adjusts the levels based on its evaluation of the tonal range. However, this is usually not satisfactory. Try it, but be prepared to undo.

Adjusting with the Curves Dialog Box

Adjusting curves is much like adjusting levels, although a bit subtler. You can use the Curves dialog box instead of the Levels dialog box to adjust the brightness. The big difference is that, instead of adjusting at only three points (black, middle, and white), you can adjust at any point (see Figure 6.7).

When you open the Curves dialog box, you won't see a curve. You won't see the histogram either. Instead, you see a different kind of graph, one with a grid and a diagonal line. The horizontal axis of the grid represents the original values (input levels) of the image or selection, whereas the vertical axis represents the new values (output levels). When you first open the box, the graph appears as a diagonal line because no new values have been mapped. All pixels have identical input and output values. As always, be sure to check the Preview box so that you can see the effects of your changes.

FIGURE 6.7
On this kind of graph, the zero point is in the middle.

As with the Levels dialog box, you can click Auto or use the Eyedroppers to adjust the values. Because the Curves method gives you so much more control, you might as well take full advantage of it. Hold down the mouse button and drag the cursor over the portion of the image that needs adjusting. You'll see a circle on the graph at the point representing the pixel where the cursor is. If there are points on the curve that you don't want to change, Command+click them (in Windows, Control+click) to lock them down. For instance, if you want to adjust the midtones while leaving the darks and lights relatively untouched, click (in Windows, Control+click) the light and dark points on the curve to mark the points at which you want to stop making changes. Then, drag the middle of the curve until the image looks right to you. Dragging up lightens tones, whereas dragging down darkens them. Figure 6.8 shows what this actually looks like. To get rid of a point that you have placed, click and drag it off the grid.

A Fine Thing
To see the curves displayed in a finer grid, press and hold Option (Mac) or Alt (Windows) and click the grid.

Adjusting with the Color Balance Dialog Box

To really understand color balance, you have to look at the color wheel. In case you don't remember the order of the color wheel, just flip to the color section and take a look at the example provided.

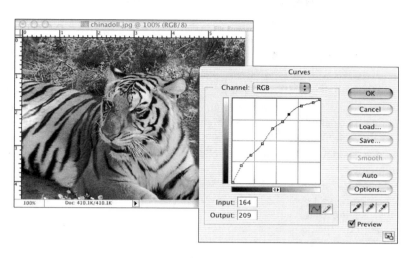

FIGURE 6.8
You can add up
to 16 points on
the curve.

Every color on the wheel has an opposite. If you follow the line from one color through the center of the wheel, you reach its opposite. Cyan is opposite to red; green is opposite to magenta; and yellow is opposite to blue. When you use the Color Balance dialog box to adjust colors in a picture, you're adding more of the color opposite to the one you want to reduce. Increasing the cyan reduces red. Increasing red reduces cyan, and so on, around the wheel.

Figure 6.9 shows the Color Balance dialog box. Color Balance is intended to be used for general color correction rather than for correcting specific parts of an image, although you can use it that way by selecting only the part to correct. It's especially helpful if you have a scanned image that is off-color, such as an old, yellowed photograph. It's very simple to apply the Color Balance tools to remove the yellow without altering the rest of the picture.

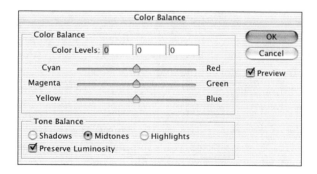

FIGURE 6.9
Move the sliders in the direction of the color you want to add.

In addition to Color Balance, you can use the sliders to adjust tone balance. As with the Variations dialog box described earlier, you can concentrate your efforts on adjusting shadows, midtones, or highlights by clicking the appropriate button.

▼   **Try it Yourself**

Apply Color Balance

Color balance can rescue pictures that have faded, and it can turn red roses blue or blue ducks red. It's fun to play with.

1. Select the image or portion of the image to correct. Open the Color Balance dialog box by choosing Image→Adjustments→Color Balance or pressing Command+B (Mac) or Control+B (Windows).

2. Choose Shadows, Midtones, or Highlights. Generally it's advisable to start with midtones, if you are correcting the whole picture, because the midtones comprise 90% of an image.

3. Check Preserve Luminosity so that you don't change the brightness of the image as you shift colors. If maintaining the brightness isn't important, don't enable the check box. Be sure to select Preview so that you can see how your changes affect the image.

4. Move the sliders to adjust the colors. The numbers in the boxes change to indicate how much of a change you are making. They range from 0 to +100 (toward red, green, and blue) and from 0 to –100 (toward cyan, magenta, and yellow).

5. Adjust the shadows and the highlights; repeat the corrections until the image looks correct to you.

▲   6. Click OK to apply the changes.

If Color Balance doesn't seem to do what you want, undo it.

Adjusting with the Hue/Saturation Dialog Box

The Hue/Saturation dialog box is a very powerful tool with a slightly misleading name. Sure, it lets you adjust the hue (colors in the image) and the saturation (the intensity of the colors), but it also gives you control over the lightness.

First, look at the controls in the Hue/Saturation dialog box (see Figure 6.10). The first pop-up Edit menu lets you select either a single color to adjust or the Master setting, which adjusts all the colors in the image or selection at once. For now, work with the Master setting. Check Preview so that you can see the effects of your changes in the picture you're working on.

There are three sliders: Hue, Saturation, and Lightness. The Hue slider moves around the color wheel. With Master selected, you can move all the way from red (in the middle of the slider), left—through purple to blue or blue-green—or right through orange to yellow and to green.

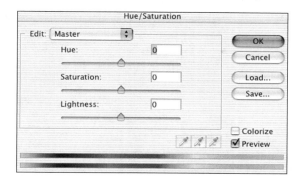

FIGURE 6.10
Small adjust-
ments to
Lightness and
Saturation are
usually all that's
needed.

The Saturation slider takes you from 0%, in the center, to 100% saturated (pure color, with no gray) on the right, or 100% unsaturated (no color) on the left.

The Lightness slider lets you increase or decrease the brightness of the image, from zero in the center, to +100 on the right, or –100 on the left.

As you move these sliders, watch the two spectrum strips at the bottom of the window, as well as the image itself. The upper strip represents the current status of the image, and the lower one changes according to the slider(s) you move. If you move the Hue slider to +60, for example, you can see that the reds in the picture turn quite yellow and the blues turn purple. In effect, what you are doing is skewing the color spectrum by that amount. If you move the Saturation slider to the left, you'll see the lower spectrum strip become less saturated. If you move the Lightness slider, you'll see its effects reflected in the lower spectrum strip as well.

Light Is Bright

Lightness is technically the same as brightness. The Hue, Saturation, Brightness (HSB) color model uses these terms to define a color, as opposed to the RGB and CMYK models that define it as percentages of the component primaries. These primaries, of course, are red, green, and blue for RGB, and cyan, magenta, yellow, and black for the CMYK model.

By the Way

Instead of selecting Master from the pop-up menu, if you select a color, the dialog box changes slightly, as you can see in Figure 6.11. The Eyedroppers are now active, enabling you to select colors from the image, and adjustable range sliders are centered on the color you have chosen to adjust. You can move these back and forth to focus on as broad or narrow a range within that color as you want. This might not seem like a big deal, but it's really very powerful, especially if you want to create a pink tiger, or maybe a blue one.

FIGURE 6.11
Click and drag to move the sliders. You can extend the range of colors to be affected by dragging the edges of the range selector between the two color bars.

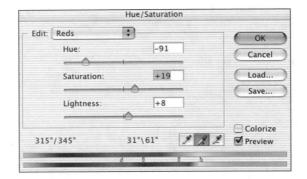

▼   **Try it Yourself**

Adjust an Image Using the Hue/Saturation Dialog Box

This powerful tool is best applied in small doses.

1. Open the dialog box by choosing it from the Image→Adjustments menu or by pressing Command+U (Mac) or Control+U (Windows). Click Preview to see your changes as you make them.

2. Use Master (the default setting) to adjust all the colors, or use the pop-up menu to select the color you want to adjust.

3. Create the desired adjustments by moving the three sliders to the left or right. The following are some tips for getting the effect you want:

   ▶ Drag the Hue slider left or right until the colors look the way you want. The numbers displayed in the Hue text box refer to the degree of rotation around the color wheel from the selected color's original location.

   ▶ Drag the Saturation slider left to decrease the saturation of the colors and right to increase it.

   ▶ Drag the Lightness slider to increase or decrease the lightness of the image.

▲   4. Click OK when you're done.

Adjusting with the Brightness/Contrast Dialog Box

If you need to make a simple adjustment to the tonal range of an image that scanned too dark, the Brightness/Contrast dialog box (choose Image→Adjustments→Brightness/Contrast) provides an easy way to adjust everything at once (see Figure 6.12). Instead of separately correcting the dark, middle, and light values, it applies the same correction throughout the image.

Although the Brightness/Contrast dialog box doesn't give you the same control that you would have if you made the adjustments using Levels or Curves, or even the Variations dialog box, it's quick and easy. Sometimes it's all you need. Many images are improved by just raising the brightness and contrast by a couple of points. As always, be sure to check the Preview box so that you can see the effect your changes have on the image.

FIGURE 6.12
Use the sliders to adjust the brightness and contrast.

Dragging the sliders to the right of the middle point increases brightness or contrast. Dragging them to the left decreases it. If you're not happy with the results you get with this tool, undo your changes and use the Variations dialog box, or Levels or Curves, to adjust the brightness and contrast.

Auto Contrast is occasionally helpful. It automatically maps the darkest and lightest pixels in the image to black-and-white, causing highlights to appear lighter and shadows darker. It might not be the best way to make the necessary adjustments, but, if you are in a hurry, it can save you some time.

There's another Auto tool: Auto Color. This tool, quite simply, analyzes the color in an image and makes an educated guess as to what it should be. If you're easily satisfied, it might be all the correction you ever need. As for me, I like things perfect, and Photoshop's sense of color is often different from mine.

Desaturate removes all of the color from an image, without changing the color mode. If you want a quick look at how something will reproduce in black and white, this is the command to use. Then, simply undo it to go back to the colored version.

Correcting the Shadows and Highlights

One of the coolest features in Photoshop CS2 is the Shadow/Highlight dialog box. It allows you to control the amount of highlight and shadow on an image without changing the contrast. If I apply it to the tiger photo, I can let her sit in deeper shade without changing the intensity of her stripes, or turn up the sunlight without washing the color out of her pale cream fur. Be sure to check the Show More Options box to open the full set of sliders, as shown in Figure 6.13. See the corrected tiger in the color section, and compare her to the original picture in Figure 6.6.

FIGURE 6.13
Experiment with these sliders on both high-contrast and low-contrast images.

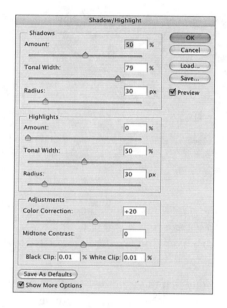

Photo Filters

When a photographer wants a special effect, he or she might use a colored filter over the camera lens. With this feature, you can do the same thing to any image, whether from a camera, scanned, or created from scratch. In Figure 6.14, I have expanded the list of filters so you can see the many options available. Serious photographers will recognize the numbers after the warming and cooling filters, because they are the same as on the glass filters you might buy at a good camera store. Use the slider to control the strength of the filter. Typically, you would use no more than 10–20% to warm up daylight or to take the excess yellow out of an indoor shot. To open the Photo Filter dialog box, follow this path: Image→Adjustments→ Photo Filter.

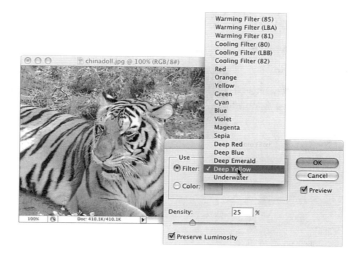

FIGURE 6.14
You can also
use any color as
a filter.

Adjustment Layers

An important point to remember about color correction is that you can apply it to the whole picture, to a selected single area, or to all but a selected area. When you apply a correction to the whole picture, it might improve some parts and make others worse, so you really need to look carefully at the end result and decide whether the good outweighs the bad.

Fortunately, there's an easy way to apply a correction and then change your mind. One of the best features of Photoshop is the capability to work in layers. (You'll learn all about layers in Hour 11, "Layers.") For now, you can think of layers as sheets of transparency film that you place over your image and paint or paste on. If you like what you do, you can merge the layers so that the additions become part of the image. If not, you can throw them away and try again. In addition to the layers that you paint on, Photoshop lets you apply *adjustment layers*. These work like normal layers except that instead of holding paint or pasted pictures, they hold the color adjustments that you make to the image.

There are a couple of ways to add an adjustment layer to your image. (This is Photoshop. You'll soon find that there are several ways to do almost anything you can think of.) First, and most logically, you can choose New Adjustment Layer from the Layer menu shown in Figure 6.15. They're also on a pop-up menu you reach by clicking a button at the bottom of the Layers palette (look for the button with the half-black, half-white circle).

▼ **Try it Yourself**

Using the Adjustments Layer Submenu

To open an adjustment layer:

> 1. Click the black-and-white circular icon at the bottom of the Layers palette or choose Layer→New Adjustment Layer (see Figure 6.15).

FIGURE 6.15
The New Adjustment Layer submenu and the Layers palette.

> 2. Select the particular kind of adjustment that you want to make from the pop-up menu. Click OK to open the appropriate adjustment dialog box.
> 3. Make whatever adjustments are necessary. You can delete the layer if you're not pleased with the changes, or change the layer opacity to effectively change the strength of the corrections you have made.

▲

Understanding Channels

Channels are another way of looking at color. Each image has one or more channels, the number depending on the color mode chosen. CMYK has four separate channels plus a composite. RGB mode has three plus the composite. Each channel holds information about a particular color element in the image. Think of individual channels as something like the plates in the printing process, with a separate plate supplying each layer of color. You can often create interesting textures or special effects by applying filters to just one channel. Figure 6.16 shows the Channels palette (twice) with RGB and CMYK channels.

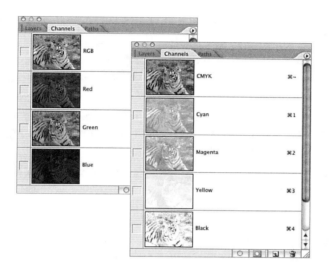

FIGURE 6.16
You can set preferences to show channels in grayscale or in their colors.

There are also alpha channels, which have several uses. They are used to define the placement of spot colors (PANTONE, FOCOLTONE, and so on). They also contain the maps for masks you create and want to save with the image to which you have applied them.

Summary

In this hour, you looked at working with color. Variations make simple, "by eye" adjustments, letting you choose from differently enhanced thumbnails. Levels and curves apply adjustments more scientifically. You now know how to make the sky a perfect blue and the grass a greener green. Now you know that adjusting levels lets you set limits for dark, middle, and light tones in an image. You have learned about color balance and how to apply changes to hue and saturation. You have seen how to change the brightness and contrast of an image.

Color adjustment is one of Photoshop's most-used features, and one that you'll rely on whenever you need to touch up a photo or a scanned image. Practice with it as much as you can, using your own favorite images.

Workshop

Q&A

Q *Levels and Curves seem to do more or less the same thing. How do I know which to use?*

A If the picture seems to have the right color balance (not too red, green, and so on) but is too dark or light, use Levels. If the colors aren't right, adjust the Curves for individual colors and for the RGB (full-spectrum) channel.

Q *I have a sepia-tinted photo (brown tones) that I have scanned into the computer, but the scan came out yellow. Is there a way to get rid of the yellow cast without losing the sepia?*

A The easy way is to convert it to grayscale so that you get rid of *all* the color. Then convert the image back to RGB. Open the Image→Adjustments→Curves dialog box. Instead of RGB on the Channels pop-up menu, select red and drag the curve up until you have added an appropriate amount of red. Then set the pop-up menu to green and drag the curve up until you have added enough of that color. Finally, set the pop-up menu to blue and drag down until you have removed the blue and achieved a reasonable amount of sepia. Experiment until you get the color you want, and then click OK.

Q *If the picture's going to be printed in black-and-white for a newsletter, do I really need to adjust the color balance and stuff?*

A Always leave your options open. Adjust a *copy* of the picture in Grayscale mode, just to make sure that the contrast is good for reproduction. For that, you don't need to think about color. But keep a copy in color in case you want to put the same picture on a web page or do something else with it later.

Quiz

1. A picture came out too green. What should you do?

    a. Open Variations and choose more red.

    b. Open Variations and choose more magenta.

    c. Say you took it in Ireland.

2. A picture was taken on a foggy day, and its colors look washed out. Is there any way to fix it?

    a. Increase the saturation.

    b. Lower the lightness.

    c. Paint over the picture with brighter colors.

3. How can you lessen the amount of change in the Variations dialog box?

    a. Hold Shift+Control+P while you click the thumbnail.

    b. Use the Fine/Coarse slider.

    c. You can't.

Quiz Answers

1. b. On the color wheel, magenta is opposite green, so adding more magenta removes excess green.

2. a. Weak colors lack saturation. Increasing saturation slightly brightens the picture, but don't overdo!

3. b. Moving the slider toward Fine lessens the amount of correction applied each time. (Trying to implement answer a. would probably sprain a finger.)

Exercise

Download some of the photos from the Sams website. To get to the website, point your web browser to http://www.samspublishing.com/. In the Search box, type **Photoshop in 24**. Find this book in the list that appears, and click the link. On the book's main page, find and click the Related Materials link to get to the files. Then see how much further you can go. Turn a cloudy day into a sunny one and vice versa. Experiment. Try your hand at changing the colors by eye, and then see whether you can duplicate your efforts by using the histograms.

HOUR 7

Paintbrushes and Art Tools

What You'll Learn in This Hour:

▶ The Brushes Menu
▶ The Painting Tools

You are already a quarter of the way through, and now it's time to have some fun. Photoshop, as I'm sure you realize, is mainly an image editor. It was created for that purpose, and it accomplishes its purpose very elegantly. Yet there is more to Photoshop than just editing. You can also create artwork here from scratch, just as in any good graphics program. Although many of Photoshop's tools can be used to create an image where none existed before, tools that are explicitly intended for painting include the following:

▶ Clone Stamp and Pattern Stamp

▶ Brush

▶ History Brush and Art History Brush

▶ Eraser, Background Eraser, and Magic Eraser

▶ Pencil

▶ Gradient

▶ Paint Bucket

Figure 7.1 shows the Painting tools. We'll look at the Brushes, the Pencil, the Paint Bucket, the Gradient tool, the Art History tools, and the Eraser in this hour. We'll cover other tools you may find useful as we need them in the next couple of hours.

Each tool is highly configurable. You can easily adjust such settings as diameter, hardness, roundness, angle, opacity, and so on. You'll learn about using these tools in the next few pages.

FIGURE 7.1
Tools for painting and drawing.

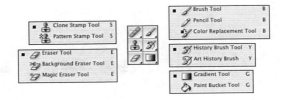

The Brushes Menu

Before discussing specific brushes, take a brief look at the Brushes menu, which you can pull down from the Tool Options bar after you select a tool that uses brush shapes. To open it, click the downward-pointing arrow next to the field that shows the current brush shape. Although each tool has its own set of options, the Brush menu (shown in Figure 7.2) works with most of the art tools, from the Brush to the Clone Stamp tool. (The Pencil's brushes are different, and the Paint Bucket and Gradient tool don't use brushes.) It gives you the capability to select any of Photoshop's preset brush shapes.

Just click to select one of the preset brush shapes. The size and shape you see in the box are the size and shape of the brush. The only exceptions are the brushes with numbers beneath, which indicate the diameter of the brush in pixels. You can use the slider to change the size of the brush without changing any of its other characteristics. A brush can be up to 999 pixels wide. Remember, clicking a brush shape doesn't select a brush tool. You have to do that in the toolbox or by typing a letter shortcut. The Brush menu just influences the shape of the tool you select.

Photoshop comes with many kinds of brushes. You can install the additional brush sets by using the pop-up menu on the Brushes palette. To view the brush shapes by name or by the shape of the stroke they make, use the pop-up menu.

Brushes Palette

The Brushes palette is shown in Figure 7.3. It's usually docked in the Tool Options bar's palette well, but if you prefer to have it accessible elsewhere on the screen, you can do so. Open the Brushes palette by first selecting any painting tool and then clicking the preferences button on the Options bar, or by choosing Window→Brushes. The Brushes palette can then be dragged to a convenient spot on the screen or "docked" by dragging its tab back to the palette well. After it's been docked, it will stay there until you remove it.

The left column displays a list of brush attributes, from tip shapes to dynamics. Clicking each of these items opens a different pane on the right side of the palette. (Shown in the figure is the Brush Tip Shape pane.) With this palette, you can select the qualities of each brush you alter or develop from scratch. Here you can select the diameter, hardness, spacing, angle, and roundness of the brushes.

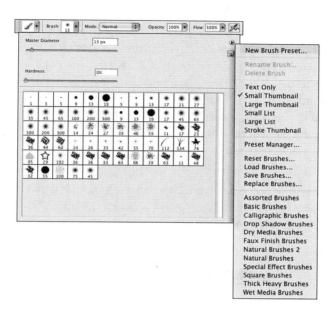

FIGURE 7.2
The Brush menu, extended to show the texture brushes and brush options.

The first two brush attributes to consider are the size and shape. Adjust the diameter with the slider, and drag the brush tip proxy to the appropriate angle and roundness.

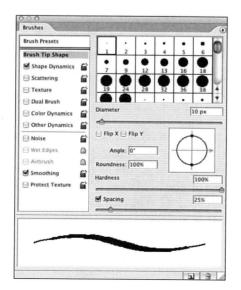

FIGURE 7.3
The Brushes palette enables you to design custom brushes.

Next, set the hardness. The harder a brush is (closer to 100%), the more defined the edges of paint will be. A brush with a setting of around 20% has a much more diaphanous or translucent appearance. The next option is for spacing.

By selecting the Spacing check box, you can set a standard spacing of paint, no matter how fast you drag the mouse. Anything around 25% should give you a very smooth line of paint. If the Spacing check box is left unselected, the speed of your mouse movements determines the spacing of discrete drops of paint. If you move more slowly, paint appears in a continuous line. If you move the mouse more quickly, dabs of paint appear with spaces between them. As you increase the percentage (either by dragging the slider or entering a number into the box), the spaces increase. You can even see the differences as you move the spacing slider (see Figure 7.4).

Play around with these settings. With a little experimenting, you can end up with a brush that behaves just as a real brush does—painting thicker and thinner depending on the angle and speed of your stroke.

FIGURE 7.4
Spacing set at 25%, 100%, and 200%, respectively, from top to bottom.

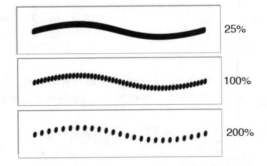

To make adjustments, you can enter values in the fields provided, drag the sliders, or click and manipulate the graphic proxy in the Brush Tip Shape section of the Brushes palette.

When you find a brush you are comfortable with, save it. Choose New Brush Preset from the Brushes palette menu. Use the Brush Name dialog box to give it a name, and the brush will be available to you from then on (see Figure 7.5). If you create an assortment of brushes, you can save them as a group. There's a pop-up menu on the right side of the Brushes palette. (Look for the right-pointing triangle.) Choose Save Brushes to save a brush set.

Using the Opacity Slider

The single most important control in the Tool Options bar is the slider that sets the opacity. Click and hold the right-pointing arrow next to the Opacity field to enable the slider. A low setting applies a thin layer of paint—nearly transparent. The closer you come to 100%, the more concentrated the color is. Figure 7.6 contains some examples of different opacities. I've drawn lines on top of the gradient with both a soft and hard brush, and changed the percentage of opacity for each set of lines. See this figure in color in the color plate section.

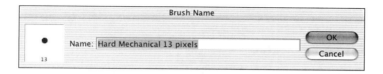

FIGURE 7.5
The Brush Name dialog box.

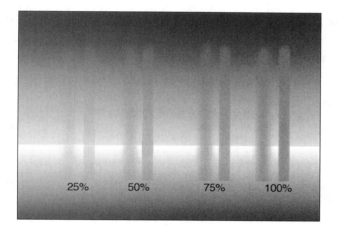

FIGURE 7.6
I've applied magenta stripes over a blue gradient. The opacity percentage is listed below its stripes.

Brush Options

In addition to the brush shape options, Photoshop also gives you some options for brush behavior. Unfortunately, unless you have a pressure-sensitive graphics tablet, you won't be able to enjoy the full effects of these options. The brush behavior options are accessed as check boxes, in the list on the left side of the Brushes palette. Click the name of the action, such as Scattering, to reach the sliders to adjust it. After you've made the adjustments, use the check box to turn the effect on or off.

Using the Wet Edges Setting

Wet Edges creates a sort of watercolor effect when you paint. Figure 7.7 shows an example of the same brush and paint with Wet Edges on and off. Paint builds up at the edges of your brush, and, as long as you are holding the mouse down and painting, the paint stays "wet." In other words, you can paint over your previous strokes without building up additional layers of color. If, however, you release the mouse button and begin to paint again, you will be adding a new layer of paint, which creates an entirely new effect. Notice the overlapped strokes in the figure.

FIGURE 7.7
The Wet Edges effect darkens the edge of a stroke and makes the middle somewhat translucent.

— Wet Edges on

— Wet Edges off

Setting Brush Dynamics

If you use a graphics tablet and stylus, you can get the same sort of fade-out effect that you'd get in the real world by easing off the pressure on a brush or pencil. You have five options for each of these settings: Off, Fade, Pen Pressure, Pen Tilt, and Stylus Wheel. Figure 7.8 shows the Color Dynamics pane of the Brushes palette and some sample strokes with the dynamics on.

FIGURE 7.8
Each line is one brush stroke with different settings applied.

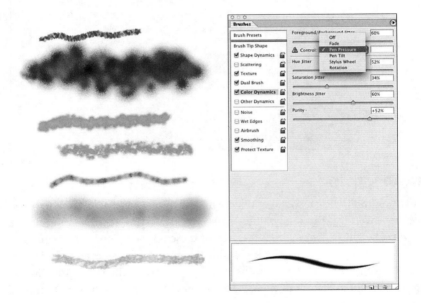

If you're not using a tablet and stylus, you can get a similar effect by closing Fade from the pop-up menu shown in Figure 7.8.

The Painting Tools

Now turn your attention to the Painting tools. For the rest of this hour, you'll be working with the Brush, Eraser, and Pencil tools.

Working with the Painting Tools

Before you go any further, why not stop and try some of these tools? Follow these steps:

1. Create a new document, making the page big enough so that you have some elbow room. The default size, 7 by 5 inches, is fine.

2. On the right side of the screen, look for the Swatches palette. If it's missing, open it from the Window menu. Click the tab to bring it forward, if necessary. Clicking Swatches opens an electronic paintbox. For now, just click any color you like.

3. Press B to select the Brush from the toolbox.

4. Click the down-pointing triangle next to the Brush icon in the Tool Options bar to open the Brushes menu. Choose a brush tip.

5. Press and hold the mouse button as you drag the brush over the canvas to paint.

6. Try the Pencil and Eraser tools, too. Press Shift+B to switch from the Brush to the Pencil and then press E to switch to the Eraser. See what changing the options does for each tool. ▲

The Airbrush

The Airbrush is represented as an icon on the Tool Options bar when the Brush tool is active. Simply click the icon to change the Brush tool's behavior to that of an airbrush. It applies paint by spraying, rather than brushing. It's like an artist's airbrush that uses compressed air to blow paint through an adjustable nozzle. The Airbrush applies paint with diffused edges, and you can control how fast the paint is applied. You can adjust it to spray a constant stream or one that fades after a specified period. Experiment with different amounts of pressure and different brush sizes and shapes.

Remember that the longer you hold the Airbrush tool in a single spot, the darker and more saturated a color becomes, just as if you were spraying paint from an aerosol can.

Figure 7.9 shows a drawing done with just the Airbrush. The spotty effect comes from using a blending mode called Dissolve. (You'll learn about blending modes in Hour 8, "Digital Painting.")

The Brush

The Brush tool is the workhorse of all the Painting tools in Photoshop. Press B to use the Brush, or select it in the toolbox. The Brush behaves very much like the Airbrush, except that paint is applied more evenly. That is to say, if you hold the mouse clicked in one area, paint does not continue to flow onto the canvas.

FIGURE 7.9
Varying the pressure and changing brush sizes gives the picture some variety.

Did you
Know?

Better Brushes

Although you can press Caps Lock to get a precise painting cursor, there is an even better way. Instead, choose Edit→Preferences→Display & Cursors (Windows) or Photoshop→Preferences→Display & Cursors (Mac OS). In the dialog box that appears, look at the Painting Cursors section. There's an option that allows you to choose from the following choices: Standard, Precise, and Brush Size. Choose Normal Brush Tip—this changes your painting cursor from a paintbrush or a crosshair to a shape that is the size of your brush.

If you need to paint a straight line, constrained either vertically or horizontally, hold down the Shift key as you drag the brush. To draw a straight line between two points at any angle, click the canvas once to set the first point, and then Shift+click to mark the end point. A line draws itself between the two points. Figure 7.10 shows some work with the Photoshop brushes. The artist started with a gradient. Then she used a smooth, moderate-sized, Wet Edges brush, and finally she used a brush that simulates grass. These are included in the default brush set.

FIGURE 7.10
This picture was painted with several different brushes.

The History Brush

The History Brush is a very useful tool when you're making changes in an image and aren't sure exactly how much change to make or where to make it. It enables you to selectively restore parts of the picture in which you've made a change, by selecting a brush size and painting out the new image with the old one. In Figure 7.11, the glass distortion filter has been applied to a photo, and then the History Brush was used to undo the effect of the filter in one area of the photo.

FIGURE 7.11
Notice that only the area where I've applied the History Brush is clear.

To use the History Brush, click the box at the left side of the History palette next to the image or state you want to use as the source. In Figure 7.11, I clicked the original image because I wanted to restore parts of it in the altered version. Then, click the History Brush, choose a brush shape, and start painting.

The Art History Brush

The Art History Brush shares space on the toolbox with the History Brush, and you can press Shift+Y to toggle between them. The Art History Brush tool paints with a variety of stylized strokes, but—like the History Brush—it uses the source data from a specified history state or snapshot. Following the motto "different strokes for different folks," it enables you to choose from a menu of different kinds of strokes. Then you paint onto the image with the chosen stroke and change your image into something perhaps resembling an impressionist watercolor, pointillist oil, or some other artistic style. Figure 7.12 shows the Art History Brush's Styles menu on the Tool Options bar.

FIGURE 7.12
Curls imitate Van Gogh at his wildest; Dab does Monet; and Loose Medium resembles a Renoir. Experimenting with these is fun!

In Figure 7.13, I've applied the Art History Brush to a photo, and then gone back into it with the History Brush to restore some of the edges and detail.

FIGURE 7.13
Combining the Art History Brush and the History Brush enables you to restore some of the original image after you've changed it.

Try it Yourself

Apply the Art History Brush

Try the Art History Brush by following these steps:

1. Start with an open image that you've modified extensively since you opened it (such as by applying a filter). On the History palette, click the left column next to the state you want to use as the source for the Art History Brush tool. You'll see a brush icon appear next to the thumbnail image.

2. Click the Art History Brush. The Art History Brush tool is grouped with the History Brush tool in the toolbox.

3. Set the blending mode to normal for now (you'll learn more about blending modes later). Set the opacity to 75%. You can change it as you see the effect.

4. Choose an option from the Style menu. This choice controls the shape of the paint stroke.

5. For Area, enter a value to specify the area covered by the paint strokes. Larger sizes mean larger areas covered and more paint strokes.

6. Enter a Tolerance value or drag the slider to limit the regions where paint strokes can be applied. A low tolerance lets you paint unlimited strokes anywhere in the image. A high tolerance limits paint strokes to areas that differ significantly from the color in the source.

7. Select a brush shape and start painting.

The Art History Brush is capable of some really nice effects, if you spend time learning to work with its settings. Like any complex tool, it takes practice to use correctly.

Color Replacement Tool

This is one of the most useful tools in Photoshop CS2. It functions like any other paintbrush, except that when you paint over an existing scene, it replaces the predominant color with whatever happens to be the foreground color in the toolbox. More importantly, it only changes the color, not the saturation or value. If you had a blue sky with lots of white fleecy clouds, and you wanted an orange sky with the same white clouds, no problem. Choose your shade of orange and apply the brush to the sky. Go ahead and paint right over the clouds. The orange won't affect them except to the same natural degree that the blue did.

Red Eye Tool

Similar to the Color Replacement tool, this tool is designed exclusively for fixing the photo problem known as red eye. You've seen it—glowing red "devil" eyes in portraits of people, and blue or green "alien" eyes in pictures of animals. It's caused by light reflecting off of the back of the eye, and usually happens only with flash photography or in a very bright light. To fix red eye with this brush, just choose an appropriate eye color, dark brown or black, and paint over the red eye. We'll discuss this in greater detail in Hour 22, "Photo Repair—Color."

The Eraser

The next tool in the toolbox that we'll investigate is one that most of us, unfortunately, have to use far too often: the Eraser tool. You'll quickly learn that the hotkey to switch to the eraser is E. One nice thing about the Eraser is that its actions, too, can be undone, so if you happen to rid the canvas of an essential element that you wanted to keep, just choose Edit→Undo to restore.

The Eraser tool is unique in that it can replicate the characteristics of the other tools. It can erase with soft edges as if it were a paintbrush painting with bleach. It can erase a single line of pixels, as if it were a pencil, or it can erase some of the density of the image, as if it were an airbrush. Of course, it can also act as an ordinary block eraser, removing whatever's there. The Options bar settings enable you to determine how the eraser will work: whether it will be a block or a brush, how much you want to erase, and even whether you want to erase to a step on the History palette or to the background color. The Eraser's Options bar is shown in Figure 7.14.

The Opacity slider controls how much is erased. This is useful for blending parts of images, and it also can create a nice watercolor effect.

FIGURE 7.14
The Eraser and its options.

The Fade option, found in the Control pop-up meu in the Brushes Palette's Color Dynamics section, works just like the Fade option when you're using the Airbrush option with a painting tool. When the Fade option is turned on, after a specified number of steps the Eraser no longer erases. This is useful to create feathering around irregularly shaped images. Set the Opacity slider to around 75%, set the Fade to about eight steps, and then drag away from the image you want to feather.

Instead of erasing to the background, you can choose Erase to History. This option (which appears as a check box in the Options bar) lets the Eraser work with the History palette, so you are actually erasing to an earlier version of the picture. Before you begin to erase or make any other drastic changes to your picture, you can take a snapshot of it by choosing New Snapshot from the History palette.

Experiment with this tool until you really understand what it's doing. It can save you lots of time when you're trying new techniques.

The other two erasers in the set are the Background Eraser and Magic Eraser. They share space in the toolbox with the regular Eraser. These erasers make it easier for you to erase sections of a layer to transparency. This can be helpful, for instance, if you need to delete the background area around a hard-edged object. The Background Eraser tool lets you erase pixels on a layer to transparency as you drag. By specifying different Sampling and Tolerance options, you can control the range of the transparency and the sharpness of its boundaries. In Figure 7.15, with the Sampling: Background Swatch option turned on in the Options bar, I've set the background color to the color of the background in my photo and am using the Background Eraser to remove only the card and the table beneath the mug. I can drag the eraser over the mug handle and remove only the stuff that shows through the hole in the handle.

FIGURE 7.15
You have to be very careful when the foreground object has colors similar to the background.

When you click in a layer with the Magic Eraser tool, the tool automatically erases all similarly colored pixels to transparency. You can choose to erase only contiguous pixels or all similar pixels on the current layer.

Try it Yourself

Use the Magic Eraser Tool

Now, you can try the Magic Eraser. Pick any image that has an area of fairly even color, such as the sky.

1. Select the Magic Eraser. The Options bar will change to show its options.

2. Enter a Tolerance value. The tolerance defines the range of colors that can be erased. A low tolerance erases pixels within a range of color values very similar to the pixel you click. A high tolerance erases pixels within a broader range.

3. Specify the Opacity to define how much is erased. An opacity of 100% erases pixels to complete transparency. Lower opacity erases pixels to partial transparency.

4. Set up the remaining options as needed:

   ▶ Choose Sample All Layers if you want to sample the erased color using combined data from all visible layers.

   ▶ Choose Anti-alias to smooth the edges of the area you erased.

   ▶ Choose Contiguous to erase only pixels of the same color contiguous to the one you clicked, or leave it unselected to erase all similar pixels in the image.

5. Click in the part of the layer you want to erase. All similar pixels within the specified tolerance range will be erased to transparency.

In Figure 7.16, you can see the results of using the Magic Eraser tool. First, I isolated the sky by lassoing it. I did this because it was otherwise too close to the color of the pond. I've clicked three times to remove this much of the background. You might have to make several selections to erase all of the area you want to remove. You might also need to use the regular Eraser to clean up pixels that the Magic Eraser misses. But this tool is by far the fastest way to remove the background from an image. You'll use it a lot in Hour 20, "Compositing," when you work on composite images.

FIGURE 7.16
The Magic Eraser removes all pixels that are similar to the one you click.

The Pencil

The Pencil tool, in large measure, works like the Brush tool, except that it can create only hard-edged lines—that is to say, lines that don't fade at the edges as paintbrush lines can. Click the Pencil tool in the toolbox or press B to select it. (Press Shift+B if the Brush tool or the Color Replacement tool is selected.) The Pencil tool shares space in the toolbox with the Brush and the Color Replacement tool. Selecting it activates its options on the bar, as shown in Figure 7.17.

You can set the diameter of your Pencil in the Brush menu on the Options bar. You can also set all the other options, just as you have with all the other tools up to now—I won't bore you with a recap.

The Pencil tool does have one option, though, that you haven't seen in the tools you've read about so far.

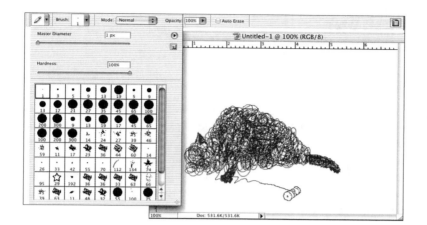

FIGURE 7.17
The drawing
was done with a
one-pixel pencil.

In the Tool Options bar, there is a check box for Auto Erase. When you turn on Auto Erase, any time you start to draw on a part of the canvas that matches the current foreground color shown in the toolbox, your pencil becomes an eraser and will erase to the current background color until you release the mouse button.

Summary

Photoshop's painting tools are easy and fun to use. In this hour, you took a look at the Airbrush, Brush, History Brush, Pencil, and Eraser tools. Brush shapes apply to all the tools, not just to the Brush. You can alter the brush shape or its behavior by using the controls on the Tool Options bar. You learned to activate the Brush, Pencil, or Eraser by pressing a single keyboard letter. You learned about some of the tool options and how they affect the quality of the brush stroke.

Workshop

Q&A

Q *Can I make a custom brush that's not round?*

A Sure. You can even make part of your image into a custom brush. Use the Rectangular Marquee to select a portion of an image. (You can use the Pencil tool to draw a particular brush shape if you want.) With the selection active, choose Edit→Define Brush Preset. The new brush appears on the Brushes palette. Select it and click Brush Tip Shape to set its spacing option. When you're done creating brushes, choose Save Brushes from the Brush menu's pop-up menu to save your current brush set.

Q *Real airbrushes can spray a very light mist of color. How can I duplicate this effect?*

A On the Options bar, set the Flow very low. A large brush and a Flow setting of 10 or less will give you the effect you want.

Q *How do I make my brush strokes look like a watercolor?*

A Easy. Just click the Wet Edges check box. If you'd rather use "oil paint," leave the check box unchecked.

Quiz

1. Are there other brush sets? If so, where?

    a. No, but you can make your own.

    b. Photoshop comes with many sets of pre-made brushes. Check the pop-up menu on the Brushes menu.

2. What happens if you hold the Airbrush in one spot?

    a. Nothing.

    b. You deposit more paint in that spot.

    c. The paint runs down the screen.

Quiz Answers

1. b. Actually, answer a is only partly wrong. You can make your own brushes and brush sets, and you can use the ones Adobe provides.

2. b. Just like with a can of spray paint, if you hold the Airbrush in one spot, the paint piles up.

Exercises

Here, you'll get some more practice with the Airbrush, Brush, and Eraser tools. Follow along with these steps:

1. Start by opening a new document. Make the page at least 6 inches square so that you have room to work.

2. Click the Brush in the toolbox. Set your opacity to 100%, choose a medium-sized, hard-edged brush, and draw a star.

3. Click the check box to turn on Wet Edges and draw another star.

4. Choose a soft-edged brush and draw another star.

5. Now turn off Wet Edges and draw another star with the soft-edged brush. Your result should look something like Figure 7.18.

   Okay, it's not great art, but you have four distinctly different brush looks.

FIGURE 7.18
Four kinds of brush strokes.

6. Scroll to the top of the History palette and click the blank page labeled New. This returns to your freshly opened page, minus stars. (It's a quick way to erase everything.)

7. Press B to activate the Brush, then click the Airbrush button on the Options bar. Set the Flow to 100%, and draw a star.

8. Set the Flow to 50%, by typing the number 5, and draw another star. (You can change Brush Opacity settings by typing a number, too.)

9. Change brushes. If you have been using a soft-edged brush with the Airbrush, try a hard one, or vice versa. Draw more stars with different brushes and pressure settings.

10. Press E to bring up the Eraser. Set the Eraser mode to Brush and the Opacity to 50%. (Type the number 5.) Try to erase one of your stars. Don't click the mouse more than once while you're erasing.

11. Change the Opacity to 100%, and erase another star.

12. Experiment with different settings until you are comfortable with these tools.

HOUR 8

Digital Painting

What You'll Learn in This Hour:

▶ Foreground and Background Colors
▶ Selecting Colors
▶ Blending Modes

Now that you know a little bit about brushes and painting tools, you need to know how to choose some colors with which to paint. Some of the nicer characteristics of digital paint are that it doesn't get under your fingernails, it doesn't smell like turpentine, and you don't have to clean your brushes after you're done painting.

In this hour, you're going to learn about choosing and applying color. There are several ways of choosing colors, and the chapter also discusses blending modes, which affect the way colors (and layers) interact.

Foreground and Background Colors

At any given moment while working with Photoshop, you have two colors available. Only two? Don't worry—that's really kind of misleading. Perhaps it's better to say that you have two colors *active*: a foreground color and a background color. The *foreground color* is the one you use to paint, to fill or stroke a selection. It's the color that's currently on your brush or pencil. (You'll learn about filling and stroking later when you read about paths.) The *background color* is the color Photoshop uses when you erase or delete a selected area on the background layer. You might think of it as the color of the canvas under your painting.

Selecting Colors

The fastest and easiest way to select color is to use the foreground or background swatch in the toolbox (see Figure 8.1). The color swatch to the upper left is your foreground color, and the one to the lower right is the background color. You can set either color by clicking its swatch.

Swatches are those two little squares of color at the bottom of the toolbox—not overpriced wristwatches.

FIGURE 8.1
Click to select the foreground or background color.

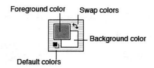

The small icon to the lower left of the swatches, which looks like a miniature version of the swatches, resets to the default colors (black and white). The little curved arrow to the upper right of the swatches swaps the background and foreground colors.

Did you Know?

> **Use Your Keys**
>
> Here are a couple of quick keyboard shortcuts for you. You can reset the default colors by pressing D. Press X to toggle between the background and foreground colors.

To change the color of either of these swatches, click the swatch. This opens the Color Picker that you selected in the General Preferences dialog box. If you haven't made a choice, the Photoshop Color Picker is selected by default. Your other choice is either the Apple or Windows Color Picker, depending on which operating system you use. The examples in this hour use the Photoshop Color Picker.

The Color Picker

Photoshop's Color Picker enables you to select a foreground or background color in any of several ways. Figure 8.2 shows the Color Picker window. You can click the color spectrum to select a color, or drag the triangle slider up or down if you'd rather. You can click the color field to select a color, or you can enter numbers in any one of the color model boxes.

By default, the Color Picker opens in HSB model, which stands for Hue, Saturation, Brightness, with the Hue radio button active. This makes the color field show you all the possible saturation and brightness variations of the particular hue that's selected. If you click anywhere in the color field, you'll see the Saturation and Brightness numbers change, but the Hue setting remains the same.

What's Hue, Pussycat?

Hue—Color, measured as its location on the color wheel in degrees.

Saturation—Strength of the color measured as percentage from 0% (gray) to 100% (fully saturated color).

Brightness—Relative lightness of the color measured as a percentage from 0% (black) to 100% (white).

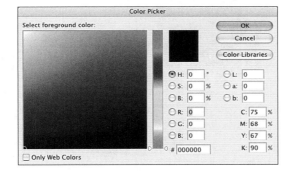

FIGURE 8.2
The Photoshop Color Picker.

If you click the Saturation button, the color field changes to something like the one in Figure 8.3. It shows you all the possible hues at the designated saturation value. If you click anywhere in the color field, the other numbers change, but the saturation stays the same.

HSB mode is the one artists generally prefer because it's easy to understand. You're not stuck with it, though. Feel free to select RGB as a working model. This is the model that governs how your computer displays color. (It uses red, green, and blue, just like a projection television, for instance.)

It's a little bit more complicated to choose a color in the RGB mode. When you click the Red radio button, the color that you see in the color field is just as likely to be blue or green. Here's where the spectrum slider and the numbers start to make a difference.

Remember, in this model, colors are made from three components, red, green, and blue, in amounts from 0 to 255. Pure red has a value of 255 Red, 0 Green, and 0 Blue. If you set those numbers in the Color Picker, the pure red will be way down in the lower-left corner of the color field. Colors representing mixes of green and blue with red will fill the rest of the field. Click up and to the right a little to add small amounts of green and blue to the basic red. Because you're dealing with relatively small amounts of green and blue, the colors you'll actually see mixed with the red are yellow and magenta. The yellow comes from the addition of green, and the magenta from the addition of blue. Figure 8.4 shows what this looks like in the Color Picker.

FIGURE 8.3
Saturation Color Picker.

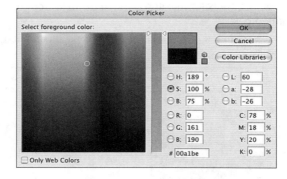

FIGURE 8.4
The selected color is mixed with percentages of the other two primaries.

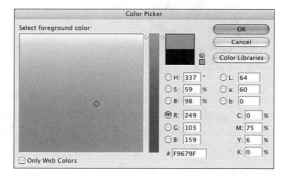

The best way to learn about this color mode is to work with it. Open your Color Picker and click a color. Then watch the numbers as you click a different one. Explore the different radio button settings and their color fields.

Ever wondered about those little letters and numbers at the bottom of the window? You can see the HTML code for any color you select, right there at the bottom of the dialog box. Those codes are in hexadecimal format, ready to enter in your web page HTML source, if you're one of those brave Web warriors who hand-code HTML. If not, don't worry about it. When you place your Photoshop picture into your web-creation program, it'll all happen automatically.

The Color Palette

The Color palette has several advantages over the Color Picker when you're working in Photoshop. First of all, you can leave it open, so you can change colors without having to go through all the fuss of clicking a swatch in the toolbox, finding the color, and verifying your choice. You can also dock it in the palette well at the far right of the Tool Options bar, just by dragging its tab to the well.

Housekeeping Tip

Don't dock too many palettes in the palette well, or they'll be just as hard to locate as on the desktop. Try to limit yourself to the most frequently used ones, such as Brushes, Color, and Layers.

By the Way

For those of you who are mathematically challenged, the Color palette has fewer numbers to contend with, and the ones you see, as in Figure 8.5, are logically related to the sliders. By default, the Color palette opens in whatever mode you used last, but you can set it to Grayscale, or whichever color model you prefer to work in, by using the pop-up menu as shown in Figure 8.6. You can even choose Web colors as a variant of RGB.

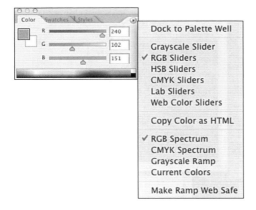

FIGURE 8.5
The Color palette and its menu.

The menu also enables you to reset the color ramp at the bottom of the Color Palette window, according to the color model with which you are working. If your work will be printed and you want to avoid using colors that are *out of gamut* (can't be achieved with CMYK inks), you can set the color ramp to the CMYK spectrum and know that any color you click will be printable. Similarly, if you click Make Ramp Web Safe, the only colors displayed on the color ramp will be the 216 colors that all current Web browsers can display.

FIGURE 8.6
If you're using your pictures on the Web, use the RGB Spectrum color ramp and Web Color Sliders options, as shown here.

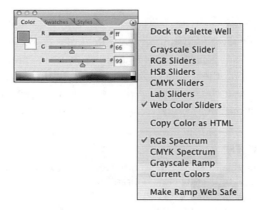

The Swatches Palette

Remember I said at the beginning of the hour that Photoshop gives you several ways of choosing colors? Well, here's the easiest one of all. The Swatches palette (shown in Figure 8.7) works like a box of watercolor paints on your screen. You simply dip your brush in a color and paint with it. To choose a foreground color, simply click the one you want. To choose a background color, Option+click (Mac) or Alt+click (Windows) to select the color you want to use.

FIGURE 8.7
The Swatches palette and its pop-up menu.

The Swatches palette, by default, opens with the current system palette. You can choose colors from the Color Picker to add to the Swatches palette, or you can select a color system, such as PANTONE, Focoltone, TRUMATCH, or Toyo, and have an additional 700 to 1,000 or more printing ink color swatches appended to the palette. You can also add custom colors to it using the Eyedropper tool described in the next section.

Try it Yourself   ▼

Add New Colors from the Color Picker onto Your Palette

Swatches are easy to work with, but Photoshop's choices won't always match yours. Here's how to add your own colors to the swatch set.

1. Click the foreground color swatch in the toolbox.
2. Use the Color Picker to select the desired color and click OK.
3. Open the Swatches palette (Window→Swatches).
4. Clicking the lower-right corner of the Swatches palette, drag the window out so that it resembles the one in Figure 8.8.

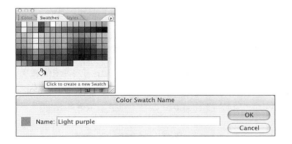

FIGURE 8.8
Adding a new color to the Swatches palette.

5. Move your cursor into the space below the existing swatches. It changes into the Paint Bucket tool.
6. Click anywhere in the unused space, and the new color is added after the existing colors. You'll be asked to give the new color a name.   ▲

If you use a lot of the same colors over and over, and they are not represented in any of the palettes that ship with Photoshop, just elect to save a palette. You can copy colors from photos, from scanner art, even from your desktop. Choose Save Swatches from the Swatches palette menu. This saves you time and the headache of having to reselect all your favorite colors each time you open Photoshop. You can also use the Swatches palette menu to open any of the 15 or so swatch palettes that ship with Photoshop. Color swatches are saved in the Presets folder.

The Eyedropper Tool

You've seen the Eyedropper appear when you moved the pointer over a color swatch or over the color ramp in the Color Palette window. Its function, quite obviously and intuitively, is to pick up a bit of whatever color you touch it with, making that the active color. What's neat about this tool is that it works in the same way on a picture—you can pick up a bit of sky blue, grass green, or skin, without having to identify a match for it with the Color Picker.

The Eyedropper tool is extremely helpful, especially when you are retouching a picture and need to duplicate the colors in it. Click it on any spot in the image and the color underneath its tip becomes the new foreground color. Use Option+click (Mac) or Alt+click (Windows) to select a background color instead. If you drag the Eyedropper across an image, the swatch of color in the toolbox changes each time the Eyedropper touches a new color. If you begin dragging in the Photoshop window you can keep the mouse button down and drag anywhere on the desktop to pick up the colors of your wallpaper or icons.

Did you Know?

Hitting the Hot Spots

Remember that the Eyedropper, like all the tools, is active only at its *hot spot*, in this case, right at the tip. If you find it hard to work with the hot spot, just go to Preferences→Display & Cursors, and change the display to Precise in the Other Cursors area.

Eyedropper Options, on the Tool Options bar shown in Figure 8.9, enables you to select how much of a sample to pick up with the Eyedropper. You can take a single pixel sample, or average a 3×3 pixel or 5×5 pixel color sample.

FIGURE 8.9
Set the
Eyedropper
Options here.

You can convert any other Painting tool (except the Eraser and the History Brushes) into an Eyedropper to change foreground colors on-the-fly by pressing Option (Mac) or Alt (Windows) while you're working.

▼   **Try it Yourself**

Choose a Color and Save It as a Swatch

Here's another way to add to the Swatches palette. This time you'll borrow colors from a photo.

1. Click the Eyedropper tool in the toolbox, or press I to select it.

2. Click the image at the spot where you want to capture the color. If you're saving a background color, Option+click (Mac) or Alt+click (Windows) the color you want.

3. Open the Swatches palette, if it's not already open. Put the Eyedropper on any empty (gray) space in the Swatch palette. It turns into a Paint Bucket.

▼

4. Click once to put a swatch of the selected color into the palette.

5. Choose Save Swatches from the palette's pop-up menu.

6. Follow the usual procedure to name your swatch file, and save it in Photoshop Presets.

To load a saved swatch file, use the Swatches palette's pop-up menu. Choose Load Swatches. Locate the swatch file you want to use in the Presets folder, as shown in Figure 8.10, and click OK.

FIGURE 8.10
The swatches are identified with swatch icons and an .aco extension.

Try it Yourself

Using the Eyedropper and Paintbrush

Let's take a few minutes to do some practicing with the Brush and Eyedropper. Pick out a picture that has lots of color and open it in Photoshop. Then perform the following steps:

1. Before you begin, choose Save a Copy from the File menu and save a backup copy of your picture, just in case you accidentally save and close a messed-up version.

2. Press B to activate the Paintbrush tool. Open the Brushes palette and choose a medium-sized brush shape.

3. Put the Paintbrush on an area of color in the picture, as I have in Figure 8.11. Press Option (Mac) or Alt (Windows). The Paintbrush turns into an Eyedropper and copies the color to the foreground.

4. Release the Option or Alt key and drag the mouse to paint on the picture with the color you've just picked up.

5. Open the Color palette (Window→Color) if it's not already open. Hold your brush over the color ramp at the bottom of the palette. It turns into an Eyedropper.

6. Click to choose another color and add something else to your picture. Use the same brush or switch to the Pencil (press Shift+B) or Airbrush (click the button on the Tool Options bar). Experiment with colors and brushes until you feel comfortable with them.

7. If you run out of space to paint, choose File→Revert to go back to the original version of the picture and start over.

FIGURE 8.11
Click to copy
the color.

The Right Tool for the Task

As you get accustomed to using Photoshop, or any other graphics program for that matter, you'll begin to realize that drawing with a mouse isn't really the best way to draw. As for using the trackball and touchpad—well, they're even more difficult. They simply weren't designed for artwork.

The natural way to draw is to pick up a pencil or pen or brush and draw on something. People have been doing it for thousands of years, all the way back to cave painters at Lascaux, who used crude crayons made of animal fat and colored clays; the ancient Sumerians, who used a stylus and slab of wet clay; and the Egyptians, who wrote and drew with squid ink and feathers on papyrus.

Today, we have something much better: graphics tablets that work with Photoshop and programs like it. These consist of a flat drawing surface, tethered to the computer by a cable, and a stylus about the size and weight of a ballpoint pen. The drawing surface is sensitized to "read" the motion and pressure of the stylus and send the input to the screen. A tablet like the Wacom Graphire3 4×5 costs less than $100 and will save you a good deal of time and frustration. Try one at your friendly local computer store, and you'll be sold on it, too.

Blending Modes

In the real world, when you place a second brush full of paint over paint that's already there, different things happen, depending on the color of the paint you're applying—how opaque it is, whether the first layer is wet or dry, and so on. In Photoshop, you can control all these factors by applying what's called *blending modes.* You'll find them on a pop-up menu in the Tool Options bar, as shown in Figure 8.12. Blending modes apply to all tools that can draw or paint, including the Pencil, Clone Stamp, and Gradient tools, as well as the more obvious ones. As you can see, there are quite a few modes. Take a quick look at the blending modes and how they work.

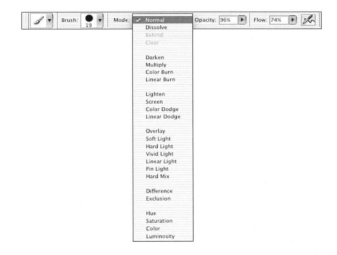

FIGURE 8.12
This list shows the Brush blending modes. Other tools have similar choices.

Suppose that you're working with only two colors. One is the *base* color, the one that's already in place. The second is the *blend* color, the one that you apply with each blending mode enabled. You get a third color, a *result* that varies according to how you blend the first two.

Figures 8.13–8.35 display what happens when you choose each of the options. (The examples were painted with a firm brush in hot pink on a lime-green background, except for those with the letter *R*, which have the colors reversed.)

FIGURE 8.13
Normal—This is the default mode. The blend color replaces the base color.

FIGURE 8.14
Dissolve—A random number of pixels become the blend color. This gives a splattered or "dry brush" effect.

FIGURE 8.15
Darken—Evaluates the color information in each channel and assigns either the base color or the blend color, whichever is darker, as the result color. Lighter pixels are replaced, but darker ones don't change.

FIGURE 8.16
Multiply—Multiplies the base color by the blend color, giving you a darker result color. The effect is like drawing over the picture with a Magic Marker. Where the background is light, you see the original blend color.

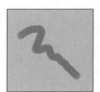

FIGURE 8.17
Color Burn—Darkens the base color to match the value of the blend color.

FIGURE 8.18
Linear Burn—Darkens the base color to reflect the blend color by decreasing the brightness. Blending with white produces no change.

FIGURE 8.19
Lighten—Evaluates the color information in each channel and assigns either the base color or the blend color, whichever is lighter, as the result color. Darker pixels are replaced, but lighter ones don't change. This is the exact opposite of Darken.

FIGURE 8.20
Screen—Multiplies the base color by the inverse of the blend color, giving you a lighter result color. The effect is like painting with bleach. The symbol was drawn with the brush set to Wet Edges.

FIGURE 8.21
Color Dodge—Brightens the base color to match the value of the blend color.

FIGURE 8.22
Linear Dodge—Brightens the base color to reflect the blend color by increasing the brightness. Blending with black produces no change.

FIGURE 8.23
Overlay—Evaluates the color information in each channel and assigns either the base color or the blend color, whichever is darker, as the result color. Lighter pixels are replaced, but darker ones don't change.

FIGURE 8.24
Soft Light—Darkens or lightens depending on the blend color. The effect is said to be similar to shining a diffused spotlight on the image. With a light blend color, it has very little effect.

FIGURE 8.25
Hard Light—Multiplies or screens the colors, depending on the blend color. The effect is similar to shining a harsh spotlight on the image.

FIGURE 8.26
Vivid Light—Burns or dodges the colors by increasing or decreasing the contrast, depending on the blend color. If the blend color (light source) is lighter than 50% gray, the image is lightened by decreasing the contrast. If the blend color is darker than 50% gray, the image is darkened by increasing the contrast.

FIGURE 8.27
Linear Light—Burns or dodges the colors by decreasing or increasing the brightness, depending on the blend color. If the blend color (light source) is lighter than 50% gray, the image is lightened by increasing the brightness. If the blend color is darker than 50% gray, the image is darkened by decreasing the brightness.

FIGURE 8.28
Pin Light—Replaces the colors, depending on the blend color. If the blend color (light source) is lighter than 50% gray, pixels darker than the blend color are replaced, and pixels lighter than the blend color do not change. If the blend color is darker than 50% gray, pixels lighter than the blend color are replaced, and pixels darker than the blend color do not change. This is useful for adding special effects to an image.

FIGURE 8.29
Hard Mix—Combines the effects of Hard Light and Vivid Light modes.

FIGURE 8.30
Difference—Compares brightness values in the base and blend colors, and subtracts the lighter. Overlaps are interesting in this mode. They cancel the previous action.

FIGURE 8.31
Exclusion—Similar to the Difference mode, but has a softer effect.

FIGURE 8.32
Hue—Gives you a result combining the luminance and saturation of the base color and the hue of the blend color.

FIGURE 8.33
Saturation—Gives you a color with the luminance and hue of the base color and the saturation of the blend color. Unless you reduce the saturation of the blend color significantly, nothing shows in Grayscale mode.

FIGURE 8.34
Color—Combines the luminance of the base color with the hue and saturation of the blend color. Useful for coloring monochrome images because Color mode retains the gray levels.

FIGURE 8.35
Luminosity—Gives a result color with the hue and saturation of the base color and the luminance of the blend color. Opposite effect of Color Blend mode.

Summary

In this very full hour, we covered the different ways to choose and apply color to a picture in Photoshop. First, you learned the difference between the foreground color (the color that's on your brush or pencil) and the background color (the color of the canvas under the painting).

The Color Picker, Color palette, and Swatches palettes all contain colors with which you can paint. The Color palette and Swatches palette are easier to use than the Color Picker because you can leave either one of them open as you work. You learned to use the Eyedropper tool with the Brush to choose colors from the palette or from the picture itself.

Finally, we covered blending modes, the way that two layers of paint or image interact with each other.

Workshop

Q&A

Q *The Color Picker has too many buttons and numbers in it! Which ones should I use if I want to change colors?*

A If picking colors by numbers is difficult for you, as it is for me, use my solution. Forget the numbers and click directly on the color you like. Either click the color ramp at the bottom of the Color palette, or click a swatch to open the Color Picker.

Q *Is it better to use the Photoshop Color Picker instead of the Apple or Windows version?*

A I think so. Even though the Macintosh Color Picker gives you lots of different ways to choose colors, I think the Photoshop version is easier to understand and to use. The same is true of the Windows Color Picker.

Q *What happens when I have the Eyedropper set to sample a 5×5 pixel area, and there is more than one color there?*

A Photoshop takes an average of all 25 pixels in the square and makes that the selected color.

Q *Under the Swatches listings, I've heard of PANTONE, but what are all the others?*

A Like PANTONE, most of them are sets of spot color inks. Printing systems can use many brands of inks. If you are sending work to a print shop, be sure to ask what spot color system it uses.

Quiz

1. Blending involves

    a. Taking paint and mixing it in a bucket

    b. Using home appliances

    c. Being able to blend colors in different ways in Photoshop

2. How many *active* colors do you have to work with in Photoshop?

    a. 16 million

    b. 256

    c. 2

3. How do you set black and white as the foreground and background colors?

     a. Select them from the Color Picker

     b. Press D

     c. Sample them from the image with the Eyedropper tool

Quiz Answers

1. c. Photoshop can blend colors much as you can on a canvas with real paint.

2. c. Remember, your foreground and background colors are the active colors, not the total number of colors available.

3. b. Actually, any of these will work, but b. is the easiest.

Exercises

To further explore this hour's topic of picking color and blending modes, fire up your Web browser and visit the Museum of Modern Art (www.moma.org). Navigate to the painting and sculpture section and look through the collection. Pay special attention to the use of color and blending effects. (Click the small images on the index page to see larger versions.)

Compare and contrast the use of color and blending in Van Gogh's *The Starry Night* and Rousseau's *The Dream*. See whether you can duplicate Van Gogh's brush strokes. (Wet Edges are part of the secret.)

HOUR 9

Moving Paint

What You'll Learn in This Hour:

▶ Smudges
▶ Focus Tools
▶ The Toning Tools

Did you ever wonder why artists always have those paint-soaked rags lying around, and why they always have paint on their hands, under their fingernails, and all over their clothes? It's because you don't just paint with a brush; you sometimes paint with your finger, or with a piece of cloth, or with your elbow or some other tool that will help you blend the paint or lighten or darken it just a little bit. In this hour, you will learn the tricks that painters and darkroom technicians have been using ever since their respective art forms were invented.

Smudges

Smudge is the artist's term for blending two or more colors. In Photoshop, there are, naturally, several ways of smudging. There are several ways of doing virtually anything in Photoshop. Be that as it may, using the Smudge tool is the most obvious and the quickest way to blend something into its background.

Using the Smudge Tool

The Smudge tool looks like, and works like, a finger. It's in the same toolbox compartment with the Blur and Sharpen tools. The Smudge tool picks up color from wherever you start to drag it and moves it in the direction in which you drag. Honestly, nothing could be much simpler. You do, however, have to use the Tool Options bar's Strength field to set the pressure of your smudging finger. At 100%, the finger simply wipes away the paint. At 50%, it smears it. At 25%, the smear is less pronounced. Figure 9.1 shows these different smear settings. Photoshop considers the Smudge tool to be a brush, so you can set the width of the finger by choosing an appropriate brush size from the Brush menu.

FIGURE 9.1
Smudges at different Strength settings.

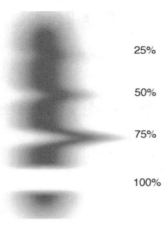

25%

50%

75%

100%

You can also use the Smudge tool to mimic finger painting. This option starts each stroke with the foreground color. You'll find it quite handy if you need to blend some color into an existing picture, perhaps to hide something that's part of the original photo that you'd rather do without. Figure 9.2 shows an example of finger painting. This is a picture I'm quite fond of. Mom and kid were adopting a cat from the SPCA, and you can see them falling in love. But someone gave that cat a really odd name, which shows up in the cage card behind the boy's shoulder.

FIGURE 9.2
The Smudge tool can help change the cat's name, and blurring the letters makes it less obvious.

Setting Smudge Options

Strength and finger-painting options and blending modes are set in the Tool Options bar, shown in Figure 9.3. Click and hold the arrow next to the Strength setting to access the setting slider, and drag the slider to set the strength. If you'd rather not access the slider, type a single digit to set it to a multiple of 10. For instance, type 4 to set to 40. (That trick works with all of Photoshop's sliders, as long as there's only one relevant slider visible at a time.) If you like that shortcut but want more precise control, simply type the digits of the measurement you desire in quick succession.

FIGURE 9.3
The Smudge Tool Options bar.

Check Finger Painting if you want to use the Smudge tool to add some smudged color as you drag. Otherwise, leave the check box empty.

The blending modes are on a pop-up menu. This tool doesn't give you all the blending mode options you learned about in the previous hour, but you can choose— aside from Normal—Darken, Lighten, Hue, Saturation, Color, or Luminosity. Of these, Darken and Lighten are obviously the most useful. The Darken and Lighten modes affect only pixels that are lighter or darker, respectively, than the beginning color. The Darken mode changes lighter pixels and the Lighten mode affects darker pixels.

Did you Know?

Which Smudge Is Best?

If the Smudge tool doesn't achieve the effect you intended, there's also a Smudge Stick filter, which you'll learn about in Hour 15, "Filters to Make Your Picture Artistic." *Filters*, in case you haven't encountered the term before, are tools that apply special effects to your picture. Photoshop has over 100 filters. Each filter applies a different effect to the image, ranging from a blurring or sharpening filter to one that adds clouds to a sky, lights to a backdrop, or turns the image into a Japanese brush painting. You can adjust most of them, and you can fade them so they have less effect.

Focus Tools

Now focus your attention on the Focus tools. These tools, Blur and Sharpen, are great for touching up an image, fixing tiny flaws, and bringing items into sharper contrast. They can't save a really bad photo, but they can do wonders for one that's just a little bit off. Sharpen can increase the contrast to create the illusion of sharper focus, whereas Blur is most useful to rid the background of unwanted clutter and to de-emphasize parts of the picture that you don't want viewers to notice. The Focus tools can be seen in Figure 9.4.

FIGURE 9.4
The Focus tools,
with Smudge
thrown in for
good measure.

The Blur Tool

The Blur tool, simply put, creates blurs in images. By blurs, I mean a softening or evening out of pixel values. Select the Blur tool from the toolbox. The Tool Options bar will show you the Blur tool's options (see Figure 9.5). When you are working with the Blur tool, you can temporarily select the Sharpen tool (and vice versa) by pressing Option (Mac) or Alt (Windows). The Sample All Layers option is available only when your image has more than one layer.

FIGURE 9.5
The Blur Tool
Options bar.

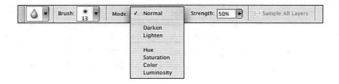

Options for the Blur and Sharpen tools are much the same as those for the Smudge tool described earlier. You have the same choices of blending mode and the same Strength settings.

Figure 9.6 shows a close look at the Blur tool's effect. The flowers were perfect, but the leaves looked as if they'd been hit with a weed whacker. Some careful blurring can hide the damage. Figure 9.7 shows the picture before and after retouching.

Make sure that, as you blur, you cover the entire area that you intend to blur. A missed spot stands out very conspicuously. Also don't forget that you can change the size of your Brush tool by choosing a different brush from the Brushes menu.

For the Blur tool, I recommend using a brush with a soft edge, but not for the Sharpen tool. When sharpening, I prefer to use a small brush with hard edges so that I know exactly where I am. You'll also find it helpful to work with a magnified view of your picture, just so you have better control over the tool.

FIGURE 9.6
The Blur tool in use.

FIGURE 9.7
Before blurring (top) and after (bottom).

By the Way

A Touch of Retouching

One of the things you'll begin to notice as you become more accustomed to working with Photoshop is the use of image-manipulation techniques in advertising and even in magazine and news editorial photos. You'll begin to recognize—in magazines and other printed pieces—pictures that betray the work of a digital retoucher. You should also begin to examine them for technique and skill. Take note of the next automobile advertisement you see in a flashy, four-color magazine or brochure. Note the foreground. Check the highlights. Examine the reflections in the headlights. Do they look good? Too good? Almost all advertising images are retouched (mainly in Photoshop), and the people doing this are professionals. Learn from them. Notice how the backgrounds fade, how the trees blur, or how the highlights appear. Evidences of Photoshop are all around you. Just keep your eyes open....

The Sharpen Tool

The Sharpen tool is the exact opposite of the Blur tool. Where the Blur tool softens pixel values, the Sharpen tool hardens them and brings them into greater relief by increasing the contrast between adjacent pixels. Because of their equal-but-opposite relationship, they share a space on the toolbox, with a pop-up that lets you choose either one, or the Smudge tool. You can also activate the Blur, Sharpen, and Smudge tools by pressing R (for *retouching*?). Press Shift+R to toggle among the three. Figure 9.8 shows a dogwood blossom, before and after having its center sharpened.

FIGURE 9.8
Applying the Sharpen tool. Compare the area inside the circle to the same picture before sharpening.

Sharpening is best done in very small doses. If you go over a section too much or have the Strength set too high, you can end up burning the color out of an image, which will probably make it look worse than it did initially. See Figure 9.9 for an example of over-sharpening.

Remember, too, that not even the magic of Photoshop can put back what wasn't there originally. Always work with the clearest, sharpest pictures you can manage. Rather than trying to salvage a bad scan, do it again. If your photo is fuzzy all over, instead of trying to sharpen it, set it aside until you start working with filters (see Hour 15).

FIGURE 9.9
Too much sharpening.

Try it Yourself

Using the Focus Tools

Let's take a quick break here and try out these tools. Open any convenient picture in Photoshop and follow these steps:

1. Select the Zoom tool and click once in the image window to zoom in on your picture.

2. Select the Blur tool. Choose a soft-edged brush shape from the Brushes palette on the Tool Options bar.

3. Type **5** to set the Strength to 50% in the Tool Options bar.

4. Drag the Blur tool across the picture. Notice the effect (see Figure 9.10).

5. Switch to the Sharpen tool by pressing Shift+R. Choose a hard-edged brush. Drag it over a different part of the picture. Try to drag it along the edge of an object and note the effect (see Figure 9.11).

FIGURE 9.10
Blurring a leaf with the image (and tool) enlarged.

FIGURE 9.11
Sharpening is
more obvious
than blurring.

6. Try sharpening the area you previously blurred. Can you restore it to its previous appearance? (Probably not.)

7. Now, just for fun, switch to the Smudge tool and see for yourself the difference between Blur and Smudge.

8. Practice with these tools at different Strength settings and with different brushes. Use Revert (File→Revert) or click the snapshot at the top of the History palette to restore the picture if you run out of practice room.

The Toning Tools

Photoshop is primarily a digital darkroom program, so it makes sense that some of its most useful tools mimic the darkroom techniques that photographers use to lighten and darken portions of an image or to brighten colors. The Toning tools include the Dodge, Burn, and Sponge tools. Dodge and Burn are opposites, like Sharpen and Blur, but instead of affecting the contrast between adjacent pixels, they either lighten or darken the area to which the tool is applied. Sponging changes the color saturation of the area to which you apply it.

Dodge and Burn Tools

Dodging, in the photographer's darkroom, is accomplished by waving a dodge tool, usually a cardboard circle on a wire, between the projected image from the enlarger and the photographic paper. This blocks some of the light and makes the dodged area lighter when the print is developed. It's also called "holding back" because you effectively hold back the light from reaching the paper. Photoshop's Dodge tool, shown in Figure 9.12, looks just like the darkroom version.

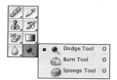

FIGURE 9.12
The Toning tools: Dodge, Burn, and Sponge.

Burning has the opposite effect to dodging—instead of lightening a small area, it darkens the area. In the darkroom, burning in is accomplished either by using a piece of cardboard with a hole punched out (the opposite of the Dodge tool) or by blocking the enlarger light with your hand, so the light only reaches the area on the print surface to be burned. Photoshop's Burn tool icon is a hand shaped to pass a small beam of light.

Click the Dodge tool and look at the pop-up menu in the Tool Options bar. As you can see, it gives you three choices:

▶ Shadows

▶ Midtones

▶ Highlights

These options indicate the types of pixels that the tool will affect. If you want to adjust the shadows, such as making them lighter and leaving the lighter pixels untouched, select Shadows. The default option for the Dodge tool is Midtones. This is a good choice when you want to affect the midtone pixels, or when you are unsure of how to proceed. Select Highlights when you want to lighten already light-colored areas, leaving the darker areas untouched. Figure 9.13 shows the effects of dodging and burning on a picture shot outdoors in shade on a sunny day. This photo is also included in the color section.

Sponging

Surprisingly enough, sponging is also a darkroom trick. When a picture in the developing tray isn't turning dark enough or looks to be underexposed or weak in color, the darkroom technician can often save it by sloshing some fresh, full-strength developing chemical on a sponge and rubbing it directly on the wet print in the tray. The combination of the slight warmth from the friction of the sponge and the infusion of fresh chemical can make the difference between a useless picture and an acceptable one. It's no substitute for a proper exposure, of course.

FIGURE 9.13
I lightened the tree and darkened the overexposed leaves.

Photoshop's Sponge does much the same thing. On a color image, it increases (or reduces, versatile tool that it is) the color saturation in the area to which you apply it. On an image in Grayscale mode, it increases or decreases contrast by moving the grayscale level away from or toward middle gray. When you use the Sponge, you also need to adjust its setting in the Options bar to determine whether it intensifies color (saturates) or fades it (desaturates). Figures 9.14 and 9.15 show before and after views of a woodland scene with the Sponge applied. See it in its full glory in the color section.

By the Way

Caught in the Middle

Have you ever wondered what's meant by *middle gray*? If you consider the grayscale as going from 0% (white) to 100% (black), middle gray is the tone that's exactly 50%. In practice, highlights are anywhere from 0 to about 20%–25%. Shadows are 70%–100%. So anything between a 25% gray and a 70% gray is considered a *midtone*.

These tools are great for fine-tuning images and creating shadows or highlights. Use them in small doses to enhance the appearance of your images.

See What You're Doing

For this sort of precision work, I strongly recommend that you change your cursors to Normal Brush Tip in the Edit→Preferences→Display & Cursors (Windows) or Photoshop→Preferences→Display & Cursors (Mac OS) dialog box. This permits you to see exactly what you are doing, when using these precision tools. Enlarging the picture is also helpful.

FIGURE 9.14
Before using the Sponge, the colors are somewhat dull.

FIGURE 9.15
After using the Sponge, the colors are much brighter.

Summary

Photoshop provides several ways to move paint around after you have applied it. The Smudge tool is useful for blending small areas of color. It has the same effect as dragging your finger through wet paint. Sharpen and Blur are two sides of the same coin, so to speak. One increases the contrast between adjacent pixels, whereas the other diminishes it. The Toning tools (Dodge, Burn, and Sponge) are the digital darkroom equivalents of real darkroom tools and procedures. They can darken or lighten an image, or change the color saturation by either adding more color or removing some. These tools are mostly used for retouching pictures that you have scanned or shot digitally, rather than for creating your own art.

Workshop

Q&A

Q *What's the difference between the Smudge and Blur tools?*

A The main difference is in the way you apply them. Smudging, because you're moving the pixels from point A to point B, tends to show the direction of the move. Blurring decreases the contrast between adjacent pixels, so they seem to blend together visually but with no hint of movement.

Q *Can I saturate and desaturate on the same object? I want to make one side lighter and the other darker.*

A Of course, you can, but the Sponge tool might not be your best choice for darkening an object. Remember, it makes the color more or less saturated, which is not quite the same as darkening it. Try it and, if the effect isn't what you're looking for, try burning instead.

Q *I understand the Sharpen tool, but there also seem to be Sharpen filters. (Okay, I peeked ahead.) When should I use the tool and when should I use the filters?*

A Use the tool when you have a small area that you want to sharpen. Use the filters when you have a soft focus image, or one that needs all-over sharpening. You'll learn how to work with the filters in Hour 14, "Filters That Improve Your Picture."

Q *My scanned picture has a very dark shadow. Should I desaturate it or dodge it?*

A Yes. Try both approaches and see which works best for you.

Quiz

1. What effect does 100% Strength have on the Smudge tool?

    a. None.

    b. It turns the smudges black.

    c. Rather than smudging, it completely replaces color in the path of the stroke with the adjacent color.

2. If you sharpen a piece of the picture too much, what happens?

    a. It turns into a seemingly random collection of black and colored pixels.

    b. It turns white.

    c. It turns black.

3. What should you do if you oversaturate part of your picture?

    a. Use the History palette to backtrack to the step just before you used too much saturation.

    b. Set the sponge to desaturate and use it on the bright spots.

    c. Choose Edit→Fade Sponge Tool, and use the slider to back off the color.

Quiz Answers

1. c. You can use the Smudge tool set at 100% almost as an eraser, dragging background color over the object you're trying to smudge out.

2. a. This effect is not recommended.

3. a., b., or c., if you used the Sponge Tool in one long continuous stroke, but the first is usually the best method.

Exercises

Find a photo that's too light and too fuzzy. Apply the Sharpen tool and the Dodge, Burn, and Saturate tools as needed until you've fixed it. Now do the same with a photo that's too dark. Which was easier to adjust?

PART II

More Tools and Tricks

Advanced Painting Techniques

What You'll Learn in This Hour:

▶ Simulating Different Media
▶ Imitating Watercolor and Oil Paint
▶ Imitating Pencil, Charcoal, and Chalk

Digital paint is so much easier to work with than the real kind. It doesn't smell, it never spills on the table, and there are no messy brushes to wash out when you're done. It doesn't get all over you and you don't even have to wait for it to dry. In Photoshop, you can either paint a picture from scratch, starting with a blank page and using it as if it were any other graphics program, or you can take an existing image and convert it into a painting. In the course of this hour, you'll explore both ways of working.

When I talk about "paint" in the digital realm, I'm talking, of course, about image manipulation that mimics real-life painting techniques. Because we're imitating real life, you might think that you'd be limited in the number of painting techniques that you can use—but this isn't the case. You're not limited to just watercolor or oil paint, for instance. Under the broad category of painting, you can include colored pencil drawing, pastels, chalk, charcoal, and even neon tubing, as many of today's artists and art students are doing. Even though digital painting is the most spectacular part of Photoshop, as well as the most fun, you'll be amazed at how easy it is. More important, mastering Photoshop's Painting tools will take you a long way toward becoming a more proficient digital artist.

By the
Way

Okay, It's Not Perfect

Quite honestly, Photoshop wasn't designed to be an all-purpose graphics program. It lacks some of the tools that you'll find in Adobe Illustrator or Corel Painter (to name just two of the very best programs). However, it can be used very effectively for many kinds of graphics. Because of its plug-in filters, which you'll learn about shortly, it can do some very remarkable things with graphics, most of which would be way beyond the capability of an ordinary painting or drawing program. Should Photoshop be your only graphics program? Probably not, if you need to do a lot of drawing. Although the last few releases have added some limited vector drawing tools and immeasurably better type-handling than previous versions had, Photoshop is still not the perfect multi-use graphics program. But for digital darkroom work and retouching, nothing can top it.

Simulating Different Media

One of the remarkable tricks Photoshop can do is simulate the appearance of other media. The effect can be achieved through the use of a filter (I jump ahead a little in this hour and introduce you to some of Photoshop's "artistic" filters). It can also be achieved through the use of the Smudge and Blur tools, or by choosing custom brushes and carefully applying paint with a particular blending mode. You can create a picture from scratch, or you can start with a photograph and make it look like a watercolor, an oil painting in any of a half-dozen styles, or even a plaster bas relief. Whatever the method, the results will amaze you.

Watercolors

Artists who work in conventional media have a great deal of respect for those who choose watercolors. It's probably the most difficult medium of all to handle. You have to work "wet" to blend colors, but not so wet that the image turns to mud. Doing it digitally is much easier. We'll start with a filter technique that makes a photo appear to have been created as a watercolor painting.

Converting a Photograph to a Watercolor

Photoshop has a watercolor filter that converts a picture to a watercolor version of itself. You can find the filter in the Filter→Artistic submenu, as shown in Figure 10.1.

Filters, in Photoshop terminology, are sets of instructions built into the program (or "plugged-in" as added features) that apply specific effects to your pictures. For instance, one of Photoshop's filters converts your image to a pattern of dots. Another simulates a colored pencil. Dozens of filters are available. Some come with the program, whereas others are sold by third-party vendors or distributed as shareware or freeware. In Hours 14–16, you'll learn more about what kinds of filters you can get and where.

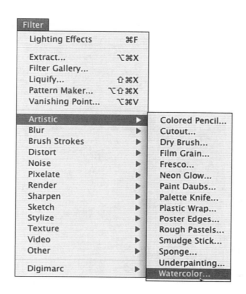

FIGURE 10.1
Watercolor is one of 15 artistic filters.

The Watercolor filter works most effectively on pictures that have large, bold areas and not a lot of detail. Because it also tends to darken backgrounds and shadows, it's best to start with a picture that has a light background. The photo in the figures that follow features some very white flowers. When you select the Watercolor filter (or virtually any other Photoshop filter, for that matter), you open a dialog box like the one shown in Figure 10.2. This Filter Gallery has a thumbnail view of your picture and a set of sliders that enable you to set the way in which the picture is converted. As of Photoshop CS, many of the filter dialog boxes also show you the list of available filters and a thumbnail-sized sample of the effects they produce. If you click and drag on the thumbnail image, you can slide it around to see the effect of your settings on different parts of the photo. Most Photoshop filters have dialog boxes and settings very much like this one. After you have tried even one, the rest will be just as easy.

Filters can take anywhere from a few seconds to a minute or more to apply. If you don't see the effects of the filter on the thumbnail view immediately, look for a progress bar in the status bar at the bottom of the filter window. It grows as the computer calculates and applies the Filter effect. When the bar is filled, the effect is in place.

Brush detail varies from 1 to 14, with 14 giving you the most detail, and 1 being a sort of Jackson Pollock splatter effect. Depending on the nature of the picture you are converting and your own preferences, you might want to start experimenting with settings around 9 to 12. Shadow intensity can be adjusted from 0 to 10, but, unless you are looking for special effects, leave it at 0. The Watercolor filter darkens shadows too much, even at the 0 setting. By the time you move it past 3 to 4, the picture is almost totally black. Texture settings vary from 1 to 3. These are actually quite subtle, and you might wonder whether they have any effect at all. They do, but the effects are more noticeable combined with less detailed brush settings. In Figure 10.3 (in the following Try it Yourself), I've gathered samples of different brush detail and texture settings so that you can see the differences.

FIGURE 10.2
Use the + and – buttons to zoom in and out on the thumbnail.

Try it Yourself

Converting a Photograph to a Watercolor

You might not want to convert all your photos into imitation watercolors, but some look really good with this treatment.

1. Find a picture that you think might look good as a watercolor, or download the one shown in the "Try it Yourself" section from our website. It's called rhodies.jpg. To get to the website, point your web browser to www.samspublishing.com, and type the book's name or ISBN.

    After the main book page has loaded, click the Downloads link to get to the files. Open the downloaded file in Photoshop and make any color adjustments you think necessary. I think it could be lighter, so that's what I did. (If you've forgotten how, turn back to Hour 6, "Adjusting Color," to refresh your memory.) Remember not to let the colors get too dark before you start applying filters. Photoshop filters, in general, tend to add more black to the image.

2. Choose Watercolor from the Filter→Artistic submenu.

3. In the Watercolor filter window, shown in Figure 10.4, use the sliders to choose a combination of texture and brush detail that you like.

    Set the shadow intensity to 0, unless you want a lot of black in the image.

4. Move the thumbnail image to check details by clicking and dragging the hand symbol that appears when you place your cursor in the thumbnail window.

5. Click OK when you're done to apply the changes.

6. If the picture seems drab, use the Sponge tool set to Saturate to bring out the colors.

Brush Detail 1
Texture 1

Brush Detail 1
Texture 2

Brush Detail 1
Texture 3

Brush Detail 7
Texture 1

Brush Detail 7
Texture 2

Brush Detail 7
Texture 3

Brush Detail 14
Texture 1

Brush Detail 14
Texture 2

Brush Detail 14
Texture 3

FIGURE 10.3
All three texture settings have been applied to each sample brush setting.

FIGURE 10.4
I've set the Brush Detail to 1 and Texture to 2. You can see this version in the color section.

Watercolors from Scratch

Sometimes you either don't have a photo of what you want to paint, or you just want to do it yourself. Perhaps you want a different style of watercolor than what's possible with the filter. If you work patiently and with some forethought, you can produce watercolors that you'd almost swear were painted with a brush on paper. Let's open a new document in Photoshop and do some painting.

You learned about working with the Brush tool in Hour 7, "Paintbrushes and Art Tools." As you recall, using the Tool Options bar, you can switch from a large brush to a small one, or change the opacity, with just a click. I also like to open the Swatches palette and use it as a paintbox to select colors, rather than going to the Color Picker each time. Please feel free to flip back if you need to refresh your memory about any of these issues.

Sort Your Palettes
If you drag on the tabs at the top of the palettes, you can move them around so you can use the Layers, History, Color, and Swatches palettes all at once, or whatever combination of palettes you need. Close the ones you aren't using to make more room. Dock the palettes you're most likely to need—for instance, Brushes, Layers, Color, and History—in the docking well at the right end of the Tool Options bar.

Transparency is one of the distinguishing features of real watercolor. To make a "synthetic" watercolor, you'll want to set the Brush opacity at no more than 75%. Because transparent is the opposite of opaque, this means that your paint will be 25% transparent, which is about right for watercolors. Try the brush on a blank page, and you'll notice that, as you paint over a previous stroke, the color darkens. Click the Wet Edges check box in the Brushes palette for even more authentic brush strokes. This option adds extra color along the edges of a stroke, making it look as if the pigment gathered there, as it does when you paint with a very watery brush.

Watercolor artists painting on paper often start with an outline and then fill in the details. Figure 10.5 shows the beginnings of a watercolor painting of an apple. I've drawn the fruit and its stem and leaves, and now I'm working on filling in the leaves with a small brush. It's often easier to work in a magnified view when you're doing small details like this.

Another useful trick for creating a watercolor is to use the Eraser as if it were a brush full of plain water to lighten a color that you have applied too darkly. Use it at a very low opacity to lighten a color slightly, and at a high opacity to clean up around the edges if your paintbrush got away from you. Don't forget that the Eraser always erases to the background color. If you have been changing colors as you paint, make sure to set the background color to what you want to see when you erase, or keep your painting on a separate layer from the textured background layer.

Take One Tablet

For this kind of task, a pressure-sensitive graphics tablet, although not an absolute must, is certainly helpful. Drawing with a stylus is far more natural than drawing with a mouse or trackball, and the pressure-sensitive function permits you to make brush strokes that trail off like the real ones, rather than having to rely on the less versatile Fade Steps option to create the effect.

Did you Know?

Most real watercolors are painted on heavily textured watercolor paper. If you would like yours to have the same grainy character, you can use the Texturizer (Filter→Texture→Texturizer) filter to add the watercolor paper texture to the picture after your painting is completed. Don't apply it until everything else is done, though, because additional changes you make will alter the texture. Figure 10.6 shows the Texturizer filter being applied.

The Canvas texture comes the closest to replicating watercolor paper, especially if you scale it down some. Sandstone works well, too. I like to set it at 70%, with a relief height of 3. Use the sliders to set relief and scaling. I find that applying the same texture a second time with the light coming from the opposite direction gives me the best imitation of textured paper. Of course, you can also print your images on real watercolor paper. Lighter weight papers run through an inkjet printer very nicely.

FIGURE 10.6
The direction
of the light
affects the
shadows that
make up the
texture.

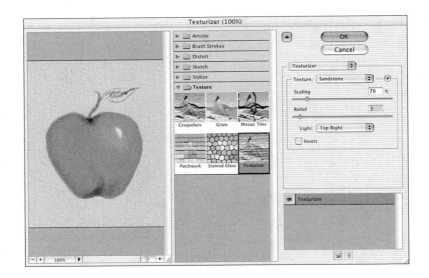

Oil Painting

Oil paint has a very different look from watercolor, and it's a look that Photoshop duplicates particularly well. The qualities that distinguish works in oil are the opacity of the paint, the textured canvas that adds a definite fabric grain to the image, and the thick, sometimes three-dimensional quality of the paint. To get the full effect in Photoshop, you might have to combine several techniques. We'll start, as artists do, with underpainting.

Underpainting

When an artist starts an oil painting of a landscape or a seascape, she usually sketches out the subject with a few lines, often working with charcoal or a pencil to locate the horizon and major land masses. Then she dips a big brush in thinned-out paint and begins the process of underpainting. This blocks in all the solid areas; the sky, the ground, the ocean, and any obvious features like a large rock, a cliff, or whatever else might be included. Underpainting builds the foundation of the picture, establishing the colors and values of the different parts of the image. After that, all that's left is to fill in the details.

Photoshop's Underpainting filter looks at the image that you're applying it to and reduces it to the same sort of solid blobs of color. In Figure 10.7, I'm applying the filter to a photo of a pond. If you want to download this photo and work along, it's called `fallpond` and it's at the Sams website discussed earlier in this hour.

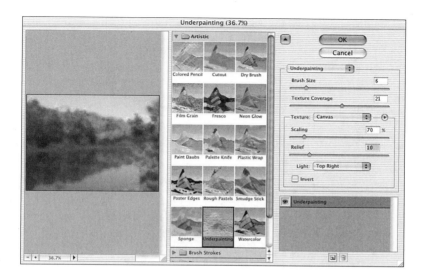

FIGURE 10.7
Check your set-
tings in the
Preview area
before you apply
them.

Underpainting gives you the basic elements of the picture, minus the details. Using
the Underpainting filter requires making some settings decisions. The Texture settings are exactly the same as in the Texturizer filter used on the watercolor. Here,
though, you want to bring out more of the texture, so you use a higher relief number, and possibly a larger scale on the canvas. You can also paint on burlap, sandstone, or brick, or on textures that you import from elsewhere. The Brush Size setting
ranges from 0 to 40. Smaller brushes retain more of the texture and detail of the
original image. Larger brushes give a somewhat spotty coverage and remove all the
detail. Texture Coverage also ranges on a scale from 0 to 40. Lower numbers here
reveal less of the texture; higher numbers bring out more of it. In underpainting, the
texture is revealed only where there's paint, not all over the canvas.

Try it Yourself

Turn a Scene into an Oil Painting

The character of an oil painting is quite different from that of a watercolor. Let's
try to apply the oil paint technique to a photo.

1. As always, start by preparing the picture. Adjust the colors if necessary and
   crop as needed.

2. Open the Underpainting filter dialog box (Filter→Artistic→Underpainting).

3. Set the Brush Size to 6 and the Texture Coverage to 21. These settings will
   retain most of the detail in the picture.

4. Set the Texture to Canvas and Scaling to somewhere around 70%. You want
   to keep the texture small so that it doesn't interfere with the detail you will
   be adding to the picture later.

5. Set the Relief to 7 and the Light Direction to Top Right. This shows just enough texture to establish that your painting is on canvas rather than stone. The Light Direction matches the position of the sun.

6. Click OK to apply the filter. Figure 10.8 shows the result so far.

FIGURE 10.8
The scene with just the Underpainting applied.

Overpainting

The Underpainting filter leaves you with a somewhat indistinct picture, fine for some purposes but definitely unfinished. An artist would proceed to go back and overpaint the areas that need to have detail, so that's what you'll do to complete this autumn scene.

Because oil paintbrushes tend to be rather stiff, choose a hard brush rather than a soft-edged one. Be sure to turn off Wet Edges in the Brushes palette, if it happens to be on. You'll probably also want to change the blending mode, although Normal will work fine for some parts of the painting where you want to make actual strokes of paint. However, Dissolve might be the most useful mode for working into the trees. Use it, as shown in Figure 10.9, to stipple colors into the underpainting. (*Stippling* means to paint with the very end of a hard round brush, placing dots rather than strokes of paint. Dissolve does this effect very well.) Vary the Brush Size and Opacity to add more or less paint with each stroke.

You can go on painting into this picture until it looks exactly like an oil painting, or you can use it as a basis to experiment with other filters and effects. In Figure 10.10, I've applied the Texturizer filter (Filter→Texture→Texturizer) and used it to restore the texture lost from the overpainting process. See it completed in the color section.

FIGURE 10.9
I've added orange and brighter greens to the trees, and sharpened up the close evergreens.

FIGURE 10.10
Placing a canvas texture under this image makes it much more like an oil painting.

Pencil and Colored Pencil

The Pencil tool has been part of every graphics program since the very first ones. It's an extremely useful tool when you know how to use it properly. The Pencil tool shares a space in the toolbox with the Brush tool. You can use it (or any of the brushes) in a sort of connect-the-dots mode. Click where you want a line to begin, and Shift+click again where it should end. Photoshop draws the line for you. Keep Shift+clicking to add more line segments. The Pencil can also serve as an eraser if you click the Auto-Erase function on the Tool Options bar. With Auto-Erase enabled, when you click the Pencil point on a colored pixel that is the same color as the current foreground color, you erase it to the background color. Use this feature to clean up edges or to erase in a straight line.

Pencils are great for retouching and drawing a single pixel-width line, but difficult to use for an actual drawing. (Yes, you can set the Pencil to any of the brush shapes, but if you do that, it's functionally a brush.) The Pencil is easier to use if you zoom in to 200% so that you can see individual pixels. Setting the mouse acceleration to Slow will also help, but it's even better to use a graphics tablet instead of a mouse.

If you want to get the look of a pencil drawing without all the effort, try the Colored Pencil filter (Filter→Artistic→Colored Pencil) or the Crosshatch filter (Filter→Brush Strokes→Crosshatch). The Colored Pencil filter, shown in Figure 10.11, gives you a light, somewhat more stylized drawing from your original image. It looks even better if you convert the drawing to grayscale after applying the filter. The Crosshatch filter, applied to the same image in Figure 10.12, retains much more of the color and detail, but still looks like a pen-and-ink drawing.

FIGURE 10.11
The Colored Pencil filter adds a light, airy feel.

Chalk and Charcoal

Chalk and charcoal drawings are found in museums and collections all over the world. Artists love these materials for their ease of use and versatile lines. You can make sharp lines or smudged ones just depending on how you hold the chalk or charcoal twig.

FIGURE 10.12
Crosshatching uses a different, more detailed drawing style.

Chalk drawings can be found on virtually any surface, from grained paper, to brick walls, to sidewalks. Chalk drawings in Photoshop enable you to take advantage of the capabilities of the Texture filters. You can place your drawing on sandstone, burlap, or on a texture that you've imported from another source.

Chalk and charcoal are linear materials, which is to say that they draw lines rather than large flat areas like paints. Choose your subjects with that in mind. You can, of course, apply shading as a pattern of lines or a crosshatch, and you can smudge to your heart's content. If you're drawing from scratch, start with a fairly simple line drawing and expand on it. If you're translating a photo or scanned image into a chalk or charcoal drawing, choose one that has strong line patterns and well-defined detail.

The Chalk & Charcoal Filter

When you apply the Chalk & Charcoal filter, which is found on the Filter menu (Filter→Sketch→Chalk & Charcoal), you'll see that it reduces your picture to three colors, using a dark gray plus the foreground and background colors that you have set in the tool window. Chalk uses the background color and Charcoal becomes the foreground color. Areas that aren't colored appear in gray. You will probably want to do some experimenting to find the right colors.

Figure 10.13 shows the Chalk & Charcoal dialog box, which controls how this filter works. In it you can set amounts for the chalk and charcoal areas. These sliders have a range from 0 to 20. Start somewhere in the middle and adjust until you get a combination that works for your picture. The Stroke Pressure varies from 0 to 5. Unless you want the picture to turn into areas of flat color, keep the setting at 1 or 2. Intensity builds up rather fast with this filter.

FIGURE 10.13
Move around in the preview window to see the filter's effects on different parts of the image.

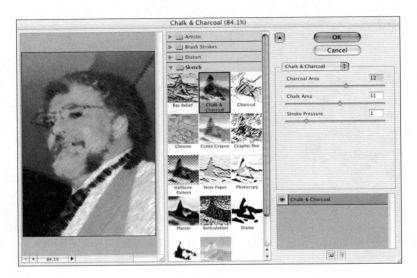

▼

Try it Yourself

Convert a Photograph to a Chalk and Charcoal Drawing

The Chalk & Charcoal filter looks great with any reasonably high-contrast subject. Try it on a portrait.

1. Open the image and then the Chalk & Charcoal filter dialog box (Filter→Sketch→Chalk & Charcoal).

2. Set the Charcoal and Chalk areas to 10 or less. When you work with a filter for the first time, always start in the middle of the settings range and increase or decrease as necessary.

3. Set the pressure to 1 or 2. Move on to step 4 if you like the view in the Preview window, or experiment with other numbers.

4. Click OK to apply the filter. Figure 10.14 shows this filter applied to the same portrait as in the previous example.

5. Study the result. Decide what areas need touching up.

6. Select the Eraser tool and erase to bring up more of the background color.

7. Select the Brush tool to apply more of the foreground color.

8. Use the Eyedropper to select the gray tone, if you need to apply more of it. (The gray is an arbitrary color used by this filter and can't be adjusted.)

9. When you're satisfied with the drawing, save it.

▼

FIGURE 10.14
After applying the filter, I adjusted the overall contrast of the photo.

The Smudge tool works nicely with chalk and charcoal. Use it exactly as you would use your finger or hand on paper to soften a line or blend two colors. Photoshop's Blur and Sharpen tools can also be used to define edges or to soften a line without smudging it.

Lots to Learn

Photoshop CS2 includes over 100 filters! If you master one each week, within two years you'll know them all.

By the Way

The Charcoal Filter

Use the Charcoal filter (Filter→Sketch→Charcoal) to convert an image to a good imitation of a charcoal drawing. Because charcoal doesn't come in colors, your charcoal drawings will be most successful if you set the foreground to black and the background to white, or to a pale color if you want the effect of drawing on colored paper. The Charcoal filter dialog box is shown in Figure 10.15. You can adjust the thickness of the line from 1 to 7 and the degree of detail from 0 to 5. The Light/Dark Balance setting ranges from 0 to 100 and controls the proportion of foreground to background color.

Figure 10.16 shows before and after versions of a portrait converted into charcoal and lightly retouched with the Brush, Blur, and Sharpen tools. Using a graphics tablet instead of a mouse makes it easier to reproduce the filter's crosshatched lines.

FIGURE 10.15
Experiment with these settings. Every image is different.

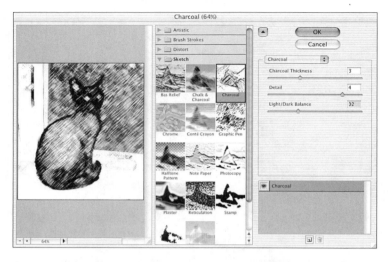

FIGURE 10.16
Retouching brought back the details that were lost in translation.

Summary

Whew! This has been a very full and intense hour. Spend some time trying these techniques before you move along.

In this hour, you saw that digital painting is an area where Photoshop truly excels. You can work from scratch or convert images you have uploaded as digital photos or scans or have created in some other compatible program. After you have the image in Photoshop, the various filters and brushes enable you to turn your work into a good imitation of an oil painting, watercolor, or drawing. The Artistic filter set includes filters that can do much of the work of conversion for you. For best results, though, you'll want to go in and touch up the picture after the filter has done its work. Choose tools and colors that are appropriate to the medium you're trying to imitate. Experiment, and if you find a technique or filter combination that works especially well, make notes on it. Yes, you can even write in this book! (Well, not if it's a library book....)

Workshop

Q&A

Q *How do I know which pictures will make good digital paintings?*

A For digital watercolors, look for photos with large plain areas and not a lot of detail. In general, try lighter colored pictures because the Watercolor filter tends to darken images. Although almost any picture makes a good oil painting, I like to use the technique to rescue otherwise bland landscapes. It helps if the subject has interesting contrasts (such as ocean and rock) or if there's a good deal of color.

Q *Can I use more than one filter on a picture?*

A You can, and many times you might want to use a combination of several filters to achieve a particular effect.

Q *In the watercolor discussion earlier in this hour, you recommended waiting until the very end to apply the texture because any changes made before the final save would alter the texture's appearance. Shouldn't those same rules apply to oil paintings as well?*

A Actually, no. Texture is an integral part of oil painting. Paint builds up and hides the canvas or is thinned to bring out the canvas texture. The canvas texture should be applied with the underpainting so that, as you go back and add more paint, you will naturally obscure some of the texture. This makes the picture look less digital and more "painted."

Q *Why do some filters have ellipses after their names, but others don't?*

A There are two kinds of Photoshop filters. The ones with an ellipsis (...) open a dialog box with parameters to set before the filter is applied. The filters with no ellipsis are one-step filters. You have no control over the way the filter is applied. When you select a one-step filter from the menu, it's applied—period. You can apply it a second time to double the effect.

Quiz

1. The Watercolor filter works best on pictures with

   a. Large flat areas

   b. Lots of detail

   c. Dark backgrounds

   2. The Wet Edges option makes a brush stroke that is

     a. Drippy

     b. Fuzzy along the edges

     c. Darker at the edges

   3. Oil painting and watercolor look

     a. Very different

     b. Very similar

     c. A lot like colored pencil

   4. Charcoal comes in many colors.

     a. True

     b. False

     c. True only in Photoshop

Quiz Answers

   1. a. Detail tends to get lost in a watercolor, and the process darkens the image somewhat, so lighter ones come out better.

   2. c. Try it and see.

   3. a. In Photoshop, as in the fine arts world, oils emphasize texture, whereas watercolor is flat.

   4. c. You want pink charcoal? Go for it.

Exercise

Find a picture with a good range of light and dark colors and moderate detail. Apply the filters discussed in this hour to the picture, and be sure to experiment with different background and foreground colors, as well as with various settings for brush width, pressure, and so on.

HOUR 11

Layers

What You'll Learn in This Hour:

▶ Using the Layers Palette
▶ Working with Multiple Layers

You're almost halfway through. You've already learned a great deal about Photoshop, but there is, as always, more to learn. From this point on, most of it's fun stuff, too. Right now, we are going to discuss one of the most important and useful features of Photoshop: layers.

At first, layers might seem confusing, but don't worry—they're not as bad as they sound. In fact, they are exactly what their name implies—layers within one image—and each layer can be adjusted and edited separately from the others. That's what makes this feature so cool.

If it helps, consider a Bugs Bunny cartoon. Imagine Bugs walking through the woods. The artists at the Warner Bros. Studios created the backdrops and then drew Bugs on pieces of transparent cellophane, which they laid over the background. They often put his body on one layer and his arms and legs on another, and as they cycled through the several sets of arms and legs they made the animated Bugs appear to move through the woods or chase Elmer Fudd, who was on yet another layer or two of cellophane.

Photoshop has a capability similar to this animation technique, and you can create as many layers as you need, up to 999, in Photoshop CS2. You can hide layers while you work on others. You can link layers together. In Hour 6, "Adjusting Color," you learned how to use adjustment layers that enable you to make color and tonal corrections in your images. Now, you'll learn the rest of the story about layers.

Using the Layers Palette

Step one is to create a new image file and then open the Layers palette. Just choose
Window→Layers. The Layers palette (see Figure 11.1) is where you control your layers' behavior—creating, adding, deleting, hiding, and showing. Think of the Layers
palette as "command central" for working with layers. The small versions of your
images on the left of the palette are called *thumbnails*. Each of these small rectangles
displays a separate layer. For the moment, because you have not created any new
layers, you should have only one blank thumbnail in the Layers palette. That's the
Background layer.

FIGURE 11.1
The Layers
palette.

If the thumbnails are too small for your liking, choose the Palette Options command from the palette's menu (the arrow in the upper-right corner) and check out
Figure 11.2.

Deep Background

The difference between the Background layer and a regular layer is this: When you
erase pixels on a regular layer, the erased area is transparent, and when you
erase on the Background layer, the erased area is filled with the background color
shown in the toolbox.

You can choose from three sizes or choose no thumbnail image at all. Remember that every image on your screen consumes a certain amount of the RAM available to run Photoshop. If you can get by with the smallest thumbnail, try to do so. The smaller the thumbnail, the less space the palette will take up on your desktop. This is an advantage as you begin to work with three, four, five, and more layers at a time.

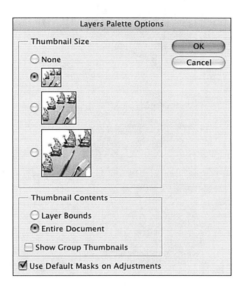

FIGURE 11.2
Optional thumbnail sizes.

Try it Yourself

Creating a New Layer

Now let's make some layers. First of all, let's put something on the Background layer, just so we'll know where it is. Follow these steps:

1. Create a new document. Use the Elliptical Marquee to select a large circular area on the page. Fill the circular selection with a color. Press Command+D (Mac) or Control+D (Windows) to get rid of the selection marquee.

2. Look at the thumbnail called Background. (It's the only one on the palette.) It should look something like Figure 11.3.

3. Click the small page icon at the bottom of the Layers palette. You've just added a layer! Now your palette should look like Figure 11.4.

FIGURE 11.3
The Background layer is your blank canvas when you open a new document. Once you put something on it, it's not blank anymore.

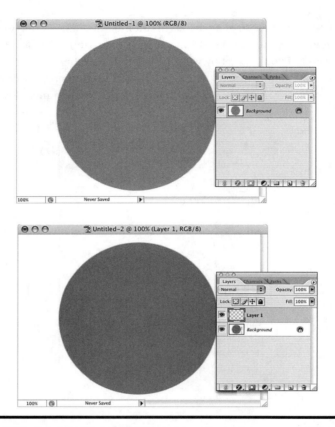

FIGURE 11.4
Adding a layer.

Let's pause here for a moment and take a close look at the new layer's thumbnail. Compared to the thumbnail for the Background layer, it has a double-lined frame around it. The double frame indicates that this is the *active* layer. Paint all you want, but only the layer with the double frame receives the paint. Of course, the active layer's entry in the Layers palette is also highlighted.

To change the active layer, click the name of the layer to which you want to change. Figure 11.5 shows what the palette looks like after the active layer change has been made.

FIGURE 11.5
Changing the active layer requires a single click.

Try it Yourself   ▼

Getting Started with Layers

Let's make some layers to see how they work. Download the following files from
the website: Plate, Bread, Lettuce, Tomato, and Bacon. To get to the website,
point your Web browser to www.samspublishing.com and type the book's ISBN.
After the main book page has loaded, click the Downloads link to get to the files.
Then follow these steps:

1. Open the files called Plate and Bread. Bring the bread image to the front, if
   necessary, by clicking it. Copy the bread by first clicking the crust with the
   Magic Wand, and then pressing the Shift key and clicking again to add the
   center of the slice. You might need to click more than twice to get it all. After
   the slice of bread is selected, press Command/Control+C to copy it. Bring the
   plate image to the foreground. Press Command+V (Mac) or Control+V
   (Windows) to paste the bread on the plate. Look at the Layers palette. You've
   added a new layer! Close the Bread file. (You don't want it to get stale, do
   you?)

2. Open the file called Lettuce. Notice that the background is a checkerboard,
   indicating that it's transparent. Align the two images so that you can see
   both. Click the lettuce with the Move tool and drag it onto the plate. Use the
   Move tool to center it on the slice of bread. Notice, in Figure 11.6, that it's
   also on a new layer.

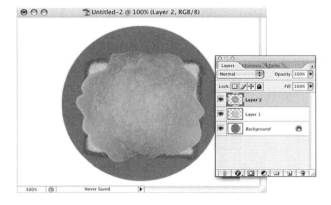

FIGURE 11.6
Drag the lettuce
onto the bread.
It will appear as
a new layer.

3. Copy and paste the Tomato next. Now, let's add some mayo. Click the New
   Layer button on the Layers palette. Choose a medium brush and a nice, pale
   yellow mayonnaise color, and paint it on. It looks okay, but it doesn't stand
   out. Let's add a layer style here. (See Figure 11.7.) Under the Layer menu,
   choose Layer Style→Bevel and Emboss. Set the Style to Inner Bevel, and the
   Technique to Smooth. Make the Depth 121% and the Size 5 pixels. Soften
   should be at 0. You can ignore the Shading area for now, or change the shading color to a deeper yellow, if you want.

▼

▼

FIGURE 11.7
Applying a style
to the layer.

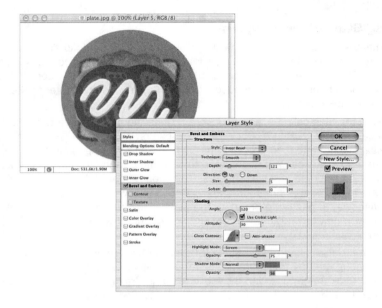

4. Open the Bacon file, and drag the bacon onto the sandwich. Bacon should be slightly translucent if it's not cooked crisp, so change the opacity on the Layers palette to 80%, as shown in Figure 11.8.

FIGURE 11.8
Either use the
slider to change
the opacity, or
double-click the
Opacity field
and type 80.

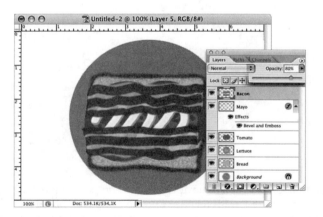

5. Click the lettuce layer to activate it. Choose Layer→Layer Properties and change the name of the lettuce layer from Layer 2 to Lettuce. (There's no good reason why you should do this except to show you that you can name your layers.) Figure 11.9 shows the Layer Properties dialog box and Figure 11.10 shows the completed open-faced sandwich.

▼

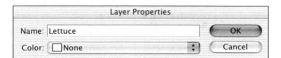

▼
FIGURE 11.9
Naming your layers is especially helpful when you have a lot of them.

FIGURE 11.10
You could duplicate Layer 1 and put a second slice of bread on top, but then you couldn't admire the bacon.

▲

You can move, add to, or erase anything on the active layer, but doing so doesn't affect layers above or below it. For instance, if you make Layer 2 the active layer, you can use the Move tool to slide the bread around, but you can't move the lettuce until you make its layer active.

Reordering Layers

You also can change the order of the layers. You might want to do this if one is supposed to look as if it's on top of another, but wasn't created in that order. (New layers are always created above the current active layer.) To do so:

1. Click the thumbnail of the active layer and hold. The active layer changes color.

2. While holding the mouse button down, drag the layer up to the top of the stack. It then becomes the topmost layer. (Note that you can't move the Background layer—by definition, it has to stay at the bottom of the stack unless you convert it to a regular layer by double-clicking it.)

If you want to move a layer up or down one level, select it and press Command+] (Mac) or Control+] (Windows) to raise it, and Command+[(Mac) or Control+[(Windows) to lower it. The left bracket lowers the layer's level, and the right bracket raises the layer's level. Remember: **Left** to **Lower**, **Right** to **Raise**.

Hiding/Showing Layers

Another great feature of layers is that when you want to concentrate on one part of your image, you can hide all the other layers. To the left of the thumbnails, you will notice small icons that resemble eyes. These indicate that a layer is visible. If you see the eye, you can see the layer. If you click the eye, however, the eye disappears, and the layer becomes hidden. In Figure 11.11, you can see that I've turned off the lettuce, but the bread, tomato, and bacon are still visible.

FIGURE 11.11
To make a layer visible again, click the space where the eye should appear.

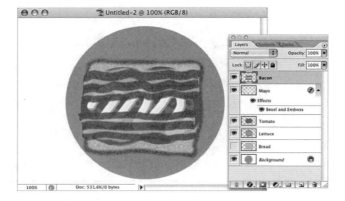

Let's try it. Click the eye icons next to the bread and lettuce layers. They disappear, as will the corresponding layers in your image. Click again and the icons reappear—with the layers. While the layer is hidden, you can't paint on it or do anything with it, except drag it up or down (or use the commands detailed previously) to change its order.

Removing Layers

The simple way to remove a layer is to click to make it active and then click the small trash can button at the bottom of the palette. You can also choose Delete Layer from either the Layer menu or the Layers palette pop-up menu. When you do this, you'll see a warning dialog box asking whether it's really okay to delete the layer. If you Option+click (Mac) or Alt+click (Windows), you can skip the warning. (You can also skip the warning by dragging the layer to the palette's trash button.) Undo brings back the layer, if you have done nothing else in the meantime. If you have performed other steps, you need to use the History palette to return to a previous state.

Working with Multiple Layers

You have seen how to create, move, and remove layers, but the hour still hasn't really addressed the question of what they're good for. You will use layers in many situations. Whenever you are combining two or more images (in Photoshop terms, *compositing*), the elements you paste or drag in from another document over the background image are added on separate layers. You can use the Layers palette to control precisely how these elements are combined. You can control the opacity of objects you paste onto a layer or paint that you apply to it. (The layer itself is transparent, even if you set the paint on it to 100% opacity.) You can also control the blending modes that affect how one layer appears on top of another, just as you can when painting over an image or background.

Opacity

The Opacity slider at the top of the Layers palette controls the opacity of the active layer. You used it briefly earlier to change the opacity of the bacon. Make the slider appear by clicking the triangle to the right of the percentage window. It can be adjusted from 0%–100% by dragging the slider. If you'd rather not access the slider, enter a value by typing 0 for 100%, 1 for 10%, 2 for 20%, and so on. If you desire more precise control, simply type the digits of the measurement you desire (57, for instance) in quick succession. This trick works with any tool that doesn't have its own Opacity setting—with tools that *do* have Opacity settings, use the keyboard to adjust the setting for the tool rather than the layer.

Let's practice some more with the Opacity slider. You should still have the sandwich open on your screen. Make the tomato layer active and drag the Opacity slider (by clicking and holding down on the arrow button to make it appear) to about 75%. Can you still see the tomato? Yes, but it's sliced very thin. Drag the slider down to 10% and then to 0%. Then move it back to 100% again. Pretty cool, huh?

The Opacity slider has no effect on the Background layer. It always remains at 100% opacity. There is, however, a way around this. There is a difference between the background of your image and what Photoshop sees as the *background* to your layers.

You can create a document with a transparent background by choosing File→New. For the contents, choose Transparent, as shown in Figure 11.12. When the canvas opens, you'll see a checkerboard pattern as a placeholder, indicating that there's nothing on the layer. If you look at the Layers palette, you'll notice that the blank page is called Layer 1 and not Background. That's to help you remember that you can change the opacity. Anything you paint on that layer will have a transparent background. Anything you copy from another source and paste in will go on a new layer that can also be made transparent.

If you don't see the checkerboard pattern, open Edit→Preferences→Transparency & Gamut (Win) or Photoshop→Preferences→Transparency & Gamut (Mac), and change the Grid Size to Small.

By the Way

What's Layer 0?

The Background layer can be changed into a regular layer simply by double-clicking and renaming it, or accepting the default name, Layer 0. The layer can be renamed Background, but it will in fact act as a regular layer. Real Background layers have the name italicized.

FIGURE 11.12
Making a transparent background.

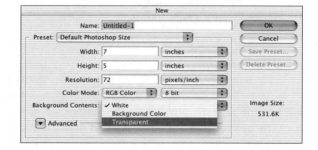

Now that you have a document with a transparent background, let's create another layer for the sandwich. I happen to like pumpernickel bread, so I'll make a slice of that, using a brush and some brown paint, and applying the Grain filter and the Blur filter to complete the look. Then I'll make a second layer, with a toothpick to hold the sandwich together, like they do in the delicatessen. I can make the toothpick translucent plastic by reducing the opacity. As a final touch, I'll add a third layer with an olive. In Figure 11.13, you can see the top of the sandwich, set in place.

FIGURE 11.13
Each layer can have a different transparency. If you look closely, you can see the sandwich through the toothpick, but not through the olive.

Layer Blending Modes

In Hour 8, "Digital Painting," you learned about blending modes and how they affect the way paint is applied. Almost the same set of modes is available to you for blending layers, and they produce the same general effects, but only on the layers beneath the one to which you have applied the blending mode. (If you're not clear on what the effects are, refer back to Hour 8.) The layer in this case is the blend color, and the image below is the base color. As with the painting tools, the layer blending modes are found on a pop-up menu on the Layers palette.

Just as a reminder, the blending modes are

- ▶ Normal
- ▶ Dissolve
- ▶ Darken
- ▶ Multiply
- ▶ Color Burn
- ▶ Linear Burn
- ▶ Lighten
- ▶ Screen

- ▶ Color Dodge
- ▶ Linear Dodge
- ▶ Overlay
- ▶ Soft Light
- ▶ Hard Light
- ▶ Vivid Light
- ▶ Linear Light
- ▶ Pin Light

- ▶ Hard Mix
- ▶ Difference
- ▶ Exclusion
- ▶ Hue
- ▶ Saturation
- ▶ Color
- ▶ Luminosity

You can apply blending modes directly from the Layers palette or by using Layer→Layer Style→Blending Options. This opens a dialog box that gives you a great deal of control over the way blending happens. When you're ready to tackle the Advanced Blending controls, consult the user manual or Help screens.

Linking Layers

If you select more than one layer in the Layers palette (Command+click or Control+click), you can click the Link Layers button at the bottom of the palette. Each linked layer will have a piece of linked chain next to its name. This indicates that the layer is linked to the active layer, meaning that if you move the contents of the active layer, the linked layers move with it. Figure 11.14 shows the Layers palette with sandwich layers linked to the bread.

Layer Groups

Layer groups help you organize and manage collections of layers. After you define a group of layers, you can collapse them or reveal them as necessary, without actually flattening the image. With the sandwich example, you could have designated everything between the slices of bread as a group. If you needed to move the individual elements or change their size or color, you'd do so to the whole set rather than a layer at a time. Layer groups must be contiguous. You can't make a set of layers 1, 3, and 5 unless you move layers 2 and 4 to above or below the layer group. To create a layer set, select the layers you want to group, then use the command Layer→New→Group. To make the set easier to locate, you can assign it a color. All the thumbnails in the set will show on the Layers palette with the assigned color as a background around the eyeball area.

FIGURE 11.14
Layers linked to the active layer move with it. In this case, the fillings move if you slide the bread off the plate.

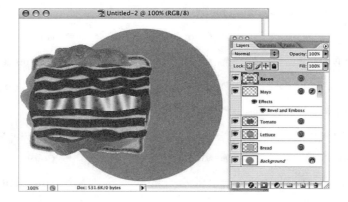

Merging Layers

The more layers you add to an image, and the more effects that you add to those layers, the larger your image file will become. If you have a large capacity hard drive and can back up to removable media, size isn't a problem.

It does, however, make a big difference if you want to use your files for anything else, such as publishing in print or on the Web. The only formats in which you can save a multilayered image are TIFF and the Photoshop native format, which is great for Photoshop, but bad for other uses. For the Web, you need to save images as GIF, PNG, or JPEG. For print, you probably will need to save as TIFF, although layered TIFF files can be very large. That's why you need to either merge layers or flatten the image when you're done working with it.

The differences between merging and flattening are as follows:

▶ *Merging* multiple layers without flattening the entire image conserves memory space but still allows you to work on the layers that you haven't yet finished. Merging Down merges a layer with the one directly below it. You also can merge just the visible layers by choosing Layer→Merge Visible.

▶ *Flattening*, on the other hand, compresses all visible layers down to one layer. Any layers that you have made invisible at the time of flattening are lost. To flatten an image, simply choose Layer→Flatten Image, but make sure that you are done. At this point, all the layers are reduced to one. Transparency is lost and the single layer you've created becomes a Background layer.

You can use either the Layer menu or the Layers palette menu to merge or flatten layers, or the keyboard combination Command+E (Mac) or Control+E (Windows) to Merge Down. Figure 11.15 shows the Layer menu with the Flatten Image command highlighted.

FIGURE 11.15
This compacts all the layers to one.

Using Layer Comps

"What the heck is a layer comp?" you're probably asking. Comps, or composites, are familiar to advertising artists. They are the mock-ups made so the client can see how a print ad will look, and include rough illustrations, sample type, the product logo, and so on. Often, several comps are made of the same ad, with elements in different colors or different positions, to see which looks best.

One of the most useful features introduced in recent versions of Photoshop is the capability to create and save layer comps. Layer comps in Photoshop and

ImageReady save multiple configurations of a file by recording the visibility, layer style, and positions of selected layers. Instead of needing to create a half dozen examples of something like a logo as six separate documents, you can create one, and then add as many comps as you need. To save a layer comp, first open the Layer Comps palette. When the image is where you want it, with the right layers showing and the others hidden, click the New Layer Comp button at the bottom of the palette. (It looks just like the New Layer button on the Layers palette.) You can name the layer comp, and select the attributes to preserve in the resulting dialog box, shown in Figure 11.16. You can also add notes about the image by typing them into the Comment field.

FIGURE 11.16
Naming layer comps helps you keep track of which is which.

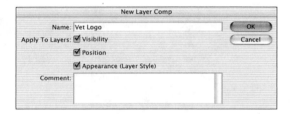

In Figure 11.17, I've created a bunch of possible logos for a local veterinarian. They are all listed on the Layer Comps palette, and if you look at the Layers palette as well, you can see that they are simply different combinations of visible layers.

FIGURE 11.17
To switch to a different comp, click it on the Layer Comps palette.

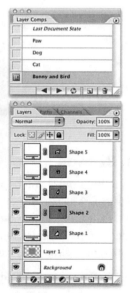

Transferring Layered Images to ImageReady

If you're working on an image for use on a web page, you'll probably want to do the initial work in Photoshop and then jump into ImageReady to save it for Web use. You can transfer layered images between Photoshop and ImageReady by simply clicking the Edit in ImageReady button at the bottom of the toolbox. All layers, layer masks, layer effects, and adjustment layers are preserved. (Adjustment layers can be applied and edited only in Photoshop, but can be viewed in ImageReady.)

Layer Styles

Photoshop and ImageReady both include *layer styles*, a number of automated effects that you can apply to layers, including drop shadows, glows, beveling, and embossing, as well as a color fill effect. You've already tried the Inner Bevel style on the mayonnaise. ImageReady also includes pattern and gradient layer effects. Figure 11.18 shows the Photoshop Layer Style submenu.

FIGURE 11.18
Most of these styles are best used with type or with a selected object.

We'll apply these effects to type and to composited images in Hours 16, 18, and 20.

Summary

In this hour, you learned the mechanics of working with layers. You saw how to use the Layers palette and how to create, delete, and move layers. You also learned about layer comps. Layers are an important part of the Photoshop interface, and knowing how to apply them will help you a great deal, especially when you work with type and composite images later.

Workshop

Q&A

Q *How can I convert a Background layer to a transparent layer?*

A The easy way is to rename it. If you double-click the Background layer in the Layers palette, you open its dialog box. By default, it appears as Layer 0. If you click OK, it is renamed and won't be a Background layer.

Q *Can I add a Background layer to an image that doesn't have one?*

A Yes. Use Layer→New→Background From Layer to convert the active layer into a Background layer.

Q *Can I have more than one Background layer?*

A Sorry, only one per document.

Q *How many layer groups can I have?*

A As many as you have layers, for all practical purposes.

Q *When I went to change the size of the thumbnails by opening Palette Options, I also pressed the Option/Alt key by mistake. Something strange happened. What was that about?*

A Congratulations! You discovered one of Photoshop's hidden Easter Eggs! Easter Eggs are little goodies put in by the programmers to add some extra fun for users. You discovered Merlin! If you open the About Adobe Photoshop screen and wait for a bit, you'll see another one. After a while, the credits will begin to roll. You can speed them up by pressing Option (Mac) or Alt (Windows). Watch for the last credit. It's a good one. Macintosh users: Click over the word Adobe and wait after the credits scroll. There are some cute quotes. (Sorry, PC folks. It's a Macintosh thing.)

Quiz

1. How many layers can you have?

    a. 10

    b. 100

    c. 999

    d. It depends on how much RAM you have.

2. The active layer is

    a. The layer on top

    b. The layer that's highlighted on the Layers palette

    c. The layer with an eye icon

3. To hide a layer

    a. Drag it to the trash can.

    b. Press H.

    c. Click the eye icon to close it.

Quiz Answers

1. c. (at least theoretically); d is probably also true.

2. b. If it's not highlighted, you can't do anything to it. The eye simply means it's visible.

3. c. Think of it as playing peek-a-boo. If the eye can see you, you can see the layer.

Exercises

Let's do some more experimenting with layers. First, click the background color swatch and choose a medium-light color for a background. Then create a new document. Be sure to choose the Background Color from the Background pop-up menu. Choose a contrasting foreground color, make a new layer, and use a medium brush to write the number 1. Add layers, with a number on each, until you have about 10. Then, starting with the first one, apply different blending modes. Try changing the transparency of a layer. Move the number 5 to the upper-left corner of the screen. Merge Layers 2 and 3. Play around until you understand how the layers are working.

Using Masks

What You'll Learn in This Hour:

▶ Applying Masks
▶ Using Quick Mask
▶ Layer Masks

Masks can be your best friends when you're working on a complicated picture. They can also be a darned nuisance, simply because there are several kinds of masks that you can apply to your image, and they do somewhat different things. So you not only have to create a mask, you also have to know ahead of time what you want the mask to do for you, and then you have to apply the right kind of mask.

So, what exactly *is* a mask? In a sense, any selection that you make is a mask because it permits you to do something that affects only the selected area, effectively masking anything that's not selected. A *mask* enables you to change one part of a picture, without changing all of it.

You can select a single flower from a picture of a garden, for instance, and change its color, without changing everything else. Masks can cover the part of the picture you don't want to change, much like masking tape covers the woodwork you don't want to paint when you're painting the walls.

The confusion about masks comes from there being so many types. You can have layer masks, mask channels, transparency masks, vector masks, and clipping masks; and there's also Quick Mask. All can be used to isolate an area that you want to protect while you make changes to the rest of the picture. Masks are well worth learning because they can save you a lot of time and effort.

Applying Masks

Masks can hide either a selected object or the background, and can be opaque or semitransparent. If the mask is totally transparent, it isn't masking anything. Masks—and channels, which you'll learn about later—are actually grayscale images. An opaque mask is black, a 50% transparent mask is 50% gray, and so on.

In Figure 12.1, I have a nice photo of a lighthouse that was shot on a cloudy day. (It's somewhere on the south coast of Nova Scotia, although I'm not sure where. Perhaps a Canadian reader will enlighten me.) To my eye, this would be more interesting if I could do something with that sky. The lighthouse and woods are accurate for color, as nearly as I can remember, so I don't want to change them. If I select just the sky, I can work on it without affecting the rest of the photo. Of course, that wire will have to come out at some point, but that's a job for another hour.

FIGURE 12.1
I've done my best to select the sky around the lighthouse and trees, so I can work on the background without disturbing them.

This is the most basic kind of masking. It's not always perfect, though. In Figure 12.2, you can see that the Lasso tool and Magic Wand didn't really give me a very accurate mask. The edges aren't very smooth, and there's a lot of the top of the lighthouse missing. What's needed is a way to edit the mask.

FIGURE 12.2
Up close, you can see that the selection isn't very accurate.

Using Quick Mask

Photoshop provides a very quick and easy way to make a temporary mask that can, in fact, be edited. It's called *Quick Mask,* and one of its advantages is that you can see both the image and the mask at the same time. You can start with a selected area and use the painting tools to add to it or take away from it, or you can create the mask entirely in Quick Mask mode. Let's apply a Quick Mask to an image.

Try it Yourself ▼

Create a Quick Mask

Quick Masks are a great time-saver, as you'll soon see. Follow along to try them.

1. Find a photo with a subject who stands out against the background. Using whatever selection tool seems appropriate, select the part of the image you want to change—in this case, the background. It's okay if your selection isn't perfect. (Don't forget that you can select the object, and then invert the selection, if that's the easiest way.)

2. Click the Quick Mask Mode button in the toolbox.

   You see a color overlay indicating the mask on the protected area, which is to say, the area *not* selected. If you compare Figure 12.3 to the first picture of the lighthouse, you can see that the mask has covered the trees and structure with a red layer. Of course, it looks like gray in the picture. (By default,

▼

the mask is 50% opaque red, imitating a piece of the rubylith film that artists use to mask photos for retouching. If you have a red object or red background that you are masking, you can change the mask's color by double-clicking the Quick Mask Mode button and using the Quick Mask Options dialog box to select a contrasting color.)

FIGURE 12.3
Clicking the Quick Mask Mode button masks the area not selected.

3. If the mask needs editing, as this one does, click the Brush tool, or press B to activate it, and select an appropriate brush size from the Brushes palette. You can use any of the painting tools or selection tools to work on a mask.

   Because masks are essentially grayscale images, painting with black adds to the mask. Painting with white (or erasing) takes it away. Painting with gray gives you a semitransparent mask. You will notice that the foreground and background colors change to black and white when you enter Quick Mask mode. (If, for some reason, they didn't, press D for Default.) Figure 12.4 shows the edited mask.

4. When the mask is edited to your satisfaction, click the Standard Mode button in the toolbox (to the left of the Quick Mask Mode button) to return to your original image. The unprotected area (in this case, the background) is surrounded by a selection marquee (see Figure 12.5). Now you can apply any change you want to make to this area without affecting the lighthouse.

5. You can try other ways of changing the sky, such as increasing the saturation or spraying on some transparent color over the clouds; this was a quick and easy fix.

FIGURE 12.4
The mask, touched up and ready to use.

FIGURE 12.5
Here the Render→Clouds filter has been applied to beef up the sky.

If you think you might need the same mask again, you can save it after you've returned to Standard Mode by going to the Channels palette and clicking the Save Selection as Channel button at the bottom of the palette. (It looks like the Quick Mask button.) This saves your mask as an alpha channel. You can come back and reapply it as needed by Command+clicking (Mac) or Control+clicking (Windows) the channel.

Keep It Straight

If you need a straight edge on your mask, use the Line tool to draw a single-pixel line. It appears in the mask color as long as you are in Quick Mask mode when you draw it.

Layer Masks

A layer mask allows you to hide and reveal parts of a single layer. Layer masks, like Quick Masks, can be edited. One advantage of working with a layer mask is that, if you don't like the result, you simply discard the mask, and your image is left untouched. If you like what you see, apply the mask to make the changes.

*By the
Way*

Not on the Background

You can't place a layer mask on the Background layer. If the image is on the Background layer, you can double-click it in the Layers palette and rename it. This removes the associated properties of a Background layer.

To make a layer mask, select an area of the image to mask and click the Add Layer Mask button (the second button from the left at the bottom of the Layers palette). When you do, you see a layer mask thumbnail next to the layer's image thumbnail. Figure 12.6 shows an example. Black indicates the portions of the layer that are covered and white shows the parts that are revealed. If the mask were made to be semi-transparent, the partially masked areas would be shown in gray.

Notice the links between the two thumbnails, indicating that the mask is linked to the layer. After you create the mask, you can edit it simply by making the layer containing the mask the active layer and clicking the mask icon. The foreground and background colors revert to the defaults. You can then apply black to add to the mask or white to remove parts of it.

If you create your mask using the Layer menu, you have the choice of whether the selected area will be shown (and the rest of the image masked) or masked (and the rest of the image shown). Choose Layer→Layer Mask, and choose either Hide Selection or Reveal Selection, depending on whether you're masking the area around the selected piece of image or the image itself. Figure 12.7 shows the menu for this.

FIGURE 12.6
The mask hides the background that I copied in with the brindle greyhound.

FIGURE 12.7
The Layer menu with the Layer Mask submenu expanded.

Hide Selection hides the area that you have selected, so you can work on the rest of the image. With this mask, you can protect part of the picture while you work on the rest. Reveal Selection obviously does just the opposite of Hide Selection. This command hides everything on a layer *except* that area within the Marquee selection. The other commands, Hide All and Reveal All, work a little differently. These, as the names suggest, are based on the entire layer.

In Figure 12.8, I've masked the beach and water and then scribbled across the entire picture. The scribbles are visible only on the unmasked area.

FIGURE 12.8
The black area is masked; white areas of the image can be edited.

By the Way

Only One to a Customer

Each layer can have only one layer mask. If you need to do additional masking on the same layer, activate the layer and apply Quick Mask.

▼   **Try it Yourself**

Adding a Mask to a Layer

The business of making masks can seem very confusing, so it's best to try the process step-by-step.

1. Open the Layers palette, if it's not already visible.

2. Select the layer to which you want to add a mask. Make sure that there are no masks already applied to that layer.

3. To hide the entire layer, choose Layer→Layer Mask→Hide All.

4. To make a mask that hides or reveals a selected area, first make the selection on the active layer.

5. Choose Layer→Layer Mask→Hide Selection *or* choose Layer→Layer Mask→Reveal Selection, whichever is appropriate for your needs. After you have made the mask, you can edit it as necessary with the painting and selection tools.

▲

Take some time now to open a picture and practice applying masks. Try Quick Mask first, and then make a selection and turn it into a layer mask. If you practice these skills while they're fresh in your mind, you'll remember them later when you need to do a quick color change or preserve an object while changing its background.

Editing Layer Masks

If you click the layer mask thumbnail in the Layers palette to make it active, you will see the thumbnail outline move to the mask thumbnail from the layer thumbnail. This indicates that the mask is able to be edited. Press Option+click (Mac) or Alt+click (Windows) on the thumbnail of the mask to display the mask in the image window. Select a painting tool and paint the mask with black to add to it. Paint with white to subtract from the mask, or paint with gray to make the layer partially visible, and the mask thumbnail displays your changes. Figure 12.9 shows a mask being edited. I switched the Layers palette to the larger thumbnail to make it a little easier to see what was going on. Just as a reminder, you can do this in the Layers palette options dialog box, which you access from the Layers palette pull-down menu. Remember that you can use any of the painting tools to edit your mask. Using a soft-edged brush will give you a feathered mask.

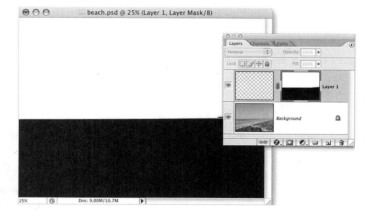

FIGURE 12.9
Here, I've masked the sky.

To edit the layer instead, click its thumbnail. You can turn the layer mask off by going to the Layer menu and choosing Disable Layer Mask, or Shift+clicking the mask's thumbnail in the Layers palette. This option puts a large X through the mask thumbnail so that you know it's inactive (see Figure 12.10). You can still paint on it while it's inactive, though, so be careful!

FIGURE 12.10
The mask is
temporarily dis-
abled.

FIGURE 12.10
The mask is
temporarily dis-
abled.

Did you
Know?

Now You See It, Now You Don't

Using Layer→Layer Mask→Disable lets you get rid of the effects of the layer mask temporarily. When you want it back, just choose Layer→Layer Mask→Enable, and you're back in business.

Removing the Layer Mask

There are two ways to get rid of the layer mask when you are done with it or you want to start over. The first way, possibly the easiest, is simply to drag the layer mask's thumbnail onto the small trash can button at the bottom of the Layers palette. You also can get rid of a layer mask by choosing Layer→Layer Mask→Delete or Layer→Layer Mask→Apply (see Figure 12.11). If you drag the mask to the trash, you are presented with the dialog box, shown in Figure 12.12, in which you are also prompted to apply the effects of the mask or discard the mask without applying it.

By the
Way

A Quick Look at Channels

Even though a detailed explanation of channels and how to use them is somewhat beyond the scope of this book, a few words about channels might prove helpful to you at this point. Photoshop creates color information channels when you open a new image. An RGB document starts with four channels: one for each color and the composite that merges them. These are akin to the color separations used in four-color process printing. You can also create additional channels, called *alpha channels* in Photoshop parlance, which hold information about the masks you create for the image. Photoshop also enables you to add additional colors in "spot color channels." Spot channels are used primarily in commercial printing.

Channel thumbnails can be viewed in the Channels palette, which shares a position with the Layers palette. Click the Channels tab to display it. The composite is listed first, and then the color channels, and finally the masks or alpha channels show up at the bottom of the list. If you have made several layer masks, you will probably need to use the scroll bars or resize the palette to see them all.

As with the Layers palette thumbnails, you can increase the size of the Channels palette thumbnails to see them more easily. You can also click the eye icons in the Channels palette to hide or show single channels in the image window. This is the function of the Channels palette you will use most.

By default, individual channels display in grayscale, but you can change this to see them in their own color by opening Edit→Preferences→Display & Cursors (Win) or Photoshop→Preferences→Display & Cursors (Mac) and checking Color Channels in Color.

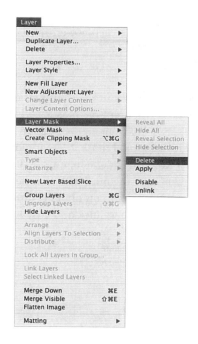

FIGURE 12.11
Apply the layer mask or delete it without applying it.

FIGURE 12.12
Choose Delete, Cancel, or Apply.

Making Layer Masks Visible with Channels

Masks appear both on the screen where you create them and also on the Channels palette, where you can see them as a silhouette of the selection. The mask that you add to an image creates a new channel in your image, called an *alpha channel*.

Channels are Photoshop's way of storing color and mask information. (See the preceding "By the Way" for more information about channels.) If you add a mask to a layer and choose Window→Channels, you will see something like the example in Figure 12.13.

FIGURE 12.13
The Channels palette with a layer mask at the bottom.

Click the eye icon to the left of the mask in the Channels palette and the mask appears as red, representing a transparent red plastic called rubylith (a carryover from the old days when this stuff was done in the real, and not the cyber-, world). You can also edit the mask as a channel mask. More importantly, you can save it by choosing Duplicate Channel from the palette menu. You'll get a dialog box like the one in Figure 12.14, letting you save the mask either as part of the document, or as its own document. To turn a selection into an alpha channel, use the menu command Select→Save Selection. It's another quick and easy way to make a mask.

FIGURE 12.14
If you click New, the alpha channel becomes a separate document.

Summary

In this hour, you looked at using masks. Masking enables you to apply changes selectively, while protecting parts of the picture that you don't want to change. You learned about the Quick Mask function and how to edit a mask with the Brush and Eraser. Then you learned about layer masks and how to turn a layer into a mask. You learned how to view your mask, and save it as an alpha channel.

Workshop

Q&A

Q *My picture has a lot of red in it, and the red mask is hard to see. Is there a way to change it to some other color?*

A Of course. If you're working in Quick Mask mode, double-click the Quick Mask Mode button on the toolbox to open the Quick Mask Options dialog box. If you're working on a layer mask, Control+click (Mac) or right-click (Windows) the layer mask icon in the Layers palette. This opens a contextual menu that gives you access to the Layer Mask Options dialog box. In either one, you can set the color and amount of opacity for your mask. In the Quick Mask dialog box, you can also set a radio button to determine whether the selection or the mask is indicated by the colored area.

Q *If I'm doing catalog photos of small objects and want to mask the back-grounds, is it easier to select the background or to select the object and invert the selection?*

A That depends on how complicated and/or how colorful the object is. If it's all one color, you can probably select it with one Magic Wand click and invert it to make your mask in a couple of seconds. If the background is simple and the object isn't, select the background.

Q *I carefully painted in a mask, but the edges look wrong. They seem to have a dark line around them. Why?*

A You probably had the brush set for Wet Edges. You can fix it, if it's an opaque mask (not painted in gray), by pouring black into the masked area with the Paint Bucket tool.

Q *The selection tools missed some of the petals on the flower I'm trying to mask, but my hand's not steady enough to draw them in. What can I do?*

A Enlarge the image to 200% or even more. Then you can see what you're doing and draw or erase more precisely.

Quiz

1. A mask can hide

    a. An object

    b. The background

    c. Either the background or an object

   2. Masks can be opaque, semi-opaque, or transparent.

      a. True

      b. False

   3. You can have up to 12 masks on a single layer.

      a. True

      b. False

   4. Masks are saved with the picture and, therefore, increase file size. To save disk space, always

      a. Apply and discard the masks after you're sure you're done with them

      b. Flatten the image

      c. Hide the layer masks

Quiz Answers

   1. c. Masks hide anything you want to protect.

   2. b. If the mask is transparent, it's not hiding anything. Parts of a mask can be and often are transparent, but not the whole mask.

   3. b. Sorry, only one layer mask per layer. Use Quick Mask for additional masking.

   4. a. and b. both work. Flattening the image compresses the layers and applies the masks.

Exercise

Find a picture with several similar objects in it. Mask them separately and experiment with changing the colors of the objects, one at a time, without changing the background.

Paths

What You'll Learn in This Hour:

- ▶ Creating Paths
- ▶ Editing Paths
- ▶ Using Paths

Congratulations! You're halfway through, which is to say that you've seen only half of what Photoshop can do.

Early on, you learned about selections and how selecting part of an image isolates that part so that you can work on it and not the entire image. Last hour, you learned about converting selections to masks to protect the parts of your image that you don't want to work on.

The problem with a selection is that, as soon as you remove the selection marquee, it's gone. The only way to reselect something is to use the appropriate tools (Marquee, Lasso, and/or Magic Wand) and make the selection all over again, use the Select/Reselect command, or use the History palette to revert to the last Selection tool used. This, however, means that you lose whatever you did to the selection.

Paths are one way to solve this dilemma. Using paths, you can create and save specific selections for future use, much like saving a mask. The paths are saved right within the Photoshop file, very much as a layer is saved. Because paths are vector-based rather than pixel-based, you aren't restricted to the shapes you can drag with the marquees. You can create very precise shapes and smooth curves with the Pen tools. Then you can use them as selections, or stroke and fill them as objects or lines in your picture.

Photoshop comes with a complete set of Path Shape tools. These tools can draw rectangles, rounded rectangles, ellipses, polygons, and straight lines. They also have a default set of 250 custom shapes, ranging from stars, arrows, animal silhouettes, and frames to talk balloons, foot and paw prints, and symbols for almost anything you can think of. The path shapes can be filled and stroked just like the shapes you draw yourself. Let's start by exploring the different ways to create paths, and then go into techniques for editing and using them in Photoshop.

Creating Paths

There are three paths you can take when creating paths (sorry, I couldn't resist):

▶ Create a path directly from a selection you've already made.

▶ Create a path from scratch by using the Pen tools and drawing the path by hand.

▶ Create a path using the Shape tools.

Paths via Selections

Depending on the image at hand, simply making a selection and converting it to a path can be the easiest and quickest way to create a path.

Let's look at an example. Figure 13.1 shows the test image, a tire gauge. We'll select the object, and make what's called a *clipping path,* clipping it out of the background. Without Photoshop, you would achieve the same effect with a photographic print and a pair of scissors.

FIGURE 13.1
The test image. The goal is a clipping path that outlines the gauge.

As you remember, selection can be accomplished by using a number of tools. For this image, I selected the background with the Magic Wand and then cleaned up the selection using the Quick Mask. Other objects might be selected more easily by using a combination of the Elliptical Marquee and the Polygonal Lasso. You might even need to combine the results of several selection tools to get it all. Just keep the Shift key pressed to merge the selections. Figure 13.2 shows the selection.

FIGURE 13.2
The tire gauge is now selected.

Try it Yourself

Convert a Selection to a Path

Now that you have a selection, follow these steps to convert it to a path:

1. Make sure that the Paths palette is visible. If not, choose Window→Paths.

2. Choose Make Work Path from the pop-up menu on the Paths palette (see Figure 13.3).

FIGURE 13.3
The pop-up menu of the Paths palette.

3. The only option to set in the Make Work Path dialog box is Tolerance (see Figure 13.4). *Tolerance* refers to how closely Photoshop follows the outline of your selection in creating the path. The smaller the tolerance, the more exact the path is.

FIGURE 13.4
The Make Work Path dialog box.

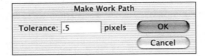

Make Work Path
Tolerance: .5   pixels   OK   Cancel

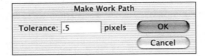

Watch Out!

It's a Long and Winding Path

Be aware that complex paths can be resource intensive. More complexity means more points, angles, curves, and so on. The result can mean slower processing of the image, bigger files, and possible problems when printing.

For this image, I first tried a Tolerance of 5 pixels. As Figure 13.5 shows, the results were unacceptable. Photoshop was too flexible and approximate in creating the path at this setting. You can see that the smoother line of the path doesn't follow the outline of the stem closely enough.

FIGURE 13.5
When the path doesn't match the selection to your satisfaction, the Tolerance is set too high.

When this happens, I simply reach for my favorite Photoshop command: Undo. Undo the path conversion and try a lower Tolerance setting. After some experimentation, I found that a value of 1 pixel worked quite well (see Figure 13.6).

FIGURE 13.6
When Tolerance
is set correctly,
the path match-
es the selection
satisfactorily.

4. Note how the path also appears in the Paths palette in Figure 13.7. Photoshop has named it *Work Path*. You can rename the path by simply double-
   clicking it in the Paths palette. In the Save Path dialog box that appears, simply type the new pathname and click OK, as shown in Figure 13.7.

5. Choose Clipping Path from the Paths palette pop-up menu, and specify the
   path you just created as the clipping path.

FIGURE 13.7
Rename paths
by using the
Save Path dia-
log box.

Although renaming the work path isn't required, it's a good idea, especially if you
might need the path again. If the path is left as a work path and you start a second
path, one of two things will happen. First, if the work path is still active in the Paths

palette, the new path will be added to it as a subpath. Second, if the original work path is no longer active in the Paths palette, the new path will replace it. (Undo and the History palette give you opportunities to recover the original path, but it's easier to simply rename it and transform it into a regular path at the time of creation.)

Another Path to Travel

There's also another way to create a path from a selection. Make a selection and then simply click the Make Work Path button at the bottom of the Paths palette. Photoshop automatically creates the path by using the same Tolerance setting you used for your last conversion.

Paths via the Pen Tools

Sometimes, making a selection is too difficult or requires too much work on a particular image. In that case, consider using the Pen tools and drawing the path by hand.

If you've used vector-based illustration programs, such as Adobe Illustrator or Macromedia FreeHand, you already know about Bézier-based drawing tools such as Photoshop's Pen tools. If you haven't used these kinds of tools before, you should know right up front that it takes a little practice, but the payoff is worth the effort. In addition to the standard Pen tools that draw a line and add or remove points on the line, Photoshop provides two additional Pen tools. The Freeform Pen tool gives you the power to draw any kind of line you want—straight, curved, or squiggly— and turn it into a path. And, when used with the Magnetic option, the Freeform Pen tool makes drawing around a complicated object much easier.

A *Bézier curve* is defined by three points: one on the curve and two outside the curve at the ends of handles that you can use to change the angle and direction of the curve. If this sounds like gibberish, don't worry; you'll see some examples.

▼   **Try it Yourself**

Using the Pen Tool

The best way to learn how to use the Pen tool is simply to play around with it in a new Photoshop document.

   1. First, create a new Photoshop document big enough to move around in. Photoshop's default size (7×5 inches) sounds good, and a plain white background looks good.
   2. Select the Pen tool. (It looks like an old-fashioned fountain pen nib.) Also make sure that the Paths palette is visible.

▼

3. In the Options Bar, click the Paths button. It's the middle one in the first cluster of three.

4. Click somewhere near the left edge of the page. This is where your path begins. (Notice that Photoshop immediately creates a path called *work path* in the Paths palette. This path can be renamed later in the same way described in the previous "Try it Yourself.")

5. To draw a straight line, simply move your cursor and click somewhere else. (Don't hold the mouse button down!) You've just created a *corner point,* which means that Photoshop connects the two points with a straight line (see Figure 13.8).

FIGURE 13.8
Just two simple clicks create a corner point and a straight line.

6. To continue the path (but now with a curved line), move your cursor to the middle bottom of the window and then click and drag left. You'll see a curve immediately appear and change as you drag it (see Figure 13.9). You've just created a *smooth point,* which means that Photoshop creates a smooth curve where two curved line segments meet.

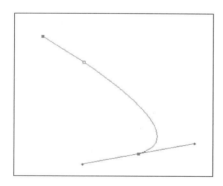

FIGURE 13.9
A click-and-drag action creates a smooth point and a curved line.

7. To make this clearer, draw another smooth curve. Move your cursor to a point that is up and to the right of the second point; click and drag to the right and a bit down. Again a smooth point and a curve are created (see Figure 13.10).

Notice the point you created in step 5. It creates a nice smooth curve between the point you just created and the point you created in step 4. That's what a smooth point is all about.

As you have no doubt noticed, creating smooth points also results in the appearance of two *handles* for each point. These handles can be used to change the angle and direction of a curve after you've initially established it. You'll learn more about them in the "Editing Paths" section, later in this hour.

FIGURE 13.10
Click and drag
to create anoth-
er smooth point
on the same
path.

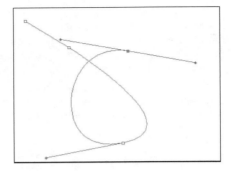

▲   **8.** Switch to another tool or click your starting point to end the path.

Okay, those are the basic ideas: straight lines via corner points and curved lines via smooth points. But there's more that you have to know about each one to use them effectively.

Corner Points

Corner points are easy. No matter what kind of line is coming into a corner point, the result is always an angle, not a curve. If a curved line comes into a corner point, it's the smooth point at the other end of that line that affects the line's angle (see Figure 13.11).

Did you Know?

Restraining Order
If you want to constrain corner points so that they appear only at 45- or 90-degree angles, hold down the Shift key while you click to create the point.

FIGURE 13.11
Corner points
surround
smooth points.

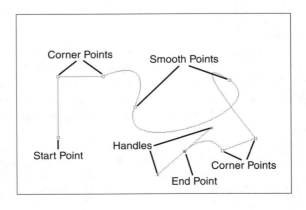

Corner Points   Smooth Points

Start Point

Handles

End Point

Corner Points

Smooth Points

As you saw in the first Pen tool example, the behavior of smooth points is a bit more complicated and takes some getting used to. A smooth point always tries to create as smooth a curve as it can between two meeting lines (see Figure 13.12).

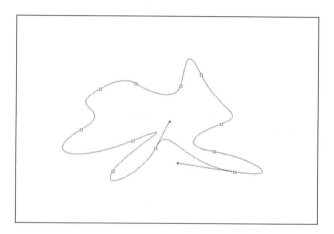

Try it Yourself

Creating a Sharp Curve

There is a less smooth kind of curve you can create when you need it. It's called a *sharp curve*. It looks like a pair of arches, or the top half of a heart, or a stick seagull, and the following steps show you how to create one:

1. In a new Photoshop document, begin a path with an initial point.

2. Create a smooth point as you normally would, by dragging after you click to set the point, making one curve.

3. Move the pointer so that it's exactly over the smooth point you just created. Hold down Option (Mac) or Alt (Windows) while you click and drag the mouse in the direction of the intended bump in the new curve. Release the key and the mouse button. Your screen should now look something like what you see in Figure 13.13.

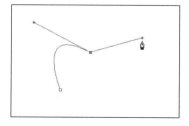

FIGURE 13.13
Creating a sharp curve. The rightmost line is what I just created by using the Option or Alt key. It becomes a handle for the first curve.

4. Move the cursor to where you want the line to end; then click and drag in the opposite direction that you dragged in step 3. The line will draw itself from where you ended the first arch to where you just clicked at its end point. As you drag, the line will expand upward. Figure 13.14 shows the resulting sharp curve. If you didn't get it right where you wanted, you can use the handles to reshape it.

FIGURE 13.14
The final sharp curve.

Previewing the Path

When you're creating all these points and lines, there's a preview feature that can be very helpful. Look at the Tool Options bar. There's an option called Rubber Band, which you can access by selecting the Pen and clicking the down-pointing arrow next to the strip of tool icons. Activating this feature enables you to preview both straight lines and curves before you click to create them. Experiment to see this feature at work. Take a look at the other options, too. Each tool and shape on the strip has different settings accessible via this arrow.

Completing the Path

To complete a path, you have two choices: *close* the path by connecting the final point to the initial point, or leave the path *open*.

A *closed path* means you have created a loop, so the final path has no beginning or end. To close a path, use the following steps:

1. Create a path by using whatever points you need.

2. After the last point, move your cursor so that it appears on top of your initial point. You'll see a small circle next to the Pen pointer.

3. Click to create a final corner point, or click and drag to create a final curve (see Figure 13.15).

FIGURE 13.15
The start and stop point is the gray one.

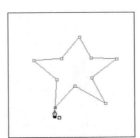

An *open path* means the path has a beginning and an end. Figures 13.8 through 13.14 have all been open paths. To end a path that you want to keep open, use the following steps:

1. Create a path by using whatever points you need.

2. After the last point, simply click the Pen tool icon in the toolbar. The path now has an end.

   The next time you click in the image, you'll be starting a new path instead of continuing your previous path.

Paths Are Composed of Subpaths

Saying that you've created a "path" is a little misleading. The line between each pair of points on a path is a path segment or subpath. Together, they make a path. You can manipulate the points and subpaths to change the shape of the path. One point to remember is that any path you create is not really part of the image. It's not a line drawn on the page. Until you add color to it, it's merely a theoretical line. That is, you aren't changing the actual image. When you stroke a path, it becomes a visible line. If you fill a path, it becomes a shape.

By the Way

Editing Paths

Most of the time, the initial path you create, whether produced by converting a selection or drawing with the Pen tool, won't be perfect. It's often too difficult to get the selection just right or the lines and curves perfectly placed on the first try. You have probably already realized this while following the previous steps in this hour.

Fortunately, you can easily alter paths after they are created and, once again, you use the Pen tool (and its associated tools) to do this.

The Path Tools

First, look at the various Path tools available in Photoshop. Click and hold the Pen tool (see Figure 13.16).

FIGURE 13.16
Photoshop's Path tools.

▶ Pen tool—You already know this tool intimately. It's used to create new paths.

▶ Freeform Pen tool—As the name suggests, you can use this tool to draw a freeform path in any shape or direction. Photoshop will add the necessary points and handles as you go, so you can adjust any part of your path that's not quite what you had in mind.

> **It's Magnetic...**
>
> Remember the Magnetic Lasso that formed itself around what you were trying to select? The Freeform Pen has a magnetic option, on the Tool Options bar, that works the same way. Use it for tracing a shape. It's under that down arrow to the right of the strip of tool icons.

▶ Add Anchor Point tool—Use this tool to add points to a path.

▶ Delete Anchor Point tool—Use this tool to cut points from a path.

▶ Convert Point tool—Yes, you can even change the *type* of point after you have initially created one. For example, you can turn a corner point into a smooth point, a smooth point into a sharp curve, and so on. You'll learn more about this tool in the next section.

There are also two Path Selection tools to help you work with paths. They're found in the toolbox right above the Pen tools. One is the Direct Selection tool and the other is the Path Selection tool. The Direct Selection tool (represented by a hollow arrow) moves individual segments of the path. The Path Selection tool (the black arrow) moves all the components of a single path at once. If you have several sub-paths within the same path, the Path Selection Tool will move one path at a time. If you want to move them all together, use the Select All command first.

You can switch between the Pen and Freeform Pen tools in one of two ways: either by clicking and holding down over the Pen tool in the toolbar so that the other Pen tools appear, or by pressing Shift+P on the keyboard. Press A to switch to the Path tools, and press Shift+A to switch between the Direct Selection tool and the Path Selection tool. And, if you're already using a Pen tool, press Command (Mac) or Control (Windows) to temporarily switch to the Direct Selection tool.

Basic Path Techniques

You've probably already figured these out on your own, but just in case, here are a few basic techniques for navigating among and using paths:

▶ To select a path, simply click its name in the Paths palette, just as you would click a layer to activate it. Selected paths show up in your image, as you would expect.

▶ To deselect a path, click another path name or click in the empty area of the Paths palette. This makes the path disappear from the main window.

▶ To delete a path, select the path in the Paths palette and drag it to the trash button at the bottom of the palette, just as you would delete a layer.

▶ To create a new path, you can do one of four things:

Simply start drawing the path with one of the Pen tools in the main image window. This makes a work path or, if an existing path is selected, adds to the existing path.

Before using the Pen tool, choose New Path from the palette's menu. This also lets you name the path before you draw it.

Click the Create New Path button at the bottom of the palette. This places a new path on the Paths palette.

Create a selection and then use the Make Work Path command or button.

▶ To duplicate a path, select the desired path in the palette and drag it to the Create New Path button. This works in the same manner as duplicating a layer.

Using Paths

What can you do with paths after you've gone to all the trouble of creating them? Well, a lot of things. In Photoshop, you can use paths to remember selections you want to use repeatedly. You can also fill a path area or define the color, border, and so on of the outline of the path. Paths indicate selections or lines, but they don't actually appear on your canvas unless you add some paint to them to make them show up. You can fill a path or stroke it, or both. *Stroking* adds a stroke of paint over the path. *Filling* places a color or pattern inside the path. Figure 13.17 shows a freeform path that has been stroked with red and filled with a pattern.

Use the Active Layer

When you fill or stroke a path, you are adding pixels to the active layer of your picture. Make sure that the layer you want to put the paint on is the active one.

Turning Paths into Selections

In Photoshop, paths one way to permanently save selections. This can be incredibly helpful when you think you might want to reuse a specific selection later. When in doubt, create a path so that the selection will always be available.

▼   **Try it Yourself**

Convert a Path into a Selection

You already learned how to convert a selection to a path. The following steps show you how to convert a path into a selection:

1. Create a path through whatever means suits your fancy.
2. Activate the path you want to convert by clicking it in the Paths palette.
3. Choose Make Selection from the menu at the top-right of the Paths palette (see Figure 13.18) or click the Make Selection button, third from the left in the bottom of the Paths palette. (This bypasses the dialog box described in the next step.)

FIGURE 13.18
Turning a work
path into a
selection.

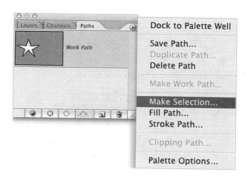

4. In the Make Selection dialog box that appears, you can set the feathering radius of the selection that Photoshop creates (see Figure 13.19). The higher the Feather Radius setting, the more partially selected pixels will appear along the edges of the selection.

▼

COLOR GALLERY

COLOR PLATE 6.2

The Variations dialog box shows variations in the hue and saturation of a picture.

Hour 6, page 93

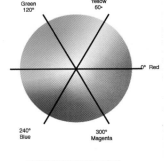

COLOR PLATE 6.8

The Color Wheel and the Gray Ramp

Hour 6, pages 100-101

COLOR PLATE 6.6

Isn't she pretty? Her name is China Doll and she lives at Wildlife on Easy St. in Tampa, FL.

Hour 6, page 98

COLOR PLATE 6.12

Color correction brings out her subtle shadings and puts her in a sunnier spot.

Hour 6, page 105

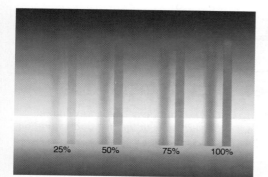

COLOR PLATE 7.6

I've applied magenta stripes over a blue gradient. The opacity percentage is listed below its stripes..

Hour 7, page 117

25%   50%   75%   100%

Normal   Dissolve   Darken   Multiple

COLOR PLATE 8.13

All of the blending modes.

Hour 8, pages 142-143

Color Burn   Linear Burn   Lighten   Screen

Color Dodge   Linear Dodge   Overlay   Soft Light

Hard Light   Vivid Light   Linear Light   Pin Light

Hard Mix   Difference   Exclusion   Hue

Saturation   Color   Luminosity

COLOR PLATE 9.13

I've lightened and brightened the leaves.

Hour 9, page 156

COLOR PLATE 9.14

Here's the original version. It's kind of drab.

Hour 9, page 157

COLOR PLATE 9.15

After sponging, the colors seem to glow.

Hour 9, page 157

Brush Detail 1
Texture 1

 Brush Detail 1
Texture 2

 Brush Detail 7
Texture 1

 Brush Detail 1
Texture 3

 Brush Detail 7
Texture 2

 Brush Detail 14
Texture 1

 Brush Detail 7
Texture 3

 Brush Detail 14
Texture 2

 Brush Detail 14
Texture 3

COLOR PLATE 10.3

All three texture settings have been applied to each sample brush setting.

Hour 10, page 167

COLOR PLATE 10.4

Painting something like this is easier in Photoshop than using real brushes and paint.

Hour 10, page 167

COLOR PLATE 10.10

The Canvas texture makes it look more like a real painting.

Hour 10, page 173

COLOR PLATE 14.13

The Spin and Zoom filters work especially well on round objects.

Hour 14, page 245

COLOR PLATE 15.1

The basic photo, a fishing boat passing Cape Forchu Lighthouse.

Hour 15, page 254

Image with various filters applied. Filtered images are shown larger on following page.

COLOR PLATE 15.6

The Cut Out filter makes the boat and lighthouse look like a silk screened poster.

Hour 15, page 257

COLOR PLATE 15.16

The Rough Pastels make almost everything look good.

Hour 15, page 264

COLOR PLATE 15.19

This filter can make things look too spotty. Be careful with it.

Hour 15, page 266

COLOR PLATE 15.25

This reminds me of looking through small pebbly glass.

Hour 15, page 269

COLOR PLATE 16.1

Hand-forged iron chain.

Hour 16, page 280

COLOR PLATE 16.2

Applying the Diffuse Glow filter makes the chain look radioactive.

Hour 16, page 281

COLOR PLATE 16.6
The Glass filter applied.
Hour 16, page 283

COLOR PLATE 16.8
Ocean ripples are fun.
Hour 16, page 285

COLOR PLATE 16.17
This scene would be very difficult to draw.
Hour 16, page 290

COLOR PLATE 16.18
Reminds me of neon tubing…
Hour 16, page 291

COLOR PLATE 16.23

In real life, it would be difficult to paint on sandstone.

Hour 16, page 295

COLOR PLATE 16.24

This one has only the Rough Pastels filter added.

Hour 16, page 295

COLOR PLATE 16.25

Same beach, with Film Grain added.

Hour 16, page 296

FIGURE 17.14

Notice how the text casts a shadow on the baby and the bed, and the baby in turn casts a shadow on the background.

Hour 17, page 315

COLOR PLATE 17.21

The difference between Bevel and Emboss is obvious.

Hour 17, page 320

Carved in Stone

SCRAWLED IN JAM

COLOR PLATE 18.1

My crystal ball, bright but not glowing.

Hour 18, page 329

COLOR PLATE 18.3

The glow seems to come from within the ball.

Hour 18, page 330

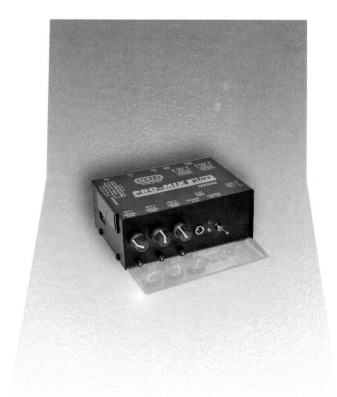

COLOR PLATE 18.14

The highlight on the box makes a big difference.

Hour 18, page 338

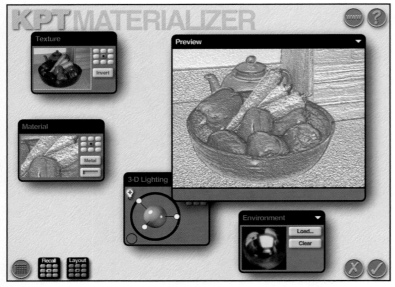

COLOR PLATE 19.8

KPT Materializer hard at work.

Hour 19, page 356

COLOR PLATE 19.9

These are truly unique effects.

Hour 19, page 357

COLOR PLATE 19.11

The New Orleans skyline as I've never really seen it before.

Hour 19, page 358

COLOR PLATE 20.12

I'm sure she'd rather be back at the casino.

Hour 20, page 374

COLOR PLATE 20.21

Now it's looking like a day at the beach.

Hour 20, page 381

COLOR PLATE 20.23

Art for over the couch in less than two minutes.

Hour 20, page 382

COLOR PLATE 21.11

I think the Healing Brush does a neater job.

Hour 21, page 397

COLOR PLATE 21.24

The most important thing to know about hand coloring is not to overdo it.

Hour 21, page 407

COLOR PLATE 21.25

The oval vignette goes with the mood of the photo.

Hour 21, page 407

COLOR PLATE 22.3

You can put back the colors by working with the saturation and brightness sliders.

Hour 22, page 413

COLOR PLATE 22.4

Blue eyed cats have red eye. Yellow eyed cats have green eye.

Hour 22, page 414

COLOR PLATE 22.6

Now he looks quite tame.

Hour 22, page 415

COLOR PLATE 22.14

A less distracting background.

Hour 22, page 420

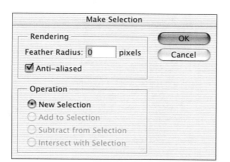

FIGURE 13.19
The Make
Selection dialog
box.

5. Click OK, and you'll see the path turn into a selection.

Filling a Path

Filling a path means just what you would expect. Select a path, choose Fill Path
from the palette menu, and you'll get the same kinds of options you get for filling a
selection, plus a couple of extras. In the Fill Path dialog box (see Figure 13.20), you
can choose a color, a pattern, or a snapshot to fill the area. You can also choose a
blending mode, opacity percentage, optional transparency, anti-aliasing, and a
feathering value. If the path consists of two separate subpaths, only the one selected
will be filled or stroked.

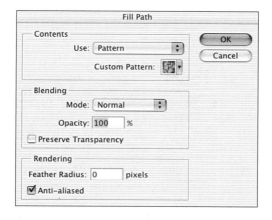

FIGURE 13.20
The Fill Path
dialog box has
many options.

Stroking a Path

Stroking a path affects the outline of the path, not the entire area enclosed within a
path. Select a path and then choose Stroke Path from the palette menu. The dialog

box enables you to choose the tool you want to use, from Pencil and Brush to Blur and Sponge (see Figure 13.21).

FIGURE 13.21
The Stroke Path dialog box allows you to determine which stroke you'll use.

Whatever tool you pick, Photoshop uses that tool's current settings to create the result. So, for example, if you want to airbrush the path outline with only 60% pressure, make sure that value is set in the Tool Options bar and that the Airbrush option is selected *before* you choose Stroke Path.

Did you Know?

Take the Shortcut

There are shortcuts for filling and for stroking. Hold your mouse pointer over the buttons at the bottom of the Paths palette, and you'll see the tooltips. Press Option (Mac) or Alt (Windows) as you click a button to open its dialog box.

Using the Shape Tools

In a hurry? Can't draw? Don't despair. Photoshop provides a handy arsenal of predrawn shapes, which it calls its *Shape tools*. These can be used as paths and be filled or stroked as needed. They can be resized, to a certain extent reshaped, and placed wherever you need them. The rounded rectangle is great for masking photos. The polygons are useful if you need a bunch of stars or other unusual shapes. The custom shapes will amaze you. Figure 13.22 shows the Shape tools.

FIGURE 13.22
These tools can draw filled or unfilled shapes.

To draw a shape, first specify a foreground color, which can be used to fill the shape. Select the appropriate tool. (If you are using the Custom Shape tool, you need to click its icon on the Tool Options bar and choose one of the available shapes.)

A Multitude of Shapes

Photoshop comes with piles and piles of custom shapes. To pick through your choices, click the arrow on the Tool Options bar's Custom Shape menu to see yet another pop-up menu. Scroll to the bottom of the menu and choose a shape library, such as Animals, Ornaments, and TalkBubbles. The resulting dialog box asks you whether to replace the existing shapes with the ones from the new library (OK) or just add the new shapes in (Append). You can always return to the default Shape menu by choosing Reset Shapes from the pop-up menu.

Did you Know?

To create a new shape, click the Shape Layers, the Paths, or the Fill Pixels button in the Options bar, as shown in Figure 13.23. Use Create New Work Path if you want to make a path with a particular shape. Use Create Filled Region to produce a filled shape. Use Create New Shape Layer to draw a shape on a new layer.

Create New Work Path

Create Filled Region

Create New Shape Layer

FIGURE 13.23
Select one of these options.

To edit a shape after you've drawn it, make sure that the shape layer is selected and choose the Add, Subtract, Intersect, or Exclude option in the Tool Options bar. If you choose Add and draw a second shape, they'll both be filled. If you choose Subtract and draw a second shape touching the first, you can cut out part of the filled shape. Intersect fills the shapes only where they overlap. Exclude *removes* the color where two shapes overlap. Figure 13.24 shows some examples.

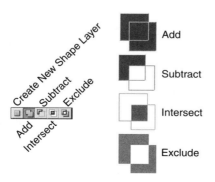

Create New Shape Layer

Add

Subtract

Exclude

Intersect

Add

Subtract

Intersect

Exclude

FIGURE 13.24
These options aren't available until you've drawn the first shape.

Dragging as you draw determines the size and orientation of a shape. Hold down Shift as you drag to constrain a rectangle or rounded rectangle to a square or to constrain an ellipse to a circle. Hold down Option (Mac) or Alt (Windows) as you drag to draw from the center of the object.

If you need a precisely sized shape, click the down arrow at the end of the row of Shape tools on the Tool Options bar. This opens a dialog box. Depending on the shape you chose, you can set height and width, corner radius, or the number of sides in a polygon or points on a star. Use the Tool Options bar to specify a blending mode and opacity for the shape.

Add a Shape to the Custom Shapes Palette

Create a shape using the other Shape tools, or select the path containing the shape you want to use. In Figure 13.25, I've used the star, drawn a path around it, and filled it. To add it to the Custom Shapes palette, make sure the path is selected in the Paths palette, then choose Edit→Define Custom Shape and enter a name for the new shape in the dialog box (see Figure 13.25). When you click OK, the shape will be added to the palette.

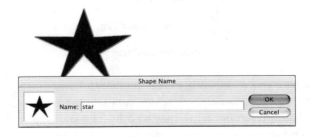

FIGURE 13.25
Give the shape a name to add it to the palette.

To select your new custom shape, choose it from the shape list in the Tool Options bar. To restrict the shape to its original size, choose Fixed Size in the Tool Options bar.

Summary

The path is a magical Photoshop feature that has many applications in your daily Photoshop existence. You can use paths as permanent Photoshop selections that can be reused anytime, as the means to fill or stroke part of an image, as a way to convert areas of an image, as a way to draw a line or shape, or as clipping paths for images that will be exported into a page layout program. Photoshop provides an array of tools and options for creating paths. You can create a path by converting a selection you have already made, or by drawing a path from scratch by using a Pen tool. You can also edit existing paths with the assorted Path tools, and you can create shaped paths with the Shape tools. You can even make and use custom path shapes.

Workshop

Q&A

Q *How can I use paths to draw shapes onto my pictures?*

A Choose the Shape tool that's appropriate, and choose Shape Layer on the Tool Options bar. Your shape will appear on a new layer in the foreground color. To draw a custom shape, select the appropriate Pen tool and draw the path you need. After you have placed the path, stroke it or fill it as necessary.

Q *What does the Magnetic Pen do that the other Pen tools don't?*

A The Magnetic Pen bases its selection on contrast. This automates path creation to some degree because you don't have to rely on your own hand-eye coordination to follow a complex path.

Q *How do I know what tolerance to set when I convert a path to a selection?*

A That depends on how smooth—or how accurate—you want the finished path to be. A tolerance of 1 pixel or less will make the path follow the selection as precisely as possible. A tolerance of 5–10 will give you a smoothed-out path, following your selection to within 5 to 10 pixels.

Quiz

1. What does it mean to *stroke* a path?

    a. Using the points and Bézier handles to refine its shape

    b. Adding a color to it so it becomes a line

    c. Painting over it with short strokes

2. How do you turn a selection into a path?

    a. Select it and press Command+P

    b. Select Make Work Path from the Paths palette menu

    c. Line it with bricks

3. What does the Rubber Band option do?

    a. Makes your paths visible as you click the mouse

    b. Makes paths spring back to a straight line when clicked

    c. Makes lines "stretchy"

Quiz Answers

1. b. Think of stroking it with a paintbrush.

2. b. Don't try a. unless you want to make a printout.

3. a. All paths are visible as you draw them (while you drag to set the handles), but the Rubber Band mode makes the path visible as you move the mouse.

Exercises

Start a new page and use the Pen tool to draw a star-shaped path and a freeform path with lots of curves. Stroke both of these paths with a color. Then use the Magnetic Pen tool to trace around them. Notice that as long as you stay fairly close to your original line, the Pen tool places a path right at the edge of the line. Fill these shapes with a color. Draw two more paths inside these shapes, and fill them with a different color. Add a couple of shapes with a Shape tool. Try a custom shape. Practice with the Path tools, adding points and refining your paths until you're comfortable with them all.

PART III

Fun with Filters

HOUR 14

Filters That Improve Your Picture

What You'll Learn in This Hour:

- ▶ Sharpen Filters
- ▶ Blur Filters
- ▶ Fading Filters

I'm not sure whether Photoshop's creators pioneered the idea of plug-in filters or just took the ball and ran with it. In either case, they've given us a wonderful tool for altering the all-over appearance of a picture. Some of Photoshop's filters are strange; some are beautiful; some are merely useful—it's this last group that we'll look at in this hour.

The title for this hour's lesson doesn't really tell the story. Presumably you wouldn't apply a filter that *didn't* improve your picture. What would be the point? It might be more correct to say that the filters we'll be looking at will fix common photographic problems.

Sharpen Filters

One of the most common problems photographers face is the out-of-focus picture. There are many reasons why a picture might be fuzzy. Either the subject or the photographer might have moved slightly when the picture was taken. Perhaps the camera wasn't focused correctly, or possibly the picture was taken with an inexpensive camera that had a poor quality plastic lens. Some of these problems are easier to compensate for in Photoshop than others.

If a photo is way out of focus, there's not much that can be done to bring it back. If it's just a little bit soft, Photoshop can at least create the illusion of sharper focus. It does this with a set of filters called *Sharpen*. Like all the filters described in this hour, they're found on the Filter menu (see Figure 14.1).

FIGURE 14.1
The Filter menu
showing the
Sharpen filters.

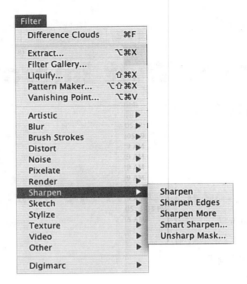

Sharpen, Sharpen More

Two of the Sharpen filters, Sharpen and Sharpen More, provide different levels of the same function. They work by finding areas in the image where there are significant color changes, such as at the edges of an object. Whenever such an area is found, Photoshop increases the contrast between adjacent pixels, making the lights lighter and the darks darker. Figure 14.2 shows three views of a slightly fuzzy picture of rocks in the desert. The top example is before sharpening. The middle example has had Sharpen applied, and the bottom example has had Sharpen More applied. If you don't enlarge the picture too much, the effect looks quite good.

Be careful not to overdo the sharpening. With many Photoshop filters, a little is good but more is better. Alas, this is not the case with the Sharpen filters. Because of the way that the filters enhance contrast in adjacent pixels, you might be just a click away from turning your photo to patchwork, as in Figure 14.3.

By the way, Sharpen More is approximately the same effect as applying the Sharpen filter twice to the same picture. Keep in mind that you can do this any time a filter has less than the desired effect. The easy way to apply the same filter again is to press Command+F (Mac) or Control+F (Windows). This keyboard shortcut applies whatever filter and filter settings (if any) you applied last.

Try the Sharpen filter on one of your own fuzzy pictures and see what you think. Does it help? Try the Sharpen More filter also. They are great for adjusting slightly out-of-focus photographs or scans, but don't rely on these filters too much. They can only do so much. They can't add what is missing from an image—namely, focus and good contrast. They can, however, help bring back a photo that's just a little bit off. Don't forget that you can apply filters selectively, using masks or selections to only filter part of the image.

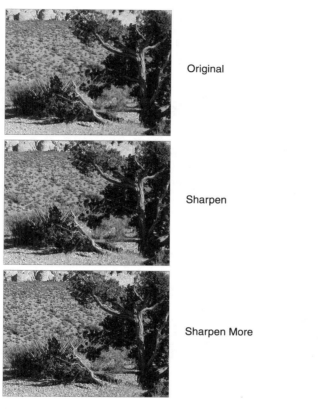

Original

Sharpen

Sharpen More

FIGURE 14.2
Before and after sharpening.

FIGURE 14.3
An image that has been over-sharpened.

Sharpen Edges

Sharpen Edges is a truly useful filter. It doesn't affect the whole image, so you don't get as much of a sense of that harsh blocky effect as with Sharpen More. Rather, Sharpen Edges "sees" and enhances the contrast at whatever it perceives to be an edge. Figure 14.4 shows before and after versions of the desert, using Sharpen Edges. Sharpening the edges has a slight but noticeable effect on the quality of the photo.

FIGURE 14.4
You can really see the Sharpen Edges effect in the foreground grass.

Unsharp Mask

Unsharp masking is a traditional technique that has been used in the printing industry for many years. It is probably your best bet for precision sharpening. It corrects blurring in an original image or scan, as well as any blurring that occurs during the resampling and printing process. The Unsharp Mask filter works by locating every two adjacent pixels with a difference in brightness values that you have specified, and increasing their contrast by an amount that you specify. It gives you real control of the sharpness of an image.

Set the level of sharpening you need in the Unsharp Mask dialog box shown in Figure 14.5; the dialog box appears when you select the filter. The Radius control sets the number of surrounding pixels to which the sharpening effect is applied. I suggest that you keep the radius fairly low—around 2.0. The Threshold setting controls how different the pixels must be to be sharpened. The lower the setting, the more similar the pixels can be and still be affected by the filter. The higher the setting, the greater Photoshop's tolerance of differences will be. (Of course, as always, feel free to go wild and try all the settings. That is the best way to learn.) Be sure that you check the Preview box so that you can see the effect of your changes.

Many Photoshop experts recommend applying the Unsharp Mask filter to every image that you process, whether it's going to be printed or used on the Web. (I personally don't like to say *always* or *never* because there can be exceptions to any rule.) You should probably *try* it on every image, to see whether you like the effect.

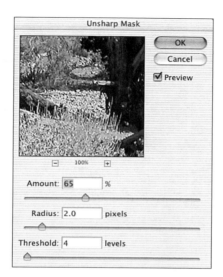

FIGURE 14.5
The preview
area lets you
see the effect
your settings
have.

FIGURE 14.5
The preview
area lets you
see the effect
your settings
have.

Double Duty Filters

Photoshop filters aren't restricted to Photoshop. Other Adobe products, such as PageMaker and Illustrator, can use many of them also. Even Paint Shop Pro and Macromedia's Director can employ many Photoshop filters. If you find particularly useful or interesting filters or filter combinations, try using them with other Photoshop plug-in-compatible programs.

Did you Know?

Smart Sharpen

For the ultimate in sharpening power, you can turn to the Smart Sharpen filter, which is new to Photoshop CS2. With this filter, you can choose different sharpening algorithms, or styles, for different kinds of images, and you can control the amount of sharpening in dark and light areas of your image.

Choose Filter→Sharpen→Smart Sharpen to see the Smart Sharpen options (see Figure 14.6). First, choose an option from the Remove pop-up menu. To fix a generally soft image, choose Gaussian Blur, which uses the same sharpening technique that the Unsharp Mask filter uses. If your image has a lot of detail and needs a pretty hefty amount of sharpening, choose Lens Blur to sharpen edges without adding "sharpening halos" (as shown back in Figure 14.3). And if your camera moved just as you shot the photo, choose Motion Blur and set the angle to match the angle of the blur you see in the image. Finally, unless you're in a hurry, check the More Accurate box so that Photoshop will take a little more time on its calculations and produce the best possible result.

FIGURE 14.6
The Smart
Sharpen filter
packs a lot of
power into a
single dialog
box.

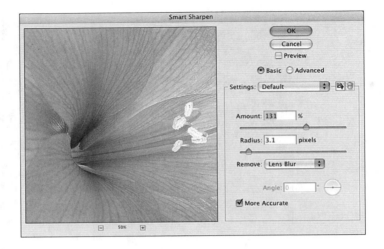

In Advanced mode, you'll see two tabs in addition to the Sharpen tab, where you've just made your basic settings. If you're seeing too much effect from the basic settings, but only in the shadows or only in the highlights, drag the Fade Amount slider to the left to reduce the amount of sharpening just in those areas. Drag the Tonal Width slider back and forth to determine how much of the image constitutes "shadows" or "highlights"—the higher the setting, the greater the area affected by your Shadow and Highlight tab settings. And the Radius slider controls how much of the area around each pixel Photoshop uses to decide whether that pixel falls into the category of a shadow or a highlight; unless you're feeling adventurous, you can leave this setting alone and get perfectly fine results.

Blur Filters

The Blur filters (Filter→Blur) are useful tools when you want to soften effects, either of a filter you have just applied or of brush strokes in a painting. Blurring can gently smooth a harshly lit portrait or, when used on a selection instead of the whole image, can throw an unwanted background out of focus, making it less obtrusive. The Blur filters are shown in Figure 14.7.

Blur, Blur More

There are two basic Blur filters: Blur and Blur More. They do exactly as their names suggest. Blur is very subtle. Blur More is only a little less so. Figure 14.8 shows a comparison of the two filters in use, against a nonblurred original. As you can see, the changes are minor. Blurring doesn't make much difference, but it can smooth out wrinkles in a portrait or soften a hard edge.

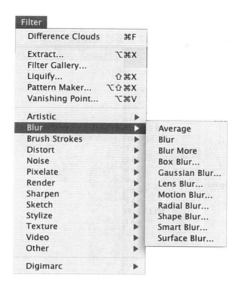

FIGURE 14.7
The Blur menu.

Gaussian Blur

You can apply the Blur filter several times to get the effect you want, or you can move on to Gaussian Blur (Filter→Blur→Gaussian Blur), which is a more controllable filter. It uses a mathematical formula (the Gaussian distribution equation, which results in a bell curve) to calculate the precise transition between each pair of pixels. The result of this is that most of the blurred pixels end up in the middle of the two colors or values, rather than at either end of the spectrum. This produces a generalized blur that neither darkens nor lightens the image.

FIGURE 14.8
Blur is applied on the top right; Blur More, on the bottom right. You have to look carefully to see the effect.

The Gaussian Blur dialog box, shown in Figure 14.9, lets you determine exactly how much blur to apply by setting a Radius value from 0.1–250. You can also use it to anti-alias the edges of an object, and to blur shadow areas when you want to create a drop shadow effect. Even at fairly low settings, it has quite a dramatic effect. In Figure 14.9, notice how the subject's eye and cheek wrinkles, obvious in the previous picture, are almost gone in the Blur preview area.

FIGURE 14.9
Smaller numbers give you less blur.

Gaussian Blur is a useful retouching tool when applied to an area within the picture that you want to de-emphasize. In Figure 14.10, there's a small lizard sunning herself on the rocks, but her protective coloration makes her kind of hard to see in the image on the left. If I select the lizard and apply a mask to hide her, I can blur the rest of the scene and call attention to the critter (see the image on the right).

FIGURE 14.10
Selective blurring is a helpful tool.

A quick application of the Blur tool, with Pressure set to 75%, helps to blend the blurred and unblurred areas.

Which Blur, When?

Use the Blur filters when you have a large area to blur. Use the Blur tool when you want to soften just a small area because it's more controllable in terms of the degree of focus change it applies.

Smart Blur

The Smart Blur filter (Filter→Blur→Smart Blur) is probably the most useful one of the bunch, especially for image editing and photo repair. It blurs everything in the image, or selection, except the edges. Smart Blur calculates the differences between color regions to determine boundaries, and it maintains these boundaries while blurring everything within them. It's the perfect filter when you need to take 10 years off a portrait subject's face, smooth out teenaged skin, or get rid of the texture in a piece of cloth without losing the folds.

Figure 14.11 shows the Smart Blur filter dialog box. The original photo is in the background, and you can see the improvements in the filter window. You can set Radius and Threshold to determine how much blur is applied and set Quality, as done earlier, to determine how the effect is calculated.

FIGURE 14.11
Experiment with the settings until you find the right combination of Radius and Threshold.

The Smart Blur filter has three modes:

▶ In Normal mode, the preview area shows the effects of the blurring.

▶ Edge Only shows you the outlines with which Smart Blur is working.

▶ Edge Overlay shows the outlines as white lines on top of the image.

You can use the Edge Overlay or Edge Only to help you determine which Threshold value to set. Convert the mode back to Normal before you click OK to apply the effect.

Surface Blur

Even more than Smart Blur, this filter blurs an image's surfaces and background areas without obscuring edges. It's a good way to get rid of "noise" in old or re-scanned photos, although it doesn't offer as much control as Smart Blur. The controls work just like those in the Gaussian Blur dialog box.

Radial Blur

The Radial Blur filter can be interesting, if you carefully choose how to apply it. It gives you two choices: Spin and Zoom. Spin mode gives you a blur that looks as if the image is spinning around its center point. Zoom mode theoretically gives you the effect of zooming the camera into or away from the image.

In the Radial Blur dialog box, shown in Figure 14.12, you can set both an amount for the blur effect (from 1–100) and a quality level (Draft, Good, or Best). Amount refers to the distance that the pixels are moved to create the blur. You can see the difference in the Blur center area as you set the blur amount. You can click and drag in the same area to determine a center point for the blur effect.

The Quality settings determine the manner in which the blur effect is calculated; you can choose Draft, Good, or Best. There's very little difference between Good and Best in the resulting images. The biggest difference, in fact, is not in the image quality, but in how long it takes Photoshop to compute and apply the blur in each mode. Best can take quite a long time if the image is complex and your computer is an older model.

FIGURE 14.12
The same dialog box applies both the Zoom and Spin methods.

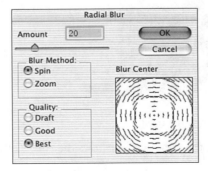

In Figure 14.13, I've applied Spin (left) and Zoom (right) blurring to a picture of a yellow lily. After experimenting with the settings, I used 20 as the amount for Spin and 50 as the Zoom setting. You can also see these pictures in the color plate section.

FIGURE 14.13
Spin and Zoom obviously aren't for everyday use, but, as a special effect, they're certainly interesting.

Motion Blur

When we see lines drawn behind a car, a cat, or a comic strip character, we instinctively know that the subject is supposed to be in motion. Those lines represent *motion blur*, which is actually a photographic mistake caused by using a slow shutter speed on a fast subject. The image's subject appears totally or partially blurred against the background because the subject actually traveled some distance during the fraction of a second that the camera shutter was open.

In the early days of photography, motion blur was a common occurrence, primarily because shutter speeds were slow, and film sensitivity was not very great. Today, motion blur is unusual, unless the photographer is capturing the subject this way on purpose by using the least sensitive film available or by using a small lens opening and a correspondingly slower shutter. If you want to try to approximate the effect of motion blur, Photoshop gives you a tool that can do it.

The Motion Blur (Filter→Blur→Motion Blur) filter can add the appearance of motion to a stationary object by placing a directional blur for a predetermined distance. In the Motion Blur dialog box, shown in Figure 14.14, you can set both the distance and direction of the blur according to how fast and in what direction you want the object to appear to be traveling. The distance sets how much of a blur is applied—or how far the original image is "moved." The angle sets the direction of the blur. To adjust, drag the Radius slider or enter precise values into the field next to it. The trick, however, is to select the right area to which to apply Motion Blur. To get a convincing blur, you need to blur the space where the object theoretically was, as well as to where it theoretically has moved.

FIGURE 14.14
Using the Motion Blur filter is tricky at best.

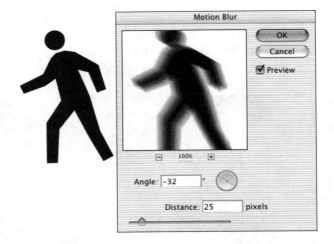

The Motion Blur filter doesn't do much for most photos. After all, the blur caused by the camera shaking is the kind of thing we usually try to avoid—not add. But, for some special effects, and for doing tricks with type, it has interesting possibilities. Figure 14.15 shows one possible use. First, I rendered the type and applied the Perspective transformation to give it some depth. Adding Motion Blur lets me run faster, but I could even take this further.

FIGURE 14.15
You can't run standing still.

For Figure 14.16, I set the type, placing each letter on a different layer. I then applied a different number of pixels (increasing left to right) to each Motion Blur, from 6 pixels on the *R* to 30 pixels on the *N*. The resulting image almost seems to be running off the screen, as shown in Figure 14.16.

FIGURE 14.16
Using layers lets you apply different filters or different degrees of filter to the same image.

Lens Blur

The lens blur filter attempts to simulate the "real-world" phenomenon in which lens flares and highlights take on the shape of the camera iris. Depending on the number of leaves in the camera shutter, the shape can be a hexagon or pentagon. Photoshop takes it a step further, letting you select from three to eight sides on the highlight, and how much of the image is involved. You can apply it to the entire photo, to a selection, or to a layer.

The most important thing about lens blur is that it can vary the amount of blur in different parts of the image based on the current selection. This adds depth of field to the image, so you can focus attention on the objects in the foreground and blur the objects in the background.

Average Blur

Taking blurring to the max, the Average Blur filter mixes all the colors in an image or the selected area to come up with the color that's the average of them all. Among other applications, it's a great way to choose a color that goes with everything to use for backgrounds and type.

Shape Blur

If you have some playing-around time, consider devoting some of it to this filter. Shape Blur bases its blur on an irregular shape of your choosing, repeating that shape throughout the image and applying the blurring effect more in darker areas of the shape. This results in a very subtle effect—for example, a slight starry sparkle can show up in an image blurred using a star shape. In addition to choosing a shape, you can determine how large the "kernel" image is using the Radius slider. The larger the kernel, the greater the blur effect.

Box Blur

I'm really not sure what Adobe intended Photoshop users to do with this new filter. It works like the Gaussian Blur filter, and it does pretty much the same thing, only less smoothly. An image blurred using Box Blur has more pronounced detail than the same picture blurred using a Gaussian blur with the same radius setting. Feel free to experiment, and if you figure out what Box Blur is good for, drop me an email!

Fading Filters

Filters are cool, but sometimes they just do a little too much to the image. Many, like the Motion Blur filter, are variable. You can set their effects to be as subtle or dramatic as you want. Others, like the basic Blur and Sharpen, don't have dialog boxes and don't give you the opportunity to apply any less than the full amount of effect that Photoshop thinks is right. Well, Father Photoshop *doesn't* always know best, but you do have an option.

You can apply a filter and then open Fade to fade the effect anywhere from 1%–100%. You can also use the Fade dialog box to set a blending mode for the filter effect. Even more important, you can fade whatever else you last did in the same dialog box (see Figure 14.17). You painted something, but the color was too strong? Fade it 50%. That's quicker than redoing it with a different color. You overdid an image color adjustment? Fade it. The Fade command changes whatever tool or action you just applied. Experiment with this feature. It can save you hours of work.

FIGURE 14.17
The Fade dialog box allows you to back off an effect that's too much.

Try it Yourself

Fade a Filter Effect or Color Adjustment

Let's try putting the Fade command to practical use.

1. Open any convenient image. Apply a Blur filter or make any color adjustment (Image→Adjustments).

2. Choose Edit→Fade. (The command will give the name of the filter you applied in step 1—for example, Fade Gaussian Blur.) If you're working on a selection, rather than the whole image, don't deselect it.

3. Set the Preview option so that you can see the effect of the fade.

4. Drag the slider to adjust the opacity.

5. Choose a blending mode other than Normal, if you want a particular effect.

6. Click OK. Deselect the selection if necessary.

Summary

Photoshop's filters are the one tool that makes the program a must-have for anyone working with photos. In this hour, you looked at the Photoshop filters that can help you rescue a bad photo or bad scan. The Sharpen filters can restore out-of-focus photographs by increasing the contrast between adjacent pixels. The most useful of these is the Unsharp Mask filter, which lets you set the parameters for how it finds and adjusts contrasts.

Blur filters come in several varieties and are most useful for putting unwanted parts of the picture out of focus and for softening hard edges. The Motion Blur filter enables you to create the illusion of movement in stationary objects and can do interesting things to type.

The Fade dialog box works with filters and with other Photoshop tools to decrease the effect of your action by a percentage that you can set.

Workshop

Q&A

Q *What's the difference between the Blur filter and the Blur tool?*

A You can apply the Blur tool as if it were a paintbrush to as small an area as you want. The Blur filter blurs the entire image or selection evenly.

Q *If I change my mind about applying a filter, can I stop the process?*

A To cancel the filter as it's being applied, press Command+period (Mac) or Esc (Windows). To undo a filter, use the Undo command: Command+Z (Mac) or Control+Z (Windows). If it's too late to undo, use the History palette to revert to a stage before you applied the filter.

Q *I have a photo that's slightly out of focus. Is there any way to make the subject stand out more?*

A Select the subject and copy it to a new layer. Use Gaussian Blur on the original, and Sharpen on the subject only.

Quiz

1. Sharpen More applies _____ as much correction as Sharpen.

    a. Exactly

    b. Twice

    c. Half

2. Gaussian Blur uses a _____ to determine how blur is applied.

    a. Mathematical formula

    b. Random memory algorithm

    c. Prismatic crystal filter

3. Many experts advise applying which filter to every photograph you bring into Photoshop?

    a. Sharpen

    b. Gaussian Blur

    c. Unsharp Mask

4. Fading a filter has this effect:

   a. It fades an action such as applying a filter according to a percentage you determine.

   b. It applies the filter at half strength.

   c. It applies a 50% gray tone over the filter.

Quiz Answers

1. b. To get the same effect, apply Sharpen twice.

2. a. The blur follows Gaussian distribution (the bell curve).

3. c. The Unsharp Mask filter is especially helpful with scanned images.

4. a. You can fade from 100% down to 1%.

Exercises

Find or shoot a picture of yourself or a friend, and load it into Photoshop. (If you don't have a digital camera or scanner, download a news photo from the Web, or a portrait from the Web site—see the Introduction for the URL.) Use the Blur and Sharpen filters to improve it. Find and remove wrinkles, eye bags, uneven complexions, and any other flaws. (In Hour 21, "Photo Repair—Black and White," you'll learn more techniques for improving photos.)

Filters to Make Your Picture Artistic

What You'll Learn in This Hour:

- ▶ Artistic Filters
- ▶ Brush Strokes
- ▶ Sketch Filters

In Hour 10, "Advanced Painting Techniques," you saw how Photoshop's filters could help imitate other media. You looked specifically at the Watercolor, Colored Pencil, Charcoal, and Underpainting filters. But those are still just the tip of the iceberg. Under the general headings of Artistic and Sketch filters, Photoshop offers approximately 30 filters that you can apply alone or in combinations to turn your so-so picture into a masterpiece. In this hour, you run through the alphabet of the Artistic, Brush Strokes, and Sketch effects. You will be amazed, boggled, confounded, delighted, and ecstatic.

Try It Anyway

I've deliberately left out step-by-step "Try It Yourself" exercises in this hour. You apply all these filters in the same way: Filter→Artistic, and so on. Use the dialog box and its preview window to judge the effects of the filter as you change the settings. The key to success with any of these filters is to experiment until you get the effect you want. If you don't like what you see when you apply a filter to the whole picture, undo, revert, or partially fade the filter. The Fade command (in the Edit menu) reduces the strength of the filter, or any other tool or effect, by a percentage you set in its dialog box.

By the Way

Artistic Filters

Artistic filters apply a certain amount of abstraction to your image. How much depends on the kind of filter and, to an even greater degree, on how you set the filter's variables. Many of these filters ask you to set Brush Size, Detail, and Texture. Brush Size affects the thickness of the line. Detail determines how large a "clump" of pixels must be so that the filter will, in effect, notice it and apply its changes. Texture, not to be confused with the effect of the Texturizer filter, simply adds a random smudge here and there in your image. Most of Photoshop's filters have a preview window in which you can see the effects of changing the settings before you actually apply the filter. To move the image inside the preview window, click it. The cursor turns into a hand, enabling you to slide the picture around to see the effect on specific parts of the image. If you change settings and the preview doesn't change right away, you'll see a progress bar grow at the bottom of the window. Click the plus or minus symbol to see a reduced or enlarged view within the preview window, but it's always a good idea to preview your image at 100% before you click OK.

One of the more useful features in Photoshop CS is the Filter Gallery. It's a new look for the dialog box that shows up when you're using Photoshop's more "artistic" filters, and it shows you how the various filters look when applied to a fairly typical photo. If you would rather see a larger preview pane and skip the thumbnail images, clicking the triangle just to the right of the gallery pane toggles the thumbnails on and off.

For the sake of consistency, let's apply all the Artistic filters to the Cape Forchu, Nova Scotia lighthouse. See Figure 15.1 and the color plate section for the unfiltered view.

FIGURE 15.1
Basic, non-artistic photo.

Colored Pencil

The Colored Pencil filter goes over the photo with a sort of crosshatched effect (see Figure 15.2). It keeps most of the colors of the original photograph, although any large, flat areas are translated to "paper" color, which you can set to any shade of the current background color. The filter's dialog box, shown in Figure 15.3, asks you to choose a Pencil Width and the pressure of the stroke. Paper Brightness can be set on a scale of 1–50, with 50 being the lightest, and 1 being completely black.

FIGURE 15.2
Colored Pencil filter applied.

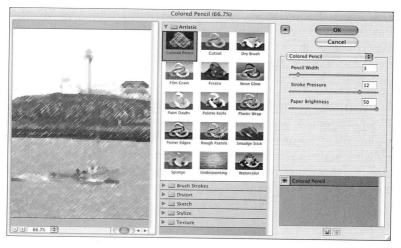

FIGURE 15.3
Colored Pencil filter settings.

Using a narrow pencil (low number) gives you more lines. Greater stroke pressure picks up more detail from the original picture. In Figure 15.2, I used a large pencil and light pressure. In Figure 15.4, I tried a compromise: a small pencil and heavy pressure, using a Pencil Width of 2 and a Stroke Pressure of 14. As you can see, the results are quite different.

FIGURE 15.4
Less pencil width, more stroke pressure.

Cutout

The Cutout filter is one of my favorites. It can reduce a picture to something resembling a cut paper collage or a silk screen print. The Cutout filter does this by averaging all the colors and shades and converting them to just a handful. You can decide how many by setting the number of levels from 2–8 in its Options dialog box. You can also set Edge Fidelity (1–3) and Edge Simplicity (1–10) in the dialog box, which is shown in Figure 15.5.

Low Edge Simplicity and high Edge Fidelity settings produced the picture in Figure 15.6, which seems to be the most pleasing variation for this filter and photo combination. It's important to experiment with different settings every time you apply a filter to a new photo. What works with one picture might be totally wrong for another that is more or less complicated. In one combination or another, this filter manages to make almost any picture look good.

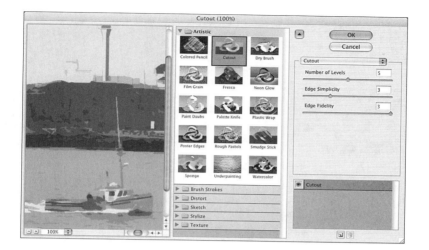

FIGURE 15.5
The Edge Simplicity setting refers to how much the edges are simplified.

FIGURE 15.6
Cutout filter applied.

Dry Brush

Dry brush is a term used by watercolor painters to denote a particular style in which the brush is loaded with heavily concentrated pigment and dabbed, rather than stroked, on the paper. Figure 15.7 shows the Dry Brush dialog box with a small Brush Size and a high Brush Detail. You can see the result in Figure 15.8.

FIGURE 15.7
Dry Brush filter
dialog box.

FIGURE 15.8
The Dry Brush
filter can look
very cool when
applied to the
right picture.

Film Grain

One reason that many commercial photographers are turning to high-resolution
digital photography is to get away from the problems caused by film grain. Film
grain is the inevitable result of applying a layer of chemicals to a piece of plastic.
When a picture is enlarged a great deal, you see the graininess of the chemicals as
specks in the picture. It can add an interesting texture to your pictures, if you apply
it carefully. It's often better to apply the Film Grain effect to selections, rather than
to the whole photo. Figure 15.9 shows what happens when it's misapplied.

Notice how the Film Grain filter picks up the texture on the water (see Figure 15.10). It makes the picture look gritty. The dark specks tend to concentrate in flat dark areas. If I use Film Grain on a photo with more contrast, it works much better.

Fresco

Fresco is an Italian term for a mural painting done on a wet, freshly plastered wall. The results of using Photoshop's Fresco filter have little resemblance to the classical fresco works by such artists as Botticelli or Michelangelo. However, it's an interesting filter—and potentially useful. It gives a spotty but nicely abstract feeling. You need to be careful not to let the picture get too dark because the Fresco filter adds a good deal of black to the image in the process of abstracting it. Figure 15.11 shows an example.

When I first applied the Fresco filter to this picture, it turned almost totally black. To make the picture and filter combination work, I first had to adjust the curves to lighten it overall. If you've forgotten how to do this, or jumped ahead to the fun chapters, go back to Hour 6, "Adjusting Color," and review it. Finally, I applied the Fresco filter with a setting of 1 for the Brush Size and Texture, and a Detail setting of 3. Remember that if some filter doesn't seem to work for you with the picture as is, you can change the filter's settings and then try again.

FIGURE 15.10
Grain applies dark specks to dark areas and light specks to highlights.

FIGURE 15.11
A fresh approach, but not exactly a fresco.

Neon Glow

It's hard to understand how the Neon Glow filter got its name; it has no resemblance to neon. As you can probably tell in Figure 15.12, the Neon Glow filter reduces the image to shades of two colors (the current foreground and background colors) and adds highlights around the edges of objects. You can choose a color in the dialog box and specify the width of the glow. If you use a very light color or gray, it can produce an interesting watermark effect. It turned the seascape into something like an x-ray. With the lime-green color applied, it was definitely weird.

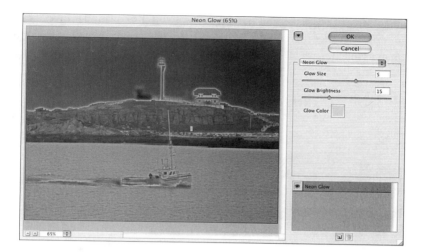

FIGURE 15.12
Neon Glow filter
applied.

That's a "No Glow"

The Neon Glow filter, more than most, should be applied to only certain kinds of pictures. Although it might give you an interesting spaced-out, surrealist land-scape, it does nothing at all for portraits, or other photos in which you want to pre-serve the character of the original. The Neon Glow filter is best used with a raster-ized type or blocks of color or shapes.

Paint Daubs

The Paint Daubs filter adds a square or wavy crosshatch texture to the image. You can set brush size and sharpness, and choose among several brushes. The Simple brush was used in Figure 15.13. Experiment with the settings for this filter; some set-tings work much better than others. In this example, I used a Brush Size of 4 and set the Sharpness to 11. I liked the result.

Palette Knife and Plastic Wrap

When a painter uses a palette knife, the result is large areas of smudged color blending interestingly at the edges. The Palette Knife filter, alas, doesn't do that. Instead it reduces the picture to blocks of color by grouping similar pixels and aver-aging them. The result, in my opinion, is not very interesting. However, you might have better luck with it than I did. Try it. If you don't like it, there's always Undo.

Plastic Wrap is another filter that I seldom use. It places a gray film over the whole picture and then adds white highlights around large objects. The Plastic Wrap filter is supposed to look as if you covered the scene with plastic film. Instead, it looks more like you poured liquid latex over it. The overall effect can be overwhelming.

Still, some of my friends have had good luck applying it to a smaller area, or in combination with other filter effects. It can be very effective as a way of making type look metallic.

FIGURE 15.13
Paint Daubs fil-
ter applied with
a Simple brush.

Poster Edges

Here's a filter that *is* worth playing with. Poster Edges locates all the edges in your image, judging by the amount of contrast between adjacent pixels, and *posterizes* the areas around them, placing a dark line around the edges. It does really nice things to parts of the sample photo, as you can see in Figure 15.14. But it's not so great on large flat areas, like the sky. The posterizing process tends to break up these areas into patches of dark and light tone. In such a case, apply Poster Edges to a selected part of the photo, rather than the entire image. For instance, the best way to use the filter on this seascape might be to apply it to the ocean and ground but not to the sky.

Rough Pastels

Rough Pastels is a terrific filter with an interface that's a little bit more complicated than the others because you can specify texture as well as the stroke length and detail. Figure 15.15 shows the Rough Pastels dialog box. Choose from the textures supplied or import one from another source. (You can create or import textures and save them as Photoshop documents; then you can open them and apply them as textures through this dialog box or the Texturizer filter dialog box.)

FIGURE 15.14
Poster Edges fil-
ter applied.

FIGURE 15.15
Rough Pastels
filter dialog box.

The Stroke Length and Stroke Detail settings seem to give the best results in the low to middle portion of their respective ranges, but, as always, experiment to see what works best for your image. Figure 15.16 shows the Rough Pastels filter applied to the sample picture. See it also in the color plate section.

FIGURE 15.16
Rough Pastels
filter on Canvas,
scaled to 80%.

Smudge Stick

Smudge Stick is a tricky filter. On light-colored areas, the Smudge Stick filter adds a
subtle, rather spotty texture that can be quite nice. On dark areas and lines, it adds
a smudge, making the lines heavier and the edges blurry. Figure 15.17 shows an
example.

FIGURE 15.17
Smudge Stick
filter applied.

Sponge

Have you ever tried painting with a sponge? It's a technique that's taught in some of the finer preschools and kindergartens. Basically, you dab a sponge into poster paint and then dab it on the paper. The results can be very nice, especially if you skip the poster paint and go straight to Photoshop's Sponge filter. On large flat areas, the Sponge filter gives a good imitation of a coarse, natural sponge (the kind they sell in the Sponge Market in Key West). In areas of detail, the sponge is a smaller one. You can, in fact, set the Brush Size, Definition, and Smoothness in the Sponge filter dialog box. One possible result is shown in Figure 15.18. This, again, is a filter that might be better used selectively, rather than on an entire image.

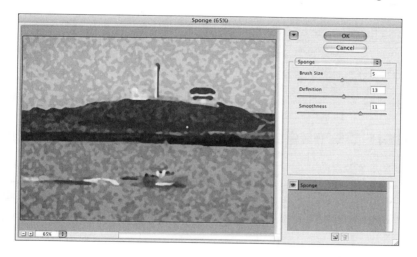

FIGURE 15.18
Sponge filter applied.

Underpainting

The Underpainting filter, which you read about in Hour 10, reduces everything to a somewhat grayed out, paler, and soft-focused version of itself. Use it as an intermediate filter on the way to an effect, rather than by itself.

Watercolor

In Hour 10, you learned ways to make a photo look like a watercolor. Unfortunately, applying the Watercolor filter isn't necessarily one of them. Figure 15.19 shows this filter applied to the sample image. The look isn't really watercolor, but it might have some uses. If you like the general effect of the Sponge filter, but it distorts your picture too much, try the Watercolor filter instead. It has the same "clumping" effect, but with smaller clumps. Both of these filters—Watercolor and Sponge—tend to darken the image quite a bit. You might need to lighten the picture before applying the filter. The color plate shows the same photo, with first the Watercolor filter, and then the Smart Blur filter applied to soften the edges of the clumps of paint.

FIGURE 15.19
Watercolor filter
applied.

Brush Strokes

I'm not sure why the Brush Strokes filters aren't part of the Artistic set. Artists use brushes, don't they? However, Photoshop's creators isolated these eight filters as the Brush Strokes set. What do they do? Cool stuff! Figure 15.20 is the original picture of a fishing shack, to which we'll be applying the next several filters.

FIGURE 15.20
Fisherman's
shed, unfiltered.

Accented Edges

Best if applied subtly, the Accented Edges filter enhances the contrast of edges. The dialog box lets you choose Edge Width, Edge Brightness, and Smoothness. The Brightness setting darkens edges if the amount is 25 or less; from 26–50, it progressively lightens them. Figure 15.21 shows the filter applied, with settings as follows: Edge Width, 2; Brightness, 17; and Smoothness, 6.

FIGURE 15.21
Keep edge width small for best results.

Angled Strokes and Crosshatch

These filters give a crosshatched effect, similar to but darker than the one applied by the Colored Pencil filter. The Angled Strokes filter is less dramatic than the Crosshatch filter. Figure 15.22 shows both.

FIGURE 15.22
The Angled Strokes filter applied on the left and Crosshatch filter applied on the right.

Dark Strokes

You can use the Dark Strokes filter with many images only if you set the Black Intensity to 0 and the White Intensity to 10 in the dialog box. Otherwise, it tends to turn the whole picture black. Even with a relatively light picture, you might need to keep the black number low and the white setting high. Figure 15.23 shows a carefully balanced application of dark strokes. My settings were Balance, 5; Black Intensity, 5; and White Intensity, 5.

FIGURE 15.23
Dark Strokes filter applied.

I never used to like this filter, but it does surprisingly nice things to the stuff on the workbench and the hanging fish net. Perhaps it will do wonders for one of your photos, or possibly it will just muddy things up. You really never know what will happen until you try some of these filters, even though you can theoretically define what effect they'll have on specific dark or light areas. After years of Photoshop use, I am still frequently surprised (and often delighted) by what a filter like this can do to a photo.

Ink Outlines

The Ink Outlines filter places first a white line and then a black line around every edge that it identifies (see Figure 15.24). You can set Stroke Length and Intensity in the dialog box.

Applied to a still life or landscape, the Ink Outlines filter can give you the look of an old woodcut or steel engraving. If you use it on a portrait, however, it might add warts, blobs, and other potentially undesirable effects.

Spatter

I really like the lacy effect on the fishnet in Figure 15.25. (Check it out in color, too.) My settings were Spray Radius 5, and Smoothness 5. Spatter is a filter that's potentially useful but, depending on the subject, might be better applied to selections rather than to the whole picture.

FIGURE 15.24
Ink Outlines filter applied.

FIGURE 15.25
Spatter filter applied.

Sprayed Strokes

Sprayed Strokes looks like Spatter, but less messy. The interesting thing about the Sprayed Strokes filter is that you can control the direction of the spray. Figure 15.26 shows what it does to the fishing shack. The settings for this variation were Stroke Length 15, Spray Radius 7, and Direction, Left Diagonal.

Sumi-e

Sumi-e is Japanese for brush painting, but the results of the Sumi-e filter can often look like the work of a crazed sumo wrestler, rather than a Zen master. This filter turns any area with any sort of detail almost completely black, even at the lowest settings. It renders all dark areas in black angled strokes. Use this filter to rescue a very light (underexposed) picture.

Sketch Filters

Photoshop has 14 filters lumped under the Sketch heading. Some, such as Bas Relief, must have landed there by default. They have little or nothing to do with the process of sketching. Others, such as Conté Crayon or Chalk and Charcoal, definitely mimic sketch media. Figure 15.27 shows the sample image: one of my cats, Reebok.

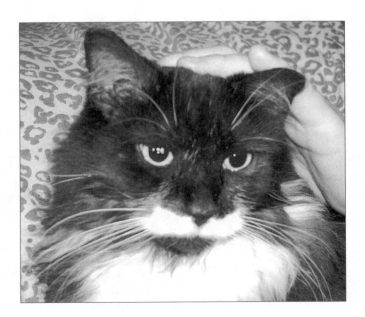

Bas Relief

The Bas Relief filter uses the foreground and background colors to create a low-relief rendering of your picture. If you choose colors carefully, it can look like copper foil, hammered metal, or carved stone. It's best used on pictures that have contrasting textures, or a textured subject against a flat background. Figure 15.28 shows the result. Perhaps it could have worked better if I had separated the cat from the bedspread.

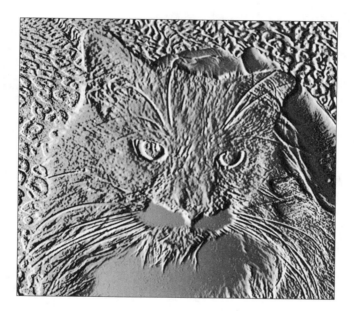

FIGURE 15.28
Use a dark background color for best results with the Bas Relief filter.

Chalk and Charcoal

With the Chalk and Charcoal filter, which reduces the image to three tones, you need to set the foreground to a dark color and the background to a light one. The third color, by default, is a medium gray, so choose colors that work with it. This filter can produce really beautiful drawings. Figure 15.29 shows the filter applied; notice how nicely it retained the highlights on the cat's face.

Charcoal

The Charcoal filter does much the same thing as the Chalk and Charcoal filter, but uses only the foreground and background colors. It's more difficult to control because there are only two colors. Experiment until you are satisfied. It helps if you beef up the contrast in the image, especially if there's detail to bring out.

FIGURE 15.29
Chalk and
Charcoal filter
applied.

Chrome

The Chrome filter appears to be a close relative to the Plastic Wrap filter described previously. It's only slightly more successful. As you can see in Figure 15.30, it's not really chrome-like. Perhaps, as my editor suggested, it's closer to looking into a choppy ocean of mercury. The Chrome filter removes the color from the image as part of its process. It also adds a large amount of distortion, as you can see. This filter is more useful on type.

FIGURE 15.30
Can you find the
cat face? I
can't.

Conté Crayon

I *love* this filter—it's done good things to every picture I have ever used it on. Conté Crayon works like the Chalk and Charcoal filter described previously but with the addition of background textures, using the same interface you saw in the Rough Pastels dialog box. Figure 15.31 shows the cat rendered in Conté Crayon on a sandstone background. For authenticity, the crayon colors are always in earth tones: a dark iron oxide red, black, or sienna brown. But feel free to use your imagination. Hot pink or lime green could be just what your photo needs.

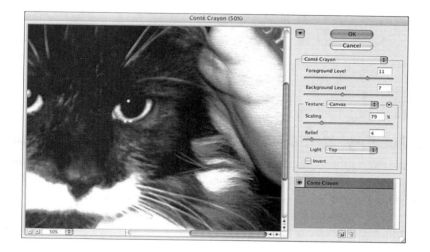

FIGURE 15.31
The Conté Crayon filter applied.

Graphic Pen and Halftone Pattern

These two filters do very similar things. Both reduce the image to whatever foreground and background colors you set. Graphic Pen then renders the image in slanting lines, whereas Halftone Pattern renders it in overlapping dots. On the proper subject, the Graphic Pen filter can be very effective. Halftone Pattern, however, merely looks like a bad newspaper photo.

Note Paper and Plaster

I don't understand the name of the Note Paper effect. I would have called it Stucco or maybe Flocked Wallpaper. See for yourself in Figure 15.32. The Note Paper filter uses the background and foreground colors, plus black for a shadow effect. Interesting, but note paper? The Plaster filter is very similar but smooth instead of grainy with the look of wet, runny, freshly poured plaster.

FIGURE 15.32
Note Paper filter
applied with a
low relief set-
ting.

Photocopy, Reticulation, Stamp, and Torn Edges

These four filters can be grouped together. Like many of the filters in this set, they
all convert an image to a two-color copy of itself. The Stamp filter loses most of the
detail, attempting to replicate a rubber stamp—but not very successfully. Photocopy
keeps most of the detail, resulting in the somewhat confusing image in Figure 15.33.
Reticulation adds dot grain to the Stamp filter, so it looks as if you stamped the picture on coarse sandpaper. Torn Edges is the Stamp filter again, only with the edges
of the image roughened.

FIGURE 15.33
Photocopy filter
applied.

Water Paper

The last filter in the Sketch set is a strange filter. Once again, I don't know how they named it. To me, the Water Paper filter produces an effect more like needlepoint, at least in the background. Unlike most of the filters in the Sketch set, Water Paper keeps the colors of your original picture, adding cross-hatching in the background and softening what it identifies as the subject of the picture. Figure 15.34 shows this filter applied to the portrait of Reebok.

FIGURE 15.34
Water Paper filter applied.

Summary

None of the filters described in this hour can produce a work of art from a lousy photo. The old proverb about silk purses and sows' ears applies. However, these filters can, when carefully and thoughtfully applied, elevate an ordinary picture to something quite extraordinary. Photoshop's filters are well worth taking the time to master. Spend some time with this hour's activity to work through the filter sets, so you can see—with your image in color and enlarged—exactly what the filters can do.

Workshop

Q&A

Q *How do I decide which filter to try?*

A As you've seen, you can't always judge a filter by its name. If you want an "art" effect, decide first whether you want full color or limited color. For the latter, look at the Sketch filters. Consider how abstract you want to get.

Cutout and Conté Crayon are both successful with most pictures.

Q *Is there a way to tone down a filter that does what I want, but does too much of it?*

A Yes. Near the top of the Edit menu is a command called Fade. It enables you to change the strength of the filter from 100%–0%.

Q *Are the filters that come with Photoshop CS all there are?*

A Nope! There must be literally thousands of filters that have been created by individuals or companies. You can locate them by searching for "Photoshop filters" or try the following Web pages:

`http://www.flamingpear.com/blade.html` (This site has several awesome sets of shareware plug-ins.)

`http://dir.yahoo.com/Computers_and_Internet/Software/Graphics/Filters_and_Plug_ins/` (This site links to many pages of filters and other useful Photoshop goodies.)

Quiz

1. The colored pencil filter applies

    a. Colored outlines around edges

    b. A crosshatched effect

    c. The color-wheel opposite of any color to which you apply it

2. Sumi-e is Japanese for

    a. A kind of painting

    b. Raw fish and rice

    c. Photoshop

3. Photoshop Artistic filters, in general, tend to _____ an image.

   a. Lighten

   b. Darken

   c. Sharpen

4. The Chrome filter is best used with type.

   a. True

   b. False

Quiz Answers

1. b. Try applying it twice with the image rotated 90 degrees between applications. It's a very cool effect.

2. a. If you knew sushi...

3. b. If an image is dark to start with, it might turn black.

4. a. At least, in my opinion...

Exercises

Use a picture you already have, or download one of the three used in this hour, and try the Artistic, Brush, and Sketch filters. (You can find them at the Sams Web site mentioned in the Introduction.) Experiment with different settings and then try applying the same filter a second time. Also, see how fading a filter can make its effect more useful. Try applying a second filter over the first. Some combinations work better than others. See whether you can find a combination that turns your photo into a work of art.

HOUR 16

Filters to Distort and Other Funky Effects

What You'll Learn in This Hour:

▶ Distort Filters
▶ Pixelate Filters
▶ Stylize
▶ Combine Filters

So far, the Photoshop filters described have been more or less useful. They corrected a fuzzy image or blurred a distracting background. Or they did something to turn your photo into an imitation drawing, painting, or mixed media construction. In this hour, we'll play with some filters that are mostly just for fun. These filters distort, stylize, and pixelate your picture. Most of these are meant for special effects. They're not for every day, but you are sure to find one or two that are helpful.

The key to success with these filters is to try as many different combinations of settings as you can with each filter and each new image that you bring into Photoshop. When you encounter a filter that relies on background and foreground colors, try several color combinations. Try a dark background and light foreground, and then reverse them. It's simple enough to do, if you just click the double-headed arrow next to the color swatches in the toolbox.

Distort Filters

Distort filters run the gamut from gentle glassiness to image-destroying twirls and even more. Want to make your picture look like it's going down the drain, melting, or being blown off the page? These are the filters for you. In this section, you'll try filters on the picture of a box of anchor chain shown in Figure 16.1 and in the color plate section.

FIGURE 16.1
Hand-forged iron chain.

Diffuse Glow

Not all the Distort filters actually distort. The Diffuse Glow filter adds a gentle haze of the background color over the lighter areas of a picture. This creates a glow that blends into the image. Hard to say why it is in the Distort family of filters, but it is cool, nevertheless.

The controls are Graininess, Glow Amount, and Clear Amount. Try to balance the Glow Amount and Clear Amount. For soft glows, I suggest that you keep the Graininess setting low. Higher numbers increase the graininess. This might be useful if you want a somewhat speckled look. In Figure 16.2, I used white as a background color, with Graininess of 9 and Glow Amount of 7 to place a glow on the chain. Using white as the glow color puts a soft foggy glow on the subject. Additional grain would make it look more like the beginning of a snowstorm.

Also, when you have a picture like this one, with limited color, you can often get a nice effect by increasing the saturation of the whole picture, either before or after you apply the glow. High saturation (90–100%) will really make the colors stand up and shout.

FIGURE 16.2
The Diffuse
Glow filter
applied.

Displace

The Displace filter is one of several Photoshop filters that requires the use of a displacement map, which works like a texture map, placing the image over a grid that creates a textured look. You can find a collection of these in the Photoshop Plug-Ins folder. Set the amount, in a percentage, for horizontal and vertical displacement in the dialog box. Higher percentages have a greater effect. After you set the amount of displacement, you're asked to choose a displacement map from the collection in the Plug-Ins folder inside the Photoshop folder. Figure 16.3 shows a partial list of maps, and Figure 16.4 shows the results of applying the Crumbles map. The effect you get from this filter depends on which map you choose. You need to try them to see their effects because the names aren't necessarily helpful and the previews don't look much like the resulting effects.

Displacement maps are images or patterns that are saved in the Photoshop format and applied as part of a mathematical formula that moves each pixel in the original image according to the values in the displacement map. You can actually use any Photoshop image as a displacement map. Just choose it instead of one of the default files.

FIGURE 16.3
Choosing a displacement map.

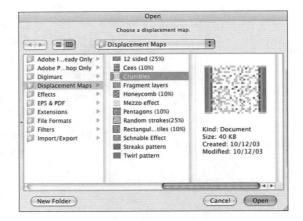

FIGURE 16.4
The Displace filter applied.

Glass and Ocean Ripple

I decided to lump the discussion of these two filters together because of the similar effects they can have on an image. They both create displacements that make the image seem as if you are looking through glass or water.

The Glass filter offers you a greater amount of control (see Figure 16.5). You can select a type of texture, such as Frosted, Tiny Lens, or Canvas, and you also can load a texture of your own. Just choose Load Texture from the pop-up menu at the bottom of the dialog box.

Use the Smoothness slider to increase the fluidity of the image. Keeping the Distortion low and the Smoothness high will create a subtle effect. Try the opposite for a much more distorted image. The scaling slider adjusts the scale of the distortion from 50%–200%.

The Invert button at the bottom of the dialog box replaces the light areas of the texture with dark areas, and vice versa. Figure 16.6 shows the results of applying the Glass filter.

FIGURE 16.5
The Glass filter dialog box.

FIGURE 16.6
The Glass filter applied.

The Ocean Ripple filter is quite similar. It creates an effect that makes your image appear as though it is under water. It is an effective filter and easier to use than the Glass filter because it has only two options on its dialog box.

Pinch, Spherize, and ZigZag

The Pinch, Spherize, and ZigZag filters are lumped together, not so much because they do the same thing but because their interfaces are so similar. Figure 16.7 shows the dialog box for the ZigZag filter.

FIGURE 16.7
The ZigZag filter dialog box.

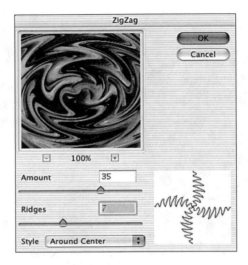

Keep an eye on the grid provided at the bottom of the box as you drag the Amount slider higher or lower. It can give you a good indication (as can the preview area) of what is going on in the image. See the final version in Figure 16.8. It turned the chain into a pool of melted iron.

This is a tough filter to master, but a good one to have in your bag of tricks. The Spherize filter can be very useful on occasion, but don't try to force it. If it doesn't look right, you can try Liquify to create a similar "bubble" effect. Also, you can set a negative amount using the Amount slider to generate a hollow instead of a bump. And if this doesn't satisfy your needs, try the Pinch or ZigZag filters.

Shear

You can tell a great deal about most filters just by their names, but this isn't one of them—unless you're an engineer. The Shear filter warps images horizontally. (It moves them in relation to the vertical line.) Drag the line in the Shear dialog box, as shown in Figure 16.9. Watch the preview to see the effect of shearing the picture. You also can add more control points on the curve by clicking it at different areas. These control points are like joints; they enable you to redirect the motion of the curve.

FIGURE 16.8
The ZigZag filter applied.

Figure 16.10 shows the results of the Shear filter. I've set the image to Repeat Edge Pixels, so it now looks as if the warping left a smudge of pixels behind.

One Way

The Shear filter works in only one direction. If you want something to shear vertically instead of horizontally, simply rotate the image before you apply the filter. Then rotate it back again.

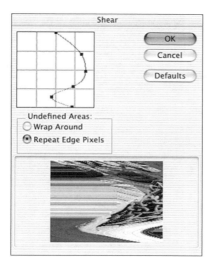

FIGURE 16.9
The Shear filter dialog box.

FIGURE 16.10
The Shear filter in use, with Repeat Edge Pixels applied.

Twirl

The Twirl filter does precisely what its name suggests: It spins an image. You can control the amount of spin with the slider within the dialog box. This is a great filter for creating special effects. So far, I haven't found very many subtle uses for the Twirl filter, but if you can, go to it. It creates wonderful, kaleidoscopic effects and can also simulate a swirling drain. It looks great with the chains, as shown in Figure 16.11.

FIGURE 16.11
The Twirl filter applied.

Pixelate Filters

When one is "pixilated," according to my dictionary, he or she is intoxicated, but in a charming, bemused, whimsical, pixyish way. Pixelation can be equally whimsical and bemusing, if applied to the right subjects. Misused, it just turns everything into a bunch of dots. *Pixelation* happens when similarly colored pixels are clumped together to form larger units, which might be square (pixel-shaped), round, or rounded off by anti-aliasing to whatever form they take. It happens, unasked for, if you're printing a picture at too low a resolution. You end up with large pixels forming jagged shapes that look like they were built out of a child's plastic block set.

When controlled, the effect can be quite interesting. Photoshop includes a set of Pixelate filters that produce different effects all based on the notion of clumping together similar pixels. It's best to apply these effects to simple subjects and to those with strong contrasts, such as the photo of the flower in Figure 16.12.

Crystallize

Most of the Pixelate filter set looks best if the effect is applied with the Cell Size quite small. Otherwise, the crystals, facets, and so on become so big that the image becomes unrecognizable. In Figure 16.13, I applied the Crystallize filter at a Cell Size of 8. It adds reasonable distortion without destroying the shape of the flower. In Figure 16.14, I pushed the Cell Size up to 50, destroying the picture. You can even set the Cell Size as high as 300, but it might turn the entire picture into one or two cells, depending on the resolution of the original image. An extremely hi-res image might require a Cell Size in the 100's.

FIGURE 16.12
A Dogwood in bloom.

FIGURE 16.13
The Crystallize
filter applied.

FIGURE 16.14
Same filter,
overapplied.

Pointillism and Mosaic

Comparing the work of Georges Seurat to that of some of the "sloppier" French
impressionists can be quite a revelation. Seurat's dabs of paint, all neatly clustered,
form elegant scenes from a distance and form equally elegant abstract patterns up
close. It would be nice if Photoshop's Pointillism filters did the job as neatly and scientifically as M. Seurat did. They don't.

This is, however, one case where the smallest setting doesn't work as well as some of the larger ones. I first tried the picture using 3 pixels as the Dot Size. I got a spotty picture, as I expected, but it looked more like video noise than pointillism. Using a slightly larger Dot Size (8) produced an image a little closer to what I was looking for. But when I tried a much larger size, approximately 25, I ended up with base-balls. Figure 16.15 shows all three effects. Be sure to set your background and fore-ground colors to something appropriate to the image because Photoshop uses them in creating the dots.

There's a Mosaic setting in the Pixelate effects, but all it does is to make larger pixels out of the smaller ones. The result is the sort of thing used to hide the faces of the people being arrested on all those late-night police shows (see Figure 16.16).

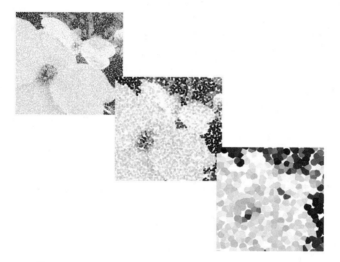

FIGURE 16.15
From top to bot-
tom, Dot Sizes
3, 8, and 25.

FIGURE 16.16
Alleged perpe-
trator, con-
cealed by the
Mosaic filter.

The Stylize Filter

The Stylize filter family offers some wonderful effects. They are creative, and you can use them to add final effects or touches to an image. This section touches on the most interesting of the filters, including the Find Edges filter, the Glowing Edges filter, and the Wind filter.

Find Edges, Glowing Edges, and Trace Contour

These three effects sound as if they should look alike. They actually do look somewhat alike, with Glowing Edges and Find Edges being much more dramatic than Trace Contour. The Find Edges filter removes most of the colors from the object and replaces them with lines around every edge contour. The color of the lines depends on the value at that point on the original object, with lightest points in yellow, scaling through to the darkest points, which appear in purple. The picture looks like a rather delicate-colored pencil drawing of itself. Find Edges works best, naturally, on photos that have a lot of detail for the filter to find. In Figure 16.17, I've applied it to a digital photo of a hot dog cart. Find Edges sometimes becomes more interesting if you apply it more than once to the same picture. If you apply it once and don't like the result, try it again before you move on to a different filter, or increase the contrast in the original photo before you try again. Touching up areas afterward with the Sponge tool can bring out colors you hardly knew were there.

FIGURE 16.17
Notice how Find Edges picks up the detail of the sidewalk and the soda can collection.

Unfortunately, you cannot set the sensitivity of the Find Edges filter. In practical terms, this means that you have to prepare the picture before you trace it. Begin by running the Despeckle filter (in the Noise submenu) so that Photoshop won't attempt to circle every piece of dust in the background. If you don't want the background to show, select and delete it, or select your object and copy it to a separate layer first. You can also use the Edit→Fade command to back off the strength of the filter. Using this filter with different blending modes can produce some spectacular effects.

Glowing Edges is more fun because it's prettier, and because you can adjust it to have maximum impact on your picture. Glowing Edges turns the edges into brightly colored lines against a black background. The effect is reminiscent of neon signs. You can vary the intensity of the color and the thickness of the line.

In Figure 16.18, I've applied Glowing Edges to the same picture. It works especially well with busy pictures with lots of edges. The more it has to work with, the more effective the filter is. Be sure to check these out in the color section. Black and white doesn't do them justice.

FIGURE 16.18
Some of the color remains, but the background goes black.

Trace Contour, like several of the previous filters, works better on some pictures if you apply it several times (see Figure 16.19). The Trace Contour dialog box has a slider setting for the level at which value differences are translated into contour lines. When you move the slider, you are setting the threshold at which the values (from 0–255) are traced. Experiment to see which values bring out the best detail in your image. Upper and Lower don't refer to the direction of the outline. Lower Outlines specifies where the color values of pixels fall below a specified level; Upper Outlines tells you where the values of the pixels are above the specified level.

FIGURE 16.19
The image was traced several times with different settings.

I like to use this filter to place different tracings on different layers and then merge them for a more complete picture.

The Wind Filter

The Wind filter creates a neat directional blur that looks, strangely enough, like wind. You can control the direction and the amount of wind in the dialog box (see Figure 16.20). This is a great filter for creating the illusion of movement and for applying to type. It works best when applied to a selected area rather than to the entire picture.

One of this book's editors adds, "My favorite Wind filter effect is making a brushed metal look by adding noise to the basic metal color and then hitting it with wind from both directions, followed by a bit of tweaking for the perfect illusion." Thanks, Jon!

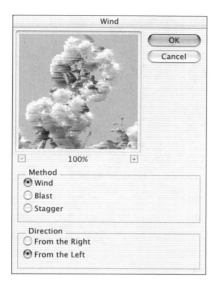

FIGURE 16.20
The Wind filter
and its dialog
box.

The Emboss Filter

Honestly, the Emboss filter doesn't do much for most photos. It turns an image into
a bas-relief, although not as well as the Bas Relief filter does. In the process, the
Emboss filter converts the image to medium gray. Photoshop also has a layer effect
called Emboss, which seems to be a lot more flexible, but it is also more complicated
to use. The Emboss filter has only three options: Shadow Angle, Height, and
Amount. Figure 16.21 shows a piece of embossed type, first embossed with the filter
and then with the layer effect.

FIGURE 16.21
On top, the
Emboss filter;
below, the
Emboss layer
effect.

Occasionally, you come across a photo, like this picture of a lion, that almost begs
to be turned into a corporate logo or advertising image (see Figure 16.22). In such
cases, the Emboss filter can do wonders to make the picture just abstract enough to
be useful. In working with this photo, I found that the angle at which the filter is
applied can make a major difference. Figure 16.22 shows two angle settings applied
to the same picture. The Height and Amount settings were the same for both.

FIGURE 16.22
On the left, the lion seems to come forward. On the right, he recedes.

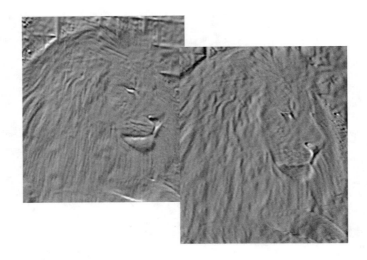

Combining Filters

Some people like things plain. I'm not one of them. I want the whipped cream, marshmallow, nuts, and cherry on my ice cream, and I'm seldom satisfied with using just one Photoshop filter. And with an arsenal of about 100 Photoshop filters (plus dozens of third-party add-ons), why shouldn't you take advantage of as many as possible? In the remaining few minutes of this hour, let's look at some interesting combinations.

Texturizer

You can add a texture to any photo, no matter what you have already done to it. The Texturizer filter (Filter→Texture→Texturizer) places a pattern resembling canvas, burlap, brick, or sandstone over your image, making it look as if it's on paper with that texture. The canvas texture is particularly nice if reduced in scale. Figure 16.23 shows a photo of a seascape, first treated with the Dry Brush filter and then texturized. Look for it in the color section.

Rough Pastels and Film Grain

The Rough Pastels filter adds a strong directional quality to Figure 16.24, another view of the same beach. A single filter is applied to it. However, because the Rough Pastels includes a texturizer, it's effectively two filters.

FIGURE 16.23
Dry Brush on
Sandstone
applied.

FIGURE 16.24
Rough Pastel
beach scene.

In Figure 16.25, I kicked it up a notch by adding Film Grain over the pastels, which lightened the image, and came up with what I think is an even more interesting result. Both beach pictures are in the color plate section.

FIGURE 16.25
The beach with
added Film
Grain.

The possibilities are endless. If you can imagine a style or treatment for a picture, chances are excellent that Photoshop can do it. As a final picture and final filter combination, here's how you can turn a photo into an instant mosaic. Start with any picture that has reasonably large areas of flat color. Figure 16.26 shows my original picture, the yellow lily.

FIGURE 16.26
Unfiltered lily.

Try it Yourself

Convert a Photo to a Tile Mosaic

To turn this picture into stained glass:

1. Apply the Crystallize filter (Filter→Pixelate→Crystallize) with a moderate Cell Size. I used 21 as the Cell Size in Figure 16.27.

FIGURE 16.27
Crystallized lily.

2. Next, apply the Ink Outlines filter (Filter→Brush Strokes→Ink Outlines) with the Stroke length set to approximately 9, and the light and dark intensity differing at 18 and 30, respectively. Figure 16.28 and its color plate show the result—a reasonable rendering of a glass tile mosaic. You can, of course, draw in any lines that Photoshop didn't trace completely, and you can go over the glass panels and change their colors if you want.

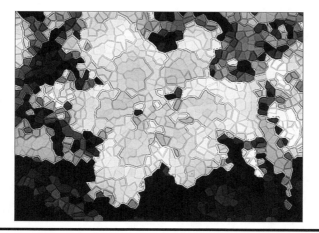

FIGURE 16.28
Lily mosaic.

At the risk of sounding like a broken record, let me leave you with a final reminder to keep experimenting. You never know what a filter or combination can do to a particular picture until you try it. The way that Photoshop calculates the filter effects means that some filters can look very different, according to the kind of picture to which they are applied. You can't always predict what will happen, but the unexpected effects are frequently wonderful.

Summary

This rather long hour has been devoted to some of Photoshop's stranger filters: the Distort, Pixelate, and Stylize filters. They're not for everyone—and certainly not for every image—but they're fun to play with and can occasionally create some interesting, unusual, and beautiful effects. Filters can add interesting dimensions to type, also.

Don't hesitate to add a second filter over the first. Many times, the second filter or second application of the original filter can turn a ho-hum picture into something marvelous. At worst, you can always undo your efforts.

Workshop

Q&A

Q *I am bored with the textures that the Texturizer adds. Can I make my own?*

A Of course. One way is to scan items with interesting textures or make digital photos of them. Save as a grayscale file in native Photoshop format, and apply them from the Texturizer filter dialog box by choosing Load Texture from the Texture pop-up menu and opening the texture file you want to use.

Q *What kinds of things make good textures?*

A Look around you. Napkins (either cloth or paper), fabrics of any kind, barn boards, sandpaper, uncooked pasta, practically anything semi-flat that you can photograph or scan.

Q *Does the Glass filter include more than one kind of glass?*

A This is Photoshop; your choices are virtually unlimited. In addition to the textures provided, you can choose Load Texture from the pop-up menu and open any Photoshop document to apply as a texture.

Quiz

1. A displacement map is

   a. Another name for a texture map

   b. A pattern applied as a mathematical formula to move individual pixels in an image

   c. A chart showing how colors shift between your monitor and printer

2. The Spherize filter can make your picture appear to bump _____.

   a. Out only (convex)

   b. In only (concave)

   c. Either way

3. Pointillism was originally a painting style introduced by

    a. Jean Luc Pontille

    b. Georges Seurat

    c. Leonardo da Vinci

    d. Jean-Luc Picard

4. The Shear filter can be used vertically or horizontally.

    a. True

    b. False

Quiz Answers

1. b. Some, like the Schnable Effect filter, are named for their creators.

2. c. It depends on how you apply it.

3. b. See an example at `http://www.ibiblio.org/wm/paint/auth/seurat/`
   `baignade/`.

4. b. If you want to apply it vertically, you must rotate the image.

Exercises

Start with a simple picture and add filters one by one until you can't recognize the image. See how many filters you can apply on top of each other before the picture disappears.

Go back to your original picture, and use the Colored Pencil filter. This should give you an interesting image. Save it. Try the other filters over it until you find at least three that work well with the Colored Pencil filter. Whenever you have time, repeat this exercise, starting with a different filter.

PART IV

Text Effects and Getting Plugged In

HOUR 17

Adding Type to Pictures

What You'll Learn in This Hour:

▶ The Type Tools
▶ Setting Type
▶ Creating Drop Shadows
▶ Cutting and Filling Type
▶ Adding Glows
▶ Creating Bevel and Emboss Effects
▶ Warping Text
▶ Setting Type on a Path
▶ Checking Your Spelling

If a picture's worth a thousand words, how many more is it worth if you add words to the picture? Well, never mind... The fact is, though, sometimes you have to add type to a picture for one reason or another. Long ago, Photoshop was infamous for its type handling, but the type problems have been long since solved. Now, you can add type directly onto a page, edit it, and control its leading, tracking, and kerning. You can set type vertically as well as horizontally, and you can warp it onto a predetermined path. You can set text either by clicking a start point on the page, or by dragging the Type tool to create a bounding box and then filling the box with type. You can even set type on a path, just like in Illustrator. There are almost too many cool type features to cover in a single hour. But, let's start with the basics.

A few things haven't changed. Photoshop still places your type on a separate type layer. Type must still be *rasterized* before you can apply filters. You can apply gradient fills and layer styles such as drop shadows, bevels, and embossing, either before or after type is rasterized.

Types of Type

At this point, a few words about type might prove helpful. You'll be dealing with two kinds of type: outline type and bitmapped type. Outline type, which is also called vector type, consists of mathematically defined shapes, in either PostScript or TrueType language. Outline type can be scaled to any size without losing its sharp, smooth edges. Bitmapped type is composed of individual pixels. The sharpness of bitmap type depends on the type size and the resolution of the image. If you scale bitmapped type to a larger size, you'll see jagged edges, or *jaggies*.

When you enter type on the screen in Photoshop, the letters are drawn as vector type. That's why you can edit them, reshape them, and play with them as much as you like. Anything you do just changes the numbers, and computers are very good with numbers. However, Photoshop is a bitmap program. It manipulates pixels, not vectors. To make the type part of the picture, it must be converted from vectors to pixels, or *rasterized*.

Think of it this way: Vector type that you set on a type layer is sort of floating. It's not nailed down, therefore it's easy to edit words or to move letters closer together. It's there, but it's not completely part of the image yet. When you rasterize type, you are, in effect, nailing it onto the layer. When you print a Photoshop image that has a type layer, the printer actually receives the image with rasterized text, even if you haven't rasterized the layer.

The Type Tools

In case you haven't noticed previously, Photoshop's creators tend to include as many ways as they can think of to do things. The Emboss effect in the last hour is a case in point. Working with type is another. There are three ways to control type in Photoshop. When you select the Type tool (the capital *T* in the toolbox), the Tool Options bar will display the basic type options: font, size, alignment, and a few other controls. The Type tool options are shown in Figure 17.1. (I had to cut the bar into two pieces so that it would fit on the page.) There are also Character and Paragraph palettes that give you even more control. Let's look first at the Type Options bar.

FIGURE 17.1
The Type Options bar.

Starting at the left side of the bar, you'll see the Type Orientation button—a capital *T* with two arrows. The arrows indicate horizontal or vertical orientation. Click the button to change the type from horizontal to vertical and back.

After that come menus listing all your available fonts, styles, and font sizes, from 6–72 points. You can set larger or smaller type by typing the point size into the entry field. Next, you can set the amount of anti-aliasing to apply: none, sharp, crisp, strong, or smooth. Anti-aliasing produces smooth-edged type by partially filling the edge pixels. As a result, the type edges appear to blend into the background. Generally speaking, anti-aliased type looks better, especially if you are working with small type sizes. (Anti-aliasing can also make small type sizes appear more readable when viewed online.) Select from four levels of anti-aliasing to modify the appearance of type online. Crisp makes your type somewhat sharper; Sharp makes it as sharp as possible. Smooth makes it smoother, and Strong makes it look heavier.

The next set of three buttons enables you to select left-, centered-, or right-alignment. The color swatch, which is the same as your current foreground color, lets you set a color for the type. Clicking the swatch opens the Color Picker, just like clicking any other swatch.

The warped *T* button with the curved line under it represents one of Photoshop's coolest type tricks. It's called Warp Text, and it gives you access to 15 preset type paths ranging from arcs and flag to fisheye. I'll go into greater detail about this tool later in the hour.

Finally, there's a button called Palettes, which opens the Character and Paragraph palettes; we'll consider these palettes next. But first, let's set some type.

Try it Yourself ▼

Getting Started with Type

Start a new image in Photoshop. Make it the default size and give it a white or colored background.

1. Click the Type tool.
2. Use the Tool Options bar to select a font and size, and a color that contrasts with the background.
3. Set left-alignment.
4. Click the Type tool on the left side of your page. You'll see a blinking black line. That's the insertion point.
5. Type your name.
6. Click and drag the cursor over the type to select it.
7. Click the colored square in the Tool Options bar and change the color of the type.
8. Change the point size.
9. Change the font.
10. Click anywhere in the toolbox to deselect the Type tool.

▼

11. Click the Type tool again.

12. Click somewhere near the top of the page, and click the Text Orientation button (the first one on the Tool Options bar). Now type your name again. It's vertical.

13. Click any type layer, then click the Text Orientation button. That type turns vertical, too. To set horizontal and vertical type on the same page, start a different type layer.

14. Play with the type options until you understand them.

The Character Palette

The Character palette (see Figure 17.2) gives you control over kerning, tracking, and shifting the baseline, in addition to the font, style, color, and size options also found on the toolbar. You can determine your type options with the Character palette before you set the type on the page, or you can use the palette to reformat type you've already entered.

FIGURE 17.2
The Character palette enables you to control the appearance of the letters.

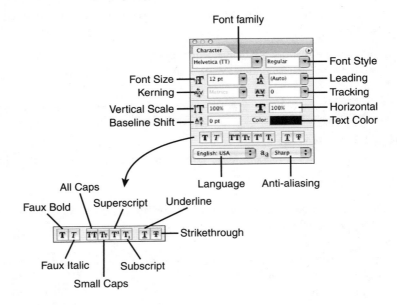

The menus on the Character palette give you access to your installed fonts, font sizes, and styles, just as on the Tool Options bar.

The entry field next to the A\V button controls kerning. *Kerning* refers to the amount of space between adjacent letters. Most fonts, in larger sizes, require some kerning to adjust the spaces between letter pairs such as AV and WA. Otherwise, you'll notice a gap. The default setting for kerning is Metrics, which means that Photoshop will apply the font metrics information built into the font. If you decide to override this, you can do so by entering a different kerning amount in the field. *Tracking* is similar to kerning, but involves evening out the amount of space between letters in a word or phrase rather than just in a pair. Tracking can be tight (enter negative numbers) or loose (enter positive numbers). Setting 0 in the tracking field means that no tracking is applied.

Leading (pronounced to rhyme with *heading* or *bedding*) determines the amount of vertical space between lines of type. If you're setting a single word or one line of type, you won't need to deal with this. As soon as you add a second line, leading becomes important. Because leading is measured from the baseline of a line of text to the baseline of the line above it, the amount of leading has to be greater than the point size of the type to keep the lines from touching or overlapping. (The *baseline* is the invisible line on which type is placed.) Photoshop's default for leading is 120%, which is to say, 10-point type gets 12-point leading, and so on up the scale.

You can set a distance from the baseline for subscript and superscript types. Why you'd be using superscripted footnotes in Photoshop, I'm not sure. Using a superscript to correctly set an equation such as Einstein's $E=mc^2$ could prove useful, though.

There's a row of buttons at the bottom of the palette for type styles, and menus for language and anti-aliasing. In addition to faux bold and faux italic, you can select all caps, small caps, superscript, subscript, underscore, and strikethrough. The language menu lets you choose fonts with foreign characters and calls the appropriate dictionary when you check spelling. (Yes, there's a spelling checker. You'll learn more about it later in the hour.)

The Paragraph Palette

What Photoshop defines as a paragraph would horrify grammarians. In Photoshop terms, any line followed by a carriage return is a *paragraph*. The Paragraph palette sets options that relate to the entire paragraph, such as alignment, justification, and indentation (see Figure 17.3).

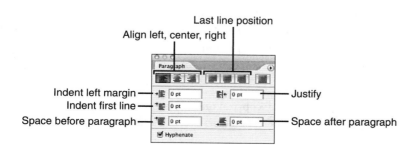

FIGURE 17.3
The Paragraph palette allows you to set alignment and indentation on any paragraph.

The buttons on the top-left side of the palette display the possible alignments: left, centered, and right. You also have these options on the Tool Options bar. Additionally, there are buttons to let you set justified type with the last line to the left, centered, right, or fully justified. These latter options are available only if you have set text in a bounding box. *Justified*, for those not familiar with the term, means that the type is artificially stretched or compressed as necessary to make all the lines exactly the same length. The opposite of justified is ragged, which is how it looks.

The other buttons and windows on the Paragraph palette let you set paragraph indents, first line indents, right indents, and additional space before or after a paragraph. These, obviously, are most useful when you are dealing with a block of text.

Setting Type

As mentioned earlier, there are two ways to set type in Photoshop. The first and simplest way is to click in the image where you want the type. If you select flush left on the Tool Options bar or the Paragraph palette, your text will stream right from the insertion point. If you select centered, Photoshop will center the words around your insertion point as you enter them. Flush right sends the text shooting off to the left from your right-side insertion point. Figure 17.4 shows examples of each.

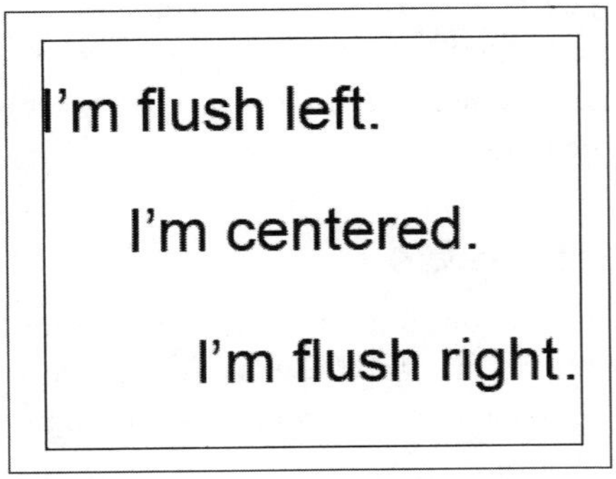

FIGURE 17.4
Text flows from the insertion point.

I'm flush left.

I'm centered.

I'm flush right.

The other way to position type, when you have to set a lot of it or when you need to fill a specific area, is to drag a bounding box. Simply select the Type tool, click it to create the corner point of the box, and drag until the box is approximately the right size and shape (see Figure 17.5). You can go back after you've entered the type and resize the box, if necessary.

Enter the text by typing it, or by copying and pasting from another program. Type always appears on a new layer. Type layers are indicated in the Layers palette by a large letter *T*, as you can see in Figure 17.6. Type layers are named according to the first word(s) you type. If you want to edit your type, switch to the Type tool and click in the text. Double-clicking the *T* also selects the type so that you can apply changes. If the type's not selected, you can't edit it.

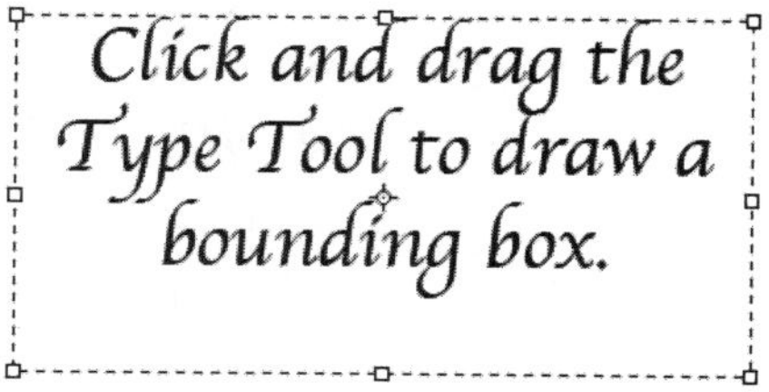

> *Click and drag the
> Type Tool to draw a
> bounding box.*

FIGURE 17.5
The type bounding box determines the shape of the block of text. Photoshop automatically breaks the line at the edge of the bounding box.

If you have set a lot of text into a bounding box, now's the time to adjust the leading, paragraph spacing, and indents, if any. The Layers palette will show you only the first few words of the type you have set, so be sure that you have selected the right type layer, if you have several.

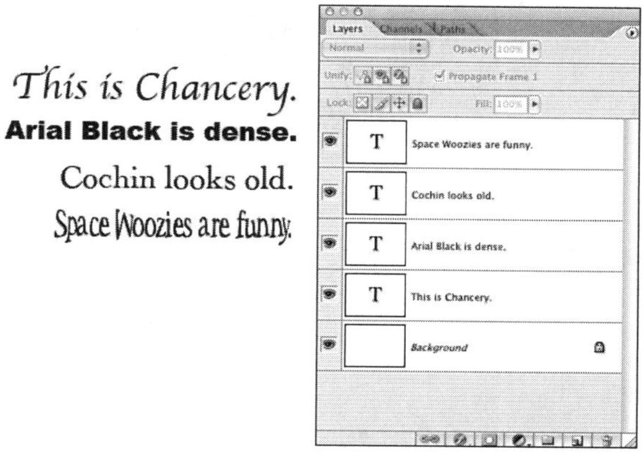

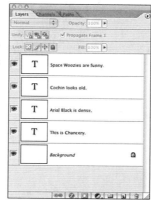

FIGURE 17.6
Each line is on a different type layer.

After you create a type layer, you can edit its text and insert new text, or delete some. You can make changes in the text itself or in the font, style, or size. You can change the orientation of the type from horizontal to vertical; you can apply or change the type of anti-aliasing. You can move, copy, or change the order of layers, or change the layer options of a type layer as you can for a regular layer. You can use layer styles. You can apply most of the Transform commands from the Edit menu, except Perspective and Distort. (To apply the Perspective or Distort commands, or to transform just part of the type layer, you must first rasterize the type layer to convert it to a regular layer.)

There's one more step to go through before your type is part of the page. The type must be rasterized before you can apply the full range of filters to it. (You can apply warps and styles to the layer before it's rasterized.) Before type is rasterized, it's as if it were placed on a separate layer but not stuck down. *Rasterizing*, in effect, sticks the type to its layer. After the type is rasterized, you can't go back and edit it again. To rasterize type, select the type layer, and choose Layer→Rasterize. You can rasterize type layers one at a time or do all the layers at once. Or you can simply flatten the image, if you're sure that you are finished making changes to the wording.

After you place the type on the screen, you can have some fun with it. Apply filters to your heart's content. Pour paint into selected letters. Select the type and distort it. Figure 17.7 shows just a few of the things you can do.

FIGURE 17.7
Filtered, dis-
tressed, and
distorted type.

By the Way

Fat Faces Are Good

Filters are most successful on bold type. Thin, delicate letters tend to get lost. If you can't read the type, it's not saying anything.

Creating Drop Shadows

As soon as you start looking for drop shadows, you'll find them everywhere: in magazines, television ads, Web sites, and in every other form of media you can imagine. Everyone is discovering that as soon as you put a shadow behind some text or an image, it takes on added dimension that can really make it pop forward into view. It's a nice and easy special effect for giving something more visual weight and making people pay attention. Drop shadows are a layer style rather than a filter, so you can apply them before or after you rasterize the type.

The following are some tips for effectively using drop shadows:

▶ Don't use them all over the place! If you use too many shadows, everything pops forward equally, and you lose the benefit of using shadows to draw attention to one particular object.

▶ Make sure that all your shadows look alike! If you use shadows on multiple objects in the same area, make sure that the shadows all go the same way, and make sure that the depth of the shadow is appropriate. If the shadows are all different and haphazard, people will notice.

▶ Don't make the shadows too dark. It's easy to go overboard and create deep, saturated shadows that overwhelm what's supposed to be getting all the attention: the foreground image. Keep shadows light and subtle. Figure 17.8 shows what can go wrong (and right).

Too Dark

Too Fuzzy

Too Far Away

Just right!

FIGURE 17.8
A too-dark shadow, a too-blurred shadow, a dark and badly positioned shadow, and one that finally gets it right.

Photoshop includes a powerful and easy drop-shadow function, along with the Glow, Bevel, Emboss, Satin, and Overlay functions, that will do wonders for type and graphics alike. You will find these effects in the Layer→Style submenu. Remember that you can use drop shadows and other layer styles on objects as well as on type. You can't apply a layer style to anything that's not on its own layer, though. Painting on the background, and then trying to add a layer style won't work.

Try it Yourself ▼

Creating a Drop Shadow for Text

Follow along to create a cool drop shadow.

1. Create a new Photoshop document with a white background.

2. Select the Type tool and enter some words. Choose any font that appeals to you. For now, don't worry about color, kerning, or setting a baseline. Figure 17.9 shows the basic type.

▼

FIGURE 17.9
The original art
in need of a
drop shadow.

Lost in the shadows...

3. Choose Layer→Layer Style→Drop Shadow to open the Layer Style dialog box, as shown in Figure 17.10. Check the Preview box so that you can see your work as you create it. The trickiest part of this operation is getting the screen arranged so that you can see both the dialog box and the type you're working on.

4. Set the Blend Mode to Normal, Multiply, or Darken. Otherwise, you won't see the shadow. Click in the color swatch next to the Mode menu to change the color of the shadow. This opens the Color Picker.

FIGURE 17.10
Applying a drop
shadow in the
Layer Style dia-
log box.

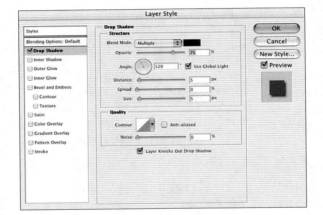

5. Adjust the shadow's Opacity and Angle as desired, by clicking the slider and dragging on the clock face to change the angle, or typing numbers into the boxes.

6. Set the Distance to determine how far away you want the shadow to be from the word or object. Set the Size according to the amount of shadow you want to see. Set the Spread according to how distinct you want the edges of the shadow to be. Click OK when you are happy with your drop shadow. You can still change it, of course. Until you merge the layers, you can make any changes you want. I've added a little bit of art to create the finished effect you see in Figure 17.11. (They're just a couple of shapes created with the Shape tools, filled and with drop shadows added.)

Lost in the shadows...

FIGURE 17.11
Drop shadow type, with symbols and more drop shadows.

Drop Shadows Should Drop

I find that shadows often work better if they're *below* the original image; that is, moved down instead of up when they're offset. When the shadow falls downward, the object looks more like it's popping up.

Drop shadows can be tricky. When it looks right, you know it. Trust your eyes to tell you what looks realistic and what looks fake, and be willing to experiment with settings. Try making your shadow twice as blurred as your original setting, or twice as far offset. You might be surprised!

Variation: Shadows on Backgrounds

Of course, drop shadows don't have to occur just over white or solid-color backgrounds. You can have a drop shadow fall over a texture, an image, or anything else that strikes your fancy.

Try it Yourself

Placing Drop Shadows on a Background

Follow these steps to apply drop shadows from text onto a background image and add depth to the background itself.

1. First, create the Photoshop image. I started with a photo of the World's Cutest Baby™. I added some type and put the baby photo on its own layer, deleting part of the background to allow a gradient to show through as a backdrop. The important thing to remember is to create a *new layer* for each element for which you want to have a drop shadow (see Figure 17.12). For a refresher on layers, refer to Hour 11, "Layers."

FIGURE 17.12
The original image before drop shadows. I've attached the Layers palette so that you can see the separate layers.

2. Add a shadow to the text first, by following the steps in the previous section (see Figure 17.13). If the background and the lettering are similar colors or values, consider adding a bit of outer glow as well.

Notice how you can actually see the texture of the background right through the new shadow. The result is a pleasant, realistic effect. You can make even more of the background show through by adjusting the Opacity slider in the Layers palette. Give it a try.

3. Now create some depth in the background itself. I'll start by adding a drop shadow to the baby layer. Then I'll scale the effect (choose Layer→Layer Style→Scale Effects) so it's more in proportion to the size of the baby. Figure 17.14 shows the final version. It's also shown in the color section.

Notice how the text casts a shadow on the baby and the bed, and the baby in turn casts a shadow on the background.

FIGURE 17.13
A drop shadow applied to the text.

FIGURE 17.14
Drop shadows at work.

Tasteful Typography

There are thousands of typefaces available. Buy them in CD-ROM collections, download them online, use the ones that come with other applications, and so on. Trying out wild typefaces can be so much fun that you might lose sight of the goal—to communicate. Before committing to a design, print out a sample page and hold it up at full arm's length. If you can't read it easily, maybe even with your reading glasses removed, try to determine why and consider tweaking the design. It might be a simple matter of making the type larger or giving the lines of type more space (leading). You might need to rethink your background or add an outline. A drop shadow might help—or might make matters even worse. Try combinations of different type and image treatment.

Remember to use "curly" quotes and apostrophes rather than the straight kind. You're setting type, not using a typewriter that has only one kind. The professionals don't use underlining very often, either. The underline habit also comes from the old manual typewriter days, when no other typographical tool was available to give emphasis to words. Use bold or italic type styles instead.

Cutting and Filling Type

The words you paste onto a picture might be filled with meaning. They can also be filled with pictures. Here's how to do some of my favorite Photoshop tricks.

Half the battle is finding a picture to work with. The other half is finding a nice fat typeface that leaves plenty of room for your pictures to show through. In this case, I'm using a photo of a pile of maple leaves.

First, I click the Type tool and hold down the mouse button to select the Type Mask tool, which is used for making type-shaped selection marquees. I've selected a bold face called Fat Man. To make it even bolder, I'll select Faux Bold from the Character palette's pop-up menu, shown in Figure 17.15. Check out the other character options on this menu, too.

When I position the cursor and start to place my letters, something surprising happens. The screen goes into Quick Mask mode, and turns pink. As I enter the letters, they appear to be in a contrasting color, but when I finish typing and deselect the Type tool, they turn into a selection marquee and the temporary mask goes away. Figure 17.16 shows how this looks onscreen.

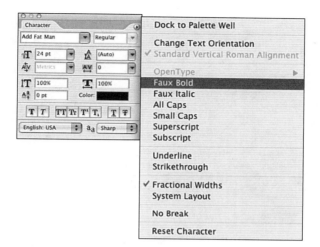

FIGURE 17.15
Faux Bold adds
extra boldness
to any charac-
ter, whether
already bold
or not.

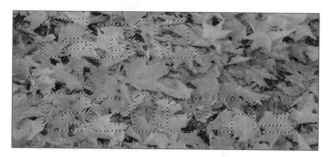

FIGURE 17.16
The letters are
active selec-
tions.

Now I can press Command+X (Mac) or Control+X (Windows) and cut out the letters.
I'll quickly open a new image file and paste them on it for safekeeping. Figure 17.17
shows the cut-out lettering and the photo it came from.

It's Automatic

If you open a new image file after having copied or cut a selection, Photoshop will
automatically insert the dimensions of the selection in the New dialog box.

By the Way

I'm going to use these letters as part of the title slide for a PowerPoint presentation.
So, I'll drag a copy onto a fall scene photo, and then add a deep red drop shadow
behind the words, and an inner glow in pale yellow to help make them stand out.
Figure 17.18 shows the final logo, after all these tricks. Be sure to see it in color, too.

FIGURE 17.17
The type's cut
out of the
photo.

FIGURE 17.18
The letters jump
right out.

Adding Glows

There are other layer styles on the menu besides drop shadows, and most are useful. In the last example, I needed a glow as well as a shadow to separate the letters from the background. Let's try working with glow styles. You can use a layer style to place a glow—or in this case an outline—around your type. You can also apply an inner glow as I just did, to make it appear as if the letters themselves are glowing. This is a great effect to add emphasis around a piece of text or to make it stand out from a busy background. Figure 17.19 shows a fairly ordinary text and photo combination.

In Figure 17.20, I've applied a light Outer Glow around the letters. It's simply another way of defining them from the background and is useful when a drop shadow isn't appropriate. (Be sure to see this image in the color section.) Other objects can glow, too, and I'll discuss these in more detail in the next hour.

FIGURE 17.19
The letters
don't quite
stand out
enough.

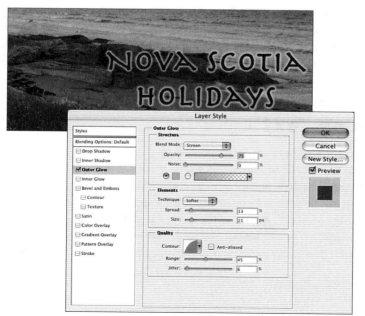

FIGURE 17.20
The glow helps
separate the
text from the
background.

Creating Bevel and Emboss Effects

These two effects are found in the Layer Style dialog box. Both produce raised type—Bevel affects the edges of the type, producing a raised, but flat, letter surface; Emboss gives the appearance of curved or rounded letters. Figure 17.21 shows examples of both. I added a little noise to the beveled stone with the Add Noise filter. Perhaps, with all that gooey jam, I should have carved a scone instead?

FIGURE 17.21
The difference between Bevel and Emboss is obvious.

You can vary the effect of these tools by changing the blending modes, by varying the opacity, and by changing highlight and shadow colors. As always, the best way to see what they do is to experiment with different settings.

Metallic Type

There are lots of ways to create metallic type using the layer styles, particularly with the Bevel and Emboss options. Choose appropriately metallic colors, such as pale blues for silver and light yellows for gold. Remember to also set highlight or shadow colors to something appropriate, not necessarily black or white. Then just start experimenting. Try adding noise and then blurring it for a brushed metal finish. Also, check out the Styles palette, which lists a great selection of prepackaged style combinations.

Warping Text

One of the major complaints about Photoshop used to be that you couldn't set type in anything but a straight line. If you wanted, say, a wavy line of text, you had to either position the letters one by one or set the type in Illustrator or something similar and import it into Photoshop. It was a nuisance, at best. Those days are long gone. As of Photoshop 7, Adobe added warped text. Rather than drawing your own path, the Warp Text dialog box allows you to select from 15 preset paths. You can also warp and distort the paths as necessary. Figure 17.22 shows a list of the presets.

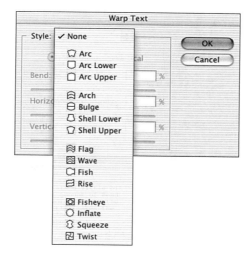

FIGURE 17.22
Multiline pre-
sets work with
one, two, or
more lines of
type.

The dialog box settings, shown in Figure 17.23, are a little bit tricky at first. Use the sliders to increase the amount of Bend applied to the path. Moving to the right bends words up; to the left (negative numbers) bends them down. Distortion makes the line of type appear to flare out on one end (Horizontal Distortion), or flare from top to bottom (Vertical Distortion).

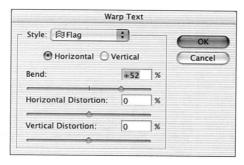

FIGURE 17.23
Move the slid-
ers left or right
to change the
settings.

In Figure 17.24, I've applied some of the warp styles to various bits of type. The best way to master this tool is to play with it. Set a line or two of type and try the differ-ent kinds of warp on it. Move the sliders around. You can't break anything.

FIGURE 17.24
Guess which
wave forms
were used on
these words?

Setting Type on a Path

Prepare to have some fun—you can put type on a path, any path, as smooth or raggedy as you care to draw it—and it's absolutely easy to do. First, draw a path. Here's mine in Figure 17.25.

FIGURE 17.25
Use the handles
to tweak the
curves until the
path is as
smooth as you
want.

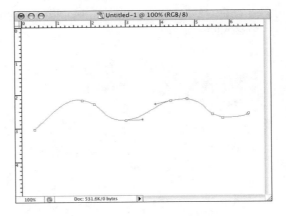

Then, select the Type tool and place the cursor at the start of the path. You'll see a little bit of thread at the bottom of the cursor. That means it's connected to the path. Just start typing and the baseline of the type will automatically align to the path, as shown in Figure 17.26.

After you've placed the type, you can use the handles to adjust the path as needed, or use the cursor to drag the type along the path, if it didn't quite line up as you had hoped. Once you've set the type, you can go on and do any of the other things we've discussed, adding shadows, glows, filters or what have you. Just one word of warning here—it's easy to get carried away. Make sure your type is readable.

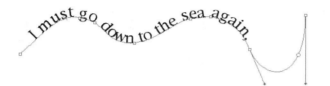

FIGURE 17.26
You can still edit this type, until it's raster-ized.

Checking Your Spelling

This isn't something you would ordinarily expect in a graphics program, but it's a big help now that Photoshop has so much type capability. When you're not sure about spelling in a headline, simply go to Edit→Check Spelling. Photoshop will check your work and, if it finds a possible mistake, will offer you choices. Figure 17.27 shows mine.

FIGURE 17.27
Most of Photoshop's guesses are pretty close.

Although Photoshop's never going to be much of a word processor, and you might never need this function, it's nice to know that you can use it to find and change words or characters in your poster text. Find and Replace Text, also accessed from the Edit menu, searches for a word, letter, or symbol you enter and then automatically changes it to whatever you have entered in its place. Naturally, neither of these functions work after you have rasterized the type.

Summary

Photoshop doesn't have all the type capabilities of a more traditional desktop publishing program, but it can handle most of your typographic needs, whether it's producing a single headline or a block of text precisely placed over a photo. Of course, getting the letters into the picture is only the beginning. After you have the type on the page, you can apply all Photoshop's filters, blending modes, and tools to it. You can warp it, distort it, punch it out of a graphic, or make the letters out of a picture. With Photoshop, your words can come alive. If all you want to do is set type, use a program such as InDesign. If you want to do strange and wonderful things to type, Photoshop has all the tools you need.

Workshop

Q&A

Q *Is there any way to improve the appearance of small type online? Anything less than 20 points looks like it runs together.*

A By default, Photoshop displays type using fractional character widths. This means that the spacing between characters varies, with fractions of whole pixels between some characters. In most cases, fractional character widths provide the best spacing for type appearance and readability. However, for type in small sizes that will be displayed on-screen, rather than printed, fractional character widths can cause type to run together, making it hard to read. Use the pop-up menu on the Character palette to turn off fractional character widths. Using a full-width character will keep small type from running together.

Q *I have a lot of fonts installed on my Macintosh, and it takes forever to scroll down the list to find the one I want. Any suggestions?*

A Despite OS X's built-in font management, I still prefer to use a font management program such as Suitcase or Font Reserve to sort my fonts into sets. I keep a set for serif type and separate ones for sans serif faces, display faces, and special-purpose fonts such as Handbill, StarTrek, and Wild West. I activate only the suitcases with fonts I am likely to need.

Q *I've typed in the text I want and have rasterized it. The problem is I found a typo and when I try to go back and edit the text, I can't. What can I do?*

A After you rasterize text, it's converted from an editable text layer to a graphic that can't be edited by any of the Type tools. Make sure that you have the type you want and that it's all spelled correctly before you rasterize it. To save your project, you might be able to go back in the History palette to a state before you rasterized the type.

Q *Is there a way to use cut-out type to reveal another picture underneath?*

A Certainly. Place the photo you want to see through the cutouts on a layer underneath the layer that will be cut. Switch to the layer you want to cut, and then enter your letters using the Type Mask tool and cut. To enhance the effect, apply a drop shadow to the top layer.

Quiz

1. Photoshop CS can set type horizontally or vertically.

    a. True

    b. False

2. Every piece of type needs a drop shadow.

    a. True

    b. False

3. Photoshop places type on

    a. The Background layer

    b. Special type layers

    c. Regular layers

    d. Adjustment layers

4. If there's a *T* in the box on the Layers palette, it means

    a. You can double-click it to open the Type tool

    b. That the layer is a type layer

    c. Layer styles have been applied to the type

    d. Both a and b

5. There's no way to set small caps in Photoshop.

    a. True

    b. False

Quiz Answers

1. a. And if you want it diagonal, rotate it.

2. b. Use them sparingly.

3. b. Type layers are editable until they are rasterized.

4. d. The italic *F* symbol indicates layer styles.

5. b. Small caps is one of the options in the Character palette.

Exercises

1. Find a nice landscape photo, and add a title to indicate where you shot it.

2. Add a drop shadow behind the lettering. Try changing the color of the type and shadow so it stands out.

3. Now, try using a glow instead of the shadow. Which do you like more?

HOUR 18

Special Effects and Useful Tricks

What You'll Learn in This Hour:

- ► Glows
- ► Lighting Effects
- ► Reflections
- ► Extracting Selections
- ► Using Notepad
- ► Contact Sheets and Picture Packages
- ► Working Efficiently

This hour is going to be a little different. We're going to kick back and explore some of the cool things you can do with the awesome tool known as Photoshop. Think of this hour as a collection of recipes—some special effects that you can add to your mental list of Photoshop tricks and use again and again, along with some timesaving tricks. You'll learn about extracting backgrounds, using stickies, and making contact sheets and picture packages. Just follow the steps, and you'll be a Photoshop wizard in no time.

Your Mileage May Vary

Very detailed instructions will be given in this hour, and I'll use very specific settings along the way. It's important to realize that, as you create these special effects with your own images, my settings might not be the best settings for you. Different resolutions, sizes, and colors call for different settings. So, when you see specifics, feel free to play with them a bit and see whether you can get even better results with your artwork.

Truly, that's the real secret of getting better and better at Photoshop: **Never stop experimenting!**

Glows

Creating a glow is an easy special effect. It's essentially a drop shadow that isn't off-set at all from the original object and is often in a color other than black. In Hour 17, "Adding Type to Pictures," you learned how to use Photoshop's Glow layer style to apply a glow to lettering. Here's a different and easy way to put a glow around type or an object.

▼   **Try it Yourself**

Create a Glow Around an Object

Let's create a basic glow around an object. I have an object that's practically screaming for a glow. It's a translucent trackball. You can download this from the book's web page. It's called trackball.jpg.

When the main book page has loaded, click the Downloads link to get to the files, or use an example from your own collection. It's helpful if the object that will glow is easy to select.

1. Select an image to which you would like to apply the effect. Figure 18.1 (and the color section) shows the original photo.

2. First, you need to select the object that will glow; in this case, the ball. The Elliptical Marquee tool does a fine job on this particular image. If there are cutouts in your object, be sure that they're selected, too.

3. Copy the object and paste it onto a new layer. Now you have two layers: one with the complete image and one with just the selected object.

4. Use the menu on the Layers palette to duplicate this layer. Now, you have the entire scene as background and two layers of the same cutout object. Select the lower of the two.

5. Click anywhere in the clear area with the Magic Wand, and choose Select→Invert to select just the ball or whatever you are using as a glow object. Expand the selection (Select→Modify→Expand) by 50 pixels (or what-ever's appropriate for your image). Feather the edges by 20 pixels.

6. Use the Path menu to make a work path around the selection. Use the Fill Path command to fill the work path with an appropriate glow color. Use the Delete Path command to lose the line around it. Now, only the color remains on the layer. Figure 18.2 shows this step.

7. Make sure that the glow is selected. Use the Gaussian Blur filter to diffuse the glow. I used a setting around 10 for a generous glow.

▼

FIGURE 18.1
Ball, bright but
not glowing.

FIGURE 18.2
I've turned off
the top layer to
show the glow
better.

▼

8. Assemble the layers so that the glow is beneath the object. If the shadows interfere with the glow, remove them. Figure 18.3 shows the final product.

FIGURE 18.3
Be sure to see this in the color plate section. It's not as effective in black and white.

Of course, this is Photoshop, so there are several ways to accomplish more or less the same result. You could skip the preceding step 6, and simply fill the selection and go on from there. You could even use the Outer Glow Layer Effect, although it doesn't look quite as good to me. It's certainly quicker and easier, and it might be exactly what you want.

We've only scratched the surface of glow effects, so I encourage you to try all sorts of settings and colors. Experiment with the brightness and size of the glow. Also try other blur filters for glows that imply movement or dimension. Have fun!

Lighting Effects

Lighting effects refers to a whole range of special effects related to how objects are lit. By illuminating objects in a unique way, you can change the entire feel of an image, drawing attention exactly where you want it.

Try it Yourself

Generate Lighting Effects on an Object

The primary tool, as you might expect, is Photoshop's Lighting Effects filter.

1. Start with an original image. Perhaps this is an image that is fairly flat as far as brightness is concerned. Perhaps it's an image that simply needs to be more three-dimensional to match its content. Figure 18.4, showing a doll and stuffed toy, is such an image. (If you want to follow along, download the image beardoll.jpg from the Sams website.)

FIGURE 18.4
The original image, in need of some special lighting.

2. At this point, I need to decide whether I want to light the entire scene or just the doll. Lighting just a selected object is more dramatic; lighting the whole canvas is more natural. I opted for a spotlight on her.

3. Choose Filter→Render→Lighting Effects to open the Lighting Effects dialog box (see Figure 18.5). From the Style pop-up menu near the top, choose Spotlight. You'll see the preview of your image on the left with the new spotlight effect.

4. Although Photoshop ships with a number of neat default settings, it's fun to play around with the various sliders and values. Don't be intimidated by the number of choices here.

FIGURE 18.5
The Lighting
Effects dialog
box.

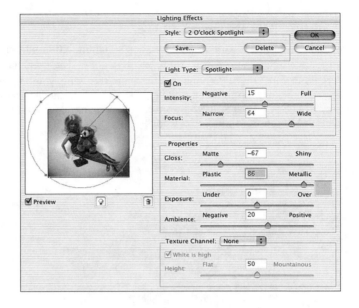

To change the direction and/or shape of the spotlight, simply grab the handles around the oval you see on the left side of the dialog box. You can move them around as you want. You can even move the center point. Move everything around so that it looks something like what you see in Figure 18.6.

FIGURE 18.6
Glamour lighting
is easy.

5. Now it looks like the non-lit parts of the image are too dark. You need to bring the overall lighting up a bit, so adjust the Ambience slider up a notch, and change the color of the spotlights.

6. That's pretty good. What if you tried something very different? Figure 18.7 shows the triple spotlights. You could make each one a different color, by clicking in the color swatch box and choosing something new. However, I think I like the previous version better.

FIGURE 18.7
This is over-done. Sometimes simple effects are best.

Reflections

If you often find yourself bringing various images together in Photoshop (and I predict you will), you can't simply toss the images together and have the new image look realistic. As you've seen, effects such as shadows are essential to create a realistic-looking environment. Creating reflections is another technique for doing this.

Try it Yourself

Add Reflections to a Surface for Realism

Let's look at an example to see how you can add reflections to your toolkit of special effects:

1. Let's say I have an object (which I do) that I want to insert into an image I've created. First, I need to create a background. I'll use the Gradient tool to lay down a very simple oblong gradient from dark to light. Then I'll add some

noise from the Noise filter so that it has a little texture. I want this to look like a photographer's seamless background, so I'll use Transform→Distort to drag the bottom out wide. Figure 18.8 shows this stage.

FIGURE 18.8
A very simple "studio" back-drop.

2. The sides of the top part should be vertical, so I'll select the backdrop part-way up and distort again to straighten the side borders (see Figure 18.9). As a final touch, I'll select the gray area and apply the Plastic Wrap filter to make the surface look like rippled plastic.

3. I have a small object that I'll set onto this background. (You can download the image from the book's website. It's called box.jpg.) I think you'll agree that the effect isn't very realistic (see Figure 18.10). It looks like the box and background came from two different sources (which they did, but I don't want it to be so obvious).

4. To start working on a reflection of the box on the background, duplicate the box layer. In the Layers palette, move this new layer below the original box layer because you want the reflection to appear underneath the original object.

5. With the Reflection layer active, choose Edit→Transform→Flip Vertical. This flips the reflected box upside down.

FIGURE 18.9
All ready to put something on.

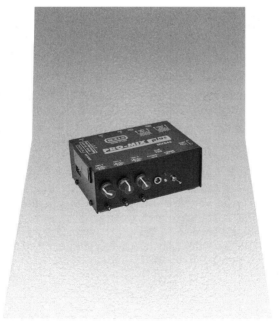

FIGURE 18.10
The box in its new environment.

▼

6. Select the box's reflection and use the Move tool to move it down. Remember that only part of the box will reflect, and use the Lasso to trim away and move the parts that won't show. You will usually find that you need to use the Distort or Skew commands to move a reflection into its proper position and shape. The adjacent edges of the two boxes should meet precisely without much backdrop visible between them (see Figure 18.11). Then you can discard the spare parts.

It looks like a reflection, right? Well, sort of. It looks like a reflection only if the surface is *perfectly* reflective, like a mirror, which it obviously isn't.

FIGURE 18.11
The box flipped
and moved
down into place.

7. To make the reflection realistic, some of the background has to show through, just as you saw with drop shadows. Adjust the Opacity slider for the Reflections layer until the reflection looks more realistic and blends in with the surface.

If you're satisfied with the reflection as it is now, you're done. Unfortunately, I'm picky and seldom satisfied. The reflection still looks too perfect to me. The background isn't that smooth.

8. To introduce a little dirtiness into the reflection, it's time for another trip to the Plastic Wrap filter. With a little fiddling, and some help from the Smudge tool, I was able to make the reflection bumps match those on the backdrop. Then I blurred the reflection slightly. Check it out in Figure 18.12.

Okay, now it's looking good. The box image is now interacting with the floor image, creating a realistic effect. There's just one more thing bugging me: the wall behind the box. Shouldn't the box and wall interact? Shouldn't the box be casting just a bit of a shadow on the wall? I think so. I can use the Drop Shadow layer style to add this shadow, being sure to move the light source so that the shadow falls on the wall, not on the reflection (see Figure 18.13).

▼

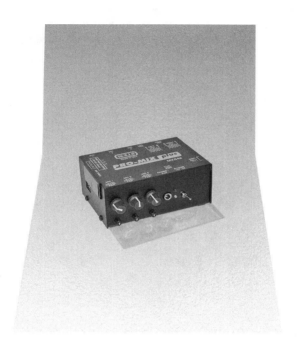

FIGURE 18.12
With its opacity reduced, the reflection looks much more realistic.

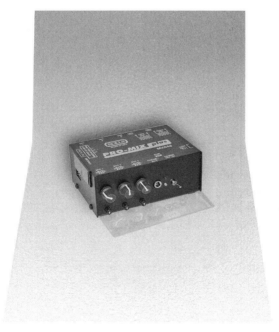

FIGURE 18.13
A touch of shadow on the wall adds to the illusion of space.

9. Finally, back to the filters. Filter→Render→Lens Flare lets you put just a little extra light reflection on the background so there's an obvious reason for the shadow. Figure 18.14 wraps it all up in one. Be sure to see it in color.

FIGURE 18.14
Now the box casts a shadow onto the backdrop as well as a reflection.

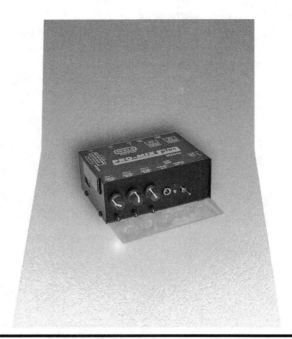

Well, I'm satisfied. The image now looks like one piece instead of a box and a handful of extra pixels thrown together. That's what special effects like reflections can do for you.

Extracting Selections

Some selections are easy to do; some are like pulling teeth. That's why Photoshop includes an extraction utility. The Extract command (Filter→Extract) enables you to isolate a foreground object from its background. Even objects with fuzzy, soft, or hard-to-define edges can now be separated from their backgrounds with very little difficulty.

To extract an object, choose Image→Extract to open the Extract dialog box. If it reminds you of Quick Mask, you're right. It's more than just a mask, however.

Extract removes whatever you don't want to keep. You can pre-select the object with the Magic Wand or use the Extract Edge Highlighter tool to draw around the edges of the object. Then you define the object's interior by using the Paint Bucket to fill in the outline. Click the Preview button to preview the extraction. You can refine and preview the extraction as many times as you want. Figure 18.15 shows the Extract dialog box. I've selected the bottle and jar, using the Extract tools to refine the selection. When you are ready to perform the extraction, Photoshop erases the background to transparency, leaving just the extracted object.

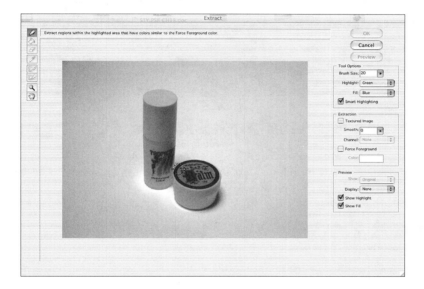

FIGURE 18.15
Many of the Extract dialog box's tools look like the regular Photoshop tools.

Notepad

If you've ever used those sticky notes (and is there anyone who hasn't?), you're going to love Photoshop's Notes tool. Click the Notes Tool icon in the toolbox, and then click the picture where you want the note to be referenced. You can even insert notes outside the picture. Notes can be any size you want, and they are even personalized with your name on top. This is a great feature if you pass pictures back and forth with other members of a workgroup. I also use it when I download a bunch of photos and want to make notes about what to work on, when I have time. Figure 18.16 shows one of my current projects.

If a note covers something you want to see in the image, you can drag the actual note to another location. To get rid of a note, drag its icon completely off the screen.

FIGURE 18.16
If you close a note, its icon remains. Double-clicking reopens it.

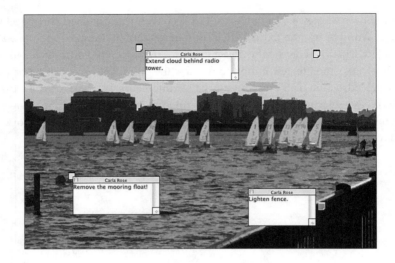

Contact Sheets and Picture Packages

In this automated world, it's only fair that Photoshop should provide ways to automate some of the more mundane tasks that we must occasionally do. Two of my favorites are contact sheets and picture packages.

Contact Sheets

If you come from a background of darkroom photography, as I do, you're already used to making contact sheets of every roll of film you process. When you download images from a digital camera, you might use a transfer program that displays your photos as slides in a sorter, or you might simply copy them from card to hard drive. If you follow the latter course, you don't know what you have until you open each picture in Photoshop and look at it. That takes time. Suppose that you could simply glance at thumbnails of your pictures, and choose the ones you wanted to use without deciphering the cryptic numbers from the camera or having to open each picture separately. Much easier? You bet.

All you need to do is to save the images for the contact sheet into a folder. You can even place several subfolders inside one main folder. Then you choose File→Automate→Contact Sheet II to open the dialog box in Figure 18.17 and select the folder you want to make contacts of.

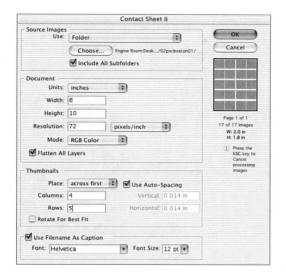

FIGURE 18.17
Click Include All
Subfolders if
you want their
contents to be
included in the
contact sheet.

If you're going to print your contact sheets, be sure that the document size is no larger than the paper in your printer. Be sure that it fits inside your printer's printable area, in fact—most printers don't print right to the edge of the paper. Low resolution (72 dpi) is usually good enough to see what's going on, and saves time and space. Decide how many thumbnails you want per page, and set them up across or down as you prefer. Finally, if you want to identify them on the contact sheet (which I strongly recommend), click the Use Filename As Caption check box and select a font and size for the caption, which is the name of the file. When you click OK, Photoshop will automatically open your files one at a time, create thumbnails, and paste them into a new document. You can then save and print this contact sheet just like any other page. Figure 18.18 shows a typical contact sheet. Note that the pictures are in alphabetical order.

Picture Packages

Remember school pictures? You got a page with one 5×7, a couple of "stick-on-the-fridge" size for the grandparents, and a couple of wallet-size photos for mom and dad. Around the holidays, your local discount store or department store offers similar deals. You don't need to bother with them. You can do your own and save a bundle.

FIGURE 18.18
Each little photo
has its filename
as a title.

Choose File→Automate→Picture Package to open the dialog box. There's a menu that
lets you locate the photo you want to package, or you can use whatever's already open.
Choose a paper size according to whatever your printer can handle. In Photoshop CS,
you have options for 10×16 and 11×17 paper as well as 8×10. Figure 18.19 shows the
dialog box and Figure 18.20 shows the photo size selection menu open.

FIGURE 18.19
Here's where
you set up the
package.

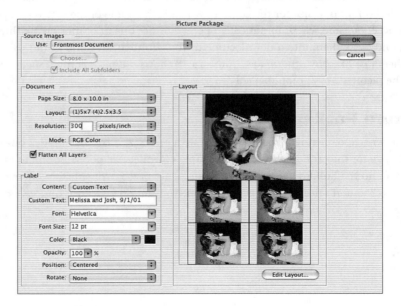

```
(2)5x7
(1)5x7 (2)2.5x3.5 (4)2x2.5
(1)5x7 (2)3.5x5
(1)5x7 (8)2x2.5
✓ (1)5x7 (4)2.5x3.25 (2)1.5x2
(1)5x7 (4)2.5x3.5
(4)4x5
(2)4x5 (2)2.5x3.5 (4)2x2.5
(2)4x5 (8)2x2.5
(2)4x5 (4)2.5x3.5
(4)3.5x5
(20)2x2
(16)2x2.5
(8)2.5x3.5
(4)2.5x3.5 (8)2x2.5
(9)2.5x3.25
```

FIGURE 18.20
Portrait sizes, wallets, little tiny ones, even passport sizes—what more could you want?

Label your photos, if you want to, with the name of the subject, your studio name and copyright notice, date, proof warning, or whatever you want to put there. Choose a font and size for this type, and decide where on the page it should go. Unfortunately, you are limited to only a few fonts, most more suitable for copyrighting or captioning than for adding an elegant title.

Set the resolution as appropriate for your printer, and click OK. Photoshop will assemble the package for you, just as it does with the contact sheets. When you're ready, save it and/or print it. Figure 18.21 shows the page, ready to print.

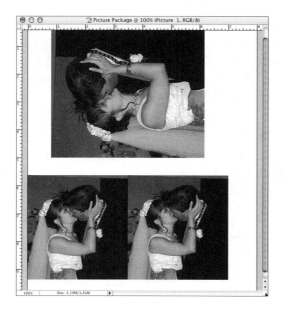

FIGURE 18.21
Be sure that you retouch your photos before you assemble them.

If none of the layouts is quite what you want, you can click the Edit Layout button and change sizes and arrangements to make your own custom package. Click a photo outline and drag to resize it, or enter a new size in the dialog box, if you prefer. Click Add Zone to add another photo to the layout. Figure 18.22 shows the Edit Layout dialog box.

FIGURE 18.22
Photoshop will rotate your photos and resize them to fit the layout.

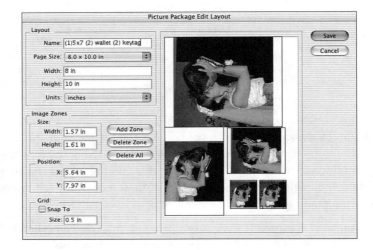

Working Efficiently

If you use Photoshop every day, and run a lot of pictures through it, you'll soon pick up some tricks of your own to work faster and smarter. The easiest trick to learn is to use the tool selection shortcuts: Z to select the Zoom tool, B for Brush, and so on. As you become familiar with the tools and what they can do, you'll find you go back to the same brush sizes or type fonts again and again.

Tool Presets

Photoshop makes it easy for you to reuse your favorite tool settings by providing a palette of tool presets. Click the Tool Preset button at the left side of the Tool Options bar, or open the Tool Presets palette. You'll see a list of the current presets for the tools you are using. The palette menu lets you add more presets, delete these, group them, rename them, and otherwise juggle them around.

To add a brush tool preset, first switch to the tool for which you want to make a preset, and then use the Brushes palette and Tool Options bar to construct the shape, action, and other attributes of the desired brush tool. Don't forget that clicking the names of the listed attributes (not on the check boxes) gives you access to their controls. The check boxes simply toggle them on or off. When you've set your brush the way you want it, give it a name. Close the Brushes palette so it's not in the way. Now, go to tool presets and open the palette menu. Again, name your brush or accept the default name, and it will be added to the current preset menu (see Figure 18.23).

Other non-brush tools such as the Crop tool and the Type tool can also have presets. These can be set and saved using the Tool Options bar and the Preset menu.

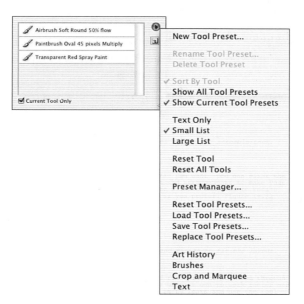

FIGURE 18.23
Tool presets for the Brush tool.

Summary

Creating a special effect isn't about specific instructions and narrowly defined settings—it's about experimenting with all that Photoshop has to offer and being pleasantly surprised by new discoveries. As you use Photoshop's features (especially its filters) more and more, you'll uncover an endless stream of special effects. This hour is just a small taste of what's possible. Have fun creating your own special effects!

The tricks in this hour are also just a taste of what Photoshop can do. Explore the menus. If you see a command you don't understand, try it. You might find something you can use.

Workshop

Q&A

Q *How do I place a reflection in water?*

A Much the same way as you did on the backdrop, except that I would apply an appropriate Ripple filter to the reflection, as well as blurring it. Depending on the kind of water, you might want to apply Blur first, and then Ripple, or vice versa. Try both and see which looks more realistic.

Q *I'm a schoolteacher, and I have taken photos of my class, which I would like to post on the bulletin board. Is there an easy way to print them all at the same size, with the kids' names underneath?*

A That's not hard. Make sure that the child's name is the name of the file, and put all the files in one folder. Then open the Contact Sheet dialog box and set it for an appropriate number of columns and rows, determined by how large you want the final photos. If you want them as large as possible, print only one image per sheet. Choose a font and size for the names and assemble the contacts. When they're ready, click Print. Ta da! There they are, and I bet they're all cute!

Q *Just how did you learn how to do all this?! It all seems so complicated—filters, effects, selecting things, changing colors, modifying options. Argh!*

A I learned the way you're learning—one step at a time. I studied my pictures and decided which effect I wanted to achieve and then kept trying things until I got the picture to look the way I wanted. When I have some free time, I like to turn on Photoshop and use it like a video game. I open a picture and see how long it takes me to completely lose the original image. It sounds silly, but I learn a lot from these sessions.

Quiz

1. How many kinds of preset lighting effects does Photoshop provide?

    a. Three: Spot, Omni, and Directional

    b. Seventeen, including colored spots and multi-light patterns

    c. Two: On and Off

2. A glow is a drop shadow that's not offset.

    a. True

    b. False

3. Which direction do reflections face, in relationship to the reflected object?

    a. The same horizontal direction, but the opposite vertical direction.

    b. The same vertical direction, but the opposite horizontal direction.

    c. Either a or b could be correct. (It depends on where the mirror surface is.)

4. How many images can you put on a letter-sized contact sheet?

    a. Up to a dozen

    b. 10

    c. It depends on how small you make them. One hundred is possible. However, if the images are at less than a half-inch wide, you might have trouble seeing them.

Quiz Answers

1. b. Take an image that's basically flat lit and try them all.

2. a. (And in a color other than black.)

3. c. Think about it.

4. c. A reasonable number is 24–30 images.

Exercises

Take some time and study reflections. Look at yourself in your coffee table. (You might have to polish it first!) Go outside and see the reflection of trees in water—even in a puddle or a pothole in the road. Find a book (or look on the Internet) of M.C. Escher's drawings and etchings and look in particular for "Three Worlds," "Puddle," and "Rippled Surface."

HOUR 19

Photoshop Plug-Ins and Add-Ons

What You'll Learn in This Hour:

▶ Where to Get Plug-Ins
▶ How to Install Plug-Ins
▶ Alien Skin's Eye Candy
▶ Kai's Power Tools
▶ Auto FX Photo/Graphic Edges
▶ Flaming Pear
▶ Genuine Fractals
▶ Andromeda
▶ Digimarc

By now, you have seen, if not used, most of the dozens of filters that came with your copy of Photoshop. There couldn't possibly be any more, could there? Well, Photoshop is kind of like those fashion dolls or action figures that kids of a certain age demand. You can't just buy Harry Potter and Hermione. You need the Hogwarts School, the Quidditch field, and Barbie's Dream House, yacht, and sport utility vehicle. After you see how much fun you can have with the basic filters, you'll want Eye Candy, Splat!, KPT (Kai's Power Tools), the Andromeda filters, and at least several dozen of the latest shareware filters, too. And the list goes on—I only wish I had time and pages enough to cover them all.

You've probably also considered buying a graphics tablet and more RAM for your computer. (You can never have too much.) Maybe you also need a faster computer to make all these tools work a little more efficiently. Of course, none of these plug-ins or add-ons is absolutely necessary, but for the next hour, let's pretend we're kids in a candy store. We'll sample everything possible.

Where to Get Plug-Ins

Commercial plug-in sets, such as the KPT, Andromeda, Splat!, and Eye Candy packages described in this hour, can be found in mail-order catalogs or at your friendly local computer dealer (who'll be even friendlier when you start buying all these goodies). Most can also be bought online from the software publishers, downloaded, and used right away.

On the other hand, you needn't spend a lot of money. It often amazes me how very many talented and generous people there are who not only write useful software, but then turn around and give it away or sell it for such a pittance that they might as well be giving it away. I am speaking, of course, of shareware, and its authors who spend many long nights polishing a program and then uploading it to the Web. If you go searching in appropriate areas for Macintosh or Windows software, you should find plenty of new and useful Photoshop plug-ins.

Finding Filters

I did a Google search on **Photoshop plug-in** and got back a list of thousands of sites that were triggered by that combination of keywords. The following are some good ones to get you started:

```
http://thepluginsite.com/
http://www.adobe.com/products/plugins/photoshop/
http://www.boxtopsoft.com/plugpage/
```

How to Install Plug-Ins

Few things could be simpler than installing an individual filter. Place it in the `Adobe Photoshop CS2\Plug-Ins\Filters` directory. Then launch Photoshop, and the new filter will appear in the list under the Filter menu. If you purchase a set of filters, such as Alien Skin's Xenofex 2, there's an installer included, which automatically places the filters where they belong. Installed third-party filters appear in the filter list after Photoshop's native filters. Try not to get too carried away. You can have so many that the list runs off the screen. Figure 19.1 shows my current collection.

FIGURE 19.1
Some filter sets
have submenus
like this one,
from Alien Skin.

Alien Skin's Eye Candy

I love this company. Not only do Alien Skin's designers produce great products, but they also have a wicked sense of humor. One of their promotional T-shirts reads, "Saturate the Industry with Freaks." Whether or not you qualify as a freak (and I'm sure some of you do), you're going to love Eye Candy. It comes in both Macintosh and Windows flavors, and can be found at your local software store or mail-order source for about $150. You can buy it online at http://www.alienskin.com, and you can also download a demo version for free.

Some of the Eye Candy effects are probably not for everyday use, unless your day job is designing covers for a science fiction magazine. Others, however, like Bevel Boss and Shadowlab, can be very useful.

The Alien Skin interface changes according to the effect you're applying, but the basic screen (shown in Figure 19.2) remains the same.

As of the current version, there are 23 Eye Candy effects, including Chrome, Fur, Drip, Melt, Smoke, Fire, Jiggle, Squint, Swirl, and a lot more. You can adjust all possible parameters of each of these effects, making the chrome shiny or dull; the fur wavy, long, or curly; the smoke dense or wispy; or whatever you can think of.

FIGURE 19.2
Alien Skin's Eye
Candy, applying
some fur to a
selection.

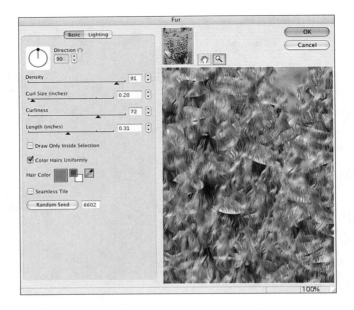

Applying many of these effects requires first selecting an area to which the effect will be applied, or adding a layer for it. A few, like Antimatter, simply do their thing. Antimatter inverts an image's brightness without affecting the colors or saturation value. Darks become light, and lights go dark, while colors and intensity stay the same. Figure 19.3 shows Eye Candy using the Fire filter to set fire to a very lazy cat.

FIGURE 19.3
You might not
use this every
day, but it's fun.

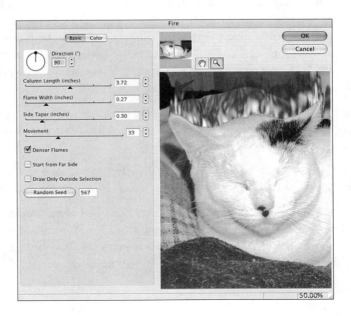

Eye Candy's Star filter, shown in Figure 19.4, is another of my favorites. It draws stars, blats (those odd-shaped, pointy designs they often use in ads to say "Sale" or "New Low Price"), and other little pointy things, with as many points as you want, shading them in three dimensions. These are great for pepping up a web page. Create them in Photoshop, and then jump over to ImageReady and assign rollover actions. (You'll learn how to do this in Hour 24, "Photoshop for the Web.")

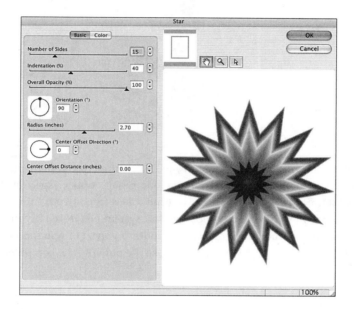

FIGURE 19.4
How many points on a star? With this filter, you can have up to 50.

Splat!

Splat! is another fun plug-in from Alien Skin. It creates frames, edge treatments, background fills and textures, surface textures, and mosaics. Splat! comes with a very large collection of images: some abstract, some strange, some beautiful and useful. Although you might not want to frame your girlfriend's portrait with cereal or teeth (complete with roots), white roses are nice. There are also lovely Art Nouveau edges, licensed from Dover Fine Arts. Of course, you can add your own image stamps, too.

Be sure to check out Splat!'s texturizers. They are much more interesting than Photoshop's canvas and sandstone. The Splat! collection's interface, shown in Figure 19.5, is easy and intuitive.

FIGURE 19.5
Splat! makes it easy to jazz up this baby portrait by filling in the background with autumn leaves.

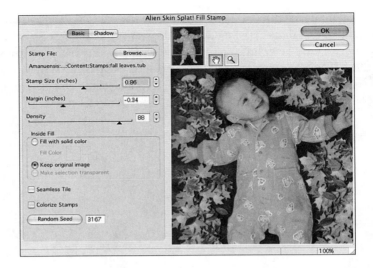

As is true of any of these tools, the more you explore, the more you'll learn about working with it. Some filters can take quite a long time to apply, especially if you push density settings to their highest points (and this is true of both third-party and Photoshop-native filters). Don't assume that your system has frozen if you don't see any movement for as much as a minute. The math involved in remapping each pixel in a swirl effect would make Einstein choke. Be patient. The computer is thinking as fast as it can.

Xenofex 2

Yet another terrific set of plug-in tools from the Alien Skin folks, Xenofex 2 is the new version of a long-time favorite. Within its 14 effects are filters to shatter, stain, burn the edges, make a mosaic or jigsaw puzzle, or cover your picture with clouds or stars, or make it look like it's printed on crumpled paper, just to name a few. Figure 19.6 shows a picture of a hot varsity basketball game, as a jigsaw puzzle. You can, of course, vary the size of the pieces, and the complexity.

Kai's Power Tools

Kai Krause is a legend in the field of computer graphics. He's the guiding genius behind Kai's Power Tools (KPT), Bryce, Convolver, Vector Effects, Final Effects, Goo, Soap, and probably many more goodies yet to be announced. The KPT 5 and 6 plug-in sets have been available for several years, although the parent company, MetaCreations, sold them to Corel Corp. Corel is now selling the KPT Collection, which includes "all the powerful Kai's Power Tools plug-in filters of KPT 5, KPT 6, and KPT effects."

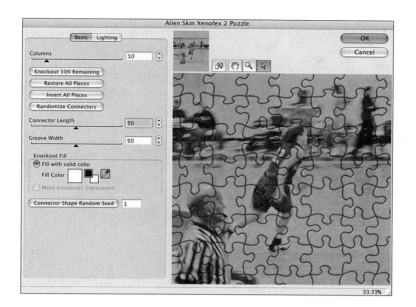

FIGURE 19.6
One of the 14
Xenofex effects.

The interfaces are designed to be as intuitive and as interesting as possible (see Figure 19.7). There are excellent help screens available within each filter (look for a question mark and click it). The goal of these filters, in addition to allowing you to do interesting things to your photos, is to change your way of working with the computer.

When you open any of the KPT filters, your screen will go blank except for the KPT logo. Then it will open with a futuristic control panel. Within the panel are smaller panels that control individual actions as parts of the filters' functions. For example, in Figure 19.7, when you slide the mouse over the panels or click a triangle, other panels drop down. The Equalizer filter enables you to selectively sharpen, smooth, or blur parts of a photo without affecting the rest. Clicking the question mark opens the PDF user guide for the selected filter. The button in the lower-left corner, which looks a bit like a calculator, takes you to the filter presets.

Materializer, shown in Figure 19.8, is my favorite KPT filter. It adds a texture by following the contours of the objects in the photo, rather than by simply covering the whole canvas with a texture. Be sure to see the materialized veggies in the color section.

There are lots more KPT filters to play with. Some can even make QuickTime movies of your actions, let you swirl and stretch the image, put it into perspective, and insert the resulting animation into a PowerPoint presentation. You can then put your movie on the Web, or do whatever you can think of with it (as long as it's QuickTime-compatible).

FIGURE 19.7
The interface for the KPT tool collection.

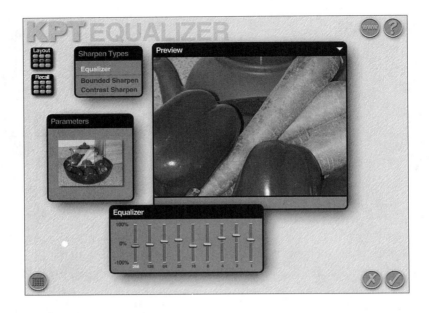

FIGURE 19.8
Materializer gave my groceries a third dimension.

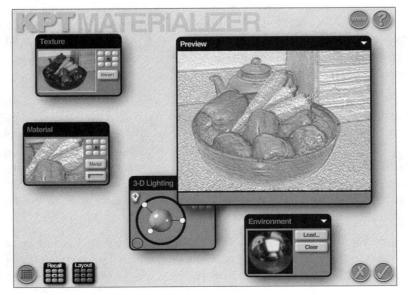

Auto FX Photo/Graphic Edges

This filter package puts the finishing touch on your pictures: textured edges. Photo/Graphic Edges has three CD volumes of edges, with more than 10,000 textures in all. You can customize them with the controls in the filter's dialog box, shown in Figure 19.9.

DreamSuite is another set of Auto FX plug-ins. Series One has 18 effects, some for type and some for graphics. Series Two adds another 11 effects. All are easy to apply and are very realistic looking. Figure 19.10 shows DreamSuite's take on liquid gold. The interface is simple and flexible, and can be opened as a standalone application as well as a plug-in. There's also Gel, as part of the DreamSuite package. It draws thick splats of jelly.

You can download a demo version of these filters from `http://www.autofx.com`, along with some other interesting and useful plug-ins. Be sure to check it out.

FIGURE 19.9
You can add color, change the size, and make any other edge adjustments with Auto FX Photo/ Graphic Edges.

FIGURE 19.10
Just move the sliders to change the effect.

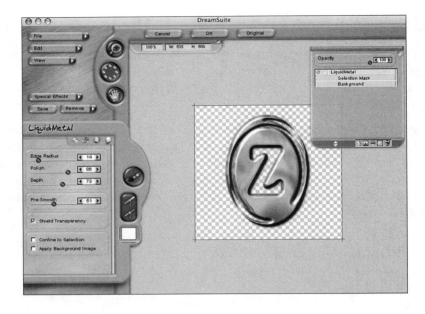

Flaming Pear

Here's another company with an interesting name and a collection of useful plug-ins. My favorite in this set is called Aetherize, part of the Designer Sextet collection. Figure 19.11 shows it being applied to the New Orleans skyline. It takes the colors and apparently changes them to their color wheel opposite hues without changing the brightness or saturation. Be sure to see the color version of this photo, too.

FIGURE 19.11
Aetherize does amazing things to color.

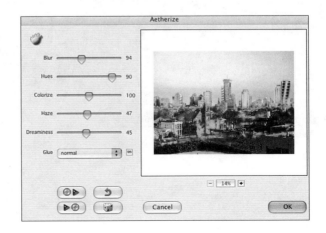

Among the other filters in the Flaming Pear set are SuperBladePro, Hue and Cry, and Melancholytron. You can download demo versions of these at http://www.flamingpear.com.

Genuine Fractals

This plug-in is a necessity if you intend to rescale images that you have scanned or imported from a digital camera. It enables you to save files at low resolution and then repurpose them as needed in high resolution, with no loss of quality. I can work at a comfortable 72 ppi, rescale to 300 ppi for a high-quality Iris print, and most viewers would never be able to spot that the file wasn't always high resolution. You can download a demo of the Genuine Fractals PrintPro plug-in—especially designed for printers and graphics pros—at http://altamira-group.com/download/dl_options.php?page=gf and judge for yourself.

Andromeda

Andromeda's filters, unlike some, are technically useful rather than just for fun. LensDoc fixes lens distortions so that straight lines don't appear to curve or slant inward. Perspective works like Photoshop's Skew, Distort, and Perspective commands, only it's easier and has a more flexible interface. Check it out in Figure 19.12.

FIGURE 19.12
This filter really puts things into perspective.

And there are more. Velociraptor puts motion trails behind moving objects; the Shadow Filter does the best drop shadows yet. I could go on. Instead, go download some demos from these nice folks and see for yourself. Find them at http://www.andromeda.com/.

Digimarc

You already have this one. It comes with Photoshop, but you might not know what it does. It's not exactly a filter because it doesn't change your picture. Instead, it protects your work by placing a digital watermark on it, and a copyright symbol © in the title bar. When you register with Digimarc, they'll send you an ID that will let you embed the digital copyright information into the file. When someone views a Digimarc watermarked file in Photoshop, they'll see a dialog box like the one in Figure 19.13, directing them to the website for more information. No one should use your work without your permission.

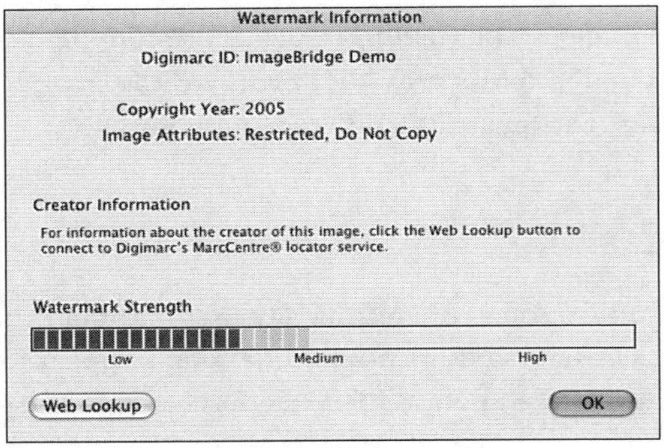

FIGURE 19.13
Prevent theft of copyrighted materials.

Summary

In this hour, you checked out some of the cool third-party filters you can use with Photoshop. The most versatile and complete package is still Kai's Power Tools (KPT 6.0), although it's probably not the easiest to use. My personal favorite, Alien Skin's Eye Candy filter set, includes a great many really odd filters, such as Fur and Fire, as well as very simple-to-apply drop shadow and glow filters. Genuine Fractals makes image scaling simple. Andromeda's lens filters and perspective should be in your repair kit. And more filters are coming out practically every day. Keep informed by checking in regularly at Photoshop Paradise (`http://desktoppublishing.com/photoshop.html`). It's a wonderful Web stop for all Photoshop users.

Workshop

Q&A

Q *Is there a way to design my own Photoshop filters?*

A There's an old plug-in called Filter Factory, which supposedly lets you do so. I've found it on the Web, but haven't really tried to do anything with it. It's a fairly complicated procedure, and the documentation is lacking. If you're really good at programming, Adobe makes specifications available for software developers who want to create plug-ins for Adobe products. Visit `http://partners.adobe.com/public/developer/photoshop/sdk/topic_sdk.html` for more information. You will need to supply your name and email address to access this site.

Q *Do these weird filters, such as Fur and Squint and Water Drops, have any practical uses?*

A Just today, I saw a sign that featured a frosty bottle of Coca-Cola on a red background. The entire image was made to look wet with Alien Skin's Water Drops filter. Anything's practical if you have enough imagination to make it work.

Quiz

1. Where do plug-ins appear?

   a. On the Plug-ins palette

   b. At the bottom of the Filter menu

   c. At the top of the Window menu

2. Which of the following is not an Eye Candy effect?

   a. Fur

   b. Fire

   c. Squint

   d. Slime

Quiz Answers

1. b. If you have many plug-ins, you might have to scroll down to see them all.

2. d. But if you start with Green Glass, you can create a reasonably slimy effect.

Exercise

Download demos of some of the great plug-ins from Flaming Pear and Alien Skin at http://www.flamingpear.com and http://www.alienskin.com. See which ones you can't live without.

PART V

Photo Repair and Enhancement

HOUR 20

Compositing

What You'll Learn in This Hour:

▶ Sources for Images
▶ Making One Picture from Two
▶ Realistic Composites
▶ Replacing a Background
▶ Composites from Nothing
▶ Photomerge
▶ Panoramas the "Hard" Way

Compositing can be known by other names. It can be *combining*, or making a collage, or photomontage. Whatever it's called, the goal is the same: To make one picture from pieces of other ones. Photoshop is the ideal program for this kind of work for several reasons. First, it has the tools to assemble pieces of different pictures. Second, it gives you the ability to work in layers. Third, its filters enable you to blend pictures and add shadows and reflections more easily and effectively than any other graphics program can.

You can use the techniques described here, along with the ones you've already learned, to produce all sorts of surrealistic images, and (for many people) this is what Photoshop is all about. For others, myself included, compositing is more often a way of making up for deficiencies in the original picture.

Image Sources

Pictures are everywhere. You can download thousands of images from the Web. You can buy CD-ROMs full of photographs and line art. And, of course, you can scan conventional photos or import pictures from a digital camera into Photoshop.

When you start thinking about combining images, you'll probably realize that some pictures are more suitable than others for this kind of use. You can even classify some as backgrounds, others as objects, and some as the raw materials from which to create special effects. As you browse through your own pictures and look at collections of stock photos, some images will jump out at you, and you'll begin to see possible combinations.

Stock photos? If you're not familiar with the term, you should be. *Stock photos* are pictures that are made available to you for a fee (a flat fee or sometimes a per-use royalty) to do with as you see fit. Under most stock photo agreements, you can use the images in your reports, in ads, or practically any way you want, as long as you're not reselling them as is or using them in any way that's libelous, defamatory, pornographic, or otherwise illegal. Be sure that you read and understand the licensing policies before you use them.

By the Way

Stocking Up

Point your web browser to www.comstock.com/ to see some really good stock photography. Alas, you can't use any of the pictures in the Comstock libraries without paying for them. The screen versions download as low-quality JPEGs, but they give you a feel for what's available and how much it costs.

The quickest route to the Land of Stock Photos is through Adobe Bridge. In Photoshop, choose File→Browse and click Adobe Stock Photos in the Favorites tab. Bridge connects to Adobe's website and serves up a flavorful collection of stock photos for your perusal. You can view various prefab collections, such as Island Travel (shown in Figure 20.1) or conduct your own search using keywords. When you see an image you like, click Download Comp to grab a low-res "sample." And when you're ready to buy, click Add to Cart.

There's no reason (as long as you pay for them) that you can't use these kinds of images in combination with your own. If you need something basic, such as a slab of concrete to use as a background, it will often be faster, cheaper, and just as effective to use one from stock rather than dropping everything and running out to find a slab of concrete to photograph yourself.

Of course, as you wander around town with your digital camera in your pocket, you can start your own stock collection, too. In fact, it's one of the ways you can make money with your pictures, allowing you to invest the profits in more software and higher-resolution cameras. Let's start compositing with a couple of images from my own stock collection.

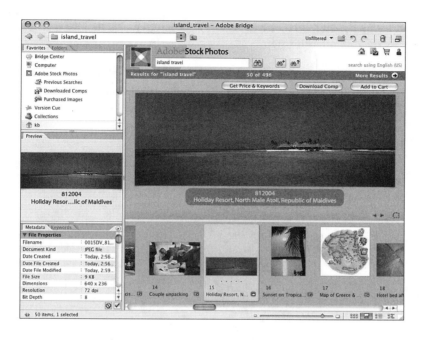

FIGURE 20.1
Easy Access to stock photos via Bridge.

Making One Picture from Two

I shot some random seagulls in a parking lot. The background was awful, but the birds stood still. A year later, I shot a Canadian Navy ship in Halifax, Nova Scotia. Nice picture, but needs something. Maybe that seagull. So, let's put him there. (The gull and the ship are available for download at the usual source, if you would like to work along. Look for gull.jpg and ship.jpg.) Figure 20.2 shows the gull.

FIGURE 20.2
Just one gull...

Select and copy the gull, then open the ship picture and paste the bird in. Figure 20.3 shows the gull after this step.

FIGURE 20.3
It's "Gull"iath!!!
We'll have to
scale him down
to size.

After reducing him down to a more realistic size, using Edit→Transform→Scale, he still doesn't look natural, but there are a few tricks that should help. First, put a drop shadow on the gull. The sun is coming from his left side, so the shadow has to be to the right. Figure 20.4 shows the Layer Style/Drop Shadow dialog box. Notice the settings, particularly the Distance. This controls the amount of offset and places the shadow under the gull, as it ought to be. Instead of using a black shadow, I've set the shadow color to match the darker parts of the piling he's standing on. That will also help the shadows match.

There's no way to determine which settings to use, other than trying them to see what works best. The only one I could set arbitrarily was the angle. That's because I knew where the light was, and shadows are usually directly opposite the light source. Setting the other parameters gives you a chance to play with the shadow, to make it harder or softer, bigger or smaller.

Finally, a tiny bit of dodging on the gull's back and burning on his face to bring out the detail will help a lot. Figure 20.5 shows the finished photo. Notice how adding the gull helps you see how big the ship really is.

FIGURE 20.4
The drop shadow must come from the same direction as other shadows in the picture.

FIGURE 20.5
He looks more real when he casts a shadow.

Controlling Transparency in Overlaid Images

It's extremely simple to paste one opaque image over another one—you just do it. Transparent images are harder to work with, although Photoshop makes it a little easier by giving you opacity controls.

When you're creating a multilayered picture, as in Figure 20.5, you have two ways to control the way the layers blend. One is the Opacity slider in the Layers palette. You can set any degree of opacity, from 100% all the way down to zero, at which point whatever's on the layer has completely disappeared. You can also control the effect by using the Blending Mode menu, also in the Layers palette. By applying different modes to different layers, you can control the way each layer overlays the others.

Realistic Composites

Creating an image that's not meant to be completely realistic is relatively easy. Faking realism is a lot harder. The main tasks to consider in making composites are

- ▶ Keeping your backgrounds simple.

- ▶ Isolating the elements on different layers for easier editing.

- ▶ Making sure that the pieces you combine are in proper scale with each other.

- ▶ When you're done, merging the layers for a smaller file.

Watch Out!

What You Add to the Image Makes It Better

Remember also that adding shadows, reflections, or other special effects can make a big difference in the end result. Watch out for perspective, too. If it's wrong, you'll know it, although you might not know why exactly. When you're walking around town or sitting in a well-lit room, notice the shadows. See where they appear and how the light source affects the angle at which they fall from the object causing them. Look for reflections, too. See what direction they reflect. When you understand how science and nature do it, you'll be able to fake it more accurately.

In my collection, I have some photos of desert scenery in Nevada—very close to the mysterious place that the government calls Area 51. It's rumored to be a landing site for extraterrestrial beings. The photos show lots of amazing rock formations but no little green men. But they got me thinking. What's the most alien life form I could imagine out there in the middle of nothing? Probably the fashion doll. So, let's send her out there.

Let's start by choosing an interesting background. Figure 20.6 looks to me most like a good spot for an alien sighting, and Figure 20.7 shows my favorite Martian, shot on a cluttered desk. When you're doing things like this, placing a piece of plain paper behind the object you photograph makes it much easier to separate the background from the subject. It's like the big rolls of seamless paper the pros use, only in a more appropriate size.

FIGURE 20.6
This is some-where in the Valley of Fire State Park.

FIGURE 20.7
She would be more at home in a Vegas casino.

First, let's prepare the background. The color could use some enhancement, and I think I would like some clouds in the sky. I can adjust the color either with Curves or with Variations, both on the Image→Adjustments submenu. A little more yellow and increasing the saturation helps a lot. Now, about those clouds... After I select the sky, and a pair of appropriate foreground and background colors for the sky, I can choose Filter→Render→Clouds, and watch the weather change. Figure 20.8 shows the result—a more interesting sky.

FIGURE 20.8
That's a little
better.

The next step is to extract the doll from her background and then to bring her into
the new setting. She'll probably need some color adjustments, too, but we'll do those
after she's in place. I can do most of the selecting with a couple of Magic Wand
clicks, but there are some cutouts and highlights that will need extra work.
Remember to zoom in when you have a complicated object to trace. As you can
probably tell in Figure 20.9, it's much easier to pick up the details when you zoom
in on the object you're tracing. Before I go on, I'll smooth the selection by one
pixel's worth (Select→Modify→Smooth). This just helps make her look less ragged.

FIGURE 20.9
I had to pick up
the hair high-
lights with the
lasso.

Now, let's put her in her place. I can either copy and paste or just drag her as a selection from one photo to the other. Either way, she'll come in on a new layer, which is exactly where I want her for now. In Figure 20.10, I've cropped her and dropped her into the desert background. But she doesn't look quite natural yet.

FIGURE 20.10
She's not really comfortable.

Trying to analyze what's wrong with this picture, I see two things. First, she's too tall. If she were standing up, she would be about 6'8". But her proportions are more suited to someone about a foot shorter. So, I'll have to scale her down a little. The other thing is that she's sitting at an awkward angle. I might be able to fix that by rotating her. Otherwise, I can move and skew her a tiny bit so she's not trying to lean on thin air. Figure 20.11 shows a close-up of this process.

FIGURE 20.11
Now she fits in better.

Of course, in the desert everything casts shadows. You'll notice that these are very sharp edged and low angle. It's late in the day but the sun is still very bright and those factors affect the appearance of shadows. I'll add a matching one with the Drop Shadow layer style. And there she is: sunning herself against a tree (see Figure 20.12). This figure is also in the color section.

FIGURE 20.12
Well, why not?

Replacing a Background

Many times you'll need to give something a different background, as I did earlier by moving the doll from my desk to the desert. The hardest parts of the job are finding appropriate backgrounds and objects to place in them, and separating the object from its original background. The doll was fairly easy to select, because I shot her against the plain paper backdrop. Suppose we took something more difficult and moved it to the same scene. Remember that hot dog wagon from New York? That would be a welcome oasis out there in the middle of The Valley of Fire. Let's do it. The cart is shown in Figure 20.13.

The Magic Wand won't be much help here. I'll begin by tracing loosely around the cart with the Lasso, and inverting so I can delete the outer pieces of the picture. Figure 20.14 shows the lassoed cart; what's left after removing the background appears in Figure 20.15.

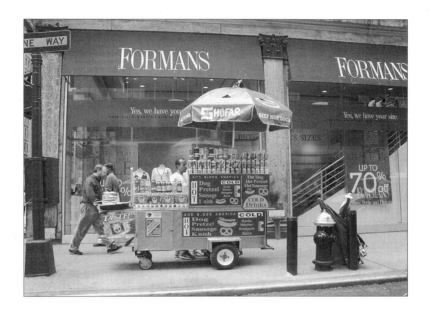

FIGURE 20.13
This image is not going to be easy to extract. There's a lot going on in the background.

FIGURE 20.14
This is obviously a rough selection.

There are several ways to get rid of the remaining edges around the cart. You can erase it, bit by bit. You can remove some small parts, but not many, by selecting them with the Magic Wand. You can use Filter→Extract. But the easiest way is to use a tool called the Background Eraser. It pops out from the toolbox when you click and hold on the regular Eraser, and it erases pixels to transparency as you drag it.

FIGURE 20.15
It still needs lots
of cleaning up.

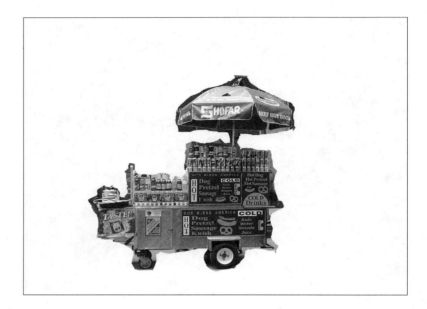

▼   **Try it Yourself**

Use the Background Eraser Tool

Let's do some practicing with this useful tool:

1. Go to the Layers palette and activate the layer containing the areas you want to erase. (It's often easier if you hide the other layers.)

2. Switch to the Background Eraser tool.

3. Set an appropriate brush size and shape using the Brush menu in the Tool Options bar.

4. Choose an erasing mode:
    ▶ Discontiguous erases the sampled color anywhere it appears in the layer.
    ▶ Contiguous erases areas that contain the sampled color and are connected to one another.
    ▶ Find Edges erases connected areas containing the sampled color, while better preserving the sharpness of object edges.

5. Set the tolerance by entering a value or dragging the slider. A low tolerance limits erasing to areas that are very similar to the sampled color. A higher tolerance erases a broader range of colors.

▼

6. To determine how erased colors are treated, choose a sampling option:

   ▶ Continuous samples colors continuously as you drag. Use this option to erase adjacent areas that are different colors.

   ▶ Once erases only areas containing the color that you click first. Use this option to erase a solid-colored area.

   ▶ Background Swatch erases only areas containing the current background color.

7. Choose Protect Foreground Color to protect areas that match the foreground color in the toolbox.

8. Drag the eraser through the area you want to erase. If you have set Brush Size Cursors in the Preferences box, the Background Eraser tool pointer appears as an outline of your brush with a crosshair indicating the tool's hot spot. Otherwise, it's a block eraser with a pair of scissors on top, just like its icon. This process is easier if you zoom in on the area to be erased.

In Figure 20.16, I've erased most of the background. I used both the Background Eraser as described, and the Magic Eraser, which determines where the chosen color ends and erases to the line of color change. (You choose the color by clicking it with the Magic Eraser.) It did a fine job on the umbrella. The cart still needs a bit of cleaning up with the regular Eraser, though. After that, I'll be able to slide it into position and rescale it if necessary (see Figure 20.17).

It's there, but it doesn't quite fit in yet. It's sitting sort of on top of a tuft of grass. I can copy the grass from the Background layer and paste it over the cart. It needs a shadow as well, but the drop shadow won't work in these lighting conditions. The shadow should be more or less under the cart. So I can add a layer between the background and the cart and use the Rectangular Marquee to create an oblong shadow shape. I'll feather the edges a little, about 3 pixels, and then fill it with black. That's too dark, so I'll slide the opacity down to about 20%, and then flatten the image. Figure 20.18 shows the finished picture.

So you see, combining pictures isn't at all difficult. You simply need to prepare them by removing unwanted backgrounds or other bits, and then assemble them in layers. Don't forget to merge the layers when you're sure that you're done working on the picture. Otherwise, your files, if they have several layers, can be quite large, and you won't be able to save them in specialized formats such as JPEG or PCX. Save copies unmerged on a Zip disk, hard drive, or CD-ROM so that you can go back and improve on your work later.

FIGURE 20.16
The Background
Eraser took
away most of
the edges.

FIGURE 20.17
The cart's
moved from
West 43rd St.
to the desert.

FIGURE 20.18
I would like a diet root beer and a pretzel, please.

Composites from Nothing

You've seen in some of the earlier hours that with Photoshop you can create art from scratch, as well as edit and alter existing photos. Let's see what you can make out of nothing.

Try it Yourself

Create a Composite Image from Scratch

Start with a new, empty document; you'll apply a gradient as a background.

Gradients can be linear, radial, angled, reflected, or diamond-shaped, and can have as many transparent or opaque colors as you want. To create a gradient, follow these steps:

1. Select the Gradient tool, which shares a toolbox compartment with the Paint Bucket. Look at its Options bar, which is shown in Figure 20.19. We want a gradient that will suggest sky, water, and beach.

FIGURE 20.19
Gradients and the Gradient Tool Options bar.

▼

2. Select a three-part gradient, and click it on the Tool Options bar to open the Gradient Editor. There's the preset three-step Blue, Red, Yellow gradient. Click it, and its settings will appear in the dialog box.

3. Click the slider at the lower-left end of the color ramp. Change its color to the deep blue sky of early evening. (Clicking the block of color at the bottom of the screen opens the Color Picker.) Then change the middle section to a sort of tropical turquoise, and the right one to sandy beige. The little diamonds indicate midpoints of each color blend. Keeping your goal in mind, slide them left or right as needed to create a horizon and a generous beach. Figure 20.20 shows the Gradient Editor.

FIGURE 20.20
The Gradient Editor.

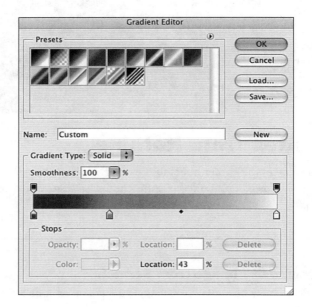

4. Drag the Gradient tool in your empty file from top to bottom to place it with the blue on top. Now turn the image into a cloudy sky. Set the foreground color to the middle value of the lighter blue and the background to the mid-point of the darker blue. Create a new layer and drag a marquee selection to define the upper third of the sky. Choose Filter→Render→Clouds to produce a nice set of clouds. Then select two related lighter colors, apply the marquee to the lower half of the sky, feathering the edges by about 10 pixels, and do it again, making a nice gradation of clouds (see Figure 20.21). If there's a line in the middle of the clouds, blend it with the Smudge tool.

▼

FIGURE 20.21
Sneak over to the color section to see this in color.

5. Now it's looking like a day at the beach. Let's add some beach grass. Switch to the Custom Shape tool and choose the Grass shape from the Options bar. Choose a pale green from the Swatches palette and draw some grass; add more grass in other shades of green and gold. The result is shown in Figure 20.22.

FIGURE 20.22
It's a cool background, but it needs a subject. Maybe some boats?

6. Finally, I'll make a new brush, and use it to put a fleet of little sailboats way out. I've used Transform to resize and distort them. Figure 20.23 shows the final result: a fleet of boats in a tropical bay.

FIGURE 20.23
Wish I were
there.

Photomerge

People have been sticking photos together to create panoramic images for close to a hundred years, with varying degrees of success. The scissors and glue method rarely succeeds. Shooting a panorama all in one photo with a wide-angle lens seems to work, until you notice that the ends of the Grand Canyon are very fuzzy, or the two outermost bridesmaids in the wedding lineup appear 50 pounds heavier than they actually are.

Distortion is the problem. Wide-angle lenses aren't good choices in situations where you want to avoid distortion. The more curve you apply to the front of the lens, the more glass the image has to pass through. Glass adds distortion. The more logical way to shoot a panorama that stays in focus from one end to the other is to take a series of pictures and splice them together. Prior to computers, that was exceptionally difficult, although it certainly was done. Now, thanks to clever software, it's easier than ever to get good results with panoramic photography.

Working with Photomerge

The first time I saw Photomerge at work, it just about knocked my socks off. It was originally part of the Photoshop Elements 2 package, but Adobe apparently got so many requests from the pros that they included it in Photoshop CS. I couldn't be happier. It makes the work of assembling a panoramic photo very easy.

Photomerge is a plug-in that automates the process of assembling a panorama. After you've gone out and taken the photos, you plug your camera or memory card into the computer and download the pictures. Then you open Photomerge and tell it where to find the pictures you want to use. By the way, it's sort of hidden near the bottom of the File→Automate submenu. The dialog box is shown in Figure 20.24. Click Browse and navigate to the folder in which your separate images are contained, select the pictures you want to use, and then click OK.

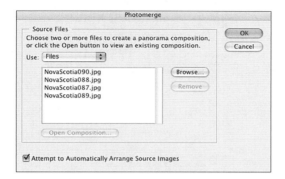

FIGURE 20.24
It's easiest if you download your pictures to a single folder. That way you don't have to go hunting for them.

When you click OK, the magic begins. First, Photoshop opens all the photos you specified and opens a new image file. Then it arranges them in order, matching the edges where images overlap. It opens a dialog box similar to the one shown in Figure 20.25, so you can watch the progress.

FIGURE 20.25
Photoshop opens the pictures as separate files, then copies them to layers in a new document.

The pictures appear to come in at 50% opacity, so the computer can easily line up areas of major contrast. In this series of pictures, the horizon seems to be the major point of reference for matching. Pictures that Photomerge can't match are left at the top of the strip, so you can drag them from the box at the top of the window into the work area at the bottom of the window and match them later. When all the pictures have been merged (see Figure 20.26), Photomerge continues the process by adjusting the brightness and contrast of each pair of pictures so you have a consistent exposure from one end to the other. If the sun has gone behind a cloud and emerged again, as it did in this set of photos, you'll have to do some extra tweaking. Apparently, it can only cope with *logical* changes.

FIGURE 20.26
It still needs
some tweaking.

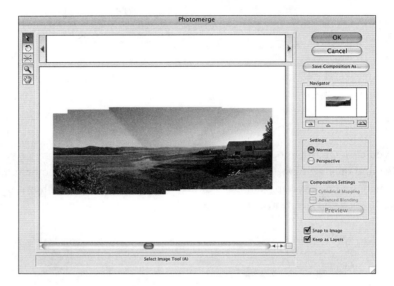

You can do some adjusting using the tools in the Photomerge dialog box. Drag a corner of any image in the work area with the Rotate Image tool to rotate it. Move the panorama within the work area by scrolling or by dragging it with the Move View tool. Zoom in with the Zoom tool.

By clicking Perspective in the Settings pane, you can make some other adjustments. To establish which image contains the *vanishing* point (which image contains the highest point on the horizon, and therefore should be treated as the "middle" image), click that image with the Vanishing Point tool. It will be highlighted with a blue border. The other images will be adjusted in relation to this new vanishing point. If needed, make your own adjustments as well by clicking the Select Image tool and scooting the nonvanishing point images up or down.

There are other options you can choose, too. The Cylindrical Mapping option transforms the panorama as if it were on a cylinder, reducing the bow-tie effect sometimes seen. This brings the viewer closer and into the panorama a bit, but you'll gain a lot of extra image space for cropping, so it's worth a look to see which view you prefer.

If your panorama has some inconsistencies with brightness and contrast, try the Advanced Blending option. It blends together areas of color, while retaining detail. The effect is a softening of these differences, making the panorama seem more like a whole image rather than a collection of images.

After choosing Cylindrical Mapping, Advanced Blending, or both, click Preview to view the results. Click Exit Preview to return to Normal view. When you're through making adjustments in the Photomerge window, click OK. The finished product is an untitled file (see Figure 20.27) with all the pictures assembled and matched as well as possible. Be sure to check the Keep as Layers box in the Photomerge dialog box. Otherwise, when you get it, the image has already been flattened, making it difficult to adjust the exposure of one frame that's a little "off."

FIGURE 20.27
Adding an adjustment layer for the middle image lets you even out the sky.

It's still up to you to crop the picture, if you want to. Some photographers argue that the slanting edges and unevenness of the "raw" panorama somehow add to the experience. Others, myself included, prefer to crop. A lot depends on whether, and how, you intend to print the picture. The four images assembled for this test of Photomerge produced a strip 6 1/2 inches high by 20 inches long. At 300 ppi resolution, that's a 34MB file. I can print it myself if I want to do so; one of my inkjet printers takes banner paper. But I would prefer to go to a service bureau and come home with a strip 3 feet long on nice shiny, heavy poster paper.

Considerations When You Shoot a Panorama

Obviously, the main thing to consider when you shoot pictures for a panorama is that you should hold the camera steady at one height. Don't take it away from your eye while you're shooting. If you get interrupted mid-sequence, start again. Better yet, if possible, use a tripod to keep the camera steady. Remember, digital photos don't waste film. Stay away from the focus and zoom buttons. Auto-focus the first picture and let that one dictate the focus for the rest.

Practice the "panorama shuffle." Start shooting with your body aimed at one end of the scene. Take small steps circling to your right as you shoot your pictures from left to right.

Don't use a flash. Particularly, don't use auto-flash, as it will throw varying amounts of light as it sees a need. These make the exposure all but impossible to correct.

Use a normal lens for best results. Set your zoom lens about halfway between zoom and telephoto, and leave it there. Don't use a wide-angle or fish-eye lens. Such lenses defeat the purpose of the panorama, which is to have everything in the same focus and not distorted. Nothing distorts more than a fish-eye.

Make sure you have enough overlap between pictures, but not too much. Somewhere around 20% is good. As you pan across the scene, remember what is on the right side of each picture you take, and just cover it again on the left of the next shot.

Take a picture of something clearly different between shooting panorama sequences. That way you won't try to assemble pictures that don't go together. Keep each set of pictures in a separate folder as you download them from the camera.

Panoramas the "Hard" Way

The process for creating a panorama without using Photomerge is time-consuming, but not especially difficult. You simply follow the same steps Photomerge uses. Locate your photos, open them, and move each one to a new layer of the document that will contain the panorama. Set the opacity of each layer to around 50% and make sure you extend your canvas to at least four times the width and twice the height of a single picture, so you have some room to work in. Slide the photos around and rotate them, if necessary, until you can line up the overlapping edges. Now's a good time to adjust the color on any layer that doesn't quite match. When everything's lined up, change the layers' Opacity settings back to 100%, flatten the image, and crop it as necessary.

Summary

Composites, montages, whatever you call them—they're simply combinations of two or more images, carefully merged. Use your own pictures or stock photos from collections, or create images by combining techniques and filters. It's fun, and it's effective. It's one of the things Photoshop does exceptionally well. Be sure to spend some time playing with compositing.

Workshop

Q&A

Q *Can I apply a filter to a gradient?*

A Certainly. It's easiest if the gradient is on a separate layer. Just make the gradient the active layer and apply any filter or combination you like. The results often make an interesting background for other pictures, too. Start by trying the Texture filters and some of the Brush Strokes. These are generally successful.

Q *I tried importing a building into another photo, but it just doesn't look right. Why not?*

A There can be a dozen reasons, but the three most obvious are scale, perspective, and lighting. The import might be too big or too small for where you put it. It might need to be skewed into a different perspective. You might also be trying to put a piece of a shadowy, noontime picture into a late afternoon background. When you select pictures to combine, try to match sizes, orientation, and time of day. If that's not possible, you can still make it work, but you will have to do more correcting.

Q *There's usually a difference in sharpness between the object I want to add and the background. It makes the object stand out like a sore thumb. Any ideas?*

A If you don't want to blur the sharper image, try selecting the object, feathering the edges of the selection slightly, inverting it, and pressing Delete. That will soften the edges of the object a bit.

Q *This is fun, but my files get so big that they take forever to save or apply a filter to. Any ideas?*

A Be sure to merge down layers when you're done with them. Save frequently. Save different stages if you think you might want to go back further than the History palette can take you.

Q *How can I get rid of that white halo around a selection I have copied and pasted?*

A Easier than you think. Select the layer and choose Layer→Matting→Defringe. Enter a value in the Width text box for the distance from the edge of the object to search for replacement pixels. In most cases, a distance of 1 or 2 pixels is enough. Click OK and that white edge is gone.

Quiz

1. Any picture you download from the Web can be considered a stock photo.

   a. True

   b. False

2. Photoshop has _____ kinds of gradients.

   a. Two

   b. Three

   c. Five

3. Name one thing you'll have to master to make good composite images.

   a. Zen

   b. Filters

   c. Layers

4. What's the easiest way to remove a plain background?

   a. Erase it

   b. Select it and delete it

   c. Fill it with clear paint

Quiz Answers

1. b. Be careful because many images are copyrighted, and you could get into legal trouble if you use them commercially or even on your personal website. If you're just messing around with Photoshop at home, you're probably safe.

2. c. Can you name them? If not, start Photoshop and explore the toolbar where the Gradient tools reside.

3. c. You'll have to know several Photoshop techniques to create composite images, but being a pro at using layers is indispensable.

4. b. Depends on the situation, but generally a plain background is easy to select.

Exercises

To experiment with compositing, find two of your own pictures or two stock photos—one landscape and one portrait. Remove the background from the portrait subject, and place the subject in the landscape. Add shadows or reflections if necessary to make the person look as if he or she were photographed on location.

Photo Repair— Black and White

What You'll Learn in This Hour:

- ▶ Easy Fixes
- ▶ Using the Eyedropper
- ▶ Using the Clone Stamp
- ▶ Healing Brush and Patch Tools
- ▶ Cleaning Up a Picture, Step by Step
- ▶ Applying Tints
- ▶ Vignetting

Fixing damaged or "just plain lousy" pictures is the number one reason why most people buy Photoshop. It can really work miracles on old, torn, faded photographs, and it can also make up for most, if not all, of the flaws in your snapshots. Photoshop can be used to recompose a picture that's off-center, tilted, or has too much empty space. You can edit out the power lines and trash cans that spoil the landscape. You can even remove unwanted former spouses, or that awful boyfriend your daughter finally dumped, from family portraits. It's nowhere near as difficult to get rid of them onscreen.

Easy Fixes

Let's start by looking at some of the things you can do to fix an old picture that might have faded, yellowed, or been damaged. First, we'll consider a couple of old family photos that need a little bit of adjusting and touching up. We'll run (literally) through the steps involved in fixing them and the tools you'll need to know how to use. (Remember, you can always flip to the front of the book to refresh your memory about these tools, too.)

Finally, we'll take an extremely damaged picture and work through it step by step, until it looks like new again.

Some pictures don't need very much work. The photo in Figure 21.1 has mainly dust and focus problems. This photo could also use a little more contrast, and it needs its vignetted corners cropped away. The original is sepia-tinted, but would probably look just as good or better in grayscale.

FIGURE 21.1
This needs relatively minor repairs. (Photo courtesy of D. Maynard.)

To fix this picture, I first crop the borders to remove the edges. I set the image's color mode to Grayscale, which removes any color information that the scan picked up. Doing this immediately eliminates the yellow and brown tones. Next, I use Curves (Image→Adjustments→Curves) to tweak the contrast a little. By using Curves, I can lighten the light tones without affecting the darks. In Figure 21.2, the very slight curve in the dialog box lets you see just how subtle this adjustment is.

In Figure 21.3, you can see the improved contrast. Now it's obvious, as it wasn't before, that the girl is holding a black kitten. A little dodging and burning will help bring out the details of her dress, and will separate the cat from the background.

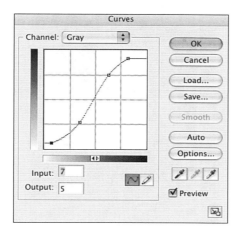

FIGURE 21.2
The curve adjustment is very slight.

FIGURE 21.3
Better but not quite there yet.

I'll get rid of the big dust spots with the Clone Stamp, using a small soft-edged brush, and copying the adjacent tone. Then I'll use the Sharpen filter to put things in better focus. The final step in this restoration is to apply the Dust & Scratches filter to remove any specks I missed. The result, shown in Figure 21.4, is much better.

FIGURE 21.4
Well-preserved photos, regardless of age, can be digitally improved.

To Dust Or Not to Dust

Many Photoshop users make a habit of applying the Dust & Scratches filter (Filter→Noise→Dust & Scratches) to every scanned photo. This is often a mistake because, although it does make dust particles less obvious, it also softens the focus of the picture. If you decide to try it, evaluate the results carefully. Use the Preview check box to toggle back and forth, turning the filter preview on and off until you're certain that it's an improvement.

Here's another fairly old photo, shot in 1948. (I know. The kid in the chair is me.) This one is in much worse shape. It is both soft and contrasty, and cracked in several places. The black tones are greenish. It has something spilled on it, too. The untouched photo is shown in Figure 21.5. Can we rescue it?

Again we'll start by cropping and then go to Grayscale mode to get rid of the green and tan tones. There's a good deal that can be cropped out of the background of this photo, improving the composition (see Figure 21.6). Just lowering the top of the photo puts the emphasis on the baby and not the big chair she's in.

The Levels dialog box shows the histogram for this picture, which tells us that there's a lot of good detail in the lights and in the darks, but the midrange is weak. The best way to learn to make these adjustments is to work on a copy of a bad picture, and simply experiment with the settings until the picture looks the way you want. Notice what happens when you move the sliders to the right or left. Figure 21.7 shows the corrections so far.

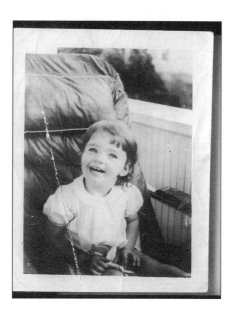

FIGURE 21.5
This one needs more serious work.

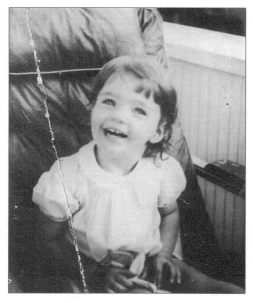

FIGURE 21.6
Cropping can remove some of the problem areas.

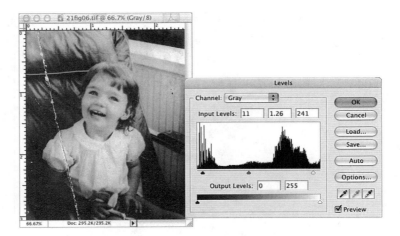

Using the Eyedropper

Taking a closer look, I'm aware of some dust as well as the creases. You can see the creases in Figure 21.7. I'll have to do some touch-up work to get rid of those.

Sometimes you need to paint over part of the image, either to fill in scratches or to remove unwanted lines, spots, or in-laws. Use the Eyedropper tool to select a color with which to paint. Simply click the Eyedropper on any color (or in this case, shade of gray) in the image that you want to replicate, and that color becomes the foreground color, ready to apply with the Brush, Airbrush, or whatever Painting tool you choose. You can also hold down the Option (Mac) or Alt (Windows) key while a Painting tool is selected to turn it temporarily into an Eyedropper, so you can change colors as you paint. A pop-up menu on the Eyedropper's Options bar gives you the choice of using a single-pixel color sample or of taking an average color from either a 3×3- or 5×5-pixel sample.

With the Eyedropper, Brush, and Smudge tools, we'll repair the damage. All you need to do is to pick up the appropriate background grays from elsewhere in the picture, paint or Clone Stamp them in, and smudge the area a little bit so that it blends. In Figure 21.8, you can see the result of these efforts.

Using the Eyedropper tool in a situation like this is much easier than trying to match an existing color or shade of gray on the color wheel. All you need to do to paint in the background is to find another spot in the picture where the color or gray shade is the one that you would like to use. Select the Eyedropper and click it to make that color the foreground color. Then use your brush to paint in the selected shade. Smudge the edges very slightly if necessary to blend in the new paint. When the area to work on is very small, I like to use a very small brush as a Smudge tool, and set it for only 20% pressure so that I don't overdo the smudges. When you are working on corrections this small, it's much easier to apply them gradually and let the effect build up, rather than trying to do it all in one pass.

FIGURE 21.8
Compare this to the original image.

Using the Clone Stamp

The Clone Stamp tool is perfect when you need to copy small pieces of a picture and paste them elsewhere. It samples from a chosen point in the image and duplicates the selection, exactly as if you had made a rubber stamp of it. Figure 21.9 shows the Clone Stamp tool and its Options bar. Choose a brush shape, blending mode, and opacity as you would with any other tool. When you select a reference point, the Clone Stamp creates a duplicate of the image anywhere you start painting, expanding the duplicated portion of the image as you go. Conceivably, you could reproduce the entire image if you had enough blank canvas.

If you don't choose Aligned, the stamp behaves differently. After you select your reference point and start painting, the duplicate portion of the image expands only while you continue to hold down the mouse button. When you release it and press it again, you start painting another duplicate image from the same reference point.

FIGURE 21.9
The Clone
Stamp tool's
icon looks just
like a rubber
stamp.

To select a point to clone from, press Option (Mac) or Alt (Windows) while you click the mouse on the spot you want to copy. Then release the key and start stamping by moving the mouse to the new spot and clicking. You can stamp as many times as you want. The crosshairs show the spot you're cloning from and the brush shows where you are stamping (see Figure 21.10).

You can define a pattern or choose an existing one, and stamp it with the Pattern Stamp tool. To make your own, use the Rectangular Marquee to select a piece of an image to use as a pattern, and select Define Pattern from the Edit menu. Now when you use the Pattern Stamp tool, if you choose Aligned, the pattern will be tiled as if you started stamping from the upper-left corner of the document, no matter where you drag. If you uncheck Aligned, the pattern will tile from wherever you start dragging each time.

When you use the Clone Stamp tool to retouch, always choose a soft-edged brush in a size only slightly larger than the scratch or blemish you're hiding. Retouching is generally easier if you zoom in on the image first.

FIGURE 21.10
If you move the
stamp slightly
as you click it, it
will smudge,
just like a real
rubber stamp.
This can be
useful.

Healing Brush and Patch Tools

Retouching has always been one of the major reasons why people buy and learn to use Photoshop. Recognizing this, the folks at Adobe have made the job easier with some tools specifically designed to touch up your photos. They are the Healing Brush, Spot Healing Brush, and Patch tools.

The Healing Brush, which looks like a Band-Aid, can be applied to any kind of spot that needs removal. Instantly, it's gone, and without affecting anything but the spot.

Sort of like digital zit cream. But it works quite differently, by using some fairly complicated math to average the texture, lighting, and shading of each group of pixels in order to locate the ones that are out of the normal range. Those nonconforming pixels represent the spot, and they're simply replaced by pixels that match the average tone that should be there. You can actually watch them change. Of course, you can heal any kind of surface, not just skin.

When using the Healing Brush, you Option+click (Alt+click) to choose a source from which to copy pixels. The difference between the Healing Brush and the Clone Stamp is that the Clone Stamp works by simply copying and pasting the group of pixels you have selected, whereas the Healing Brush melds the replacement pixels into the original ones. The changes are less obvious. In Figure 21.11, I've tried to clean up the stray hair and sweat on the man's forehead with both the Clone Stamp, on the left, and the Healing Brush on the right. Judge for yourself which one looks better. (You really have to see this in color. Flip to the color plate section.) The main thing you need to be careful about is that if you apply the Healing Brush very close to dark hair, it will pick up extra dark pixels and average them into the correction as well, making a darker spot on the face. You can mask the hair before you start, or just use the Clone Stamp on those places.

The Spot Healing Brush is like a quick-and-dirty version of the Healing Brush—or maybe that should be quick-and-clean. Instead of defining a point from which to copy new pixels, then painting, all you do with the Spot Healing Brush is click on the spot you want to eliminate. Photoshop looks at the area around the spot, averages the colors it finds, covers the spot with the average color, and blends the repair in with its surroundings—all in about half a second. For slightly larger spots, you can click and drag, but make sure that the spot you're trying to eliminate is located in the middle of a relatively uniform area so that the tool doesn't pull in different-colored pixels from an adjacent area.

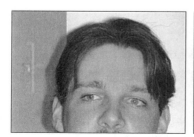 

FIGURE 21.11
On the left, cleaned up with the Clone Stamp. On the right, same skin, cleaned with the Healing Brush and Spot Healing Brush.

For larger areas, there's the Patch tool. Like the Healing Brush tool, it matches the texture, lighting, and shading of the sampled pixels to the source pixels. It's not completely opaque, so it blends the new pixels with the old ones, rather than copying and pasting. To use it, you must first decide whether the piece you select is the source or the destination. Click the appropriate button on the Tool Options bar. The tool pointer for the Patch Tool is a lasso. In source mode, select the area you want to replace. Drag the shape you've lassoed over the stuff you want to replace it with, and Photoshop does the rest. In Figure 21.12, you can see how I am using the Patch tool in Destination mode to remove the power lines in the sky. I've already done a piece on the top. I have just dragged the lassoed piece of clean blue sky over the power line on the left side. When I release the mouse button, the patch will fill in.

FIGURE 21.12
Although the lasso is the default, you can use any selection tool to make the selection. Then, click the Patch tool and continue to make the repair.

In the following exercise, you'll use the Healing Brush, Spot Healing Brush, and Patch—and probably all the tricks in the book.

Cleaning Up a Picture, Step by Step

As you can see in Figure 21.13, this picture has been ripped, faded, badly scratched, and generally beaten up. We'll go through this one step by step so that you can see exactly what happens at each stage. You can download this one from the website mentioned in the Introduction and follow along. It's called brothers.jpg.

FIGURE 21.13
This will take some work. (Photo courtesy of Suzanne Hecker.)

Try it Yourself ▼

Restore a Badly Damaged Photo

To make this picture, or any other, look like new:

1. Crop the image to remove the border, if there is one, and any unnecessary parts of the image. (Anything you remove doesn't have to be retouched.) Select the Crop tool from the toolbox. Drag it across the picture, holding down the mouse button. Use the handles on the cropping outline to fine-tune the selection, and then double-click inside the window to crop the image.

2. Set the mode to Grayscale (Image→Mode→Grayscale) to remove the colored stains and the brown tones.

3. Open the Histogram palette. Look at the histogram to see what needs to be done to equalize the contrast (see Figure 21.14). In this case, both the white and dark points need to be reset. To make these changes, you'll need to adjust the levels.

FIGURE 21.14
The histogram shows a lot of middle points and not many very light or dark ones.

4. Open the Levels dialog box (Image→Adjustments→Levels) and adjust the levels by dragging the dark slider to the right until it's under the beginning of the dark peak of the histogram. Drag the white slider to the left until it's under the beginning of the white peak. Figure 21.15 shows these adjustments.

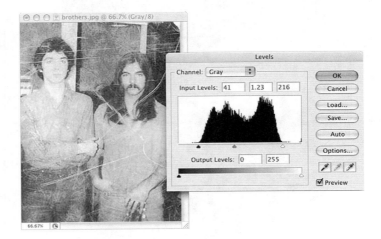

FIGURE 21.15
Adjusting the levels improves the contrast.

5. Now try the Dust & Scratches filter (Filters→Noise→Dust & Scratches). In this case, it seems that the harm it does outweighs the improvement. In removing the dust, it removes too much detail, even at a low setting. (Figure 21.16 shows the filter applied.) Click OK to apply the filter or Cancel if you don't want to use it.

Did you Know?

In the Background

If the image you're working on has a clearly delineated foreground figure and a smooth or blurry background, try selecting just the background and then running the Dust & Scratches filter. Any blurring the filter does won't matter as much on the background, and you'll save yourself a lot of picky clean-up work.

6. Because the Dust & Scratches filter didn't do what we wanted it to do, you'll have to remove the scratches by hand. Let's use the Healing Brush to cover them, starting with the background because it's a good place to practice with this tool. Select the Healing Brush and open the Brushes palette. Choose a soft-edged brush. Choose Source: Sampled and make sure Aligned isn't checked. Pick the dark tone adjacent to the scratch, and start stamping it out. Remember to set a spot to use as a source, by pressing Option (Mac) or Alt (Windows) while you click the mouse on the spot you want to copy. For small spots located far from object edges, try using the Spot Healing Brush with a small, hard-edged brush selection. Figure 21.17 shows the partially treated photo. Remember to change your source selection as the areas the damage runs through change value.

FIGURE 21.16
Removing dust can also remove detail.

FIGURE 21.17
Obviously, I am working from the top down.

7. The best way to remove the scratches across the faces is to use the Brush tool and repaint each face, rather than trying to stamp them. To make the task easier, enlarge the picture to at least 200%. Switch to the Zoom tool at the bottom of the toolbox and click it in the image window to enlarge the picture.

8. Select the Eyedropper tool and click the closest gray adjacent to the scratch. Choose a small brush and paint over the scratches, changing shades of gray with the Eyedropper as needed. Figure 21.18 shows before and after views of this step.

9. At the same time, you can use a combination of the Spot Healing Brush and the Smudge tool to remove any light spots and to blend small gaps in the image.

FIGURE 21.18
Be careful not
to apply paint
too evenly.

10. Next, apply the Dodge and Burn tools as needed to bring out details. Dodging lightens the image, and burning darkens it. Sponging, the third tool in that toolbox compartment, increases or decreases the saturation of colors. Select the Dodge tool and set its exposure to 25% so that the effect will be gradual. Figure 21.19 shows the progress to this point.

FIGURE 21.19
It's looking
better.

11. Now all that's left to do is to try a little Unsharp Masking, or possibly a small amount of Gaussian Blur. Compare Figure 21.20 with the original photo. It's not perfect. It's still a very grainy photo, but it's not scratched and torn anymore.

FIGURE 21.20
Maybe not as good as new, but darned close.

Toggle Trick

When you're applying filters such as Dust & Scratches, you can quickly toggle the filter preview on and off by clicking in the preview area. When the mouse button is down, the filter effects aren't shown in the preview area. This lets you judge the effect.

Did you Know?

Applying Tints

It was common in the early days of photography for pictures to be brown, blue, or silver instead of plain black and white. Sepia toning, which gave a warm reddish-brown color, was the most common, and the one we tend to associate with most old-time photos.

If you want to restore the sepia tone to a picture you've been working on, Photoshop gives you several ways to accomplish this. Perhaps the easiest is to reset the mode to CMYK or RGB, depending on whether the finished photo will be viewed onscreen or printed, and then use the Hue/Saturation dialog box (Image→Adjust→Hue) to add color. After you open the dialog box, as shown in Figure 21.21, check the Colorize and Preview boxes. Then move the sliders until the image looks the way you want. Click OK when you're satisfied with the color.

Duotones

A somewhat richer tone can be achieved by using Duotone mode, which combines the grayscale image with a colored ink. Duotones are often used to extend the gray range of a photograph because a typical printing press is capable of reproducing only about 50 shades of gray. (Photoshop can generate 256.)

To create a duotone look, start with a grayscale image. You needn't convert it back to RGB or whatever color space you usually work in. Choose Image→Mode→ Duotone. In the Duotone Options dialog box, you also have the option of adding colors to make a tritone or quadtone. Although duotones are usually composed of black plus a single color, as shown in Figure 21.22, there's no good reason why you can't use two colors instead, especially if the end result is to be displayed on a web page or as part of a desktop presentation, rather than in printed form.

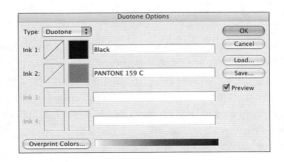

Try it Yourself ▼

Create a Duotone from a Grayscale Image

If you did the last exercise, try applying a duotone to the teenagers. Otherwise, use any photo with a wide range of gray tones. To make a duotone from a grayscale image, follow these steps:

1. Open the Duotone Options dialog box (choose Image→Mode→Duotone).

2. Choose Duotone from the Type pop-up menu, if it's not already selected (refer to Figure 21.22). This menu is in the upper-left corner of the dialog box.

3. Choose colors for your duotone by clicking the color swatches. Choose black or a dark color for Ink 1 and a lighter color for Ink 2. (Figure 21.22 shows my choices.) You must select the Adobe Color Picker, rather than the system Color Picker, to access the Custom colors (that is, colors from ink systems such as PANTONE, Focoltone, Toyo, Trumatch, and so on). If you need to switch to the Adobe Color Picker, close this dialog box temporarily by clicking Cancel, and open the General Preferences dialog box by pressing Command+K (Mac) or Control+K (Windows). Set the Color Picker to Adobe and click OK. Reopen the Duotone Options dialog box and proceed.

4. Use the curve proxies within the Duotone Options dialog box to adjust the curves for your two colors. (They're the small windows with diagonal lines, just to the right of the words *Ink 1* and *Ink 2*.) If you click one of the small curves, it expands to a full-size curve grid, which works just like the one on the Image→Adjustments→Curves submenu (see Figure 21.23). Click to set points and drag to adjust the curve. You can see the effect of your changes on the image as you work, and you can also monitor what you're doing using the strip of tone in the Duotone Curve dialog box.

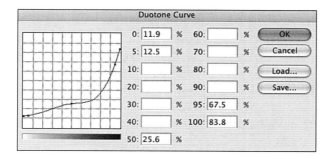

FIGURE 21.23
Here we're adjusting the curve for Ink 2.

5. Click OK to apply the duotone to the image. If you're not satisfied with the result, choose Image→Mode→Duotone again and try a different combination. ▲

That '50s Look

Using blue as the second color along with black gives you an image that replicates an old, black-and-white TV set. Using a light-to-medium brown with black gives a fairly good imitation of sepia, as does a combination of red and green. If you use red and green, though, be sure to use the same curve settings for both colors so that the image doesn't have reddish or greenish areas.

"Hand-Tinted" Photos

Years ago, before color film was readily available, it was common to see hand-tinted photos. These had been painstakingly overpainted with thinned-out special paints to add a pale suggestion of color to the picture. The Photoshop Brush and its Airbrush option are well suited for re-creating the look of a hand-colored photograph. You can even do the whole Ted Turner routine and colorize stills from your favorite Marx Brothers movie or Bogart classic. (You can find lots of movie stills and movie star pictures on the Web to practice on.)

After you have cleaned up the image that you want to hand-tint, change the mode back to color, either RGB or CMYK. Make a new layer and set the layer opacity to between 10% and 30%. Set the Brush opacity to 80% and paint your tints. Alternatively, leave the layer at 100% opacity, change its blending mode to color, and paint away!

If you have large, uncomplicated areas to tint, use one of the selection tools, such as the Lasso or the Magic Wand, to select the area. Select a foreground color and choose Fill from the Edit menu; a dialog box will appear.

Set the Opacity to about 25% and choose Multiply from the Blending Mode menu. Do *not* check Preserve Transparency. Set Foreground Color on the Use pop-up menu. Click OK to fill all the selected areas with your chosen color at that opacity. If it's not enough, either reopen the Fill dialog box and apply the fill again, or undo the Fill operation and redo it with a higher percentage. If it's too much, undo and try again with a lower percentage. Be sure to see the finished picture in the color section, as well as in Figure 21.24.

FIGURE 21.24
Use Fill for large areas. It's faster and smoother than painting. (Photo courtesy of D. Maynard.)

Vignetting

When you're working with old photos, or with new photos that you would like to look old, *vignetting* is often the trick that makes the difference. It gives that sort of cameo look as the portrait subject comes forward and the background fades to nothing. Here's an easy way to do it.

Draw an elliptical selection marquee around the portrait subject. Invert the selection so that the background is selected. Feather the selection by whatever amount looks right (choose Select→Feather). Use Edit→Fill and set the Use menu to white, Mode to Normal, and Opacity to 100%. Figure 21.25 shows the effect.

FIGURE 21.25
No more annoying backgrounds.

Summary

This chapter looked at ways to repair photographs that need help. When you have old, cracked, torn, or faded pictures, you can use a variety of Photoshop tools to cover up the imperfections and restore the image. The Eyedropper tool enables you to select a color or gray tone and apply it with any of your Painting tools. The Clone Stamp clones a selected piece of the picture and places it wherever you want it, as much or as little as needed to cover a crack, fill in an empty space, or cover objects you want to hide. The Healing Brush and Patch tools copy the characteristics of a selection and transfer them to another, maintaining the same lighting, texture, and so on. The Patch tool selects an area with a lasso, whereas the Healing Brush works with brush shapes.

Tinting old photos can be managed in any of several ways. Toning can be applied by colorizing or by turning the picture into a duotone, tritone, or quadtone. Hand-tinting can give you a different "old" picture look. Vignetting adds to the old look.

Workshop

Q&A

Q *How can I remove my ex-husband from a group shot of the family? He's right in front.*

A Perhaps you can find some other face the right size and colors to hide him. (Brad Pitt, perhaps?) Adjust the size and position of the new face on a separate layer. Blur the face you want to hide and use the Layers palette's Opacity slider to bring in the replacement. If you leave it at about 80%, it should merge right in.

Q *Printing these old photos on plain paper just doesn't look right. What should I use?*

A If you want to duplicate the look of the original photo printed on glossy paper, invest in a package of glossy photo-quality paper for your inkjet printer. If the photo was originally printed with a matte surface, try printing on card stock.

Q *Okay, I've retouched all the old family photos. What do I do now?*

A The next logical step is to buy a package of photo-quality glossy paper and print them as photos. Kodak, HP, Canon, and Epson all sell glossy paper for inkjet printers. It's about the same weight as photo paper, and it makes your pictures look really good. If you don't have a reasonably good color printer, take your photos to a service bureau and have them printed on a color laser or high-quality inkjet.

Be sure to save the files for future use, too. DVDs, CD-ROMs, and Zip disks can hold several generations of family photos and can be stored in very little space. If you keep a backup copy in a safe place, such as a bank safe-deposit box, your precious family history is fire- and flood-proof. You can also place a family album on your web page, so distant relatives and friends can see how the kids have grown.

Quiz

1. Burning is the opposite of

    a. Covering

    b. Filling

    c. Dodging

2. The Clone Stamp tool places

   a. Text

   b. A copy of the image area you have selected

   c. Random shapes and designs

3. How many colors of ink are in a duotone?

   a. One

   b. One plus black

   c. Any two, not necessarily including black

4. To remove the sepia toning from an old scanned photo

   a. Change the mode to grayscale

   b. Adjust the colors to add more cyan

   c. Click Bleach

Quiz Answers

1. c. Dodging lightens the image. Burning darkens it.

2. b. Although c. might be fun.

3. c. Although black is usually one of the two colors, it needn't be.

4. a. This also helps get rid of colored ink, coffee, or other stains on a black-and-white print.

Exercises

Find a picture in need of retouching, or download one from this book's page on the Sams website. Clean it up as much as you think necessary and save a copy. Convert the copy to a duotone. Hand-tint the original using transparent tints. Notice how the duotone looks like rotogravure pages from the 1930s, whereas the hand-colored version looks like photos from the '40s or '50s. Think about how you might use these techniques with your own work.

Photo Repair—Color

What You'll Learn in This Hour:

▶ Color Retouching
▶ Removing

Last hour, we worked on some black-and-white pictures that needed help. This hour, we'll do the same with color pictures. You can adjust the colors to fix a picture that's faded with age or has too much red, green, or some other color in it. You can compensate for slight-to-moderate underexposure or overexposure, but you can't put back an image that's just not there, unless you paint it in.

You can take the red out of your daughter's eyes or the unearthly green out of the cat's eyes. Does your teenager wonder how she would look with orange or green hair or a half-shaved head? Try it on the screen first. Maybe she'll settle for a second set of earrings.

Color Retouching

So far, all the pictures we've worked on are old, black-and-white photos. You can use most of the same tools and tricks in color. You might find that color retouching is even easier than working in black-and-white. The color tends to disguise some of the manipulation.

Figure 22.1 is a picture that was taken sometime in the late 1960s. I don't know what happened to it. Perhaps it was left on a radiator or in the sun. Maybe it wasn't processed right. It was dark to start with and as you can see in the supposedly white edge, it's turned yellow. Feel free to download the picture from the Sams website and work along. It's called momanddog.jpg.

FIGURE 22.1
This picture
turned yellow
with age.

Apply a Simple Color Correction to a Photo

First, look at the Channels palette, shown in Figure 22.2. You can immediately
see that the darkest channel is the blue one. In this case, that means that there's
not enough blue in the image. We also know that there's too much yellow. The
good news is that there's good detail on all three channels, suggesting that we
should be able to balance the colors and save the photo.

FIGURE 22.2
We need to bal-
ance the red
and blue.

Using the Curves dialog box, as shown in Figure 22.3, I can lower the curve of the green channel to remove most of the unwanted color. Rather than trying to remove it all, which would take away the flesh tones, it's better to compromise. To adjust a single color with the Curves window, follow these steps:

1. With the image open, open the Curves window (choose Image→Adjustments→Curves).

2. Choose the color that needs adjusting from the pop-up Channels menu. Choose Red, Green, or Blue if those colors need lessening. If you decide the problem is with cyan, magenta, or yellow, consider the color wheel, and work with the complementary color. If there's too much yellow, add blue. If there's too much magenta, add green. If there's too much cyan, add red. In this case, we obviously need to decrease both yellow and blue. But there's no yellow curve, so we decrease the green instead.

3. Drag the curve up to increase the amount of the color. Drag it down to decrease the amount by adding the complement. Watch the preview as you drag. Click OK when the colors look right (see Figure 22.3).

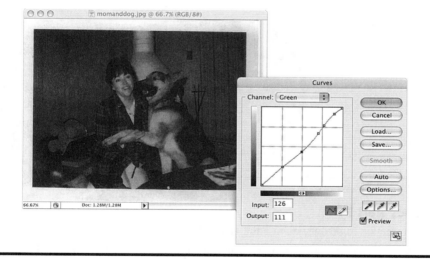

FIGURE 22.3
After correcting the green, you can also adjust the red and blue if necessary.

This photo needs some additional tweaking to increase the saturation now that we've taken out the excess color. It also needs cropping and some brightness and contrast adjustment, and some spot removal. Be sure to see the final picture in the color section. It's a big improvement.

Fixing Red Eye

You've seen red eye. It's not a problem in black-and-white photos that you colorize, but it's often a problem in color pictures of people and animals taken with a flash camera.

Basically what happens is that the flash reflects off the blood vessels at the back of the eye and puts an eerie, red glow into the pupils of anyone looking straight at the flash. Some animals, by the way, can also display a similar phenomenon called *green eye*, which is caused by the flash reflecting off the back of the eye. You can avoid this if you make sure that your portrait subject, human or otherwise, isn't looking directly at the flash. Also, make sure that there's plenty of light in the room so that the subject's pupils have contracted as small as possible.

You may think red eye is easily fixed these days with a quick application of the Red Eye tool, but this magic solution doesn't work in all cases. Figure 22.4 shows a portrait of a blue-eyed cat suffering from serious red eye. This one was shot in a dark room and the flash caught the cat staring wide-eyed. If we correct the off-color eyes, it will be a nice picture. But the large red area overwhelms the Red Eye tool—it doesn't know where to apply its magic—so we'll have to step in with a manual repair.

FIGURE 22.4
Even printed in black-and-white, the eyes look wrong. On the color plate, they're scary!

Try it Yourself

Correct Red Eye

The correction is actually quite easy. Here's how to do it:

1. Open the image and zoom in on the eyes by clicking the Zoom tool in the image window.

2. Use the Magic Wand to select the parts that need to be corrected (see Figure 22.5).

FIGURE 22.5
Cat's eye selected at 200% magnification.

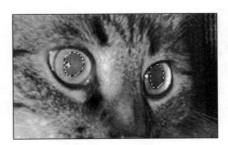

3. Choose the Paint Bucket tool. Set the foreground color to black or to a dark color from the image. On the Options bar, set the blending mode to Darken with an Opacity no greater than about 80%. This setting darkens the eye while maintaining the detail.

4. Pour the paint carefully into the pupils of the eyes, making sure not to pour it into any white or colored highlights in the pupil. You might need to click different selected parts of the pupil to cover it all. If you accidentally fill one of the highlights, undo. If you want to accent the highlights more, use a single-pixel pencil and touch up as needed.

5. Press Command+H (Mac) or Control+H (Windows) to hide the selection so that you can evaluate the effect of the change. Figure 22.6 shows the finished cat.

FIGURE 22.6
Highlights in the pupils are called catch-lights.

The semi-opaque black that we poured in effectively darkened the pupils without losing detail. You can use this technique any time you have a small area in a picture that needs to have the color changed drastically. Be careful not to select any part of the image that you *don't* want to change.

The Color Replacement Tool

If the method we just used to fix the cat's eyes doesn't appeal to you, you'll be glad to know that Photoshop includes a tool created expressly for fixing small spots that need a quick color change. The Color Replacement tool uses the foreground color to paint selectively over only the color you choose to replace. It's quicker than using the previous method, but might not give as good results around the edges of the eye. If you find a red ring around your corrected eye, you can adjust the tolerance to a higher setting so more of the color will be replaced. Figure 22.7 shows the tool in use, correcting the same eyes.

FIGURE 22.7
Which do you
think is the bet-
ter correction,
this or Figure
22.6?

*By the
Way*

How Much Change Is Okay?

Editing a picture to improve the composition is entirely reasonable, if it's a picture
for your own use, but this is precisely what got the esteemed *National Geographic*
magazine in trouble some years ago. They were doing a piece on Egypt and sent a
photographer to get pictures of the pyramids. The art director studied the pictures
and decided the composition would be better if he moved one of the pyramids
closer to the next. As soon as the issue was published, astute readers began call-
ing and writing to the magazine to complain. An apology appeared in the following
issue, but simply knowing that the manipulation was possible waved a red flag for
many people both inside and outside the publishing industry. The question has
been debated ever since. How much change is okay? How much is too much?

It's clear that you can't always believe what you see. The supermarket tabloids frequently feature pictures that stretch the bounds of believability. Remember the
one of the president shaking hands with the space alien? Or Bigfoot carrying off
the scantily clad woman? (Why was she dressed like that in the snow anyway?) On
the other hand, if a model is having a bad hair day or her face breaks out,
retouching is required and expected. Where do you draw the line?

The answer depends on how the picture is to be used. Reputable newspapers and
magazines tend to have strict guidelines about what they'll allow for photo manipulation. The general rule seems to be that, if a change affects the content of the
photo rather than its appearance, you can't do it. You can lighten a too-dark picture of the politician, but you can't change the soda can in his hand into a beer
can (or vice versa).

Drag-and-Drop Repairs

Some photos are almost perfect, except for one annoying flaw. Maybe there are
power lines running through the sky, or litter on the ground (see Figure 22.8). When
the area directly next to the troublesome spot is essentially the same as the rest of
the foreground, you can get rid of the clutter by simply lassoing a piece of sky or
street or whatever and dragging it to cover the offending objects. This technique
works well when you have things like power lines or cell phone antennae sticking
into the sky or anything against an uncomplicated background.

Here's a photo of a fishing pier in Yarmouth, NS. I like the photo, but I don't like all the wires.

FIGURE 22.8
Nice pier, but too many strings attached.

Try it Yourself

Use the Patch Tool to Retouch a Photo

To use the Patch for this purpose:

1. Select the Patch tool. Make sure Source is selected on the Tool Options bar.
2. Select the area you want to patch over by circling it with the Patch tool.
3. With the selection marquee active, drag the selection to an area of the image that would form a good patch. (See a close view of this in Figure 22.9.)

FIGURE 22.9
Be sure to cover all of the area.

4. Repeat as needed. You can also use this trick to hide any other parts of the picture that you don't want.

Did you
Know?

Another Way to Patch

You may have noticed that the Patch Tool Options bar offers you a choice of Source or Destination settings. The Source option works as just described. If you switch to Destination, the area you select with the Patch tool is dropped over the area to which you drag it, rather than vice versa. Use Destination if you have a good idea what area of the image you want to use as a patch. For example, if you want to drop Antonio Banderas's face over your cousin's face in a family portrait, select Antonio with the Patch tool and drag him right where you want him. If your goal is simply to cover something up, and you're less concerned with what you cover it *with,* use Source mode.

Editing a Picture

There are times when you have to remove more than a scratch or a small imperfection from a photo. Sometimes you have to take out larger objects to save a potentially good picture. Figure 22.10 shows just such a photo. A friend sent me this in hopes that I could remove the distracting background. There's a copy at the book's website so you can work along. It's called `family.jpg`.

FIGURE 22.10
That background needs to come out.
(Photo courtesy of Joyce Flagg.)

▼   **Try it Yourself**

Remove Unwanted Items

The first step in rescuing any photo is to determine whether it needs cropping or color correction. This one is well cropped but needs a bit more cyan. Adjusting using the Variations dialog box lets you add cyan and darken the image a little bit. Now you can move on to a trickier fix.

▼

1. Let's replace the wallpaper with a plain-colored background, choosing a color from some other part of the photo. I'll work on a new layer first, and paint the new background color on it. I've chosen a blue green from the sweater of the woman on the right, and just sprayed it on the new layer over the old background, not worrying a lot about the edges. Figure 22.11 depicts what it looks like now.

FIGURE 22.11
Be sure you catch any cutouts—small background areas surrounded by foreground elements—and put background there, too.

2. Now comes the fun part. You have to swap the position of the two layers. It will look, temporarily, as if the new background has vanished. Double-click the background layer, which is the photo of the four couples. Rename it whatever you want to call it (Layer 0, the default name, is fine in this case). Then, on the Layers palette, drag it above the layer you just put down. See Figure 22.12.

FIGURE 22.12
You want the new background behind the photo.

3. All you have to do now is to select and remove the wallpaper, thus revealing the background. For this, you can use any of the Lassos, or the Eraser tools. I prefer the Magnetic Lasso for jobs like this, but I'll still need to do some touch-ups with a small eraser. See Figure 22.13.

4. I've removed the awful wallpaper. Now is a good time to do any last-minute
    color adjustments. I tweaked the saturation up a small amount, and applied
    the Despeckle filter to remove the dust that had been on the scanner glass.
    Finally, because the painted wall looked so flat, I used the Lighting Effects fil-
    ter to add some reflected light and shadow to the wall. Figure 22.14 and the
    color plate section show the final photo, ready to go up on the wall.

FIGURE 22.14
That looks
much better.

Removing

It happens in the best of families—someone creeps into the family portrait who really shouldn't be there. Maybe it's your former spouse, or your kid's current attraction
with the green punk hairdo, leather vest, and nose ring. Well, whoever it is, you can
usually get him or her out of the picture more easily with Photoshop than in the
flesh. Figure 22.15 was shot at a trade show. The man in the foreground had a
striped shirt that photographed with a moiré pattern, and there's a woman in a
bright red shirt mostly hidden who might as well not be there.

FIGURE 22.15
Nice shirt, but it
didn't photo-
graph well.

I'm going to remove the woman, and turn the striped shirt into a nice even gray.
The first step is to select the shirt. In Figure 22.16, I've used the Magic Wand and
Lasso tools to isolate the stripes. I've also applied a small amount of the Lens Blur
filter to them. This makes the stripes blend into each other. Because it's only applied
to the shirt, the rest of the photo remains sharp.

FIGURE 22.16
Yipes! No more
stripes.

This next piece is even easier. I can just copy a piece of the background from above
the woman's head and slide it down. Figure 22.17 shows the picture after removing
the extraneous bystander.

The fixes required took only a couple of minutes, and definitely improved the picture. This kind of "candid" photo almost always has something in it that you wish
wasn't there. Thanks to the magic of Photoshop and a few minutes of work, you can
make all of your pictures perfect.

FIGURE 22.17
It's as if she were never even in the room.

Putting Back What Was Never There

The Maritime Museum in Halifax, NS, has a thoroughly intriguing *Titanic* exhibit; particularly interesting is the deck chair—one of a handful that survived the sinking. It's shown in Figure 22.18. Having been accused at least once of some useless action like "rearranging the deck chairs on the *Titanic*," it seemed as if I should take the opportunity to do so. I would like my deck chair somewhere on a nice sandy beach.

FIGURE 22.18
The deck chairs on the *Titanic* were solid oak. Having the fake deck under this one will make selecting it tricky.

The best way to select the chair seems to be to use the Magic Wand at a fairly low tolerance. I'm still going to pick up some of the floor, but I can hold the Option/Alt key down while I use the Lasso to circle and remove unwanted planks. See Figure 22.19.

I ended up using the Magnetic Lasso as well as the Magic Wand and the regular Lasso. Enlarging the image helped a lot, too, but it's still a test of one's patience. Finally, with the chair completely selected, I simply cut it out of the picture, and place it on a nice sandy beach I shot on the same trip. Because I didn't like the way it faced, I flipped it and distorted it a little so it would look more natural. Finally, a drop shadow on the chair layer adds a bit of realism, and I copied and pasted some of those strange weeds over the chair (see Figure 22.20).

The point of these exercises is that there's no picture too damaged, or too full of interlopers, to rescue. The only limit to what you can do with your pictures is your own imagination.

FIGURE 22.19
It takes a good deal of patience to select just the chair.

FIGURE 22.20
The final result.

Summary

Color repair isn't much different from black-and-white photo repair, except that you need to be a little more aware of the colors and color-blending modes. Off-color photos are fixed with Photoshop's regular color adjustment tools. Retouching to get rid of obvious flaws and red eye is best accomplished with Photoshop's special tools and with the image enlarged so that you can see what you're doing. Use layers to protect your original while you're working, and merge the changes when you are satisfied with the results.

Workshop

Q&A

Q *If the picture I need to repair doesn't have enough background to copy, or doesn't have a good background, what should I do?*

A Remember that Photoshop allows you to have more than one file open at a time. You can borrow from another picture and copy the selection onto a new layer of the picture that needs fixing. Shrink it or enlarge it so that the texture is in scale with the rest of the scene, and then copy and paste it as much as needed. If you have a digital camera, shoot lots of backgrounds and keep them in a special folder on your computer or on a Zip drive. Then when you have a problem photo, you have ready-made scenery to drop the subject into.

Q *What color mode should I be working in: CMYK Color, RGB Color, Indexed Color, Lab Color, or Grayscale?*

A If the image is grayscale, such as a black-and-white photo, and is going to remain grayscale, stay in that mode. If the image is intended for the Web or an inkjet printer, stick with RGB. If the image will be sent to a commercial print shop for four-color process printing, convert to CMYK after you've done your retouching.

Quiz

1. Red eye is caused by

    a. Excessive consumption of caffeine

    b. Impossible deadlines

    c. Light reflecting off the back of the eye

    d. Trying to finish this book in 24 hours straight

2. If a picture is too yellow, add more

    a. Cyan

    b. Blue

    c. White

3. Old color photos most often look too

   a. Blue

   b. Red

   c. Washed out

Quiz Answers

1. a., b., c., and d. Mine are almost too red for Photoshop to correct.

2. b. Blue is the color wheel opposite of yellow.

3. b. Color dyes often shift toward red as a print ages.

Exercises

Find some of your own photo portraits that have bad red eye. Scan them into the computer and use the tricks you have learned to restore normal eye colors. Next, find a group photo and remove one member of the group.

PART VI

Picture Publishing on Paper and Otherwise

HOUR 23

Printing and Publishing

What You'll Learn in This Hour:

- ▶ Choosing a Printer
- ▶ Preparing to Print
- ▶ Printing the Page
- ▶ Preparing the Image
- ▶ Picking the Paper
- ▶ Placing Photoshop Images in Other Programs

We're almost done… You've created some wonderful Photoshop art, and you would like to hang it on the walls and send copies to your friends. You want to use your pictures in newsletters and PowerPoint presentations, maybe even in databases. (You would probably also like to add these masterpieces to your web page, but you'll learn that in the next hour.) Even in this brave new world of the Web-enabled camera phone, the inexcusably cool iPod Photo, and other electronic media, printing isn't going away, and it never will. Getting your image to output correctly is as important as any other step in the process of image creation, and that's why it deserves its own hour.

Printing should be easy, right? Choose the Print command and watch your image emerge on paper. Unfortunately, getting Photoshop images to print well can involve quite a few variables and decisions. In this hour, we'll look at what those are, from choosing a printer through setting up inks, separations, halftones, and other issues.

Be warned. Some of this stuff gets into detail and gets very technical, and some of it is irrelevant if you print to only one kind of printer. Feel free to ignore the sections that don't relate to the kind(s) of printing you do. If *none* of it makes sense, stick with the default settings. Your pages will be, at the very least, adequately printed.

Choosing a Printer

You know this already: Lots of printers, as well as lots of printing technologies, are out there. How you print obviously depends a lot on what printer you're using. In fact, the printer you use can and should influence how you work in Photoshop and how you prepare your image because you'll want to create a final image that will print best from your particular printer.

> ### Printers Are Not People Who Print
>
> By the way, when I talk about printers, I mean the machines that put the image on the paper, not the people who run them. Some printers sit next to your computer; others reside in commercial print shops or service bureaus.

An entire book could be written about all the varieties of printers. In this section, we'll make do with a snapshot of what's available: inkjet printers, laser printers, dye-sublimation printers, and imagesetters.

Inkjet Printers

At the inexpensive end of the spectrum are home and office inkjet printers, almost all of which can deliver acceptable-quality color printing. Examples of inkjets include HP's DeskJet series, Canon PIXMAs, and Epson's Stylus printers.

Inkjet printers are not necessarily PostScript-compatible. This means that some of them can't print *PostScript* information that might be in your non-art documents. For most Photoshop images, however, this isn't a problem unless you've chosen to save them in EPS (Encapsulated PostScript) format.

> ### P.S.:
>
> *PostScript* is a page-description language that lets any two devices (computer and compatible printer) describe and reproduce exactly the same page.

The quality of output varies tremendously between inkjet printers, ranging from fair to excellent, depending on how much you want to spend. A lot depends on the size of the ink dot that a printer applies and whether it uses a four- or six-color process. Basic inkjets use a four-color ink cartridge, with cyan, magenta, yellow, and black inks. Many can produce photo-quality pictures. More sophisticated printers use a six-color process that adds two more inks, usually a light magenta and light cyan. In the four-color process, if you have a broad light area, such as sky, you might see the dots of cyan and magenta that color it because they're quite far apart. Using lighter values of those inks lets the printer place more color, less visibly.

High-end inkjets, like the Iris, can cost tens of thousands of dollars but can be perfect for graphics professionals. Iris and similar art-quality printers are sometimes found at service bureaus or art studios. They can produce very large prints, up to 33×46 inches, with remarkable detail and quality. You can have an Iris print made of your work, but they tend to be expensive. Prices range from $50 to $100 for a single 16×20 print.

Laser Printers

The laser printer offers a good balance of price, quality, and speed. Laser printers abound from well-known companies such as Brother and Hewlett-Packard.

Most laser printers output 300 to 600 dpi (some up to 1200 dpi), and they are particularly good with halftone and grayscale images. Some can subtly alter the size of the printed dots, thus improving quality. Laser printers are generally faster than inkjet printers, but they tend to be more expensive.

Color laser prints can be very good, if you like bright colors and don't mind the shiny surface that you're likely to get in areas where the toner is quite dense. Laser printers work by fusing powdered toner to the paper. Color lasers use a four-color toner cartridge.

Dye-Sublimation Printers

Dye-sublimation printers are expensive photographic-quality printers, but you get what you pay for. Image quality is superb, but these printers use special ribbons and paper. You can't use ordinary paper with them, and the specially coated paper is expensive. You can often find these printers at a service bureau, where you can get a single dye-sub print for a modest fee. If you're satisfied with small, but perfect prints, look into desktop dye-sublimation printers. Several companies make them at reasonable prices. The drawback is that the most affordable ones only make 4×6 prints.

Imagesetters

Imagesetters are printers used for medium- or large-scale commercial printing jobs. These large, expensive machines burn the image onto photographic film or paper. That film is then developed and used to make printing plates that are used for the actual printing. We're talking high resolution here: 1,200–2,400 dpi, or even better.

Imagesetters don't print in color, per se. Instead, you have to create a separate image for each color you want printed. These are called *color separations*; we'll talk more about them later.

Preparing to Print

It's possible to go very deeply into the theory and methodology of printing. Professionals know the power of having color-compensated monitors and color-printing profiles, which guarantee that what you see on the screen is as close as humanly possible to what you will see on the paper. For the rest of us, most of the time pretty good is good enough. We'll delve into some of the mysteries of color printing in this hour, but before we do, let's start with the most basic of the basics.

Printers (the hardware kind) use software called *printer drivers* that function as part of your operating system, whether it's Mac OS or Windows. The driver converts the output from Photoshop (or your word processor, or whatever printable software you're using) into a form that the printer can understand and reproduce on paper. (Okay, on silk or transparency, too.) So, before you can print, you need to have a printer hooked up and the appropriate driver installed.

If you have more than one printer available, be sure that you've selected the one you intend to use. If you're on a Mac, use the Printer Setup Utility or choose your printer from the pop-up menu at the top of the Print dialog box. On a PC, select a printer from the File→Page Setup pop-up menu.

Photoshop has five print-related commands. Page Setup is part of the printer driver. Print with Preview is specific to Photoshop. (It used to be called Print Options.) Print is where you verify everything you've set in the other two boxes and click OK to create the actual print. Print One Copy does just that. It immediately sends the current image to the printer, no questions asked. It will print to the selected printer with whatever settings were used on the last photo. And Print Online starts up Bridge, which displays a form you can use to order prints online from Adobe (via Ofoto.com). If you just want to print using your own printer, you can make many of the same settings in either the Print with Preview or the Page Setup dialog box. It doesn't really matter which one you use. Let's start with Page Setup. It's shown in Figure 23.1.

Each printer's Page Setup dialog box looks a little different, and of course Mac and Windows Page Setup dialogs look different, but they all provide the same basic functions. (Note that not all additional options will be available in every situation.) A Page Setup dialog box will generally display the following information and options:

▶ Printer—The name of the printer always appears somewhere in the dialog box. Make sure you've selected the right one for the job.

▶ Properties—On Windows systems, you can click this button to access a dialog box that enables you to change options such as paper size, layout, printer resolution, and halftone settings.

▶ Paper Size—Choose the size of the paper on which you're printing. You'll generally find a good selection of standard U.S. and European paper sizes, including letter, legal, A4, tabloid, and envelope sizes.

▶ Source—If your printer has multiple paper trays or gives you a choice of tray or single-sheet feed, you can choose the paper source for the printer to use.

▶ Orientation—Choose how you want the printed image to be placed on the page: portrait (the page's height is the larger dimension) or landscape (the page's width is the larger dimension).

▶ Scale—Want the image to print smaller or larger? Adjust this percentage appropriately.

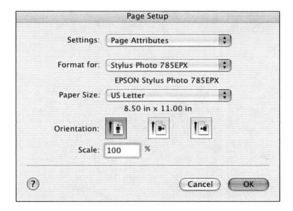

FIGURE 23.1
The Page Setup dialog box looks different depending on what printer you're using.

Too Big?

Later, when you actually click the Print button (see the next section), you might run into a problem with files that are large in dimension. If the image dimensions are larger than the dimensions of the page on which you're printing, Photoshop tells you. You can then choose to print anyway, resulting in only part of the image being printed, or you can cancel and adjust the Reduce or Enlarge value so that the whole image fits on the page.

By the Way

You can set other options in this dialog box, too, but I prefer to set them in the Print with Preview dialog box so that I can see exactly what I'm doing. Take a look at the Print with Preview dialog box in Figure 23.2.

The first option here is Position. If you uncheck Center Image, which is checked by default, you can then move the picture around on the page by varying the Top and Left position values, placing it wherever you want. This is a big change from early versions of Photoshop, which could only print an image centered. If you drag on a corner of the image, you can rescale it. The Scaled Print size values will change accordingly. You can also scale the image by typing a number into the Scale percentage window. Scaling is done relative to the original image size. If you have a photo that's 6 inches wide and you want it to print 9 inches wide, scale it to 150%. This setting can be made here or in the Page Setup box.

FIGURE 23.2
Notice that I've clicked the More Options button.

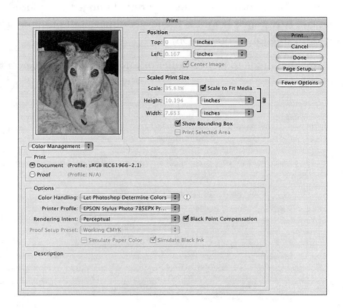

When you click Show More Options, you can choose between Output options and Color Management options. Output options are the same here as in the Page Setup box, except that you can see them on the preview screen as you apply them. In Figure 23.3, I've added crop marks, calibration marks, and a caption to my photo.

Here are some of the options and what they mean:

▶ Background—Want to print a background color around your image? Click the Background button and you'll be greeted by the standard Color Picker. Whichever color you pick is used only for printing and does not alter your actual image file. (If you're printing from Windows, be sure to turn this off after you use it. Otherwise, you'll print the background around the next picture as well.) Be careful about using this feature with an inkjet printer. It eats up a lot of ink!

▶ Border—Similarly, if you would like a border around your printed image, click the Border button. In the resulting dialog box, you can set the width of the printed border in inches, millimeters, or points. The border is always black; you can't change the color. (Like Background, using this feature doesn't affect the actual image file.)

▶ Bleed—*Bleeding* means that part of the image runs right off the edge of the paper. There isn't any border or empty space between the image and the edge of the page. (Note that this feature won't work on every printer. Some printers are incapable of printing to the very edge of a page.)

Click the Bleed button to define the bleed area of an image in inches, millimeters, or points. Higher values move the crop marks within the boundaries of the image so that less of the image gets printed. You can't bleed an image more than an eighth of an inch.

▶ Screen—Use Printer's Default Screens is checked by default, and you won't be able to change anything else. Uncheck this option if you want to customize the other halftone options. Most of the time, Photoshop's default settings work fine.

▶ Transfer—This allows you to compensate for dot gain between the image and film, when using an imagesetter. Dot gain is the increase in size that happens as ink spreads out on the paper. A 50% dot, for example, could print as a 58% dot, producing an 8% dot gain. The Transfer function makes 50% dots in the image print as 50% dots on film. Similar to dot gain curves, the transfer functions let you specify up to 13 values along the grayscale to create a customized transfer function. Unlike dot gain curves, transfer functions apply only to printing—they don't affect the image color data. If you're using a home/office inkjet printer, you needn't worry about dot gain.

▶ Interpolation—*Interpolation* refers to some printers' capability to resample an image as they print it. That is, any PostScript Level 2 printer can take a low-resolution image and resample it on-the-fly, improving the resolution so that the printout is of better quality. This is valuable only if you're dealing with low-resolution images. Interpolation is available only on PostScript printers.

▶ Calibration Bars—Check this box to print calibration and color bars next to your image. A calibration bar is a row of 11 gray squares of different values, and a color bar is a row of 11 colors. These bars can help when you're trying to calibrate to a specific printer or to see how a specific printer prints. (This option is available only if you're using a PostScript printer.)

▶ Registration Marks—Activate this feature to print a variety of registration marks around the image. You can add bull's eyes (which look like what you would expect), star targets (two crossed lines within a circle), and/or precise pinpoint marks (two simple crossed lines). These marks can be helpful for aligning color separations.

▶ Corner Crop Marks—Corner crop marks appear around each corner of your image, defining where it should be trimmed. They're simply horizontal and vertical lines.

▶ Center Crop Marks—These crop marks are centered along each side of the image, defining the exact center of the image. They look like two crossed lines. Figure 23.4 shows the registration marks and crop marks added to the image.

▶ Description—Check this box, and on the printed page you'll see the text that appears in the Description field of the File Info dialog box for that file. (To get to this dialog box, choose File→File Info and make sure that Description is selected in the top pop-up menu.) This can be helpful for providing contact info or details next to your image.

▶ Labels—This check box prints the filename next to the image. If you're printing color separations, the name of the appropriate color channel is also printed on each color plate.

▶ Emulsion Down—This setting prints your image as a horizontal mirror image of the original. Everything gets flipped left-to-right. Use this setting when you're printing on T-shirt transfer paper so that the image faces the right way when it's transferred to the shirt. Or, if you're taking the file to a print shop, the staff there can tell you whether you need to print this way for some other reason.

▶ Negative—With this option checked, the printer reverses the values of the image. That is, the whites become black, the blacks become white, and everything in between changes accordingly. You end up with a negative image. This option is useful if you're printing to film for commercial offset printing because these images usually need to be negatives.

Figure 23.3 shows the additional options I've selected in the Print with Preview dialog box. Figure 23.4 shows the resulting output.

Before you continue, make sure that whatever you want to print is currently visible on the screen. By default, Photoshop prints all visible layers and channels. If you want to print just certain layers or channels, make them the only ones that are visible.

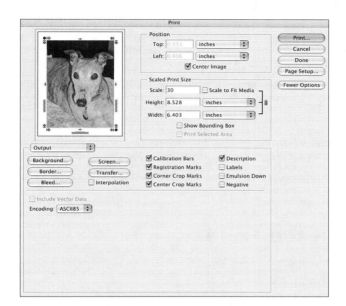

FIGURE 23.3
Now we're ready to print with the desired features.

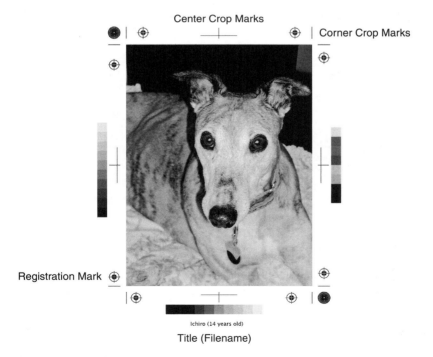

Center Crop Marks

Corner Crop Marks

Registration Mark

Ichiro (14 years old)

Title (Filename)

FIGURE 23.4
A printout showing various crop marks, registration marks, and a caption.

The Color Management options are fewer and simpler:

▶ Print—Choose Document for normal printing; choose Proof if you want to try to match the way your image would look when printed on an output device other than your own (such as a four-color printing press). Either way, Photoshop uses the device profiles specified in the Color Settings dialog box.

▶ Options—In the Color Handling pop-up menu, choose whether you want the color managed by Photoshop, by your printer, or not at all. If you choose Photoshop, specify a device profile that matches your printer. Leave the Rendering Intent pop-up menu set on Perceptual for the closest visual match in colors.

Printing the Page

Okay, now you're finally getting around to printing the image. I told you there were a lot of printing variables, didn't I?

Pull up the Print dialog box by choosing File→Print (see Figure 23.5). The first thing you should notice is that this dialog box also looks different depending on what printer you have, what platform you're running on, and the mode of the image. However, they all ask for the same information.

FIGURE 23.5
The ultimate
dialog box:
Print.

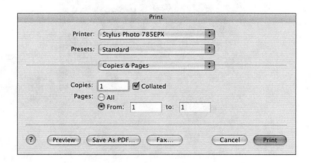

Let's look at some of the Print fields and options you might see:

▶ Copies—How many copies of the document do you want to print? Enter a number here.

▶ Pages—This area specifies the range of pages to be printed. This setting is irrelevant in Photoshop because its documents consist of only one page.

▶ Media Type—Here you enter what kind of paper or transparency film you're printing on. This setting actually determines how much ink is applied because different kinds of paper are more or less absorbent.

▶ Ink—Choose Color or Black.

▶ Print Quality (also called *Mode*)—You can often specify a printer resolution here, such as 300 or 600 dpi. Some printers enable you to specify Best, Normal, Econofast, or some variation on this theme, as well as a specific dpi setting. In this case, it's done by choosing Custom and then the quality.

▶ Destination—You can print to the printer, obviously, but you can also print to a file. This means saving the printed output as a PostScript or EPS file or an Adobe Acrobat PDF. (This option works only if you've selected a PostScript-compatible printer or are using Mac OS X.)

When you choose File, the Print button says Save. Click it to bring up the Save dialog box, where you can name the file and select the file format you want (see Figure 23.6).

FIGURE 23.6
Printing to a file.

▶ Print Selected Area—When this box (simply called *Selection* in Windows) is checked and you have a rectangular area currently selected in your Photoshop image, you can print just that area. This works only with rectangular selections created with the Marquee tool. Also, it doesn't work for feathered selections.

▶ Encoding (can also be simply a check box for ASCII format)—Here you tell Photoshop which encoding method to use when it sends the image data to the printer. ASCII is understood by all PostScript printers, so it's a safe bet. Binary encoding is more compressed and thus can be faster, but it doesn't work on all printers. JPEG encoding is even faster, but it results in some loss of data because it's a lossy compression scheme. JPEG encoding works only with PostScript Level 2 printers.

▶ Print In—Here you can decide how to print the image: in grayscale, in RGB colors, or in CMYK colors. For some desktop printers, RGB gives better results. (If you're unsure, try both and see which looks better to you.)

▶ Print Separations—This option appears in place of the Print In option, but *only* if the image is currently in CMYK or Duotone mode and the composite color channel is active. When you check this option, Photoshop prints each channel as a separate color plate. For example, a CMYK document would print as four separate pages, one for all the cyan data in the image, one for magenta, one for yellow, and one for black.

▶ Options—Strangely enough, Options isn't always one of your options. On a non-PostScript printer, such as the HP DeskJet series, you'll see the Options button as one of your choices in the Print dialog box. Options lets you choose Intensity, Halftoning, and Color Matching. Leave all three at Auto unless you're printing a photograph. If you are, choose Photographic from the Color Matching menu to get the best possible color reproduction.

At long last, when everything's set to your satisfaction, click Print to print it!

> ### Your Mileage May Vary...
>
> Each printer is slightly different, as are its dialog boxes. I have attempted to cover some of the most common print settings. Be sure to read your printer manual before you start printing. It's your best source for specific printing info.

So, that's how to print from Photoshop. But as you'll probably discover, printing directly from Photoshop doesn't happen as often as you might expect. Most of the time, images created in Photoshop are brought into another application for final placement and output. Most often these are page layout applications, such as InDesign and QuarkXPress. Photoshop images can even be brought into other image-editing or drawing applications, such as Painter and Illustrator, and printed from there.

The main thing to watch for when you're printing Photoshop images from other applications is the format of your file. Make sure that it's compatible with the program you're bringing it into. If it's not, believe me, you'll know! Other than that, any settings related to the image, such as custom colors or halftone screens, are brought with the image automatically.

Preparing the Image

Here's the best strategy if you know you'll want to print your final Photoshop image: Keep the printer in mind throughout the entire process! Different printers output differently, so knowing your printer enables you to adjust your image for its particular behavior and, thus, guarantee the best possible image on the final printed page. This is particularly true for full-color images.

With that in mind, always configure Photoshop for the monitor and printer you'll be using, and do so before even considering printing anything important! This configuration involves several different areas: setting up monitors, printing inks, separations, and separation tables.

Color management capabilities have become an important feature in Photoshop, and are managed by a collection of predefined settings for monitors and printers, and even print media. Each setting includes a corresponding color profile and conversion options, which should give you consistent color for a particular kind of printer under typical conditions. Color management is most helpful if you output your work to several printers or different kinds of printers, such as laser and imagesetter, or if your images will appear on the Web as well as in print and keeping the colors consistent from one kind of output to another is important to you.

What's Color Management?

Color management is what enables you to move color information from one device (such as a monitor) to another (such as a printer) in a predictable and measurable manner. This is what's meant by WYSIWYG color: What You See (on the monitor) Is What You Get (when the image is printed). It's not automatic.

For many printers, scanners, and monitors, color management is handled by International Color Consortium (ICC) profiles. These are made by measuring each device in accordance with a language agreed upon by the ICC (a consortium of color management professionals and vendors). To create an ICC profile for a printer, the profiling software includes a target chart with many small squares of color. The target is printed on the printer being profiled. Then, a measuring tool is placed over each of the color squares and a measurement is taken. The data goes back to the computer, which compares the printed colors against the theoretically perfect colors of the software target and defines the differences. These are all assembled and calculated, and an ICC profile for that printer, ink, and paper combination is produced. The profile is actually a set of numbers that tells the computer how to adjust the color information it sends to that particular printer to make the printed colors match as closely as possible the colors in the image file. Scanner profiles are produced by scanning a known color chart, and monitor profiles are created by displaying the chart onscreen and measuring the color squares with a tool similar to the one used for the printed chart.

ColorSync is color management software developed jointly by Apple and Linotype-Hell. ICM is a similar program for Windows. They are used to correct color spaces for both display and print. ColorSync and ICM include profiles of many kinds of monitors, so you can select yours or at least one close to it. They adjust color on the monitor so that printer color space (CMYK) is displayed correctly.

What does all this mean to the novice user with a home-quality inkjet printer? Here are a few suggestions:

▶ Do your work in RGB color. If you have ColorSync available, be sure that you've set it to your own monitor. If you don't have it, use Adobe Gamma (Windows) or Display Calibrator Assistant (Mac OS X). Adobe Gamma is a control panel that comes with Photoshop to let you adjust your monitor according to how it displays colors, and Display Calibrator Assistant is a similar program that's built in to the Mac OS.

▶ If you're printing to a low-end printer, don't convert the color to CMYK. Photoshop will make the conversion as it sends the data to the printer. It actually does this quite well.

▶ If you'll be printing on a machine that has an ICC profile, change the file color space to CMYK when you're ready to save it for printing, and apply the ICC profile. (Be sure to save an RGB copy, too.)

Figure 23.7 shows the Color Settings dialog box. You can find it on the Edit menu, or you can press Command+Shift+K (Mac) or Ctrl+Shift+K (Windows) to open it. Be sure to notice the descriptions area at the bottom of the dialog box. It can be very helpful when you're not sure which settings to use.

As you can see, you need to make several decisions, even without shifting to the Advanced mode. First, you need to use the Settings pop-up menu, shown in Figure 23.8. You need to decide whether Color Management should be on or off. If you turn it off (click More Options to see this choice in the menu), you're not left colorless. Photoshop will still apply minimum color management standards to make the color onscreen match that of noncolor-managed documents. It's most useful for onscreen presentations.

If you know that your work will be printed on standard printing presses (not a home inkjet), apply either the U.S., European, or Japanese standard prepress defaults according to where your printing company is. (It's not uncommon for some artists and ad agencies in the U.S. to send high-quality print jobs to another country where they can be done less expensively.)

Did you Know?

Customize It

You can also save and load various combinations of settings you create via the Save and Load buttons, respectively.

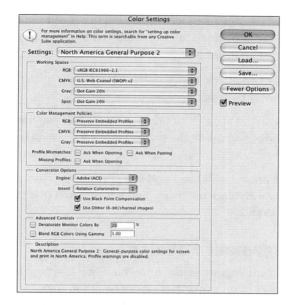

FIGURE 23.7
The default
color settings
are for images
that may be
both printed
and displayed
on the Web.

FIGURE 23.8
Choose an
appropriate
setting.

Working Spaces

The Working Spaces settings in the Color Settings dialog box are *less* complicated than they look (which is nice for a change). RGB asks for the monitor space you want to work in. Choose sRGB if you plan to share your images mostly onscreen, as web images or via email or slideshows; sRGB is a version of RGB that includes the colors that the standard computer monitor can display. If you will be printing most of your images, on the other hand, stick to Adobe RGB; it includes some printable colors that don't show up in sRGB.

The CMYK field wants you to choose the kind of printer you're using. Again, if it's all Greek to you, choose Generic.

Gray is easy. If you use a Mac, choose Gray Gamma 1.8. If you have a PC, choose 2.2. These are the basic settings for the method that each system uses to display grayscale images.

Spot refers to pages printed with black and one or two spot colors, such as duotones, or illustrations done with black and white and limited PANTONE colors. The standard setting is Dot Gain 20%.

Color Management Policies

The Color Management Policies refer to how Photoshop handles files created in another application or in an earlier version of Photoshop. Your choices are to preserve the color management profiles embedded in the file, convert to your active mode, or turn off color management. This last choice lets Photoshop display the file in Active mode, while keeping the embedded profile, until you resave it with the new color management information. You can also direct Photoshop to warn you when a color management mismatch occurs as you open a file and ask what to do about it. Figure 23.9 shows a typical warning message.

FIGURE 23.9
This happened because I opened an image created in an older version of Photoshop.

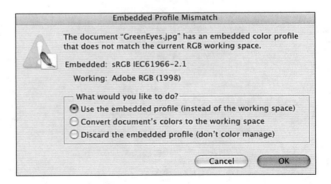

Conversion Options

If you check Advanced mode, you'll have additional choices to make. The first of these is Engine, which refers to the color conversion engine that Photoshop uses to match colors. Even if you're using a Mac, ignore the Apple ColorSync option and choose Adobe (ACE). It's designed specifically to work with Photoshop and other Adobe graphics applications. For Intent, unless you need to match another version of the image exactly, I suggest you use Perceptual. It will give you the most pleasing colors, rather than the most mechanically accurate ones. It also allows you to print a wider range of colors than, for example, Absolute Colorimetric. Check both Black Point Compensation and Use Dither, unless your print shop or service bureau tells you not to. Again, you'll see better-looking color.

However, you can usually ignore the Advanced Controls area. You don't want to desaturate your monitor or change the color-blending gamma except under rare circumstances, which is something only an expert user is likely to encounter.

Picking the Paper

What you print on makes almost as much difference as how you do the printing. You can get various types and weights of paper for all kinds of printers. There are special papers for inkjet printers and for laser printers. If you want your picture to resemble a photograph, consider investing in a pack of photo-weight glossy paper. It's a much thicker paper with a glossy surface that really does help make your inkjet or laser printed picture look like something that came out of a real darkroom rather than a computer.

You can get coated papers for printing color on inkjet printers. These give you photo-quality prints with a matte surface, rather than the glossy one just mentioned. Transparency paper is clear acetate film, specially treated to accept the inks. Use it to make overhead projection slides and overlays.

You can also get art papers for some kinds of inkjet printers. These are heavy rag papers, much like artist's watercolor paper. Find these at www.inkjetmall.com, among other places. I've had very good luck printing on Somerset Smooth and Somerset Velvet with the Epson Stylus Photo 750 and 1200 printers. These fine-art papers are ideally suited to printing pictures that you've converted to imitation watercolors, pastel drawings, and so on. This is because they are the same papers generally used for those techniques. If you use a heavy art paper, feed in one sheet at a time and set the printer for thicker paper (if it has such an option).

For some kinds of art projects, printing on canvas or foil would be ideal. You can find treated pieces of thin canvas with a paper backing that will go through the printer very well at many art or office supply stores. There are also foils, treated to accept inkjet ink, and probably more kinds of cloth and other surfaces to print on, since the last time I looked. You can even buy sheets of rice paper or sugar, as well as edible inks, and put your photos on cakes or cookies. (Check out www.computercakes.com or www.icingimages.com for these materials.)

Label stocks come in all kinds of sizes and shapes, and literally hundreds, if not thousands, of kinds and weights of paper for both inkjet and laser printers.

Finally, you can buy packs of iron-on transfer paper (for color laser or inkjet printers), which let you put your images on T-shirts, aprons, tote bags, or anything else onto which you can iron. Follow the instructions with the paper and don't forget to flip your image before you print it so that it reads correctly.

> **Paper Matters**
>
> I used to use inexpensive photocopying paper for most of my work. It's fine for printing a quick proof to see how a picture comes out. For serious proofing, though, you need to use the same paper that you'll use for the final print. Otherwise, you aren't proving that the combination works. For work that a client will see, I use a coated inkjet paper like Weyerhaeuser Satin Ink Jet paper because the colors are brighter and don't bleed into each other. If I want the picture to look more like a darkroom photo, I'll pay the extra money to print it on special glossy paper.

Placing Photoshop Images in Other Programs

Either your Photoshop images will be "standalone" works of art, or they will be incorporated into some other kind of project. Perhaps you edit a newsletter, or you do Flash movies or PowerPoint presentations. Maybe you've done a pile of product shots to go into a catalog. The question is, how do you move them from Photoshop into some other application? It's not difficult. The other programs do the importing. You simply need to save your images in a compatible format, and in a folder that you can easily keep track of.

Compatible formats for anything ending up as printed matter would depend on whether the final product is being printed on a Postscript or non-Postscript printer. To print on a Postscript printer, save the file as a PDF, DCS, or EPS. For non-Postscript printers, use TIFF when you place the picture into another file.

Using Photoshop with PowerPoint

PowerPoint supports most graphics formats, but GIF (for line art such as logos, charts, and graphs) and JPEG (for photos) are the most compact and best suited for screen display. How you insert the picture depends on whether you're using a preformatted page or making one up as you go along. You can select a slide layout (see Figure 23.10), and then choose the picture to go into it, as in Figure 23.11.

You also have the option of starting with a blank slide and placing your photo on it. To do this, you use the same dialog box as in Figure 23.11.

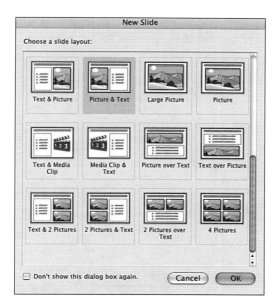

FIGURE 23.10
The PowerPoint New Slide dialog box.

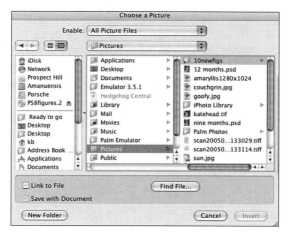

FIGURE 23.11
Locate the picture you want to use and click Insert.

Using Photoshop with a Word Processor or DTP Program

The process of adding pictures to desktop publishing documents is a little bit different. Rather than inserting the images into the program you create, you link to them from the master document you assemble in the DTP or word processor. This means that, in order to keep your pictures where they belong, you can't move or rename any image once it's been placed. If you do, you break the link, and then you have to find it and restore it again. If I'm creating something like a newsletter or ad that might have several images in it, I keep them all in one folder, and make sure that the folder goes to the print shop along with the InDesign or Word files.

To insert a picture in a Microsoft Word document, choose Picture from the Insert menu (as shown in Figure 23.12) and navigate to the picture you want to use. It opens in a box that you can move or resize as needed.

FIGURE 23.12
WordPerfect and other word processors have a similar menu.

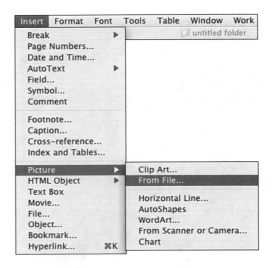

Typically, in a desktop publishing program like Adobe InDesign, the command to insert a picture is Place and it's found on the File menu. Other than that, the procedure is much the same. Navigate to the image you want to use, and (in InDesign) click the page to place it. In QuarkXPress, you'll need to draw a box to contain the picture first, but that's the only real difference. Once the picture is on the page you can scale it, move it, and wrap type around it.

Summary

Printing Photoshop images isn't difficult; there are just many decisions to make along the way. This hour discussed those choices, from initially preparing an image for printing, to setting up the page, and finally setting the printing options. The wonderful thing about printing is that if you don't get a gorgeous printout the first time, you can simply change settings and try again, provided you have enough paper and ink, of course.

Putting Photoshop pictures into other applications is also very simple. Save them in an appropriate format and then use the other program's method of importing them.

Workshop

Q&A

Q *I love the idea of putting pictures on T-shirts and so on. What should I know before I start?*

A Iron-on transfer paper works best with white or light-colored cotton or cotton/polyester blends. Transfer with a household iron on its highest setting (no steam) or in a professional heat press. Iron the fabric first and be sure that it's cooled before you place the transfer on it. Also back up the single layer of fabric you're ironing onto with a sheet of cardboard. This prevents the dye from bleeding through and giving you a second image on the back of the T-shirt. Press quite firmly and expect to iron a large, full-page image for at least two to three minutes—longer is better. Keep the iron moving enough so that you don't scorch the fabric. Small images are easier to manage and take less ironing time. To avoid fading the transfer, wash shirts inside out, preferably in cold water on gentle cycle, and do not bleach.

Q *How can I print my company logo on a hat? I only need one.*

A Use the iron-on paper and make your logo the right size for the space where it's going. Because you can't iron it directly onto your hat, put it on a piece of white cloth, trim the cloth, and sew or glue it in place.

Q *I would love to have a really big print of one of my pictures. Where can I find out about Iris printing?*

A Start on the Web. Do a search for giclée and Iris. With more than 16,000 matches, you're bound to find an affordable Iris printer (or a similar device) close to you.

Q *I want to print pictures at the top of the page that my kids can write their stories under, but Photoshop insists on centering the images. Is there any way around it?*

A Easy. Use the Print with Preview dialog box to move your pictures wherever you want them on the page.

Quiz

1. Dye-sublimation printers need special paper.

    a. True

    b. False

2. Registration marks look like

    a. The letter *R* in a circle

    b. A cross in a circle

    c. Four concentric circles in CMY and K

3. RGB stands for

    a. The initials of Roy G. Biv, inventor of ColorSync

    b. Raster, Gray, Black

    c. Red, Green, Blue

Quiz Answers

1. a. It can be expensive.

2. b. These marks make it easy to see when a color's out of register.

3. c. Those are the colors your monitor uses.

Exercises

PaperDirect is a company that sells more different kinds of papers for more purposes than you can possibly imagine. Visit its website (`http://www.paperdirect.com`) to see how to get a sample kit of its papers and envelopes.

Take a field trip to your local computer store or to a really good office supply store to see what kinds of papers they have for your printer. Also, check out art supply stores for unusual papers, such as canvas-textured, silk, and watercolor. Treat yourself to a package of high-quality paper and try printing some of your best work.

HOUR 24

Photoshop for the Web

What You'll Learn in This Hour:

▶ Jumping into ImageReady
▶ File Formats and File Size
▶ Preparing Backgrounds
▶ Building Animations
▶ Web Photo Gallery
▶ Creating Slices
▶ Preparing Text for the Web
▶ Emailing Your Pictures
▶ Making Pages Load Faster

Wow! You're almost finished; this is the last hour. You've learned enough to work effectively with Photoshop, even if you haven't yet mastered all the tricks and timesaving features. The rest will come as you do more work with the program. This final hour is devoted to one of the best uses for Photoshop: putting your work on the World Wide Web.

You've surfed the Web with Safari, Firefox, Internet Explorer, or one of the lesser-known programs. You have email and probably even your own home page. But do you know what's really going on out there in cyberspace? First of all, although the Web is what you might call a *virtual space*, it also exists in a physical space. It is composed of computers called *servers* that serve files across networks that stretch around the world. The computers can be anything from supercharged SPARC stations to minis and mainframes—or machines not unlike the one sitting on your desktop. These machines run software that can *talk* with your computer via what are known as *protocols*.

Thus, when you type a URL (Uniform Resource Locator) into your browser to access a website, a message, made up of electronic chunks of information called *packets*, goes out to these remote computers. These machines then send back the files for which you have asked. The files that make up all the sounds, pictures, and text of the Web then have to travel across phone lines or down a cable TV line.

This creates a problem that you have to keep in mind as you create graphics for your website. Phone lines are slow, and only so much information can travel at a time. If you are lucky enough to have a cable modem, DSL, or T1 connection, you have all the speed you need. Dial-up connections, in which you use a regular phone line, are slower. We used to be satisfied with 2400bps modems, but those were the pre-Web days, when we used our modems only for email and perhaps accessing chats on CompuServe or America Online.

The most popular language used to publish documents on the Web is still HTML (Hypertext Markup Language). HTML isn't really a computer *programming* language, so relax. It is, as its name suggests, a *markup* language. A series of relatively simple *tags* enables you to specify how text appears in the browser, images, and links to other sites. HTML isn't difficult to learn, but you really don't need to. (If you decide to get into it, look for *Sams Teach Yourself HTML and XHTML in 24 Hours*. It's an excellent reference.)

There are programs, including desktop publishing programs, web browsers, and word processors you might already own, that can translate your pages into HTML with just a couple of mouse clicks. All you need to do is lay out the page the way you would like it to look with your Photoshop pictures pasted in. You do have to make sure that they're in a compatible format, though. Because web pages can be viewed on all kinds of computers, the graphics have to be in a format that's common to as many as possible.

Jumping into ImageReady

One of the best features of Photoshop CS2 is the program that comes along with it, ImageReady CS2. This is the latest and greatest version of this web graphics program. You can move an image back and forth between Photoshop and ImageReady just by clicking the button at the bottom of the toolbox.

ImageReady is Adobe's web graphics program. ImageReady includes many of the basic color correction, painting, and selection tools that you've already learned in Photoshop, plus a powerful set of web tools for optimizing and previewing images and creating GIF animations and rollovers.

Figure 24.1 shows the ImageReady toolbox. As you can see, many of the icons are familiar. A few of the new ones let you create and view image maps, rollovers, and slices. (You'll learn about these interesting terms later on this hour.) The button with the browser icon opens your browser, displaying the image you're working on, so you can check to see that the actions you're inserting will work as expected.

FIGURE 24.1
Click the button at the bottom of the toolbox or press Command+Shift +M (Mac) or Ctrl+Shift+M (Windows) to switch between ImageReady and Photoshop.

Which, When?

If Photoshop and ImageReady have the same tools, and both can save images in GIF, JPEG, and PNG formats, how do you know when to use which one? If you're just dealing with one picture, you can use either. If you want to optimize several pictures so that they'll display well while using as little memory as possible, use ImageReady to do the optimization. You can edit, apply filters and type, and color correct in either program.

Did you Know?

File Formats and File Size

The first thing you need to learn about preparing web graphics is the type of file format to use. There are two standard choices: GIF (Graphics Interchange Format) and JPEG (Joint Photographic Experts Group). There's also a third format known as PNG (Portable Network Graphics). It's actually been out for several years and promises to be the best choice of all three, but it has never really caught on. Use it if you like it, but be aware that there might still be a few folks out there whose software can't read PNG files.

The most important thing to remember, regardless of the file format you decide to use, is that the Web has limited bandwidth. This means that if you create an absolutely beautiful image and it weighs in at something like 4MB, it will take forever to download on a 56K modem—better than 10 minutes. This is not to say that you *can't* create images with as large a file size as you want. I am just suggesting that few Web surfers out there will have the patience to sit and wait while your 4MB image downloads. If you know that your primary audience is surfing from home with slower modems, you might want to keep your web page images under 30KB apiece—a size that a 56K modem can download in a comfortable six seconds. This is an area where ImageReady can be a big help. It lets you decide how small you can save a file without sacrificing quality.

Can You Think Big?

If you have some big files that you want to publish on the Web, don't fret. There are ways around the big file issue. Most surfers won't mind the wait for a big file if they have a warning. Give them a thumbnail version of the image and tell them how big the file is. This way, they can decide for themselves whether they want to spend the time waiting for the download. A little courtesy, as in all aspects of life, goes a long way on the Web.

JPEG (Joint Photographic Experts Group)

Depending on your needs, JPEG could be the best file format for you. It is great for photographs and other continuous tone (full-color) images, primarily because it lets you use 16 million colors. JPEG maintains color information but does, however, employ a *lossy* compression scheme, which means that you can adjust and reduce the file size—at the expense of the image quality.

If you're creating JPEGs for the Web, you need to work in RGB mode within Photoshop. This is reasonable because RGB is the "monitor" viewing mode, and Web images are going to be seen on, guess what: an RGB monitor. ImageReady has only one mode, RGB, which is all it needs. (You can't print from ImageReady.)

When you're working in Photoshop, choosing File→Save for Web will open the dialog box shown in Figure 24.2. I selected JPEG Low from the Preset pop-up menu in the upper-right corner. I could have chosen GIF or PNG, as well. After a short calculation, and because I had clicked the 4-Up tab at the top of the window, I can see my original image, plus the image with three different JPEG settings. The file size and download time are displayed for each image.

The original Photoshop file for this image was 1.43MB. As a low-quality JPEG, it's 29.35KB and will take about six seconds to download on a phone modem—and much less time to download on a broadband connection. At medium quality, the file size increases to 50.47KB and the download time increases to ten seconds. At high quality, it's a 114.4KB file and loads in about 22 seconds. Is the quality difference worth the download time?

On the other hand, we've gone from 1.43MB down to 114.4KB. That's a tremendous difference with a relatively small loss of quality.

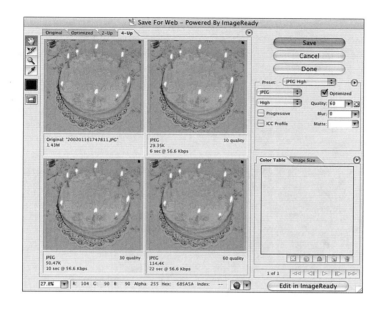

FIGURE 24.2
As a JPEG in high, medium, and low quality.

Once Is Good, Twice Is Not

Each time you save the file as a JPEG, you lose some data to compression. This can create artifacts—blocky areas or color bands in your picture. Never save a file as a JPEG a second time. If you make a conversion to JPEG, and then decide to make changes, go back to the original Photoshop file. Don't make changes and resave the previously saved JPEG. And if your digital camera produces JPEG files, be sure to resave them in Photoshop format before making any changes.

Watch Out!

To save your file, click on the version you want to save, then click OK. The usual Save As dialog box will open, enabling you to name your document and save it where you want it, presumably in the same folder with other web page items.

Opening your file as a JPEG in ImageReady opens a similar window and the Optimization palette (see Figure 24.3). After you've selected a JPEG quality level and your other settings, click the version of the image you want to save and choose File→Save Optimized.

If you are saving a JPEG file directly from Photoshop with the File→Save As command, the first thing to remember is this: Don't. Save for Web gives you much more power and control. However, if you're in a hurry and determined to just save and go, choosing JPEG in the Save As dialog box gives you a second dialog box, like the one in Figure 24.4.

FIGURE 24.3
You have the same options in ImageReady as in Photoshop.

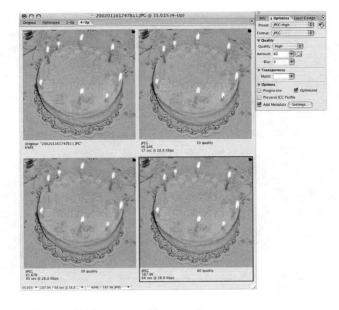

FIGURE 24.4
The JPEG Options box lets you choose image quality and how the picture is loaded into a browser.

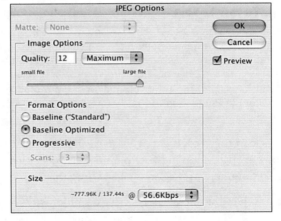

This box will prompt you for format options:

▶ Baseline (Standard)—This is the default option, if you leave the others unchecked.

▶ Baseline (Optimized)—This option optimizes the colors in the file. It creates a smaller file.

▶ Progressive—Except for very small JPEGs, this is almost a must for web work. Progressive means that your file is visible within a web browser faster and it is then refined by subsequent passes, or *scans*, as more file information is downloaded. If you select a progressive JPEG, it will automatically be optimized.

Did you
Know?

See What's Happening

Always keep your web browser open when you are creating web graphics. Doing so lets you take a look at them in context.

Don't be fooled by how quickly File→Open File in your browser opens one of your files. These files are on your hard drive—they're local. When a viewer has to go out on the Web to get your pages, the process slows down quite a bit.

GIF (Graphics Interchange Format)

GIFs are another option for web file formats. Because they're limited to 256 colors, they're not as good as JPEG for continuous tone art, but they're great for line art, logos, and anything with limited color. The GIF format also lets you save files with transparent backgrounds, which is extremely useful when you are creating buttons and other round graphics. Furthermore, you can animate a GIF.

Did you
Know?

It's Okay to Peek

A good way to select the file format that's right for you is to visit web sites that have graphics similar to what you want to publish. To find out what kind of file format an image is, simply click the image. On a Macintosh, Ctrl+click or click and hold the image (depending on your browser) until a dialog box appears. On a Windows machine, right-click the image.

In the dialog box, choose to save the image. When you are prompted for where you want to save the image, note the file extension—.jpg for JPEG, .png for PNG, or .gif for GIF. Click OK to save the file or click Cancel if you are just looking.

In Figure 24.5, I've created a simple button that I'll be saving as a GIF. Notice how much the file shrinks (from 190KB to 1.78KB) when I limit the colors in the GIF.

PNG (Portable Network Graphics)

There are two kinds of PNG: 8-bit and 24-bit. The PNG-8 format uses 8-bit color, which means that each image can contain only 256 colors. Like the GIF format, PNG-8 compresses solid areas of color very well while preserving sharp detail, such as that in line art, logos, or illustrations with type. The PNG-8 format uses a lossless compression method, with no data discarded during compression. However, because PNG-8 files are 8-bit color, optimizing an original 24-bit image—which can contain millions of colors—as a PNG-8 will degrade image quality. PNG-8 files use more advanced compression schemes than GIF, and they can be 10%–30% smaller than GIF files of the same image, depending on the image's color patterns.

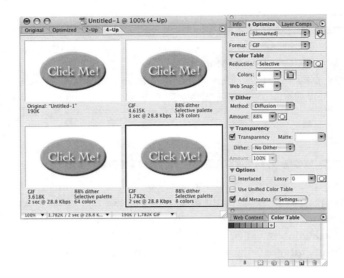

PNG-24 file format uses 24-bit color and is suitable for continuous-tone images. PNG-24 uses a lossless compression scheme, so that you never lose image data when you save in this format. However, as a result, PNG-24 files can be much larger than JPEG files of the same image. PNG-24 format is recommended only when working with a continuous-tone image that includes multilevel (variable) transparency, such as you would have in an anti-aliased image on a transparent layer. (Multilevel transparency is supported by the PNG-24 format but not the JPEG format.)

Bottom line: If you would consider GIF for an image, consider PNG-8 as well. It might give you a smaller file, and can do the job well. If you're thinking about JPEG, consider PNG-24 if your picture has multilevel transparency. If it's a straight image, JPEG will probably give you a smaller, more efficient file. Just remember that if you choose PNG, some users with older browsers may not be able to view your images.

Preparing Backgrounds

I admit that I have mixed feelings about backgrounds on web pages. These can really add personality to a website, but they also can make reading the text of your site difficult and frustrating. To quote web designer David Siegel, "Gift-wrap makes poor stationery."

That said, however, if you use backgrounds with discretion, they can add to a site's presence and look. Because HTML includes the capability to tile any image as a background, your background file can be quite small. You just have to make sure that it doesn't have obvious edges or pictures that end abruptly, unless that's what you want. In Figure 24.6, I've created a tile for a web page background, and I'm saving it as a GIF using the Save For Web dialog box in Photoshop.

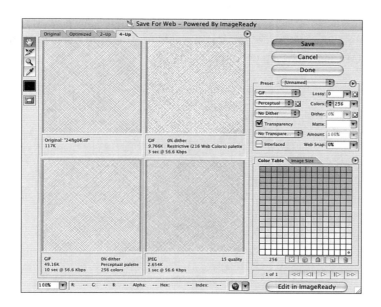

FIGURE 24.6
This tile combines several filters applied to a plain white background.

To convert the single tile into a background is easy. You simply open a page in your favorite web page layout program, and import the image. Depending on the program, you might import it as an image and click a check box in the dialog box to make it a background. Some other web page layout programs have a specific dialog box for placing backgrounds. Figure 24.7 shows how to insert a background image tile using HTML Assistant.

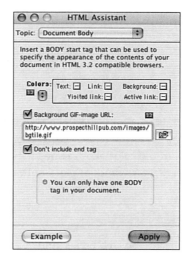

FIGURE 24.7
There are no options for background tiles; all you have to do is specify the location of the image file you want to use as a background.

Now, all you have to do is to be sure that when you upload your page to the Web, the background image is where you said it would be. Figure 24.8 shows the tiled background with some type placed over it.

FIGURE 24.8
The background looks even, and the tiling hardly shows at all.

Here's a trick for placing a stripe down one side of your page. Make a single tile that's a little wider than the width of the screen by as few pixels high as needed. Place your color and/or texture on its left side, and then save it as a GIF or JPEG. The file will probably look something like Figure 24.9.

FIGURE 24.9
When you design your HTML page, make sure you indent the text from the left margin so that it's not over the dark stripe.

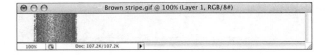

When you place this file as a background, it will be tiled vertically but not horizontally, because it's already as wide as the screen. You'll end up with a nice stripe, as wide as you care to make it, in the color and texture of your choice. It makes a good accent for a plain page, especially if you then place buttons on it.

Building Animations

GIF animations are commonplace on web pages, and you'll probably see dogs wagging their tails endlessly, cats catching mice, balls bouncing. It's enough to make you dizzy. Photoshop and ImageReady can create the graphics elements and add motion to any of these goodies. If they aren't too big and flashy, they can be cute.

Today's animation is done, as it was 50 years ago, using layers. Figure 24.10 is my animation model, a Japanese Happy Cat. This one, in black, represents good health. I'm going to make him wave at you in a very simple three-step animation.

FIGURE 24.10
This cat will soon wave his paw.

The first step is to copy the cat into a new image file in Photoshop. (If you want to work along, the cat is in the collection of images that you can download from this book's companion website. See the Introduction if you've forgotten where the downloads are.)

Duplicate the layer twice, so you have three in all. The bottom layer is the "resting" state for the animation, so you don't need to do anything to it. It will be the first frame in our animation. The second layer is the "transition" state and the third layer is the "final" state. You can insert as many transition layers as you need. More steps will give you smoother animation, and a much larger file. Unfortunately, it might not play well on some computers, or if Internet traffic is tied up, as it sometimes is.

Move to the top layer and make the changes necessary to take the picture to the final state. In Figure 24.11, you can see that I have moved the cat's paw to a fully extended wave position. To do so, I cut it loose with the Lasso, rotated it, and filled in the gaps in black and pink with a small brush.

Next, move to the middle layer. Because this is a small animation and the cat's paw has to move only a short distance, one middle step is enough. If the paw had farther to travel, we could put in more transitional steps, but the animation will look fine with just one step here. Cut the paw loose and rotate it halfway between where it is on the first and third layers. Again, use a small brush to fill in any gaps. Now your animation should look like Figure 24.12. The "art" part of the job is nearly complete.

FIGURE 24.11
The waving cat.

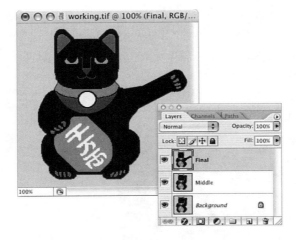

FIGURE 24.12
Midpoint of the wave.

Copy the middle layer and add it to the top of the stack, and then copy the background layer and add it to the top, so the cat's paw will end up where it started. You now have five layers.

Now, open the Animation palette. Open the pop-up menu and choose Make Frames from Layers. You will see the frames in the Animation window, and clicking the forward arrow will run through them so you can preview the animation.

From the pop-up menu at the bottom of the Animation palette, choose Forever or Other if you want it to go continuously. Otherwise, it will run its steps once and stop. If you choose Other, you can specify a number of repeats. If it seems to run too fast, you can add a delay between each frame in the animation by setting the Frame Delay value. Then save it as a GIF file with animation, either using Save for

Web or by switching to ImageReady and using Save Optimized. Figure 24.13 shows the final settings for the animation as seen in ImageReady. You don't need very many colors for this particular example, so you can make it a 16-color GIF with no noticeable change.

When saving, choose HTML and Images to let ImageReady write the code and optimize the individual frames. Then copy that HTML code into the Web page file and place the frames in the image folder. Check the animation out in your regular browser, and then if possible in other browsers to make sure it works for all.

If you want to get serious about web page design and using HTML, run to your local bookstore or computer store and look for *The Web Wizard's Guide to Photoshop*. It's a great source for tips and tricks to spiff up your website.

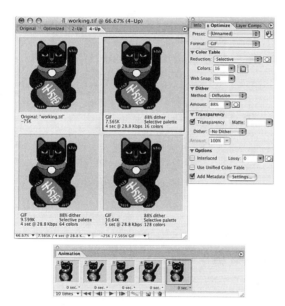

FIGURE 24.13
Here are the five frames in order.

Web Photo Gallery

Want to put your art on a web page? Sure. So do I, but those files can be huge. Wouldn't it be better to put up thumbnail images, and then let interested viewers click those thumbnails to see the large versions? Of course it would. But creating all those thumbnails, and then making the page and linking the images to it—well, that sounds like hard work.

Fortunately, there's a better way. Photoshop's Web Photo Gallery does the job for you. Layouts range from a simple page of thumbnails, each of which you can click to open a new window with a full-size view; table format, again with thumbnails; scrolling frames, to variations with patterned and colored backgrounds, including the familiar Microsoft navy and gray. You can also choose your own colors for background and type as well as for links. Last, there is a slide show format that changes images every 10 seconds. Figure 24.14 shows the Web Photo Gallery dialog box with the styles showing.

FIGURE 24.14
Each style has a thumbnail view so you can see what you are choosing.

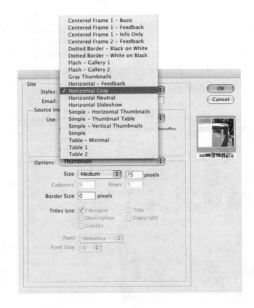

Try it Yourself

Making a Gallery Page

Let's practice making a gallery page:

1. Before you begin, make sure that all the images you want to include are in one folder. If you are planning to use the image filenames as titles, check the spellings and remove file extensions. Then choose File→Automate→Web Photo Gallery.

2. Styles, the first pop-up menu, lets you choose how the pictures will be displayed. Select one of these as described previously. Enter your email address if you want it to appear as an information contact.

3. In the Source Images section of the dialog box, Click Browse (Windows) or Choose (Mac OS) to locate your folder of pictures, and choose a destination where you'll save the web page. The Options section lets you set up a title banner for your work, determine the sizes of thumbnails and images, and set text and background colors.

4. Choose Options→Banner and enter a name for your page, as well as your own name if you want. Choose a font and size to display your type. There are only four fonts shown, all system fonts for Windows or Mac. If you try to hack the HTML code and put in your own fonts, chances are good that many of your website visitors won't have them and will see the type however it defaults. Bottom line: Don't bother.

5. Choose Large Images from the Options pop-up menu and set a size and quality for the large display images. Add a border if you want. Decide what information must be given.

6. Choose Thumbnails (see Figure 24.15) from the Options menu and choose whether to use no captions, use the filenames as captions, or add captions in the File Info dialog box for each image. You can also choose a font and size for the captions, and decide whether they'll have borders. If you're using a table or another simple layout, you might select the number of photos in rows and columns.

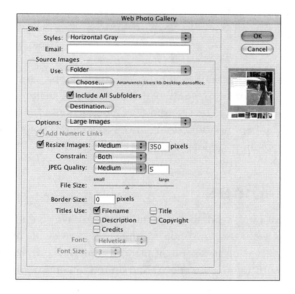

FIGURE 24.15
You don't have to have names or anything else if you don't want them.

7. Choose Options→Custom Colors and choose appropriate colors for your page's background, banner, headline, and links.

8. Options→Security lets you place a copyright or other message on each picture. When everything's ready, click OK.

Photoshop will assemble the page according to your specifications. When it's complete, it will automatically open in your default browser. Figure 24.16 shows the web page I set up to show off my husband's newly rearranged home office.

FIGURE 24.16
This office is
clearly the
home of a
sports fan.

Photoshop lists the images alphabetically. If you aren't happy with the type size or font, the background color, or any of the other settings you've made, now is the time to go back and change them. The File Info dialog box (choose File→File Info) holds captions, titles, and other important data. Once you've made your changes, run Web Photo Gallery again to update your pages.

Creating Slices

Slices are not the easiest concept to grasp, but they can save you a lot of file space, after you determine what they are about. Simply put, *slices* divide an image into smaller files. Each slice is an independent file, containing its own optimization settings, color palettes, URLs, rollover effects, and animation effects. Slices can give you increased image quality when you are working with documents that contain more than one kind of image, or text and images. They can make pages seem to load faster because each slice becomes visible as soon as it's loaded, giving the viewer something to look at while the rest of the image loads. Slices also let you create image maps that do useful things when you click part of an image. They can take you to new pages, show an enlarged view of the slice, or anything else you care to program them to do.

Slices are assembled in an HTML table in the document's HTML file. By default, the document starts with one slice that comprises the entire document. You can then create more slices in the document. Both Photoshop and ImageReady will automatically make additional slices to complete the full table in the HTML file. Note that this means you must choose HTML and Images when saving a sliced image, rather than Images Only, and you'll need to copy the HTML that ImageReady creates into your web page file.

Slices are created by dragging the Slice tool, which looks like a drawing of an X-Acto knife. Select it from the ImageReady toolbox, the Photoshop toolbox, or simply press the K key to activate it. Drag a selection box across the area you are slicing. If you make a slice across the middle of an image, by default, you have defined three slices: one above and one below where you have sliced. Slices that you create are called *user-slices*. Slices that Photoshop generates are called *auto-slices*. If you place a slice across the middle of a picture, Photoshop will place auto-slices above and below it. Slices can be vertical as well as horizontal. Subslices are created when you overlap two or more user-slices. Figure 24.17 shows a sliced image.

FIGURE 24.17
The numbers in the upper-left corner of the sections are their slice numbers.

Preparing Text for the Web

HTML Web standards include a handful of type sizes and fonts, some for headings, some for text, and some for emphasis. Uh-huh. "Bo-ring," to quote the kids. However, you're not necessarily limited to what HTML has to offer. If you want an elaborate title for your page, create it in Photoshop, using filled letters, filters, drop shadows, glows, or whatever other special effects you like. Crop it tightly and save it as either a GIF or JPEG. Figure 24.18 shows a logo created for a small business web page. Compressed, the file is only 6.3KB.

FIGURE 24.18
Eye Candy
4000's Bevel
Boss filter creat-
ed the three-
dimensional
effect shown
here.

You have the option of converting your file to JPEG or PNG or to GIF. One good
thing about text is that it usually, but not always, is applied to a white background.
If this is the case with your website, there is no need to go through the trouble of
exporting a transparent GIF89a file. Just make sure that your background is white
and save it as a plain GIF file.

GIF or JPEG?

There's one rule of thumb that professional web page designers apply to choosing
formats. With line art, or anything with a limited palette (fewer than 216 colors),
choose GIF or PNG-8. With photos or full-color art, choose JPEG or PNG-24.

Emailing Your Pictures

You have all these great pictures, and you want to share them, right? There are several ways to go about this. You can send them as email attachments, just like stuff-
ing a handful of prints into a letter. You can post them on a forum, if you belong to
one. You can set up your web gallery on your own website, or you can join a service
such as Webshots (www.webshots.com) that gives you online storage and lets you
share your pictures with others as well as make digital prints and photo gifts.

To add a photo to an email, use the Add Attachment button or command in your
regular email program and locate the picture you want to send. You can't send mail
directly from Photoshop. The photo needn't be any special format, as long as you
know your recipient has software that can open it. JPEG is always safe, because it
will open in any web browser.

To post a picture in a forum or on a service such as Webshots, follow their instructions. In any case, make sure that the picture is a reasonable size. You wouldn't
want someone to tie up your computer by sending you a huge file, so don't do it to
them.

Many computer users are rightfully suspicious of unsolicited downloads. If you want your pictures to be seen and enjoyed, send them only to people you know, and warn them first, in another note, that a picture is coming. Otherwise, your art might end up in a spam filter.

Making Pages Load Faster

The bottom line for making web pages load faster is—you can't. The page will load as fast as the server can send it and the recipient can receive it. Those are both factors beyond your control.

What you can do, though, is make sure that your page is arranged so that there's something to see while the graphic loads. Bring up a Welcome headline first, and then add the background. If there's a graphic that will take some time to load, bring up a block of text before the graphic appears. The load time for the picture will seem much shorter if the person waiting has something else to read or think about.

Keep your images small or put up a thumbnail and link the full-size picture to it, so visitors have the option of waiting to see the big picture. If the content of your picture is important, put a text description of it on the page, too. If you learn HTML, you can use the ALT tag to place an image description in place of the image. (This also helps make your website handicapped-accessible, which is important to do for the millions of visually impaired Web users.)

Summary

In this final hour, we looked at putting your work on the Web. We examined what file formats work in most web browsers and how you might best choose the right formats for your own work.

So, what comes next? You've finished your 24th hour, and you know a lot more about Photoshop than you did when you began. That doesn't mean you know it all, but you now have the tools—your imagination, creativity, and a basic understanding of Photoshop. There is still plenty out there to learn and with which to experiment. I've been using Photoshop ever since it first came out, and I'm still learning new tricks and techniques. You can spend years with this program and still not try everything it can do.

Above all else, have fun!

Workshop

Q&A

Q *Can I mix the kinds of images I use on a Web page—some JPEGs, some GIFs, a PNG—or will that cause everything to crash?*

A There is no reason not to mix image types. Choose the type depending on the content of the image. Realistic photos look best as JPEG or PNG files. Graphics with limited color are most efficiently stored as GIFs.

Q *What's the trick for using a picture as a page background?*

A Keep it small and apply the picture as a tiled background. If you keep the edges blurry, they blend smoothly, avoiding that floor tile look. Save your file as either a GIF or JPEG with the name background. Your web page creator program should be able to insert it automatically, but if not, use the HTML tag `<body background = "background.gif">` (or `.jpg`, if appropriate).

Another effect that uses the whole photo once is to make the image nearly transparent so that it looks really toned down. Use it as a nontiled background, or *watermark*.

Q *If I want to put my pictures on the Web, but only for my friends to see, can I protect them?*

A There are lots of ways to do this. The easiest is to put them on a hidden page. This is a second page on your site, not linked to the first. Instead it has a separate address, such as `http://home.myservice.net/mypage/_hidden.htm`. Give your friends the direct URL to this page. No one who doesn't know it's there will be able to reach it. However, "security through obscurity" is never a recommended policy for truly sensitive information or images. If you want to be more secure, you can learn enough JavaScript to password-protect the site. Look for *Sams Teach Yourself JavaScript in 24 Hours, Third Edition*. It's a good way to learn JavaScript.

Quiz

1. What do I have to do to a native Photoshop format file before I can put it on the Web?

    a. Attach a copyright notice.

    b. Save it as a JPEG, GIF, or PNG file.

    c. Get a model release on any recognizable people.

2. HTML stands for

    a. Hypertext Markup Language

    b. Hand-coded Type Meta Language

    c. Has Trouble Making Lines

3. What's the most important thing to remember about Photoshop?

    a. Experiment

    b. Experiment

    c. Experiment

Quiz Answers

1. b., but a. and c. are good ideas, too.

2. a. It's the language that defines web pages.

3. The most important thing is that there's no wrong answer. Keep trying new things, new combinations, and new approaches. Photoshop is a wonderful tool, but, without *your* creativity and imagination, it's just software.

Exercises

I have no assignments for you in this chapter—it's time to go forth and create. Most of all, have fun!

PART VII

Appendix

Photoshop CS2 Palette Quick Reference

Navigator Palette

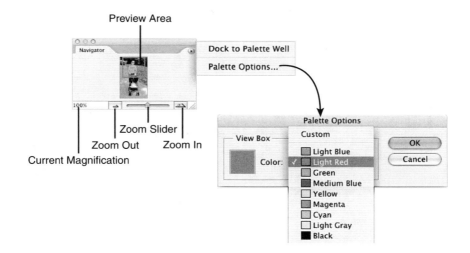

Info Palette

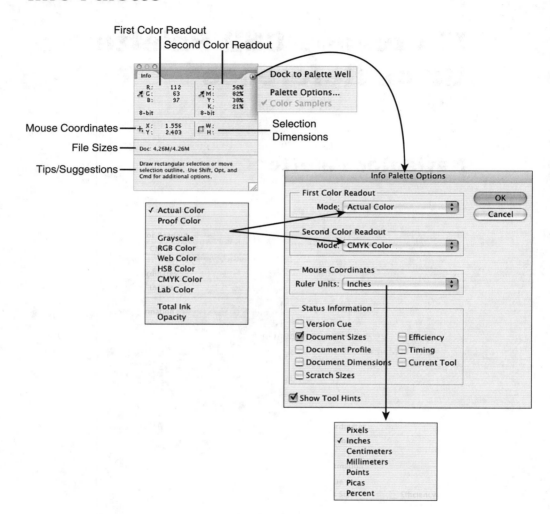

Histogram Palette

Graph

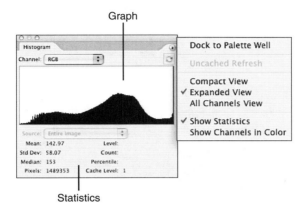

Statistics

Color Palette

Numerical Entry Fields

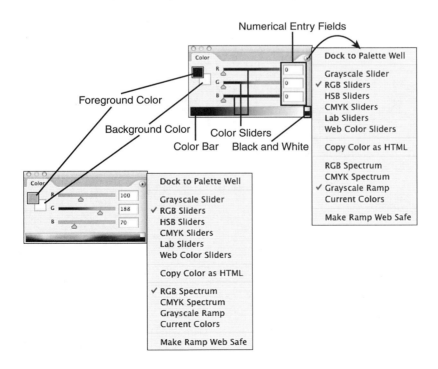

Foreground Color

Background Color

Color Sliders

Color Bar

Black and White

Swatches Palette

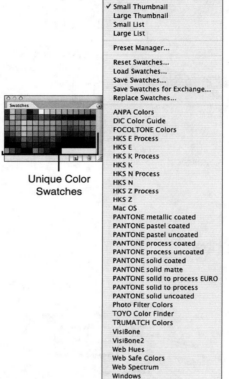

Unique Color
Swatches

Styles Palette

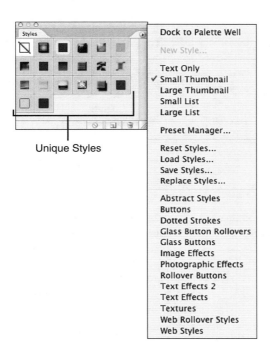

Unique Styles

History Palette

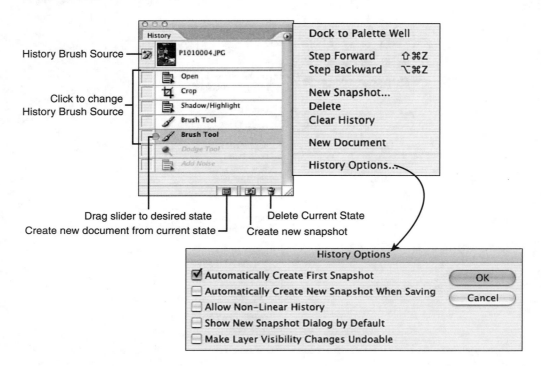

Actions Palette

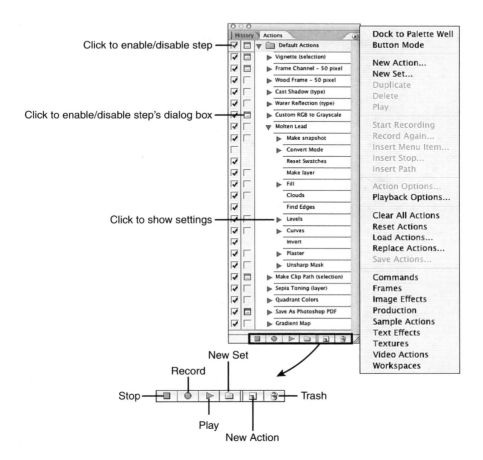

Click to enable/disable step

Click to enable/disable step's dialog box

Click to show settings

New Set

Record

Stop

Play

New Action

Trash

Layers Palette

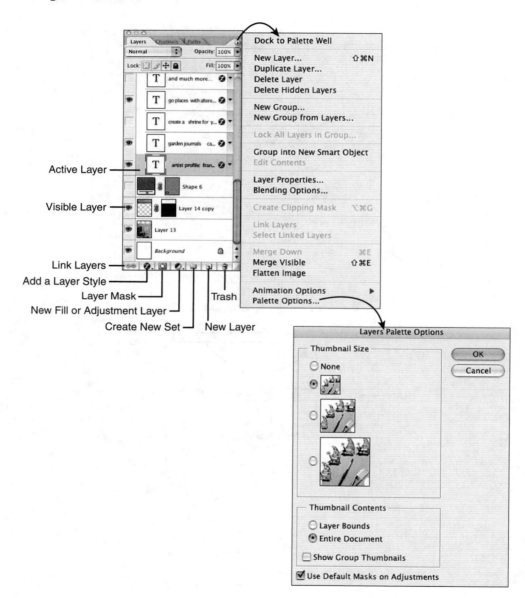

Active Layer

Visible Layer

Link Layers

Add a Layer Style

Layer Mask

New Fill or Adjustment Layer

Create New Set

Trash

New Layer

Channels Palette

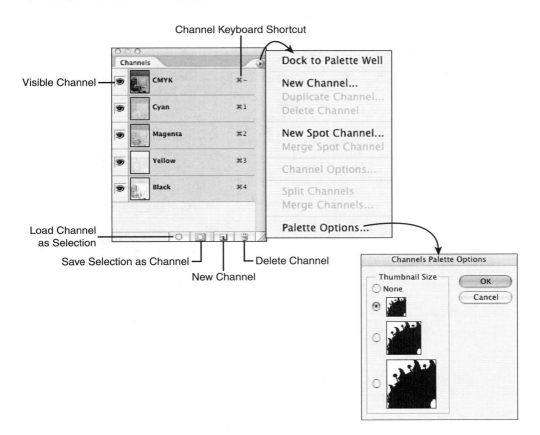

Channel Keyboard Shortcut

Visible Channel

Load Channel
as Selection

Save Selection as Channel

New Channel

Delete Channel

Paths Palette

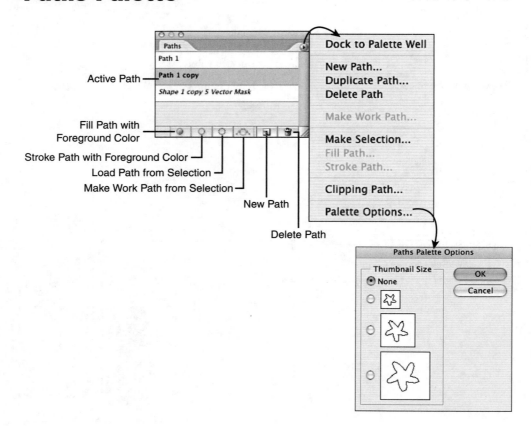

Active Path

Fill Path with Foreground Color

Stroke Path with Foreground Color

Load Path from Selection

Make Work Path from Selection

New Path

Delete Path

Character Palette

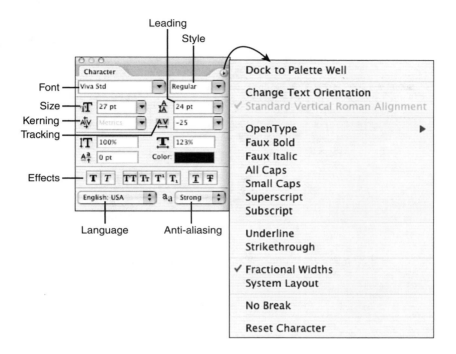

Paragraph Palette

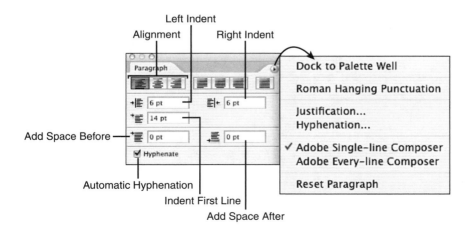

Animation Palette

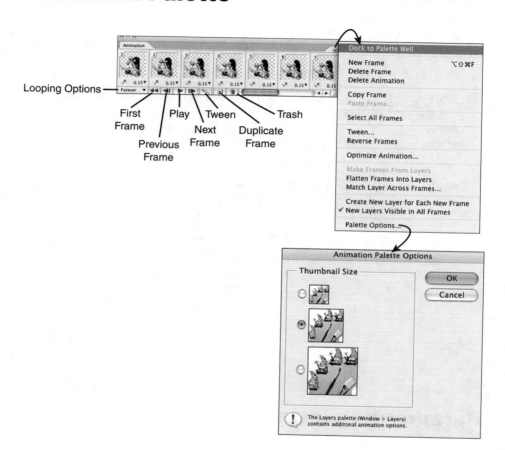

Looping Options

First Frame

Play

Tween

Trash

Next Frame

Duplicate Frame

Previous Frame

Brushes Palette

New Brush

Trash

Layer Comps Palette

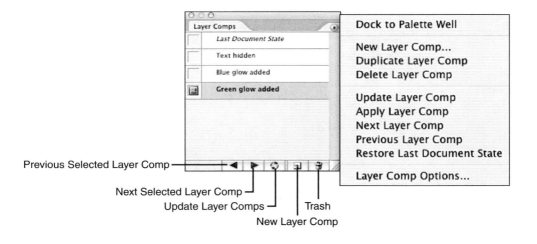

Previous Selected Layer Comp

Next Selected Layer Comp

Update Layer Comps

New Layer Comp

Trash

Tool Presets Palette

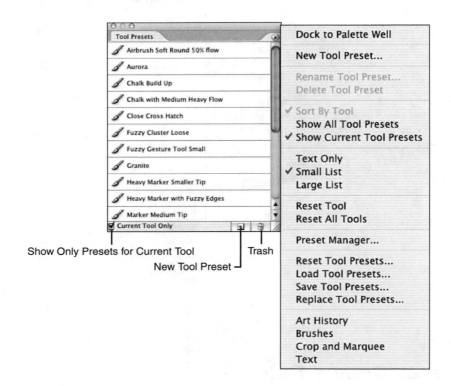

Show Only Presets for Current Tool

New Tool Preset

Trash

Index

Q - R

replacing

    backgrounds in color photos, 419-420

    removed items in color photos, 422-423

resizing

    canvases, 57-58

    images, 57-58

    selections, 60

resolution

    changing, 6-7

    reducing file size, 33

Reticulation filter, 274

retouching, 152

    black-and-white photo repair, 396-398

    charcoal drawings, 177

    color photos

        color correction, 411-413, 418

        drag-and-drop repair, 416-417

        Patch tool, 417

        red eye removal, 413-415

revealing/hiding

    layer mask selections, 204-205

    layers, 188

    palettes in Window menu, 20

reversing images, 66

RGB color model, 77-79, 82, 133-134

Rotate Canvas submenu (Image menu)

    Arbitrary Rotation dialog box, 62

    rotating images, 61

Rotate dialog box (Transform submenu), 65

rotating

    canvases

        90 degree rotation, 61

        180 degree rotation, 61

        by degrees, 62

        measuring rotation, 65

    images, 60

        90 degree rotation, 61

        180 degree rotation, 61

        by degrees, 62

        measuring rotation, 65

    selections, 65

    versus flipping, 66

Rough Pastels filter, 262-263, 294-295

roundness (brushes), selecting, 115

S

Sandstone texture (watercolor techniques), 169

saturation (color), defining, 133

saturation blending mode (color), 143

Saturation button

    Color Picker, 133

    Variations dialog box, 94

Save a Copy command, 32

Save button (Variations dialog box), 96

saving

    brush attributes, 116

    brush sets, 116

    colors as swatches, 138-139

    custom swatch palettes, 137

    files, 31

        cross-platform saves, 32

        reducing file size, 32-33

        Save a Copy command, 32

    JPEG files, 455

    layer comps, 194

    Quick masks, 203

    tool option presets, 14

Scale feature (Marquee tool), 60

Scale option (Page Setup dialog box), 433

Scale Styles feature (Image Size dialog box), 58

Scaled Print option (Print with Preview dialog box), 434

scaling images, 434

school picture packages, 341-344

scratches, removing (black-and-white photo repair), 394-395, 401

screen blending mode (color), 142

Screen option (Print with Preview dialog box), 435

Select menu, 17

selecting

    custom shapes, 230

    large areas via Magic Wand tool, 48-49

    paths, 225

    printers, 432

Selection menu

    Feather Selection dialog box, 47

    Modify submenu, 48

Selection tools, 9

    Crop tool, 51-53

    finding, 39

X - Y - Z